TABLOIDCULTURE

Console-ing Passions

·

Television and Cultural Power

·

Edited by Lynn Spigel

TABLOID
CULTURE

Trash Taste,

·

Popular Power,

·

and the
Transformation
of American
Television

·

KEVIN GLYNN

Duke University Press   Durham and London, 2000

To my mother, Joann C. Bacon,
and in memory of my father,
Gerald T. Glynn (1930–1978)

© 2000 Duke University Press
All rights reserved
Typeset in Quadraat by Tseng Information Systems, Inc.
Printed in the United States of America on acid-free paper ∞
Library of Congress Cataloging-in-Publication Data
appear on the last printed page of this book.

The tabloidification of American life—of the news, of the culture, yea, of human behavior—is such a sweeping phenomenon that it can't be dismissed as merely a jokey footnote to the history of the 1990s. Rather, it's the very hallmark of our times; if the decade must have a name—and it must, since decade-naming has become a required public exercise in the second half of the 20th century—it might as well be the Tabloid Decade.—David Kamp, "The Tabloid Decade," *Vanity Fair*, February 1999

Contents

Acknowledgments

This book began its life as a doctoral dissertation at the University of Wisconsin–Madison, so my earliest debts are to people there who helped directly or indirectly, in numerous ways large and small, to foster and shape many of the ideas expressed here. Lynn Spigel, Don Crafton, Diane Rubenstein, Murray Edelman, Richard Merelman, David Trubek, Tom Gunning, and David Morley taught me a great deal about various cultural and political practices and about the complexity of relationships between them. My warmest thanks to Julie D'Acci, Michele Hilmes, Liz Ellsworth, and Nick Mirzoeff for carefully reading a very early version of the manuscript and providing incisive, challenging, and encouraging comments on its various strengths and weaknesses. I am especially indebted to my teacher and friend John Fiske for his acuity, generosity, humor, and encouragement. I am also grateful to everybody else who helped to make the Media and Cultural Studies wing of the Department of Communication Arts at Wisconsin a site for pleasurable intellectual engagement. The earliest drafts of several chapters of this book were presented at colloquiums there, so I'd particularly like to thank those who offered helpful comments and criticisms in response to those presentations, who imparted insights and opinions that have contributed to my understanding of tabloid media, or who forwarded clips, clippings, and other useful resources my way: Lisa Parks, Steve Classen, Yong-Jin Won, Jeff Sconce, Pam Wilson, Chad Dell, Tasha Oren, Aniko Bodroghkozy, Derek Kompare, Alyssa Goldberg, Matthew Murray, Dan Marcus, Jason Mittell, Michael Kackman, Don Meckiffe, Dave Tetzlaff, Laura Kipnis, Antonette Gorro, and Elana Levine.

I would also like to express my gratitude to several other friends, colleagues, and family members who have been directly or indirectly supportive of this project in a variety of ways that include (but are not limited to) suggesting productive ideas, forwarding pertinent materials, and engaging in interesting and challenging discussions about the politics of culture and television over steins of Wisconsin's and Aotearoa New Zealand's, finest malt beverages: Christine Trost, Paula Mohan, Paul Passavant, Dan Smith, Greg White, Amy Glynn, Doug Johnson, Jami Moss, Moya Luckett, Dan Skidmore-Hess, Lisa Bower, Judith Strand, Julie White, Bob Wheeler Lane, John Schwarzmann, Jan Levine Thal, Adolf Gundersen, Ruth Lessl Shively, Erik Olsen, Tiina Vares, Gary Gibson, Dave Frame, Jane Harrison, Jodi Dean, and the late Paige Baty, whom, although we met only near the end of her life, I feel very fortunate to have counted as a friend. Special thanks to Jayne Simpson both for encouraging me during the late phases of this project and for taking the time to distract me from it.

Some of the research that has culminated in this book was supported by a Jacob Javitz Fellowship from the U.S. Department of Education. I'd like to thank Jenny Breukelaar, Thomas Zimmerman, and Cheri Goldner for their assistance with the research on the O.J. Simpson case and its media coverage. Thanks to Ken Wissoker, Richard Morrison, and Rebecca Johns-Danes at Duke University Press for their support and for believing in this project. Thanks also to Henry Schafer and Marketing Evaluations/TvQ, Inc., for their generous assistance with audience demographic data. Much of the material in the first two sections of chapter 4 appeared in an earlier form in *Communication Studies* (Kevin Glynn, "Reading Supermarket Tabloids as Menippean Satire," *Communication Studies* 44, no. 1 [Spring 1993]: 19–37). Thanks to the Central States Communication Association for permission to include this material. A version of the second section of chapter 2 appeared in *Cultural Studies* (John Fiske and Kevin Glynn, "Trials of the Postmodern," *Cultural Studies* 9, no. 3 [1995]: 505–521). Thanks to Taylor & Francis Ltd., Oxfordshire, UK, for permission to include this material.

I'm grateful to all my students and colleagues in the Department of American Studies at the University of Canterbury. They have each helped to create a stimulating intellectual environment where scholarly productivity can flourish. In particular, I would like to thank my colleagues Yvonne Reineke (unfortunately no longer at Canterbury), Ken Harris, Vernon Andrews, and Cornelia Sears for kindly and thoughtfully forwarding to me news reports and other materials pertinent to this project. I am especially indebted to Leonard Wilcox and Valerie Kuletz for generously reading and commenting on drafts of portions of this book and for many enjoyable discussions from which I have learned much and that have often pressed me to reconsider, modify, or clarify some of the ideas contained within these pages. Finally, many thanks to my administrative and secretarial colleague, Gwen Standring, for her assistance and expertise.

My greatest debt of gratitude is to my mother, Joann C. Bacon, who has given me immeasurable support and encouragement throughout the various stages of this book's development. She has been a constant source of press clippings, anecdotes, and thoughtful opinions about popular media culture. Although she has not always agreed with my viewpoints, she has always been eager to discuss them.

TABLOIDCULTURE

John Walsh

1 The Genealogy of Tabloid Television

Popular culture always has its base in the experiences, the pleasures, the memories, the traditions of the people. It has connections with local hopes and local aspirations, local tragedies and local scenarios that are the everyday practices and the everyday experiences of ordinary folks. Hence, it links with . . . the informal, the underside, the grotesque. That is why it has always been counterposed to elite or high culture, and is thus a site of alternative traditions. And that is why the dominant tradition has always been deeply suspicious of it, quite rightly. — Stuart Hall, *Black Popular Culture* [1]

Introduction: Talking Tabloids

On May 8, 1988, John Walsh looked into the television camera with sincerity and firm resolve. Behind him, men and women could be seen shuffling through papers and answering telephones in surroundings resembling a busy police precinct house or FBI office. Walsh was making an appeal for help to the twenty million or so regular viewers of *America's Most Wanted*, the prime-time program he hosts each week on the Fox Television Network. [2] The problem at hand was Stephen Randall Dye, a fugitive from justice who allegedly shot a man in New Jersey in 1986 and was wanted in connection with the 1981 death of a motorcyclist in Cleveland. A dramatic re-creation of the 1986 shooting followed Walsh's introductory remarks. Then police mug shots of the fugitive were shown, along with detailed descriptions of Dye's tattoos, his loner's lifestyle, his heavy drinking.

Included in the television audience for *America's Most Wanted* on that Sunday night was the fugitive, Dye, himself. Aware of *Most Wanted*'s growing reputation for "getting its man" and unable to cope with the stress and foreboding generated by the program's report and dramatization, Dye turned himself over to San Diego police officers on May 20, less than two weeks after the original broadcast. In any event, it may have been only a matter of time for Dye, since law enforcement officials received more than 300 calls from viewers of the May 8 broadcast, many of whom correctly placed the fugitive in the San Diego vicinity. "I'm not a cop," says Walsh. "Nor am I some kind of vigilante. But there are 280,000 fugitives out there, and this is a chance to show that Americans can make a difference."[3] A number of Americans respond enthusiastically to Walsh's implicit challenge. According to *Most Wanted*'s producers, a typical broadcast spawns about 2,000 phone calls to the program's toll-free number throughout the evening. An additional 1,500 calls come in by the end of the following week.[4]

A consistent ratings hit for the young Fox Network, *America's Most Wanted* pleases not just the "ordinary" members of its audience but many cops as well. Robert Leschorn of the U.S. Marshals Service remarks that the program has "created the largest posse in American history."[5] Thus some law enforcement officials would like to see the concept extended, perhaps in the form of an entire channel devoted to the dramatization of fugitives' crimes. "I wish we could have our own station," said John Herbert, a New York City detective, after he captured the suspected perpetrator of six drug-related murders dramatized on *America's Most Wanted* in March 1988. "We could arrest a whole lot of bad guys."[6] In the show's first two seasons, viewers' phone-in tips led to the capture of about one fugitive per week.[7] By the time the show reached its fifth anniversary on the air in 1993, *America's Most Wanted* attributed the capture of 250 fugitives to what Walsh calls "the partnership" between media, audiences, and law enforcement. By September 1999, this figure had risen to 579.[8]

The broad genre represented by *America's Most Wanted* has become one of the most significant developments in recent U.S. media. This genre has attracted attention, scorn, and a variety of labels. "Reality-based" or "actuality" programming, "infotainment," "confrontainment," and "trash TV" are among the terms by which it has commonly been designated (and then typically dismissed without serious consideration) by numerous commentators. Perhaps the term with the greatest resonance, however, is "tabloid television."[9] During the last half of the 1980s and throughout the 1990s, tabloid television "grew and developed to the point of being an expected part of the television lineup."[10] Expected though its presence may now be, however, the genre remains a slippery entity. It entails a variety of intertwined discursive formations that occupy a mobile space where journalism and popular culture intersect. It includes a highly mixed bag of typical forms, thematic concerns, image repertoires, tones of voice, and narrative patterns, many of which are traditional for television but have been reworked in specific and sometimes striking ways. This is a genre (or more accurately a collection of genres) that is not susceptible to easy definition or summary characterization, because of both its internal diversity and its many overlaps with other sets of television genres. *America's Most Wanted*, for example, is, after the fashion of eclectic postmodern hybridity, part telethon, part newscast, part documentary, part cop show, and part family drama.[11] This hybridity highlights the importance of the insight that because of the nature of the medium that it is—and of contemporary media generally—television's generic territories can never be neatly self-contained. Rather, they constantly play off of, and mutually constitute, one another, for television's intergeneric universe is fluidly interpenetrating.[12]

Television genres can be delineated only provisionally and problematically. David Morley points out that media texts are always interdiscursive: they are continuously constituted and reconstituted by (and thus dependent on) the shifting relations of meaning that make up the intertextual networks within which they exist. A text thus never occupies a fixed position; it is always "placed and articulated with other texts in different ways."[13] This is as true of generic formations as it is of individual texts. Regarding TV talk shows, for example, Sonia Livingstone and Peter Lunt note that these programs "move between diverse generic forms . . . not simply because the genre is at a formative stage of development but because it is inherently unstable, drawing on a variety of generic conventions in a provisional manner in order to achieve a diversity of sometimes contradictory aims."[14] Tony Bennett argues that a text or a genre has no "in-itselfness." Genres and texts must therefore be analyzed in terms of "the different ways in which they have been culturally activated as a result of their inscription in different social, institutional and ideological contexts."[15] The principle that unifies a genre is therefore never neatly contained within that genre or its texts themselves. It is always a product, too (and perhaps primarily), of "the full range of the ideological and cultural traffic that has been conducted around [those texts] in . . . popular culture."[16]

Bearing in mind these stubborn problems of textual classification, we can nevertheless begin by setting out some of the terms of discussion and by noting significant family resemblances that tend to be shared between the various members of the unstable generic formation at hand. We might best understand TV "tabloidism" as a tendency or a collection of inter-related, trangeneric tendencies, sensibilities, and orientations that have long and well-established histories,[17] though they are currently best embodied in a set of identifiable textual forms that include various types of "actuality programming" like *America's Most Wanted* and *Cops*; disreputable, "sensationalistic," or "offbeat" news and public affairs programs like *A Current Affair* and *Hard Copy*; and issue-oriented talk shows like *Ricki Lake* and *Jerry Springer.* TV tabloidism not confined exclusively to textual forms such as these, however. Graham Knight observes that tabloid journalism's defining affinities and preoccupations (subjectivism, moral disorder, and deviance, to name a few) are characteristic of television as a whole, so that "it is perhaps more difficult to specify a distinctively tabloid television format," and it becomes, therefore, "a question not so much of major differences in style and content as of differences in detail and the ways these are combined."[18] Hence the differences between "lowbrow" programs typically labeled "tabloid," for example, and "middlebrow" offerings likely to receive the more socially respectable designation "news magazine" are ones of degree rather than kind. Indeed, we could imagine a continuum of "seriousness" and "respectability" that stretches from television's "highbrow" public affairs forums (like the networks' Sunday morning chat shows that feature government officials and learned commentators), through its "midcult" programming (such as, perhaps, *Sixty Minutes*, *20/20*, and *48 Hours*), to the "lowbrow" fare of its tabloid shows.[19] There are two significant points to make about such a continuum. First, the designations "highbrow," "midcult," and "lowbrow" bear an important relationship to the particular social groups that consume the objects thus categorized. Typically, the most disparaged cultural objects are those consumed predominantly by the most devalued social groups. Second, categories such as "highbrow," "midcult," and "lowbrow" are differentiated only by uncertain and fluidly shifting boundaries. Moreover, they can only ever be relative, and never objective, categories (the "lowbrow" is not inherently or objectively "low" but rather low only in relation to that which is designated as "high"). It is not my primary goal here, however, to produce a taxonomy of programming categories. Rather, my aim is to conceptualize some of the complex and shifting discourses of tabloid TV and their relationships to both those broader, always-in-process currents of meaning we call culture and the power-laden system of social relations within which all cultural production is embedded.

America's Most Wanted is a complex example of tabloid television that is fueled by political contradictions. On the one hand, this program contributes to the production of a generalized ethos of fear, within which the demonization, surveillance, and repression of threatening (and often nonwhite) "others" becomes a fact of everyday life. It is part of the apparatus that generates a continuous hum of "low-level fear" that permeates U.S. popular culture: "naturalized fear, ambient fear, ineradicable atmospheric fright, the discomfiting affective Muzak that might come to be remembered as a trademark of the late-twentieth-century America."[20] One study found that regular viewers of *America's Most Wanted*, *Cops*, and two other "reality-based" law enforcement shows are significantly more fearful of becoming victims of violent crime than others are.[21] But the mass production of programmed fear targets not only those who are interpellated as "innocent (potential) victims." When fugitives like Stephen Randall Dye are driven to participate in their own policing, it would seem that the apparatus of fear, in conjunction with social discipline (in the highly dystopian sense delineated by Michel Foucault) is operating at peak efficiency.[22] We have, in the Dye case, an example of what we might call "reflexive panopticism," where the object of surveillance becomes, in front of his television screen, the subject of the same normalizing gaze that the legal apparatus has trained on him. The prisoner assumes the tower guard's perspective in an even more literal sense than that described by Foucault.[23] The Dye case illustrates the contradictoriness of some of the forces at work within a regime of social power based upon Foucauldian mechanisms of disciplinary control. Perhaps the primary one is that between submission and empowerment: to benefit from the complex nexus of rewards and sanctions that make up a disciplinary society, people must submit themselves to the power carried within prescriptions to think and behave in normalized and normalizing ways.[24] Rewards thus become contingent on submission, and in submitting to police after America's Most Wanted made him a prime-time media figure, Stephen Randall Dye was rewarded with relief from the fear generated by the very mechanisms of surveillance and discipline to which he chose to submit himself.

On the other hand, there are reasons to be suspicious of some of the suspicions that most well-spoken commentators harbor toward the popularity of America's Most Wanted, which features cinematic reenactments of the criminal violation of everyday folks and populist appeals for assistance where the official institutions of law and order have failed. Pierre Bourdieu notes that whereas elite cultural taste makes a public display of subdued, detached, contemplative, and distanced aesthetic appreciation, the popular tastes of the working classes and those fractions of the middle classes with the least cultural capital express, by contrast, a "deep-rooted demand for participation," a "desire to enter into the game, identifying with the characters' joys and sufferings, worrying about their fate." [25] In his study of British tabloid newspaper readers, Mark Pursehouse notes the "sense of lively, active engagement" conveyed through "the sheer enthusiasm with which people spoke about their uses and opinions of the tabloids." [26] An ethos of participatory engagement pervades America's Most Wanted, from the level of its sincerely melodramatic examination of the consequences of criminal victimization to its incitements to pick up the telephone. Emotional investments and participatory inclinations such as those evoked by America's Most Wanted are all too often seen as evidence of the unsophistication or manipulability of the popular classes by those with an interest in distancing themselves from "vulgar tastes."

America's Most Wanted addresses cultural tastes born of alienation from power and tempered by popular resentment of the disproportionate exposure to criminal victimization that afflicts the socially subordinated. It is not surprising that at least one Nielsen survey found the program's core audience to consist of people with relatively low incomes living in large households (households of four or more people with combined earnings of less than $40,000 annually) situated in densely populated areas.[27] *America's Most Wanted* bespeaks, however indirectly, popular dissatisfaction with institutions perceived as incapable of fulfilling the great promises of liberal democracy, and it powerfully explores the tragic consequences of vulnerability in a society where vulnerability is a condition that runs rampant. The program's emphasis on the treacherous and threatening dimensions of everyday life speaks to widely frustrated desires for some secure measure of control over one's own circumstances and conditions of existence — even as it depressingly scapegoats the "criminally deviant" and reproduces white working-class racism. The alliances facilitated by *America's Most Wanted* are, to be sure, popular alignments with the power exerted by institutions of social regulation (as police departments' enthusiasm for the program demonstrates), so there is obvious justification for the view that such programs mobilize frustrated desires in ways that produce a hegemonic sense of popular consent to the basic structural configurations of the status quo.[28] But the program also paradoxically helps to sustain and amplify frustrations capable of counterhegemonic mobilization, a tendency that is characteristic of many forms of tabloid television.

Tabloid television is the electronic descendant of the déclassé tabloid newspapers that surround U.S. supermarket checkout counters.[29] John Fiske suggests a tripartite classification that is useful for developing a map of the contemporary journalistic landscape and its audiences.[30] First, there is the serious, official news (often dubbed "the quality press"), which targets, and is mostly consumed by, the well-educated middle classes. Its class-cultural location is imprinted in its language, its characteristic tones of voice, its underlying epistemology, and its particular designation of which topics are worthy of attention and which are too "insignificant" or "trashy." Next there is the alternative press, which consistently politicizes its practices of informing and so rejects the pretense of "objectivity" that distinguishes the news work of its "quality" counterpart. If the alternative press differs from official journalism in this one significant way, however, the alternative converges with its "respectable" twin in another equally important area: both are principally concerned with speaking to middle-class audiences (although, in the case of the politicized press, the target market is a dissident, usually "liberal" fraction of the affluent and educated classes). Consequently both the quality press and its alternative foil are *almost* of one voice in their constant denunciations of the third contemporary journalistic formation: the popular tabloid media, which have learned (albeit because of market exigencies) to converse far more effectively with the subordinated classes than either of the other journalisms and so have become quite commercially successful, as many commentators have (usually gloomily) noted. The tabloid media thus serve generally as conduits for the circulation of *popular* (as opposed to elite or official) ways of knowing.³¹ *Popular* knowledges are those produced and used by social formations with severely limited access to power in their struggles to attain some forms of control over the immediate conditions of ordinary life.³²

Although the defining characteristics of tabloid news are extremely fluid and so difficult to pin down, Fiske offers some helpful provisional suggestions: "Its subject matter is generally that produced at the intersection between public and private life; its style is sensational, sometimes skeptical, sometimes moralistically earnest; its tone is populist; its modality fluidly denies any stylistic difference between fiction and documentary, between news and entertainment."³³ We might add several equally provisional observations about tabloid television to those enumerated by Fiske. It prefers heightened emotionality and often emphasizes the melodramatic. It sometimes makes heavy use of campy irony, parody, and broad humor. It relies on an often volatile mix of realistic and antirealist representational conventions. It resists "objectivity," detachment, and critical distance. It is highly multidiscursive. It incorporates voices frequently excluded from "serious" news and often centers on those that are typically marginalized in mainstream media discourse. The "bizarre" and the "deviant" are central to its image repertoire. It is generally offensive to high- and middlebrow tastes. Moreover, it is often equally offensive to masculine tastes (although tabloid discourse is itself gendered: there are both masculine and feminine varieties of address found within it). It frequently violates dominant institutional standards and procedures for the production and validation of "truth." It thrives on the grotesque, the scandalous, and the "abnormal." Its images are often stark, raw, unprettified, and unsanitized. It dwells on social and moral disorder. Among its favorite themes are the ubiquity of victimization and the loss of control over the outcomes of events, and of one's fate. Also typical are stories involving gender disturbances and ambiguities, troubled domestic and familial relationships, and paranormal phenomena that apparently outstrip the explanatory power of scientific rationalism. Tabloid media simultaneously defamiliarize the ordinary and banalize the exotic.

Tabloid television's discursive conventions and representational strategies place it at odds with the canons of official journalism, which stresses, among other things, objectivism and a proper distance—critical and emotional—from its subjects. From the perspective of official journalism, therefore, tabloid television's sins are indeed numerous. It lacks taste, decorum, and seriousness. It "panders" to the people, stressing storytelling over facts and conflating "reality" with "fiction." It eschews the mission of public edification and "enlightenment." It serves unrefined tastes for the scandalous and grotesque. It encourages video voyeurism. It sensationalizes the news, short-circuiting reason through excessive emotionality. It exists for no apparent reason but that it satisfies the needs of broadcasters' bottom lines. It threatens the viability of the "real" news. The laundry list of tabloid television's transgressions bears a strong family resemblance to the many complaints typically registered against popular culture in general by middle- or highbrows and their media spokespeople. This should come as no surprise, since tabloid television is best understood as a form of popular culture, whereas "legitimate journalism" has historically been produced according to the tastes and knowledge practices of the most privileged and empowered formations in modern Western societies.

Cultural phenomena require methods of investigation and analysis that differ significantly from those used to study industrial and economic practices. My aim in this book is to understand tabloid media *not* primarily as industrial products but rather *in terms of their popularity*. The "popularity" designated by the term "popular culture" should not be reduced to the commonplace definition of this word, which denotes merely widespread enthusiasm for something. Following Stuart Hall, I understand the popular as a "class-cultural formation" that encompasses the cultures of the socially subordinated, oppressed, excluded, and marginalized—in short, cultures that are "of the people." [34] Under the highly elaborated and commodified conditions of late-capitalist society, the people produce their cultures largely from materials provided by the "culture industries" (television, radio, cinema, mass publishing, the amusement industries, and so on). Just as people's conditions of existence differ starkly according to their forms and levels of access to social power and resources, so too do their cultural tastes and preferences differ equally starkly. The differences between the texts, objects, and discourses circulated within popular culture and those prioritized by elite cultural institutions such as museums, conservatories, and universities are symptomatically expressive of the more fundamental differences between popular and elite tastes. Bourdieu demonstrates how the taste-based distinctions created within the sphere of culture work in turn to generate inequalities and political exclusions.[35] His analysis suggests that the system of cultural distinctions is indeed no less important than the economic system as a producer and distributor of power.

The ordinary social experiences of most people living in white, patriarchal late capitalism involve a degree of subordination and marginalization (and we must keep in mind that these are always relative concepts). Thus we cannot entirely ignore the commonplace definition of popularity as widespread circulation, for popular culture is generally majoritarian in a way that elite culture is not. We must not, however, confine our understanding of the popular to this banal definition, in part because of the extreme heterogeneity of popular social formations. A more useful indicator of the degree to which a cultural object or practice is "popular" is the extent to which it is both widely enjoyed *and* reviled or trivialized by social elites and official institutions. Popular culture is then a symbolic, discursive, and actively practiced expression of the social presence of an alliance of subordinated forces and powers formed in general correspondence with categories of empowerment and disempowerment such as race, volumes of economic and educational capital possessed, gender, age, ethnicity, sexual orientation, and geographic regionality. This multitude of differences (only a handful of which I've explicitly invoked here) *within* the popular should indicate that popular culture is always and necessarily crosscut by an equally broad multitude of social and political interests that cannot always be neatly congruent but, on the contrary, often contradict and challenge one another. Therefore, the notion that the popular is formed around a set of interest-based social and cultural alliances should always be counterbalanced by an awareness of the way in which such alliances must constantly be forged and constructed and are routinely undermined by the very differences that "the popular" necessarily includes within itself.[36]

Wherever the cultural tastes and practices of some people disgust and offend others, there can be little doubt that we are in the presence of the political. We shall see that tabloid media produce nearly as much disgust and offense as pleasure. The production of disgust, offense, and popular pleasures is of primary significance for cultural theory because it is central to the general process whereby the meanings we make of ourselves and of the social world are organized and reorganized. This process has crucial implications for social change, not least because it shapes the production, diffusion, and urgency of the recognition of a need for change. The meanings we use to make sense of the world and our place within it play a key role, moreover, in the determination of the types and degrees of social change that become thinkable (and therefore possible) at any historical moment.

(Popular culture is historically unstable and variable (its objects and practices are sometimes annexed or appropriated by elite culture, for example).[37] What does, however, persist over time in a stratified society, Hall argues, is the basic distinction between the popular and the elite.[38] Thus, over and against the popular stands "the side with the cultural power to decide what belongs and what does not," that "other alliance of classes, strata and social forces which constitute what is not 'the people' and not the 'popular classes': the culture of the power-bloc."[39] Although Hall's "power-bloc" is a set of alliances whose members enjoy relatively easy access to the institutions and instrumentalities of social domination, it does not have a monopoly on historical agency. On the contrary, its agency constrains, but is also restricted by, that of the popular forces that, at key historical junctures and specific social sites, constitute the limits on which dominating power runs aground. The power-bloc is not a class or a demographic group, though in the late-twentieth-century United States it corresponds closely with the social interests, tastes, and values associated with straight, white, urban, adult, upper-middle-class masculinity. The category of "the people," by contrast, is constantly defined and redefined by the set of preferences, interests, and alliances that coalesce and disperse continuously among the social relations of the marginalized and subordinated formations.[40] For Hall, the struggles and contestation that characterize relationships between the power-bloc and the people form "the central line of contradiction around which the terrain of culture is polarised" and thus displace traditional Marxist notions of "class against class" in cultural analysis.[41]

Because of its openness to types of information and ways of knowing that are typically excluded from the "hard news," tabloid television is a cultural resource that is well suited to the sustenance of an oppositional popular stance toward the tastes, values, and "standards" preferred by the power-bloc. Although it is often accused of "cheapening" public life, its populist cultural politics cannot adequately be reduced to such dismissive terms. Although popular culture rarely traffics in radical cultural politics, it nevertheless opens spaces where some progressive forces can develop and even gain social momentum. Their producers may be concerned only with maximizing economic profits, but consumers have their own reasons for engaging with tabloid media. Insofar as these audiences are "of the people" and not the power-bloc, their cultural preferences and practices will generally express resentment and antagonism toward the forces of social domination; or they will at least seek out a cultural terrain on which their agency can be maximized—that is, one that strives to evade many of the power-bloc's multifarious techniques of discipline and control (which include the constant elaboration of cultural "standards"). Official journalism generally contains little that is of much use to the people, for the power-bloc has maximal control over the forms of knowledge considered appropriate to it (and thus over the truths those knowledges have the power to produce). Through its transgression of bourgeois "standards" and tastes, its contradiction of the truths circulated in official news, and its emphasis on voices usually marginalized or excluded from the discourse of elite journalism, tabloidism provokes, encourages, and amplifies some of the popular forces that interfere with the extension of imperializing power-bloc knowledges. While this is clearly and obviously not part of any revolutionary praxis, its significance should not be minimized. It is part of the more ordinary micropolitics of everyday culture, which, while less dramatic than revolutionary politics, could become more closely intertwined with organized democratic movements if such micropolitics were better understood, particularly by critics on the Left, than has historically been the case.[42]

Rosemary J. Coombe discusses an example of popular knowledge that implicitly challenges and ultimately denies the sufficiency of scientific rationalism, a socially powerful way of knowing that has historically been linked to a variety of hegemonic techniques and projects. In the early 1980s, she recounts, a popular rumor campaign linked megacorporation Proctor and Gamble (interestingly, television's largest single advertiser) with the forces of Satan by ascribing an "occult significance" to the "man-in-the-moon" logo inscribed on its products. One woman observed, for example, that "when you turn the logo up to a mirror, the curlicues in the man's beard become 666—the sign of the Antichrist." A leaflet of unknown origin told that a Proctor and Gamble official speaking on national TV "gave all the credit for the success of the company to SATAN," and that the folks at P&G "have placed their Satanist symbol on all their products so that they can get SATAN into every home in America." Others claimed that Proctor and Gamble's "owner" publicly admitted that he sold his soul to Lucifer in return for corporate riches.[43]

Proctor and Gamble invests huge sums into monitoring and controlling the use of its trademarks, which are designed to regulate the meanings circulating around its products and, perhaps more significantly, around its corporate identity. In 1982, then, Proctor poured millions of dollars into an all-out assault on the "hydra-headed" popular rumor. Its PR department issued a statement claiming that "Proctor is going after the rumor with all the diligence that it devotes to a new product."[44] Despite Proctor's best efforts, however, the rumor continued to spread and inflict harm on the conglomerate. Finally, Proctor admitted defeat, removing its 135-year-old trademark from all its products, an act that prompted marketing experts to describe the affair as "a rare case of a giant company succumbing to a bizarre and untraceable rumor."[45]

What's all the more remarkable about this example is that it occurred during a decade that saw high levels of *organized* opposition to Proctor's products and "rational" criticism of its corporate practices, most of which was ineffectual compared to the power of the popular knowledges brought to bear on P&G's image apparatus via the Satanism rumor. The Federal Centers for Disease Control had linked Proctor's tampons with toxic shock syndrome; white middle-class feminists protested the company's advertising campaigns; and labor unions organized boycotts of the corporation's products in conjunction with ongoing struggles for recognition. Nevertheless, Coombe notes, "it was the battle over the meaning of a tiny moon-and-stars symbol that brought the diffident corporation most prominently to public attention" and posed the most serious of threats to its "benign, if somewhat empty, public image."[46] She argues persuasively that this and similar rumor campaigns amount to a kind of "cultural guerrilla tactics" that are politically significant because they express and encourage a profound popular suspicion toward corporate social control and cultural hegemony.[47]

Rumor is politically useful because of its capacity for passing anonymously and elusively through the social world. "It belongs to no one and is possessed by everyone," as Coombe aptly puts it.[48] The social disreputability of rumormongering is a mark of the danger it poses to those whom it targets. The failures of the more organized forms of opposition to Proctor and Gamble were likely exacerbated by their organizers' inadequate awareness of the significance of popular knowledges such as those expressed through the rumor campaign, which undoubtedly inhibited their capacity to forge alliances with the people they were unable to reach through more conventional tactics of political communication. Popular knowledges, antagonisms, and suspicions are expressed in very different social accents and a different idiom from those deployed by middle-class dissidents. This can unfortunately lead many middle-class dissidents to misinterpret (and therefore dismiss) popular knowledges such as the Proctor and Gamble rumor as ostensible evidence of the extent to which people's ways of knowing have been colonized by an "irrational" and even "delusional" tabloid media culture. Such dismissive attitudes and misunderstandings of the kinds of popular knowledges circulated in tabloid newspapers and on tabloid television constitute a debilitating deficiency that middle-class progressives cannot afford to ignore. As Pursehouse puts it, "however contradictory the ground worked on by the tabloids, the kind of appeals they work on have to be tackled if the Left is to reach significantly wider than the already converted."[49]

Because of its materially rooted antagonism toward the agencies of the power-bloc, popular knowledge is often accessible to various forms of insurgency of the sort associated with the rumor campaign against Proctor and Gamble. It is an irony of late capitalism, however, that the commercially interested professionals of the "culture industries" generally have a better grasp of popular tastes and tones of voice than do most other members of relatively privileged social formations (including social dissidents), for their livelihoods depend on it. Of course, such professionals typically have no inclination to encourage popular insurgency and are indeed likely to be inclined against it. It is, however, in the interests of the people to oppose, to challenge, and to argue with the ways of knowing that are validated by the official culture (and promoted through institutions such as professional journalism).[50] The variety of forms of tabloid media currently available circulate mediated modalities of the popular voice. These media forms reveal symptomatic traces of the role taken by "the people" and their discredited popular tastes in the historical determination of the way in which institutional systems of cultural production develop.[51] Conversely, therefore, these media forms also facilitate popular cultural productivity and are easily inserted into the popular and oral cultures of everyday life. In the chapters that follow, I will examine some of the mediated popular voices articulated through the texts of tabloid television and tabloid media more generally, and I will analyze some of the controversies and struggles over meaning that have arisen around their success and proliferation.

In this book, I turn to a number of theoretical sources that many people consider to be incompatible with one another. For example, I find both Jean Baudrillard's postmodern theories of hyperreality and simulation and John Fiske's Birmingham-derived accounts of popular cultural productivity to be extremely useful for understanding tabloid culture.[52] At the same time, however, I recognize that aspects of the respective theoretical frameworks developed by these two authors differ at times so greatly as to be nearly incommensurable. With regard to questions of audience subjectivity, for example, Baudrillard and Fiske could not, perhaps, be further apart. For Baudrillard, whose penchant for theoretical excessiveness, totalization, and ironic hyperbole has frequently been noted, the audience is at times passivized in the extreme. For example, Baudrillard, like Fredric Jameson, finds the metaphor of schizophrenia to be productive. In the contemporary age, therefore, the media subject is understood as a schizophrenic who "cannot produce the limits of his very being" and who therefore "becomes a pure screen, a pure absorption and resorption surface of the influent networks."[53] This conceptualization of the media subject is far indeed from Fiske's understanding of active audience agency. For Fiske, media consumption creates opportunities for subordinated social formations to maintain a subversive sense of their own difference from the ideologically dominant through the assertion of subcultural meanings, pleasures, values, and identities. His view is that "television is so popular" because "the characteristics of its texts and of its modes of reception enable an *active* participation in that sense-making process which we call 'culture.' "[54]

My response to the objections that I anticipate regarding the simultaneous use of such apparently incompatible theorists is to suggest, following Hall, that "the problem is that it is assumed that theory consists of a series of closed paradigms" rather than to "understand theorizing as an open horizon, moving within the magnetic field of some basic concepts, but constantly being applied afresh."[55] In this book, I appeal to Baudrillard because I think that especially his concepts of hyperreality and simulation uncannily grasp something of the *cultural conditions* brought about under postmodernity and the image saturation with which its pervasive electronic networks present us. Indeed, I think this dimension of his work can productively be conjoined with aspects of the hegemony theory that lies at the center of Fiske's analyses, for such a conjunction can help to overcome Baudrillard's ideas about media subjectivity that I often find less convincing. It is therefore Baudrillard's account of the postmodern cultural landscape to which I turn and that I find most useful, although I believe that the limitations of that account can be compensated for to some degree with theories like Fiske's of audience agency and semiotic contradiction which, derived as they are from the work of Hall and others associated with Birmingham, seem better equipped to explain contestation between different cultural forces, struggles over hegemonic meaning, and aspects of popular cultural productivity and pleasure. I do, however, find something of a convergence between Baudrillard's use of the concepts of spectacle and fascination, on the one hand, and Fiske's account of resistive textual characteristics and reception practices, on the other. In his essay "In the Shadow of the Silent Majorities," Baudrillard suggests that spectacle displaces, and that the mass audience intransigently refuses, many of the controlling meanings with which they are routinely deluged.[56] While, as I point out hereafter, the way in which Baudrillard works this position out—and particularly his use of the concept of the "mass"—is problematic, it is also both usefully suggestive and not entirely incompatible with the approaches to media reception, including Fiske's, that have been derived from hegemony theory in recent years.[57]

Related to this issue is a more encompassing objection some may have to the way in which, in this book, I rely heavily on broadly materialist approaches to culture and history derived from the Gramscian Marxism developed around the "Birmingham school" of cultural studies and from the work of Pierre Bourdieu, as well as poststructuralist and postmodernist concepts and frameworks such as those of Foucault and Baudrillard. Stuart Hall again speaks usefully to this issue in his argument that cultural studies must remain ever open to external theoretical influences including those (such as, for example, psychoanalysis, he says) that may on the face of things seem to have little more than misplaced and contradictory relationships to the Birmingham projects. Cultural studies is, Hall asserts, fundamentally about "theorizing in the postmodern context, if you like, in the sense that it does not believe in the finality of a finished theoretical paradigm."[58] Although he expresses concern that the "discursive position" associated with poststructuralist and postmodern thinking "is often in danger of losing its reference to material practice and historical conditions," Hall also criticizes "vulgar materialism" in his assertion that "we need to think material conditions in their determinate discursive form, not as a fixed absolute."[59] In this book, I treat the material, the social, and the discursive as mutually informing and mutually constitutive phenomena. I therefore mobilize theories that, however incompatible in some respects, enable me to attend to the concerns pertinent to each domain and, I hope, to illuminate some of the complex relations between them.

I thus try here to explain the rapid expansion of tabloid media forms and discourses partly in terms of the material and social history of that political and cultural phenomenon known as Reaganism, and also in terms of certain changes in the media industries. I rely heavily on the idea that popular tastes are produced in part by social and material conditions, following both Gramscian and Pierre Bourdieu's approaches to that issue. I also appeal to Foucault and Baudrillard not because they provide a "method" or doctrine on which to rely but because they work with a set of concepts and concerns (including, for example, discursive relations, regimes of truth, power and knowledge, normalization, hyperreality, simulation, and obscenity) that seem particularly useful for understanding aspects of tabloid culture. Therefore, I am not so troubled as some may be about combining some of the assumptions associated with cultural materialism and social history, say, with approaches developed by Michel Foucault, a scholar who, as Lynn Hunt points out, "denied the validity of any reductive relationship between discursive formations and their socio-political contexts."[60] The key term here is "reductive." I believe my approach is ultimately consonant with that of a poststructuralist such as Foucault, who, while always wary of reductive causal arguments, remained resolutely interested in elaborating the *conditions of possibility*—some of which may be social or material—for the appearance of this or that discursive event. I believe that I follow Foucault by analyzing the knowledges circulated through tabloid media in terms of their relationship to historically specific modes of discursive power and authority. By inflecting this Foucauldian problematic with a Gramscian concern for the hegemonic relations between different knowledges that coexist within the same social formation, I seek to trace the expansion of tabloid media in terms of its consequences for the stability of the dominant regime of truth.[61]

Such an approach differs significantly from the critical theory of Jürgen Habermas and its central concern with the "public sphere" (a concept that has been both influential and controversial).[62] For Habermas, the public sphere emerged with the bourgeoisie in seventeenth- and eighteenth-century Europe, where it served as an independent arena for the formation and circulation of critical opinions that were relatively untainted by the intervention of either state or commercial interests. It could therefore function as a source of resistance to those very interests and thus as a wellspring of progressive social change. The bourgeois public sphere, however, was born dying and has long since foundered in an extreme state of accelerated decrepitude. Rapidly colonized by commercial and bureaucratic forces, "refeudalized" and shrunken to its virtual vanishing point, it exists now for all intents and purposes as little more than a dim memory and a distant hope beyond all hope. For Habermas, "critical publicity" has been replaced by public relations: the stage- and media-managed spectacle of domination masquerading as democracy and consumerism substituting for citizenship.

As noted above, however, extensive debates have developed around the very concept of the public sphere, whose ultimate origins lie in classical Greek democracy but depend heavily on modern liberal political theory and the philosophical legacies of the Enlightenment in general. The public sphere is defined in terms of the "communicative rationality" from which it is born, to which it gives rise, and on which it subsists. Anthony Giddens observes that this communicative rationality functions in Habermas's thinking as a counter to "relativism" and a basis for interpreting "the overall evolution of human society." Hence the relative "evolutionary advancement" of both individuals and whole cultures can be charted, for Habermas, according to "the range and depth of the defensible validity-claims which they incorporate."[63] The public sphere concept thus entails problematic normative assumptions about the "irrationality" of many cultural practices and configurations external to the modern West or marginalized and dominated within it.[64] Within these normative assumptions are embedded further troubling implications concerning class (the rational procedures and the models for "consensus" associated with the public sphere are explicitly bourgeois) and gender (the very distinction between public and private, and the valorization of the former at the expense of the latter, carry far from innocent consequences for sexual and gender politics).[65]

Moreover, the concept of "the public" presumes a level of coherence, consensus, and homogeneity that is highly dubious, especially under contemporary social conditions. In fact, many forms of popular knowledge that circulate through tabloid media clearly point toward some of the serious difficulties that beset the central Habermasian claim for the possibility of a universal mode of consensus rationality capable of mediating between different social standpoints. As Jodi Dean writes, statistically widespread UFO belief in the United States, for example, "challenges the presumption that there is some 'public' that shares a notion of reality, a concept of reason, and a set of criteria by which claims to reason and rationality are judged."[66] Indeed, not only do such heretical popular knowledges dispute the empirical existence of these supposedly shared concepts and rationalistic criteria; they question their very potential to exist. Some commentators assert that the *ideal* of critical publicity, however historically illusory and unattainable in current practice, nonetheless serves as a "usefully mobilising fiction."[67] However, that very ideal may also lead its adherents to misunderstand or misrecognize the at least potential counterhegemonic thrust of some popular counterknowledges that nevertheless fall short of the standards for this imagined critical rationality (such as the Satanism rumor discussed earlier). We must wonder about the relationship between the *ideal* of rationalistic critical publicity and Habermas's view that the "uncritical masses" use media as a "tranquilizing substitute for action."[68]

Still, some scholars have made use of Habermas and the public sphere concept to analyze at least one realm of the tabloid television domain: the issue-oriented daytime talk shows. One strong example of such work is Livingstone and Lunt's *Talk on Television*.[69] The authors pay careful attention to the weaknesses and criticisms of Habermas's "public sphere" concept and his social theory generally. Drawing on both Habermas and a number of his important critics and revisionists, Livingstone and Lunt retain the public sphere terminology while suggesting several significant ways to reformulate the Habermasian conceptualization of it. To this terminology, therefore, they add several key qualifying concepts and thus speak of a "proletarian public sphere," an "oppositional public sphere," a public sphere that sometimes exists only under very localized conditions. The Habermasian public sphere is thus transformed, becoming multiple, heterogeneous, contestatory, and not necessarily dependent on either consensus reality or universal rationality. Indeed, Livingstone and Lunt push this model to a point where it comes close to the poststructurally inflected version of hegemony theory adopted here, for they seek partly to recognize and listen to voices and knowledges that would likely be considered simply irrational and apolitical from Habermas's perspective. As the authors note, "the audience discussion programme may not conform to the bourgeois debate and yet may still be compatible with oppositional conceptions of public spheres as sites of discursive contestation."[70] Although I therefore find much that is indeed valuable in their approach, I don't share Livingstone and Lunt's interest in retaining the Habermasian terminology of the public sphere in light of the vexing problems to which it gives rise.

One constellation of issues and terms that I do find particularly useful for understanding tabloid culture is the one surrounding the debates over postmodernity. While it is well known that there is no settled definition of the postmodern, there is a set of issues with which this concept is widely understood to engage. Among the ones that I find most pertinent to tabloid culture are those concerning the consequences of increasing media and image saturation, including a shift of, or threat to, modern sense-making practices (and to "sense" itself, in some accounts) and the increasing prioritization of images over "the real"; a general instability and uncertainty regarding key modernist organizational categories (including, for example, distinctions between "public" and "private," "reality" and "representation"); a generalized pluralization, relativization, and fragmentation of discourses and knowledge games; an increase in cultural products marked by stylistic eclecticism and bricolage; and the growth of incredulity toward what Jean-François Lyotard has famously called "grand narratives," including those that underwrite modern claims for the universality and "objectivity" of scientific rationalism.[71] Tabloid culture, as we shall see, is immersed in image rearticulation and appropriation—among "the most widely discussed features of postmodern cultural production," as Jim Collins points out.[72] The tabloid media also exemplify the commodification of culture that lies at the heart of many working definitions of postmodernity; the consequence is a profound destabilization of differences between "news" and "entertainment." Although "postmodernity" has no settled definition, then, I nevertheless believe it is worth thinking "tabloid culture" on the terrain of the problematic that is formed by such concerns.

Before proceeding further, there is one more aspect of postmodernism that deserves special mention, for it pertains to all that is yet to come. In a famous essay, Jameson suggests that "the very function of the news media is to relegate . . . recent historical experiences as rapidly as possible into the past."[73] The one-two punch of electronic hyperspeed and image saturation renders contemporary media events ready, almost coterminously with their currency, to be jettisoned on to the scrap heap of history. On the one hand, the *hyperspeed* of electronic images means that we experience events with an increasingly enhanced sense of simultaneity and direct involvement as these events unfold in all their indeterminacy. The logic of "you are there" is taken to the nth degree. Thus, when the media responded instantaneously and en masse to the unfolding slow-speed police chase after O.J. Simpson (a chase that seemed literally frozen in time in comparison with the hyperspeed of media mobilization around it), audiences rushed from their televisions to the freeway to insert their bodies into the electronically mediated scene, extending and literalizing the effect of simultaneous (over)presence with which the contemporary media imbue events. On the other hand, the incredible volume of images and commentary that results from the saturation coverage of such events means that many audiences are already exhausted with those very events almost from the moment they begin. Consequently, many of the major tabloid media events of the last decade or so have been accompanied by high-volume spin-off discourses in the media about how overwearied with each event audiences have been. Even as they intensely covered stories such as the O.J. Simpson case (chapter 2), the death of Princess Diana (chapter 6), and, more recently, Zippergate (also known as the Ken Starr scandal), the media clamored endlessly and from the start about how fed up with these stories their audiences already were.

A media environment that is marked by such an odd yet increasingly characteristic mélange of images and discourses works to provoke a strange admixture of exhaustion and desire for the next media event, long before the present one has even reached its culmination. This process therefore primes us for the quick relegation of events to the dustbin of "ancient" history. Thus, although the modern category of "news" has always been, by definition, one that has a sort of "planned obsolescence" built into it, I believe that under current conditions distinguished by the hyperspeed of media mobilization and a hyperabundance of images and discursive output, hypers(t)imulation and overpresence produce events that verge on a necrotic form of history even before their achievement of narrative closure. However, such processes function not so much to generate "historical amnesia," as Jameson argues,[74] as to deposit residual memory traces that prepare the way for subsequent media reappropriations of those very events that have become the source of cultural exhaustion: having been thus rapidly aged, such events speedily come to constitute appropriate subjects for nostalgia-before-its-time.[75] Cultural conditions such as these help to explain how tabloid media events like the O.J. Simpson case and the Amy Fisher saga can seem tiresome, outworn, and obsolete within weeks of their appearance, let alone from the perspective of several years hence.[76] At the same time, such apparently "outworn" events remain available for retrospective reactivation from time to time, as when the three made-for-TV movies about Amy Fisher are rerun although the "real" Fisher has long since vanished from the media limelight, or the players in the Simpson murder trial resurface in a spate of "where are they now?" stories such as those that made the media rounds at the time of the fifth anniversary of the Brentwood murders in 1999.[77] Such nostalgic remembrances serve both to reactivate "dead" media events via the circuitry of dormant memory trace deposits and to further propel relatively recent happenings into the deeper recesses of the past, for questions such as "where are they now" belong to the bulwark of tropology that consigns incidents to obsolescence.

There is, therefore, a powerful confluence of forces that work to produce and regulate our perceptions of the "timeliness" of media events, and to rapidly imbue tabloid phenomena such as the Simpson affair and others with an aura of outdatedness. Adequate analysis of such phenomena demands that the analyst resist these forces and the sense of cultural exhaustion they work to generate. Because the in-built "obsolescence" of popular media events works to thwart precisely the very forms of understanding that are needed, critical analysis must defy the puissance of cultural exhaustion and expulsion in order that we may explore the tabloid forms and practices that have come to play an increasingly large and significant role in the contemporary media universe.

In capitalist societies, there is an important contradiction at the heart of the cultural process: the economic interests of cultural industrialists can be served only if the culture industries provide people with objects and texts capable of being turned into popular culture. In television news, this contradiction becomes acute. The power-bloc has an interest in producing forms of news that support its cultural authority. Therefore, *official* news is built around the circulation of the kinds of knowledge that serve long-term power-bloc interests. But it is generally in the interests of the people to argue with the power-bloc and to question its privileged modalities of knowledge production.[78] It has long been recognized that there are significant differences between official and popular news tastes and preferences. These have produced a protracted and continuing conflict between television journalists who, like cultural missionaries, strive for public "enlightenment," and those who would prefer to produce news and informational programming that people actually choose to consume.

During television's early years, however, newscasts were not typically considered to be vehicles of popularity. Instead, they served primarily as markers of broadcasters' commitment to the "public interest," as required by federal law. Accordingly, the networks committed relatively scant resources and energy to news production, which was largely regarded as a perennial money loser incapable of capturing the attention of mass audiences to any significant degree. In the wake of the quiz show scandals of the late fifties and FCC chairman Newton Minow's famous 1961 characterization of television as a "vast wasteland," the networks made a bid to improve their reputations in respectable cultural circles by vastly expanding their production of news, documentaries, and public affairs programming.[79] Although it was calculated to garner prestige and capture cultural cachet, the expansion of journalistic programming in the early sixties had the ironic effect of requiring producers to seek new ways to increase television journalism's popular appeal. If they were going to increase their financial outlays on journalistic programming, after all, they had better reap a return more tangible than cachet. Thus, in the early 1960s, the expansion of network newscasts on CBS and NBC from fifteen- to thirty-minute formats was quickly followed by imaginative experimentation with a greater variety of ways to present news with enhanced visual and narrative interest. For example, when thieves made off with $7 million during a British railroad heist in 1963 but left no videographic evidence, Don Hewitt, executive producer of the CBS evening news, ransacked the film classic *The Great Train Robbery* for surrogate images.[80] Such techniques, which had been pressed into service by the producers of newsreels dating back to the 1930s, would later become commonplace on tabloid newscasts such as *Hard Copy* and *A Current Affair*.

When the networks began covering the political and social conflicts of the 1960s, including especially the civil rights movement, the war in Vietnam, and the so-called U.S. war at home, TV news developed an unprecedented broad appeal. Broadcast historians and other commentators have associated this growth in the popularity of TV news with the development of emotionally intense narrative styles that emphasize high-impact images at the expense of official commentary and fact-based objectivism of the sort preferred by the establishment of print journalism.[81] The ensuing conflict over journalistic "quality," which continues today, was very much a conflict between conceptions of journalism as an extension of literate culture and journalistic practices that were increasingly anchored in the visual. This conflict had repercussions concerning the most fundamental aspects of journalistic epistemology. "Legitimate" print journalism linked neatly with the socially prioritized literacy of the privileged classes it mostly served, whereas television news appealed visually and emotively to the debased orality of the "masses," since its consumption and verbal recirculation required no skills of literacy. Despite photography's powerful modernist appeals to transparent truthfulness and television's claims to immediacy, the written-ness of print journalism was persistently touted as a hallmark of its superiority. In his influential analysis of the relationship between oral and literate cultures, Walter Ong helps to explain why: "Writing separates the knower from the known and thus sets up conditions for 'objectivity,' in the sense of personal disengagement or distancing."[82] The public (and private) demonstration of one's capacity for detachment and distantiation in cultural consumption is among the primary practices through which the socially powerful create and display a sense of their own cultural superiority vis-à-vis the socially weak.

Consequently the place of visual images in journalism has long been a subject of controversy, since many perceive, in the directness and immediacy of images, a threat to the pseudoscientific objectivity of official news work.[83] Moreover, throughout Western history, images have often (though by no means always) been associated with seduction and superficiality. That a vast bulk of the imagery generated by Western cultures takes "woman" as its subject suggests that such associations are more than coincidental and perhaps bespeak displaced masculinist fears and anxieties regarding the feminine and the "irrationality" it represents in the patriarchal imagination. Bourdieu notes that in the tradition of Western aesthetic criticism, condescension toward "easy" cultural pleasures often appropriates the regulatory discourses of sexual virtue, so that denunciations of "shallow" popular works and of female profligacy take place in the same register: the "easy" popular work is as "cheap," "undemanding," and inherently flawed as an "easy lay." Similar discursive convergencies occur in the criticism of debased, visually rooted journalism, especially TV news. *Washington Post* columnist David S. Broder observes tellingly, for instance, that "we cannot [afford to] reduce" news to the "close-up pictures on which television thrives. . . . [For] we *cannot think straight . . . if our emotions* are being *jerked up and down by . . .* zoom lenses." [84] Broder's commentary contains a barely—just barely—submerged sexual subtext that evinces a fear of the seductive, too-close, too-easy image. Denunciatory discourses such as Broder's are central to the production of masculine cultural spheres and identities, for the threat posed by the feminized aspects of the seductively easy image extends to convey fear for the feminization of the spectator. Thus feminist film theorist Mary Ann Doane has written of "the peculiar susceptibility to the image . . . attributed to the woman in our culture," whose "spectatorship is yet another clearly delineated mark of her excess." [85] Hence conflicts between word and image, "reason" and spectacle, have long been near the center of struggles over the popularization of journalism.

Despite the cultural disreputability of the growing imagism of 1960s telejournalistic practice, this shift had brought newscasts' increasing profit potential to the attention of network bosses. [86] So the late sixties and the seventies brought a massive economic expansion of the networks' news divisions. No longer would they be considered relatively unimportant beyond their function of demonstrating the networks' public-spiritedness to powerful observers. Instead, the news divisions became vital network organs. The conception of television news as a profit center was troubling to traditional journalists, however. Even Edward R. Murrow, who had certainly done his part to advance the popularization of television journalism during the 1950s, spoke out about the incompatibility of popular tastes and journalistic responsibility. [87] As early as 1958, Murrow had warned that television's "constant striving to reach the largest possible audience for everything" carried the potential to change the journalistic profession irreversibly and for the worse. [88]

The transformation of television news was driven not only at the network level but also by changes taking place at broadcasting stations around the country. During the late sixties and the seventies, there was an "explosion" in the production of local news as station managers began to recognize the economic potential of their in-house newscasts, particularly since all the advertising revenue generated by those shows belonged to the stations. [89] (By contrast, network affiliates received only a flat compensation fee and a limited amount of local advertising time during the networks' newscasts and, indeed, during prime-time programming hours.) Moreover, station managers discovered that broadcasters with the best local news ratings also tended to have the highest *overall* ratings within their markets.[90] As competition between local broadcasters became fierce during the recession of the early seventies, stations became ever more reliant on the capacity of their in-house news productions to convey an image capable of serving loosely as an identity marker, somewhat like a corporate trademark, but with greater personality. This spawned the local TV news "family," usually built around an attractive mixed-sex couple with a communicative style whose phatic production of an imaginary viewing community was at least as significant as its "informational" work. Graham Knight suggests that "tabloid television news began effectively in the early 1970s with the 'happy talk' format of 'Eyewitness' and 'Action News' shows in major U.S. metropolitan areas like New York, Los Angeles, and Chicago."[91]

During this period, local news began to prefigure what would later emerge as tabloid television's penchant for what we might call the hyper-visibilization of events. This had partly to do with the development of technologies of mobility and miniaturization (including satellites and Mini-cams) associated with the electronic news-gathering boom that had, by 1980, spread through the local news production industry.[92] This trend toward electronic news gathering expanded local newscasting's visual field and enhanced the sense of rawness and immediacy generated by videography. Local news programs began to use electronic news-gathering technologies to regularly "transport" their audiences to the scenes of crimes in progress, unfolding hostage situations, urban shooting sprees, raging fires, and the like. Additionally, they used satellite uplinks to bring distant events near, inflecting the far-off with a localizing accent. The development of electronic news-gathering technologies was a key phase in the evolution of a pandemic communications network increasingly approximating a global central nervous system—albeit one with localizing attributes. In such an environment, the significance and social impact of events is ever more closely linked to their visibilization—or rather hypervisibilization—in the electronic media. This idea resonates with Baudrillard's notion of "hyperreality," the social condition wherein the pace of image saturation and the rate of electronic mediatization have reached such massive proportions that the credibility of any categorical distinction between "reality" and media "representation" approaches its vanishing point. One by-product of such a condition, according to Baudrillard, is the onslaught of an "orgy of realism" and a "mania . . . for making everything appear, for placing everything under the jurisdiction of signs."[93] This is a by-product that arguably finds its apotheosis in tabloid television programming.

The hypervisibilizing tendencies of local newscasts predictably drew the ire of commentators and critics, given the low repute of imagistic journalism. Conrad Smith, for example, accused local newscasts of "overdrama-tizing" stories and "going for the visual instead of the analytical, especially now that newsgathering technology makes it easy to do 'live' coverage of otherwise unimportant" events.[94] Smith inadvertently attracts our attention to the fact that the "importance" or "unimportance" of an event is never in-herent to it but is instead culturally ascribed. Social power accrues to those who can effectively mobilize the discursive power to designate the impor-tance or triviality of this or that event or genre of events. Official journalism implicitly claims that the "newsworthiness" (or not) of an event is trans-parent and unproblematic, though its definitions of "newsworthiness" co-incide, not surprisingly (but with striking consistency), with the tastes, values, and knowledges designated most serious within the terms of the white, masculine, and middle-class public sphere. Consequently, the often visually rich but analytically thin broadcasts associated first with local and then tabloid television news provoked a great deal of what Bourdieu calls "disgust at the facile," a defining characteristic of middle-class identity and cultural consumption practices. Because classifying classifies the classifier, culturally "inferior" products are often treated by socially dominant forma-tions as "a sort of insult to refinement, a slap in the face to a 'demanding' . . . audience which will not stand for 'facile' offerings."[95] The expression of disgust at the facile demarcates a sphere of suspect cultural products and simultaneously marks the disreputability of particular audience identi-ties and consumption practices. This process can operate covertly and in-directly, as when, for example, in the early eighties, journalist Edwin Dia-mond characterized local news formats as "part of that disco beat of the visual over the analytical, of excitement over explication, of stimulation over talking heads." Here Diamond implicitly evokes the threat of sexual ex-cess that the white imagination commonly associates with both racial dif-ference and sexual minorities (in this instance via the signifier "disco," a metonym for late-seventies black and gay urban music cultures widely de-spised and disparaged for musical and cultural "inferiority").[96] Joanmarie Kalter neatly encapsulates this logic in her characterization of local news as "bang-bang," a shorthand designation that, by the mere repetition of a single word, manages to conjure both "vulgar" or "animalistic" sexuality and the threat of racial difference for which urban violence stands in white discourse.[97]

In 1980 broadcasting mogul Ted Turner launched CNN, a twenty-four-hour-a-day all-news cable network. This was one of several events that would, over the course of the next decade, undermine the dominance of net-work news programming—still television's most "official" journalistic in-stitution—and push it to alter some of its practices. Changes in television's journalistic programming and practices during the 1980s were not isolated but rather connected to wholesale shifts in U.S. broadcasting away from the oligopolistic structure dominated by the three major networks that had been in place for some sixty years. The massive expansion of cable television was one of the key conjunctural events at the core of these shifts.[98] Many predicted miserable failure for Turner's upstart cable news enterprise. The notion of an entire TV network devoted solely to news shows was quite heretical, despite some evidence that journalistic programming was capable of impressive popularity. Nevertheless, by 1988, CNN was a staple of more than eight thousand cable systems with combined access to forty million homes.[99] By contrast with the growth of cable, the three network newscasts lost fully 10 percent of their audience between 1979 and 1985. This loss was not due to lack of economic effort, for network news budgets grew expansively between 1970 and 1985.[100]

At all three network news divisions, these declines in viewership were greeted with efforts aimed at popularizing evening newscasts and altering their structures to take account of their place within a rapidly shifting media environment marked by a growing diversity of information sources. For example, the headline approach to newscasting entrenched at CBS under the Cronkite regime gave way to a features orientation characterized by fewer individual stories, each of greater length, partly because in an increasingly media-rich society, audiences were expected to have already encountered the day's primary headlines by the time they switched on the networks' evening newscasts. Furthermore, story selection criteria shifted away from abstract notions concerning what information was deemed necessary for good citizenship according to rationalistic and deliberative models of the public sphere. Instead, news producers became more interested in questions about the relevance of stories from the perspectives of "ordinary folks." More stories were evaluated in terms of their capacity to engage audiences as some network news workers apparently became less embarrassed about television's close proximity to oral popular cultures and its journalism's growing distance from elite literate ones. Consequently Cronkite criticizes the current generation of newscasters for their collective lack of training in print news work, noting dismissively that most are inept for having "learned journalism from a box." His defense of the headline approach to TV newscasting privileges the written over the spoken word and the cultures of the socially elite over those of the disempowered in its insistent prioritization of print over broadcast journalism: "Television news needs to give the headlines so that people can refer to their newspapers." [101]

Trends at the networks' news divisions during the eighties represented both a continuation of earlier developments designed to more effectively realize the profit potential of television newscasting and a movement along the news continuum toward those socially disparaged formats that had shown themselves capable time and again of engaging the imaginations of various viewing publics. Perhaps the figure who best embodies the continuation of these incremental shifts in the logic of network news production is Van Gordon Sauter, who was appointed to head the CBS news division twice during the eighties after Cronkite's retirement. Sauter's news production philosophy was unashamedly populist, and even his personal biography seems to encapsulate some of the key cultural and political contradictions inherent in many of the tabloid television formats that emerged during the Reagan decade. Sauter was a political conservative of working-class origins married to a liberal Democratic politician (incidentally, the sister of California's leftish maverick former governor Jerry Brown). He gained network notoriety by complaining bitterly about the "hopelessly corporate, upper middle-class, complacent and condescending" character of official journalism.[102] Sauter was convinced that most of what passed for news at the networks was utterly detached from the concerns of ordinary viewers. He sought to shift the emphasis of the CBS *Evening News* away from its tight focus on "soundbites from congressional hearings and the White House briefing room" [103] in order to foreground "how those institutions affected ordinary people" in the small towns as well as the cities of the United States.[104] Moreover, he argued that the conventional journalistic distinction between "news" and "entertainment" was "too restrictive." [105] He thus became, not surprisingly, subject to frequent attacks by old-school newsmen committed, like Cronkite, to a variety of traditional beliefs about proper journalism. Sauter was not shy of fighting back. Consequently he became one of the few "establishment journalists" inside the networks to publicly defend the emergence of "tabloid television" after the trend became a topic of widespread discussion in the late 1980s. In 1989, for example, he penned an article for TV *Guide* entitled "In Defense of Tabloid TV," in which he wrote:

> No longer is the delivery of news and information on television dominated by the programs produced under the imprimatur of the three networks or their affiliates. More and more upstart programs, falling into exotic and carefully calibrated categories such as tabloid, reality, talk, trash and information, are elbowing their way onto the screen. . . . The flowering of these new programs is provoking outrage from some media critics and journalists in the Turgid Triangle of Imperial Journalism, a spiritual and geographical locus embracing the District of Columbia, the West Side of Manhattan and Cambridge, Mass. The Colonel Blimps in these zones denounce the "bad taste" displayed by these obstreperous newcomers. That's a code phrase for

what really alarms these elitists: the popularization of news and information by people who don't wear the old school tie of Establishment journalism.[106]

Sauter's rhetoric and his political inclinations converge unmistakably with the conservative populism of Reagan and Reaganism. He was driven by his commitment to the idea that network news (like the federal government, in Reagan's view) had "lost touch" with ordinary folks. Also like Reagan, Sauter sought to reconnect by exploiting television's unique capacities as an image apparatus and, as his managing editor put it, "a 'feeling' medium."[107] The leadership at CBS (and, for that matter, at the other network news divisions) would allow such a strategy to be taken only so far, however, for powerful forces both within and outside the journalistic profession maintained a massive cultural investment in the distinction between "quality" journalism and the sorts of "infotainment" that "pander" to "illiterate" mass audiences. Thus in 1986 Sauter was "forced to resign" from his job at CBS. He would go on to become an independent producer of syndicated "reality-based" TV programming.[108]

Another key figure at the center of television journalism's tabloidization was Rupert Murdoch. Like Sauter, Murdoch was tuned-in to American-style populism. However, whereas Sauter was a heretical insider, Murdoch, despite his long-standing entrenchment in world media structures, represented something more of an external challenge to the classic U.S. network system. The challenge he posed was linked to two interrelated phenomena: the introduction of a fourth U.S. broadcasting network and the expansion of outlets for syndicated programming. These changes had significant consequences, for they led to a growth in the range of popular formats available in U.S. television while shifting the norms governing "taste" and "appropriateness" that were closely connected with the previously quite tightly structured relationship between the oligopolistic networks and the handful of major advertisers on whom they relied.[109] Although Murdoch's incursion into American broadcasting was linked to Reaganism via the deregulatory environment established by the FCC under the leadership of Mark Fowler, the programming on Murdoch's new network was often very much out of step with the traditional values central to Reaganism's domestic agenda. In short, as one observer put it, "Rupert Murdoch spent half a billion dollars to acquire Twentieth Century Fox. He did not spend this money to compete with the Family Channel."[110] Quite the contrary, according to another commentator, Murdoch launched a full-scale "campaign to make Fox into America's tabloid network."[111]

Murdoch was an apt figure to represent the tabloidization of U.S. media, given his long association with tabloid newspaper operations throughout the Anglophonic world. John J. Pauly has closely examined the significant place Murdoch occupies in the demonology of professional journalism, where he constitutes the Other in an epic struggle for purity and "high-mindedness." As Pauly puts it, "Murdoch provides professional journalists with someone to be normal against. His incessant presence marks the dark border at which enlightened journalism imagines itself standing watch." Consequently Murdoch is used to support, authorize, and reproduce dominant myths about the "socially edifying features" of the profession, "a conception of journalism as news work conducted by public-spirited, independent professionals." Thus he has been portrayed by editorial cartoonists as "a barbarian, a killer bee, a Godzilla-like 'creature from down under,' King Kong, a Tasmanian devil, Dracula, Dr. Frankenstein, and the Grand Acquisitor." In editorial writing, he has been repeatedly represented as "the dark Other, a vulgar Prince of Darkness, the Antichrist of Professional Journalism." [112]

The sense of threat many professional journalists experienced in the face of Murdoch's enterprise is understandable, given his refusal of the canons of taste, decorum, and seriousness that work to define "high-minded" news work. Nor is it surprising that Murdoch would provoke such classism as that expressed in the complaint that his new network dug "deep . . . past mere sleaze . . . all the way down to the bowels of the American Zeitgeist and unloosed . . . the timeless blatt of . . . lumpenprole self-loathing." [113] Fox had, after all, in many ways redefined U.S. network practices with its heavy reliance on tabloid-style shows like *America's Most Wanted* and *Cops*, both of which placed consistently among its most highly rated programs during the late 1980s. [114] The Fox strategy was partly a product of economic conditions: TV production costs increased steadily throughout the eighties, and "reality-based" programming could be produced far more cheaply than the traditional entertainment genres — about half as cheaply, according to some estimates. [115] Moreover, programs such as *Cops* and *America's Most Wanted* were produced with a minimum of pre-scripted dialogue and narration and so were considered "writer proof" — that is, unaffected by unplanned production interruptions like the writer's strike of 1988 that helped to open a space for, and solidify the place of, these very programs in the Fox lineup.

Some of the conditions of possibility for the emergence of tabloid television were the same as those on which the Fox Network's existence depended. Perhaps the most significant of these was the growth of independent broadcasting stations under Reaganism. In 1980 there were 103 independent television stations operating in the United States. Thanks in part to deregulation and other Reaganist policies, that figure nearly tripled by 1986. Consequently there was high demand for syndicated programming, which was in relatively short supply. [116] As cable and independent broadcasting services were rapidly expanding, the production of program-ming for first run in syndication, previously a relatively minor activity, became a prevalent practice. Whereas only twenty-five such productions existed in the first season of the decade, by the 1986–1987 television season there were ninety-six programs produced for first run in syndication. This nearly fourfold expansion in the production of programming for first run in syndication led to an explosion of tabloid programming, which was both cheap and popular. The exclusion of programming aimed unambiguously at culturally disreputable tastes had became more difficult to achieve with the weakening of the oligopoly once enjoyed by the three major networks. As the number of media channels expanded, audiences became more dispersed and fragmented, so that the "respectable" tastes previously enforced fairly effectively by a relatively small group of major advertisers with a firm grip on the bulk of programs aired gave way to a diversity of outlets, many of which depended on programming that appealed specifically to down-market audi-ences whose tastes and preferences the tripartite oligopoly could once (but no longer) afford to ignore. Thus in 1989, when Ron Powers (the snooty and acerbic TV critic for *Gentlemen's Quarterly*) attended the International Pro-gram Conference of the National Association of Television Program Execu-tives, he reported that the gathering, formerly "the three major networks' private little block party," was now dominated by syndicators, who had turned Houston's Brown convention center, "for a few gossamer days, into Gomorrah-by-the-Gulf—a lubricious temple to the New Television, the . . . television of . . . tablotrash and . . . docucrime." [117] Even at the three major networks, whose prime-time programming and serious news work were still envisioned as the standards for "high-mindedness" and "tasteful" re-spectability, there were movements down market. The networks could not entirely avoid these, since they had registered significant losses of upscale viewers who were increasingly drawn away by such attractions as the VCR and pay-TV.

Reaganism's Racial Mediascape

Power had to be given the instrument of permanent, exhaustive, omnipresent surveil-lance, capable of making all visible. . . . It had to be like a faceless gaze that transformed the whole social body into a field of perception: thousands of eyes posted everywhere, mobile attentions ever on the alert. —Michel Foucault, *Discipline and Punish* [118]

The emergence of tabloid television is linked to the culture of Reaganism that defined the U.S. social context of the 1980s. Tabloid television did not, of course, simply "reflect" some intact social reality played out externally to it. Jane Feuer writes that during the 1980s, "television and Reaganism formed mutually reinforcing and interpenetrating imaginary worlds."[119] Nor was Reaganism without significant internal contradictions. In the "docudramatic" and "fictional" entertainment programming of the Reagan decade, Feuer finds a great deal of "complicitous critique," a contradictory characteristic of postmodern cultural forms that are both symptomatic and critical of their historical circumstances.[120] Tabloid television, like fictional and docudramatic 1980s programming, is often, in its different forms, simultaneously an expression of, and a reaction against, key currents of meaning associated with the cultural moment of Reaganism.

Ronald Reagan's was a telegenic, pixilated, postmodern presidency. Diane Rubenstein notes that the Reagan presidency "may well be . . . remembered as the most perfect exemplar of Baudrillard's third order of simulation," the contemporary social condition marked by media saturation, the implosion of distinctions between signs and referents, and the partial eclipse of production by reproduction that accompanies the shift from representation to simulation as the dominant cultural logic (see chapter 2).[121] In such a cultural context, "comedian David Steinberg's joke that 'I'm not a president, but I play one on TV' reads as an apt empirical description."[122] Michael Rogin designates "the Reagan process," whereby the fortieth president of the United States "found out who he was through the roles he played on film."[123] This is symptomatic of an age of simulacra, where models take priority over referents. Says Rubenstein of Reagan's claim to have been present at the scene of the liberation of Nazi death camps (when in fact he had only seen the films), "Lou Cannon and the Reagan spin doctors who tried to explain or decry the Reagan 'gaffe' to Shamir simply do not realize that his episteme is not one of representation (in which the notion of 'false representation' makes sense) but of simulation, in which the signs of the real . . . [are] superior to the real itself."[124] Similarly, Michael Sorkin refers to "the Reagan switcheroo of presidentiality for presidency" that was constitutive of "the first triumphantly electronic" administration.[125] Whatever else it may have been, the Reagan effect was truly a phenomenon of electronic mediation. It was thus with no small amount of prescience that Democratic Party campaign strategist Bob Squire noted, "an election is like interactive TV": you vote "to put somebody on your television screen for the next four years and to take the other . . . off."[126]

Such postmodern analyses of Reagan remind us that he was, first and foremost, a media figure—one whose tough but reassuringly avuncular image embodied a "no-nonsense" response to the conflicts and upheavals of the post-Vietnam era in ways that cut across a range of social divisions within whiteness to produce a hegemonic coalition united in difference against various forms of racial and sexual alterity. Although Baudrillardian postmodernism often lacks an explicitly political dimension, it incisively discerns some of the key developments through which cultural politics operate in an image-saturated society: hypervisibilization, an orgy of imagism, the rapid dispersion of a technological gaze that generates such insistent reality effects that these become our most pressing political realities. Under and in conjunction with Reaganism, a mediascape emerged within which whites could express racial fears without being labeled racist, for so much "reality TV" confirmed their anxieties. Herman Gray has shown that the sign of "blackness" was indispensable for the establishment of the Reaganist hegemony, for the black body was constructed as the locus of "a continuum ranging from menace on one end to immorality on the other, with irresponsibility located somewhere in the middle." [127] Gray convincingly demonstrates that racialized representations and discourses formed the linchpin of Reaganism, as working-class whites (especially men) were drawn to Reaganist populism despite administration policies that worked against many of their economic interests. This was due in large measure to the way in which "whiteness" was successfully constructed as a racial category under siege in many of the most pervasive discourses and visible representations circulating through a variety of social and cultural domains during the Reagan decade. Thus "nightly television news reports of 'rampaging' hordes of urban black youth robbing and raping helpless and law-abiding white (female) victims" were crucial to the solidification of a white hegemonic identity politics rooted in the fear, suspicion, and resentment of racial difference.[128] Such narrative patterns as these have a long and powerful history in the white U.S. patriarchal imagination, where fantasies of nonwhite masculine sexual "animality" have conspired with fetishistic constructions of white female vulnerability to more effectively assert control over both people of color and Caucasian women.[129] During the Reagan decade and since, such fantasies and fetishistic constructions migrated from the white imagination into the hyperreal electronic media, where they form a complicitous couplet that links imaginary and imagistic processes.

There were at least two key sectors of white Reaganist identity politics that fed into the formation of the discourses of tabloid television in the late and post-Reagan years: the "war on drugs" and the "victims' rights" movement. The war on drugs saturated U.S. media with images of an urban battleground steeped in violent criminality that struck all too often at innocent (white) victims. In its 1986 report on the drug war, *Newsweek* declared:

> We realized, preparing this week's cover, that what we have been chronicling piecemeal over the years was in fact an authentic national crisis—an assault on the law and the peace, a waste of life and treasure, a test of the will and the character of a people. We plan accordingly to

cover it as a crisis, reporting it as aggressively and returning to it as regularly as we did the struggle for civil rights, the war in Vietnam and the fall of the Nixon presidency.[130]

The war on drugs thus erupted in the media, laying the groundwork for the emergence of new forms of crime journalism.[131] In essence, "drug war" was the Reagan administration's code name and cover story for covert (and overt) operations against people of color. It was stunningly successful as a set of media discourses and representations. Among the most significant products of the war on drugs was the drug crisis it created, for crises are not "recognized" but rather produced by the representational systems used to depict them. The production of crises is a political practice that typically authorizes measures that serve the interests of the powerful and are harmful to the socially weak.[132] As discursive formations, crises spread cancerlike throughout the body social, thus inciting action against the segments of that body presumed to be diseased and dangerous. In Murray Edelman's apt description, a social crisis is a "radiation of signifiers" that evokes "an exploding set of scenes and signs that move in unpredictable directions and that radiate endlessly." [133] Such was the drug crisis, which was variously labeled a "national-security threat," an "epidemic . . . as pervasive and dangerous . . . as the plagues of medieval times," the "primary culprit" responsible for a surge in urban murder rates, and the reason "we have lost . . . our [economic] edge to the Japanese." [134]

The wide range of phenomena typically subordinated to the logic of crises testifies to crisis discourses' power to spread and colonize ever widening domains of social experience and cultural production. As a discourse of crisis performs this semiotic labor, it necessarily represses competing discourses that might be used to produce alternative understandings of the events it inscribes. In the case of the drug crisis, those repressed discourses include African American discourses on white racism, the discourses on deprivation circulated by the economically impoverished, and the discourses of capitalistic enterprise and economic advancement generated by urban drug entrepreneurs.[135] Interestingly, though, although certain tabloid programs such as *America's Most Wanted* and *Cops* often seem clearly complicitous with white discourses on drugs and criminality rooted in Reaganism, as we shall see shortly, others, particularly the daytime talk shows, were among the few sites through which alternative discourses repressed by Reaganism actually gained media circulation. One consequence of its penchant for conflict, confrontation, and explosively sensational material is that tabloid television exerts only very loosely constituted discursive controls over its content. This opens it up, on the whole, to a range of competing voices and perspectives. This characteristic of tabloid television is enhanced by the fact that discursive formations such as the drug crisis paradoxically both repress and provoke the formation of *counterdiscourses*.

As the criminalizing discourses of the drug crisis radiated endlessly throughout all the forms of 1980s journalism, they intensified the emphasis on white victimization that was among the central currents of both tabloid television and the cultural moment of Reaganism. One consequence was the so-called movement for "victims' rights," one of the most successful social movements of the Reagan decade. In 1982 a California constitutional amendment gave the victims of crime the legal right to address the judge during the sentencing of their convicted transgressors.[136] Also during the same year, President Reagan signed into law the Victims and Witness Protection Act, the first piece of victims' rights legislation ever passed by Congress. This unanimous act of Congress instituted the use of "victim impact statements" during the sentencing phase of all federal trials and the payment of mandatory restitution to victims suffering monetary or property losses.[137] These measures were the first in a decade that would witness the formation of 7,000 victim advocacy and support groups and the passage of 1,500 laws "aimed at giving victims broad new rights to participate" at a number of different levels "in the cases against their assailants." [138] In 1984 Congress passed the Federal Victims of Crime Act, establishing a $100 million fund to be distributed to crime victims and the agencies that serve them. By 1986, thirty-six states had enacted "victims' bills of rights." [139] Writing in 1984, Senator John Heinz echoed sentiments that would form the central proposition of the victims' rights movement:

> For every crime counted, there are innocent victims: those directly assaulted, those whose homes and businesses are entered and rifled, as well as the families, neighbors, and loved ones who share in the victims' pain and loss or who must cope with their own losses as survivors. . . . We must all begin listening to the overly large population of victims.[140]

Betty James Spencer, whose four sons were systematically assassinated in her home in 1977 and who was herself shot and left to die during the incident, became a vocal and active victims' advocate during the eighties. Says Spencer,

> Many cannot speak out to let the public know how they feel. There are those who are suffering so from their traumatic experience that they silently wait for someone to help them, but help has been slow in coming. There are those who cannot speak out because they are dead. I feel sure that all victims are asking the same question! Where are *my* rights?[141]

Spencer's emphatic closing question implicitly reveals the extent to which the victims' rights movement was tied to the Reaganist reaction against what was widely perceived by white conservatives as two decades of liberal judicial intervention on behalf of the rights of (poor and nonwhite) criminals; this situation was in turn seen to have been exacerbated by the drug and crime crisis and the moribundity of degenerative, inefficient, bloated judicial and penal systems badly in need of streamlining and a return to "basic moral principles." The new activism of crime victims and victims' rights advocates shared elements of a common historical conjuncture with emergent forms of tabloid discourse. As we shall see, Reaganist racism was indeed often covertly underwritten and reinforced by individuating and moralizing tendencies located in the segments of tabloid media most concerned with the topic of criminal victimization.

Nevertheless, these tabloid media realms, like others, also provide evidence of complicitous critique, for they inevitably attract attention to the many forms of vulnerability that arose from the exacerbation of social inequalities brought about by Reaganism itself. Such complicitous critique is enhanced by tabloid television's emphasis on the victimization of the socially weak, a convention inherited from melodramatic traditions in popular crime reporting. Child abuse, neglect, and abduction, sexual assault, violent theft, spouse battering, kidnapping, and even gay bashing and racially motivated hate crimes have all figured into tabloid television's discursive repertoire. Even when such crimes are not posed in terms of structural or socially systemic inequalities (as, somewhat surprisingly, they occasionally are), the motifs typical of tabloid crime stories can be read as spectacular metaphors for the social subordination and brutalization of the disempowered,[142] which thus attain (displaced) hypervisibility in the media and therefore contribute to the development of ideological contradictions in the social. Just as crisis discourses radiate in endless and unpredictable ways, so the cultural emphasis on issues of victimization associated with media tabloidization spread quickly to social topic areas that could not be contained by the conservative impulses of Reaganism and the victims' rights lobbies. Although the connections between them are not direct or causal, neither is there no relationship between the abiding interest in victimization evidenced on programs such as *America's Most Wanted* and, for example, the marked openness of tabloid media arenas like the daytime talk shows to the discussion of issues such as the violent consequences of homophobia and racism (see chapter 5). While the social activism of subordinated or marginalized populations is primarily responsible for whatever public circulation such issues enjoy, the teletabloids' emphasis on victimization in general provokes heightened media attention around them. The tabloids' emphasis on criminal victimization produces some ironic consequences, then, in light of the conservative and racist social forces that undergird and flow from the movement for (white) victims' rights.

John Walsh is a media figure who has come to embody much of the spirit of the victims' rights movement. In 1981 Walsh's six-year-old son was abducted during a shopping trip in Hollywood, Florida. Walsh and his wife tried to enlist the services of state police departments and the FBI. The FBI refused to get involved in the case, and there was no established network that would enable Florida's scattered police departments to participate effectively in the investigation. "At the time, 70 percent of the police agencies in the state of Florida didn't know Adam was missing," Walsh recalls, evincing the victims' rights critiques of bureaucratic failure.[143] Frustrated, the Walshes organized their own search parties with the help of relatives and friends. After two excruciating weeks of fruitless searching, Adam's body was discovered, mutilated, in a swamp located 150 miles from the site of his disappearance. Ever since, Walsh has worked tirelessly for the passage of child protection legislation and the cause of victims' rights.

The actuality of Walsh's personal experience of victimization authorizes his role on *America's Most Wanted* and helps to constitute a powerful sense of media authenticity around the program. Media authenticity is an electronically mediated sense of the real that derives in part from the implosion of any *categorical* distinction between representation and referent that is one condition of postmodernity. After his son's murder, Walsh became something of a television celebrity similar to Reagan himself in his pervasively mediated embodiment of no-nonsense patriarchal populism. Most of the crimes chronicled on *America's Most Wanted* are ones that in some way disrupt family life and domestic relationships.[144] The program links up with Reaganism in its construction of a realm of white hegemonic identity politics that places the traditional nuclear family at the absolute center of social life. Like Reaganism, the program required that its primary spokesman be a stern but caring father figure, and it articulates neither a collectivist nor an individualist populism so much as a familial one. The grassroots populism of *America's Most Wanted* emerges against the backdrop of investigative bureaucracies and a penal system that are seen as inadequate to the task of effective law enforcement unless ordinary citizens lend assistance in the name of the family and indeed become members of its imaginary viewing family.[145] As Reaganism embodied the paradoxical view that government bureaucracies are simultaneously inept and necessary as counterforces against such malevolent entities as communism and drug lords, so is *America's Most Wanted* based on a contradictory perspective that views the police as simultaneously inadequate and indispensable to the protection of the family against a variety of threats to its very existence. In its turn, the televisual construction of an imaginary viewing family imaginarily shores up both familiality and the police against the malignant forces that would bring about their ruin.

If *America's Most Wanted* articulates a familial rather than an individualist populism, it implicitly locates the etiology of criminality, as Anna Williams observes, in what Foucault calls the discourses of "the dangerous individual." [146] Thus the signs of abnormality implicitly associated with criminality are often shown to be inscribed on the bodies of fugitives, like the "bulbous nose and crooked little fingers" of a man wanted for child molestation and murder, or the "sunken, hollow cheekbones" of a prison escapee and confessed multiple killer. Connotatively rich corporeal descriptions such as these, given by Walsh during installments of *America's Most Wanted*, serve to reinforce the logic of crime as a product of "dangerous individuals" by associating malevolence with the body's most individuating social stigmata.[147] Such descriptions also underwrite the tendency to rely on the visibilizing technologies of surveillance that have become perhaps our primary mechanisms of social regulation and control. Technologies of surveillance work by hypervisibilizing signs of abnormality while heightening our attentiveness to them. *America's Most Wanted* generates forms of imaginary surveillance through its frequent video reenactments of crime and its heavy use of computer modulation to visibilize the looks of fugitives under a variety of possible states of appearance.[148] The program hypervisibilizes the individual faces of criminality, on which the cameras dwell, even after the fugitives who own those faces have been captured through the teamwork of "the partnership."

The discourses of the dangerous individual and the centrality of the family interact with one another in interesting ways in *America's Most Wanted*, combining and combusting to expose the dangers and excesses that lurk just beneath the surface of domestic life. The program is symptomatic of cultural anxieties around family life that were heightened by Reaganism's renewal of emphasis on the normativity of the traditionally patriarchal unit. Thus many of the program's stories depict crime as something that emerges within and from the very tensions and excesses of patriarchal domesticity itself. Beneath the veneer of every happy family, in the world of *America's Most Wanted*, there lurks a volatile and potentially explosive situation. Consequently the program is awash with stories of horrible crimes that in one way or another originate with the deficiencies and dysfunctionalities of families. In some instances, the dysfunctionalities of the family form the apparent mechanism for the creation of dangerous individuals; in others, the happy family is merely the weak, unfortunate victim of such individuals.

Through its particular combination of the discourses of the family and those of the "dangerous individual," *America's Most Wanted* works hard to provoke affective investments, summoning all the emotional intensity and moral outrage appropriate to our confrontations with the morally deficient and degenerate persons who threaten the security of families. Its affective intensity is among the program's primary mechanisms for inviting audiences into its "regime of the fictive we" who must be ever vigilant in the face of pervasive dangers.[149] The affective charge generated by America's Most Wanted is resonant in, for example, the words of one man who found himself living next door to one of the program's featured fugitives: "Living next to the guy that's most wanted was, was exciting! . . . Holy geez, a guy on Most Wanted? It was just . . . exhilarating, for a little while. I was really pumped up about it! 'Cause he didn't seem out of the ordinary at all!" This affective charge is thus linked to the intervention and rapid dispersion of electronic images that visibilize and magnify signs of aberrance that had been hidden. The obverse of the affective energy generated by the successful capture of a fugitive through the intervention of the world's largest virtual posse lies in the populist appeal of knowing that one has helped another member of the electronic community. Thus, for example, when viewers' phone calls led to the capture of the man who raped a kindly grandmother in her own home, she appeared on camera and thanked "all the alert and caring people who called the hotline with tips." While I don't wish to detract from the significance of the apprehension of a rapist at large, I would like to point out as well that Most Wanted's reenactment of the events leading up to this attack expose the program's typical proximity to the white hegemonic identity politics of Reaganism, for the video segment clearly enacts a moral Manichaeanism that is decisively racialized. In this reenactment, an exceptionally cheerful, helpful, and unsuspecting elderly white woman offers, with gracious naïveté, to help the black crack addict who has knocked on her door under a false pretense. Most Wanted's reenactments are tellingly symptomatic of the mediacentricity of postmodern conditions, wherein events become amenable to constant resignification through imagistic mechanisms. Under such conditions, originary events themselves become increasingly insignificant in comparison with their videated enactments, which powerfully exploit the instability of meaning within imagistic regimes.

Above all, America's Most Wanted celebrates the everyday victories of those who rise above victimization to strike back against the combined threat posed by the deficiencies and weaknesses of bureaucratic institutions and the diabolical cleverness of the dangerous individuals who are, as the program often shows us, amazingly adept at exploiting those deficiencies and weaknesses. Its fifth-anniversary broadcast, for example, featured special segments commemorating the work of "ordinary people" catalyzed by victimization to become, like Walsh, politically active toward producing legal reforms aimed at eliminating the flaws in "the system." As Walsh states emphatically, "people can and do make a difference." It is to this populist sense of reformist activism and intervention that *America's Most Wanted* most force-fully appeals. The program regularly airs feature stories that inform viewers of the efficacy of their participation, often by bringing us firsthand accounts from callers-in, relieved victims, and even captured fugitives themselves who sometimes comment on the effectivity of the "partnership." It is a populism rooted in the expansion of surveillance toward which the program is directed. As John Walsh proclaims during one broadcast, "Every week, *America's Most Wanted* helps you become the eyes and ears of justice, making the streets of America a little bit safer. Safe havens for fugitives have become extremely hard to find."

The surveillant ethos and populist appeal of *America's Most Wanted* are ex-tended in Fox's *Cops*, which uses Minicams to place viewers in the squad cars and on the beats of men and women in blue. *Cops* is a product of the same technologies of miniaturization and mobility responsible for the imagistic "bang-bang" that transports local news audiences to the scenes of crimes in progress. Significantly, the program emphasizes the everyday struggles of the ordinary "men and women of law enforcement" against a variety of imaginary dangers that construct a crisis around U.S. urban spaces, which figure as breeding grounds of criminality, violence, irresponsibility, and aberrance. The populism of *Cops* (and its clones *American Detective* and *Real Stories of the Highway Patrol*, as well as its tabloid cousins *Top Cops* and *True Detectives*) does not center on the inadequacy of police bureaucracies but is figured in the face of the ordinary police worker. His or her job skills are depicted as wide-ranging and well developed. These are everyday folks who work hard under the most difficult of conditions but retain enough spirit to joke with one another around the precinct house or (often mockingly of a "bad guy") at the scene of an arrest. *Cops* encourages viewer identifica-tion with the featured officers (different ones in different cities on each epi-sode) as they shame, scold, and sometimes gently ridicule the reprobates who cross their paths in droves. Between calls—some adventurous, others mundane, still others quirky—the cops recount for the camera their phi-losophies of law enforcement and the hopes and aspirations that brought them to police work.

We see firsthand how concerned the cops are with those in need, par-ticularly children. Not only are these cops the foot soldiers of the drug war, then, but they also spend a great deal of time solving the difficult prob-lems of ordinary folks. The program's coupling of these two activities can readily be seen as characteristic of the hegemonic process whereby con-sent to particular configurations of social power is secured. Nevertheless, as hegemony theory reminds us, both the consent thus won and the con-figurations of power it underwrites are provisional and ultimately unstable. As Reaganism advanced and the social inequalities it exacerbated became increasingly tense, so did its hegemony become ever more insecure and contested. By the time the Reagan presidency was replaced by the Bush administration, a number of key sectors of cultural hegemony had become discursive battlegrounds fraught with tensions and contradictions. Symptomatic of this, as we shall see in chapter 5, is the way in which topical daytime talk shows—the most contentious sector of tabloid television—became the most explosive growth area within the genre during the early nineties. But even *Cops* contains its contradictory and ambiguous moments whose political valences are difficult to determine, and which clearly open the text to alternative reading relations and a range of different political inflections. At certain points in the program, for example, the cops' treatment of some individuals becomes cruel and excessive—emotionally at least, if not physically as well. Even after the program has been heavily edited (as is typical in the production of such shows, as we shall see in chapter 2), there is "enough rough handling . . . left in to raise the suspicion that producers" err "on the side of repression rather than leniency." [150] The program's moments of repressive excess, however muted in comparison with those abuses that are edited from the broadcasts, invite audiences who are more typically *targeted* rather than protected by police officers to use *Cops* to reverse the relations of surveillance that usually work *against* the socially disempowered.[151] If the surveillance of marginalized social differences serves to reinforce manifestations of suspicion among the cultures of the dominant, *Cops* can also be used as a cultural resource for the production and sustenance of defensive popular knowledges of the police among subordinated populations. Such reversals of surveillance are promoted through the Internet at the *Copswatch* Web site, which presents itself as "an electro-alchemical transformation of trash TV into a practical video handbook for true civil disobedience" and features "commentary on the unlawful police tactics routinely captured on episodes of the *Cops* television show." [152]

Paul G. Kooistra and his colleagues observe that "occasionally a thoughtful cop [on *Cops*] will describe the living conditions of victims and offenders and suggest that the lack of jobs, the declining schools, and the decay of housing and social services may explain more about crime than simply the mental state of those captured in the war on crime." [153] We should also note that at other times, the TV cops' monologues are politically ambiguous and clearly inviting of both ideologically complicit and critical readings. After busting a black teenager for selling crack, for instance, one Fort Lauderdale officer explains:

A juvenile, he's out there sellin' crack cocaine at three o'clock in the mornin'. And, uh, from his point of view, you know, why should he be goin' to work, make an honest livin', makin', uh, four dollars and

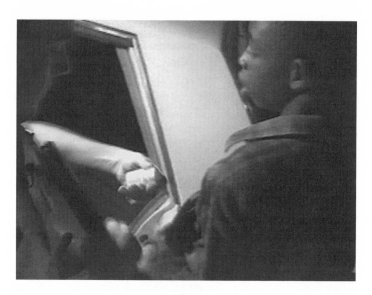

Cops: searching for visual evidence.

Cops: the search pays off.

change an hour, when he could be on the street sellin' crack cocaine and makin' two to three hundred dollars a day in profit. [Long pause.] It just amaze you to see what some, some people do to make a livin'.

The ambiguity here, of course, concerns the adequacy of the minimum wage at a time of increasing African American unemployment and urban poverty generally. The "amazement" evoked by this officer cannot be anchored securely in the antidrug discourse implied by the words "honest living," when "four dollars and change an hour" obviously enables one to do so very little of it. This monologue thus invites viewers to be amazed not at the fact that poor urban youths turn to crack dealing for financial gain but rather at the fact that anybody would instead choose the wage slavery of the legal minimum hourly pay.

Like *America's Most Wanted* and other reality-based programs such as *Rescue 911*, *Code 3*, and *I Witness Video*, *Cops* is organized around abundant images of bodies in crisis. John Langer has productively analyzed a genre of "truly awful" local TV news stories that can be seen as progenitors of these reality-based programs. This genre features "individuals who, in the process of going about their daily affairs, encounter an unanticipated turn of events which ensnares them in a state of crisis from which they cannot emerge using their own efforts and resources." [154] In tabloid television shows such as *Rescue 911*, such everyday victims pile up with a kind of deadening regularity that ultimately yields "a conception of the world which does not seem to admit the possibility of control, where life is subject to capricious external forces which strike indiscriminately, exposing people to radical changes of fortune and unanticipated disruptions to the everyday world." [155] Tabloid television's continuous accretion of victimized bodies construes contemporary social life as having gone so hopelessly out of control that we are at risk in nearly everything we do and thus in constant need of "protective" agencies, however inadequate they may ultimately be.

In *Cops*, however, ensnarement in difficult and threatening if not impossible situations is just as likely to be a product of individual weakness, foolishness, dishonesty, incompetence, or irresponsibility as it is likely to be a consequence of capricious external forces beyond individuals' fields of control. *Cops* thus frequently represents urban policing as the work of protecting people not only from their "others" but also from themselves. In contrast to the malevolent, drunken, drug-crazed, belligerent, or merely misguided perpetrators, suspects, and troubled people featured on *Cops*, the title figures represent the moral center of the urban universe and show themselves to be fonts for the articulation of common sense, which often seems to be sadly lacking in everyone else. What the cops do for a great deal of their time on camera is not so much law enforcement as *morality* enforcement, particularly where children are involved. Indeed, morality and common sense are fused into a hegemonic populist discourse that resonates heavily with Reaganism. This discourse frequently orbits around the figure of childhood, a powerful and mythically rich sign that condenses into itself complex and contradictory meanings associated with innocence, indiscipline, misbehavior, vulnerability, and the nuclear family, among others. So, like John Walsh, the cops speak often about the welfare of children, sometimes evincing an interesting slippage between the modes of sense making appropriate to that topic area and those by which perpetrators, suspects, and the "general public" are understood. An example of this is spoken by Officer Randy Sutton as he explains his philosophy of police work for the video camera:

> The citizen—the honest citizen—has rights. And those rights are that he should have the ability to conduct his life free of being molested by burglars, and rapists, and criminals, and gang members, and other scum of the Earth. And it's our job to do the best we can to protect them from these leeches. It's no different than the bullies in, in school when I was growing up. I never could stand bullies. And that's usually what, what criminals are. They're bullies. And they take advantage of the weak. And they take advantage of people that can't defend themselves. And those people look to us to defend them. And that's what our, that's what our job is.

Such discursive slippages enhance the representational logic whereby the cops on *Cops* are implicitly positioned as the adults of the urban milieu, whereas nearly everybody else they encounter (with the possible exception of occasional "responsible bystanders") is infantilized into an individual agglomeration of unrestrained appetites and impulses that endanger the fragile balance of the postmodern cityscape. Thus it is no coincidence that one of the most paradigmatic video sequences in each *Cops* segment is that when the undisciplined and unruly body of a suspect or "troublemaker" is brought under the physical control of the cops—usually two or more—who characteristically secure each untamed body (which is forced, face down, onto the ground) by driving a knee into the small of its back while its arms are twisted upward and around, where they will be met by the set of open handcuffs that waits to receive them. If the offending body continues to emit noises and convulsions, it may be carried to the carceral squad car, where the body is shut up in the backseat while the cops either continue their narration of unfolding events or offer retrospective commentary on those that have just taken place. The interminable struggle against loss of control over the U.S. body social is thus imagistically displaced and condensed into a struggle for mastery over the individual bodies of the infantilized urban populace, for those individuated and racially marked bodies are seen as the sites of dangerous impulses and destructive appetites for a variety of bodily satisfactions.[156] *Cops'* images of this struggle play to the racism and the punitive, authoritarian orientations toward criminality for which one audience study found evidence among those who most enjoy the show.[157]

The physical submission of suspects is always fully visibilized through the mediation of the *Cops* Minicam, which metonymically and crucially links the surveillant gaze with the material effectivity of the forces imposed on the subdued body.[158] This link between looking and subduction secures the social centrality of surveillance as a technique of power in the contemporary United States.[159] But our practices of surveillance may be changing. We might well read *Cops* in light of the trajectory from Foucault's panopticism to "simulated surveillance," identified by William Bogard. Simulated surveillance entails a kind of anticipatory staging of alternative scenes and scenarios. It grows from a dream of making all things transparently observable and thus enhancing one's control over as many of them as possible. It is a way of preparing for all imaginable eventualities and averting or deterring some. It becomes possible when "the panoptic imaginary" is "refined and intensified in a system geared to the frenzied, instantaneous production of images." Bogard notes that "if we could imagine a perfect simulation of surveillance, of observational control, . . . the question of its 'staging' wouldn't even arise, because everything would appear 'too real' to leave any room for doubt, for even the slightest suspicion that what was observed was 'in reality' a simulation."[160] The *Cops* videocam can be seen as a technique of simulated surveillance. It is both an imaginary surveillance-enhancement device and a reality guarantor whose cultural resonances derive in part from its situatedness within a postmodern, post-Reaganist mediascape. As I shall argue in the next chapter, *Cops* exemplifies the *hyperreality* of such a mediascape, where simulation generates unstable truths amenable to political contestation via constant resimulation. Here, I wish merely to point out the role *Cops* takes in the hypervisibilization of police work within the cultural context of the drug war, whose resonances continue to radiate.[161]

The drug war was a media event that resided not only in the rhetoric and policies of the Reagan administration but perhaps most significantly in the images generated on programs such as *Cops*—images of the subduction of unruly, noncompliant bodies, of shiny white crack rocks found in the pockets of urban youths, of chemicals and weapons stashes discovered during raids on clandestine drug factories. These are all examples of "real" events captured and authenticated on *Cops*, though it is not so much the "reality" or "authenticity" of the events themselves that matters; rather, it is the *media authenticity* to which the images of these events gave rise that has generated far-reaching social and political consequences and struggles. This media authenticity is a product of communication vectors that transport images from the sites of their origination to the living rooms and other spaces where they are received by viewers. When images are vectorally displaced into sites that differ from those of their origination, their meanings are typically reframed, recontextualized, and thus reconfigured. McKenzie Wark notes that the emanation of such images from a "real" site of origin works to legitimate and naturalize the meanings with which they become

Randy Sutton tells it like it is.

The unruly body subdued.

Cops: captured contraband.

laden through this process of recontextualization. This allows audiences to project their fantasies onto the other that is seen in these images and yet simultaneously indulge themselves in the belief that these fantasies emanate from the realities of that other. "The vector makes this other possible, and makes an 'us' possible. . . . the vector keeps throwing us together, pitting us against others, and legitimating the conflict with the contraband of images it traffics from one place to the other."[162]

Reality TV is part cause and part symptom of cultural conditions distinguished by media saturation, hypervisibilization, and the constant resignification of meanings through image generation, vectoral displacement, and recirculation. Under such conditions, images constitute a significant, if not the only, terrain of struggle over the power to produce socially effective truths. In 1989, when the pioneering tabloid newscast *A Current Affair* (see chapter 3) aired amateur footage of California police "manhandling the celebrants" after a fight erupted at a bridal shower, one commentator was inspired to remark on the new genre's inauguration of a "democracy of video" that was missing from conventional broadcast journalism.[163] I would prefer to call it a "struggle over images." In any case, the tabloidized images of bodies subdued that were generated by *Cops* videocams can be seen to have provoked the counterimages that would form one of the central media events of the 1990s: those captured by home video operator George Holliday as LAPD cops rained baton blows down on the body of an unfortunate motorist named Rodney King. If images of confiscated crack rocks and seized weaponry constituted a politically powerful video authenticity that authorized Reagan-Bushism's intensification of the policing of people of color, they also ironically helped to establish the very conditions under which, for example, the image of an ill-fitting glove could circulate widely throughout African American communities as powerful "proof" of O.J. Simpson's innocence and of LAPD corruption, ineptitude, and racism. Tabloid television is thus part cause, part symptom, and part player in the postmodern process whereby notions of a singular, objective truth give way to a fragmented multiplicity of simulated ones whose imagistic instability establishes the conditions for contestation over a variety of declared truths and even over the nature of truth itself.

2 Cops, Courts, and Criminal Justice: Evidence of Postmodernity in Tabloid Culture

Is there still reality? I would rather say that we are in hyper-reality. . . . It is as if every-thing becomes sign and image—in fact, it is more and more necessary for this to happen. . . . In my opinion our modern—or postmodern, I don't know—condition is really that of mediation and it is there that strategies are worked out.—Jean Baudrillard, *Baudrillard Live: Selected Interviews* [1]

In 1992, U.S. media erupted convulsively around the figure of a "Long Island Lolita" named Amy Fisher. At point-blank range, the telegenic six-teen year old had discharged her .22 caliber pistol into the head of Mary Jo Buttafuoco, wife of Fisher's thirty-six-year-old lover Joey. The ensuing whirligig of representations emitted by the media indicated the accelerated decrepitude of boundaries between such discursive realms as mainstream journalism, made-for-TV docudrama, and tabloid news work. Indeed, the hyperspeed with which the events around Fisher and the Buttafuocos moved between these spheres of representation was instrumental in accelerating the decrepitude of the categorical boundaries that once held them apart. As Jeff Silverman observes, "in the old days, producers usually waited for a book to be written about a true-crime story before adapting it for the small screen. More recently, however, stories have begun to go directly from courtrooms and headlines to network schedules, sometimes with as-tonishing speed." [2] Actual crimes, their journalistic renditions, their docu-dramatic fictionalizations, the trials of suspects involved, and secondary journalistic accounts and fictionalizations of all these events now often occur with virtual coextensivity and with mutual reference to one another. The Fisher-Buttafuoco story demonstrates hypertrophic mediatization to such extremes that the vortex of representations swirling around the crime events, the characters involved in the events, the characters involved in re-porting the events, the characters involved in the fictionalization of the events, and the characters involved in reporting on the fictionalization of events all become part of a single simulacrum, within which it becomes virtually impossible to neatly disentangle the various levels of reality and representationality involved. Thus the three made-for-TV movies spun off from Fisher's accusation and trial were "vigorously cross-promoted in local newscasts: Meet the real Amy Fisher! Meet the actress portraying Amy! Find out how the real people felt about the movies! Find out how the actors felt portraying the real people!" and so on.[3] The imagistic proliferation of "real news" about the "fictionalization" of a "real news" event signals the complete pulverization and dispersal of truth effects that once guaranteed at least the thinkability of anchoring the social play of images in a neatly compartmentalized reality presumed to have an objectively knowable existence independent of images themselves.[4]

Like Fisher and Buttafuoco, William Shatner and his former employee Eva-Marie Friederick found themselves at the center of a tabloidized media event, albeit on a much smaller scale. Friederick had filed suit against Shatner over a variety of abuses and breached promises that occurred during a sexual relationship between the pair. When in January 1990 the tabloid newscast A Current Affair ran its report on the lawsuit, Shatner declined to comment. Because he is a media figure, though, Shatner's is a body made not only of flesh, blood, and a self-directing mind but equally of magnetic traces and electronic pixels available for use by others.[5] A Current Affair shrewdly exploited this fact when it built its story around Shatner's fictional alter ego, Captain James T. Kirk of the United Federation Starship U.S.S. Enterprise. Thus, over filmic images of the starship, reportorial narration announces:

> California Supreme Court: the final frontier. Captain Kirk had been brought down to Earth. And now, with all those fierce intergalactic battles behind him, he faces one of his most daunting duels: a showdown with a human Klingon—a woman, determined to cling on to what she insists is rightly hers.

In its fluid movement between the "real" Shatner and the dramatic character Kirk, A Current Affair's story about the star-crossed lovers exemplifies that program's typical denial of any categorical difference between the "factual" and the "fictional," which distinguishes much tabloid television from the sensibilities of mainstream journalistic practice. Whereas mainstream journalistic realism mutes and disguises, to the extent that it can, the necessary blurriness of boundaries between the factual and the fictional, tabloid new shows such as A Current Affair delight in the provocations associated with blatant violations of such boundaries. Modernist sensibilities neatly distinguish between the credibility or veracity of different discursive modes by enacting a hierarchy of reliability that descends from the scientific through the merely realistic to the unreal and the surreal. Postmodernism has put such modernist hierarchies in question, on the grounds that in an image-saturated society, competing systems of representation interact with a kind of boundary-transgressing promiscuity that ultimately confounds any attempt to distinguish clearly and with certainty between the credibility of different ways of knowing and representing "reality" (which, in any event, has never been accessible in a direct and unmediated way).[6] Whereas mainstream journalism is unabashedly modernist in its epistemological sensibilities, tabloidism is often demonstrably postmodern in its own.

Jean Baudrillard and the Policing of Obscenity

Examples like the Fisher-Buttafuoco incident and the Shatner-Friederick affair trade, as does tabloid television generally, on the increasing instability of distinctions between "reality" and its "representations," a tendency noted by theorists of postmodernity. As Zygmunt Bauman has written, our "well structured and orderly" social habitat, which once came with "foolproof instructions on how to sift the real from the imaginary, has decomposed, or is in the process of advanced decomposition."[7] This tendency is both produced and intensified, so the theory goes, by the growing electronic overproduction of images, which saturate the fields of our social experience now as never before.[8] If distinctions between "reality" and simulacra *are* still evoked and mobilized—and they are—these discursive mobilizations increasingly privilege the authority of that which has been technologically mediated, simulated, or enhanced over that which has not been electronically processed. Increasingly large domains of knowledge and experience rely on the technological generation and modulation of artifacts whose (hyper)reality displaces the claims of the unmediated. Thus whereas "unmediated" realities once guaranteed or stood as the measure of the truth or accuracy of images, it seems that this situation has undergone something of a reversal: the electronic reproduction of an event now functions as a powerful guarantor of its actuality and incontrovertibility.

Canadian sociologist Arthur W. Frank has shown that even in hospitals, the "real" body has somehow receded from the field circumscribed by the medical gaze. The flesh-and-bone body has been displaced by the *screen body* that is a product of apparatuses that exteriorize images of the body's interior (such as fluoroscopes and ultrasounds) or code and digitize graphical on-line images of corporeal processes (such as electrocardiograms and electroencephalograms). Electronically generated images have problematized the ontological certainty of the physically real body, which has been rendered, in some sense, epistemologically obsolete in hospitals as elsewhere. "A traditional intuition suggests that at the center of medical practice we ought to find the body of the patient," ponders Frank. "Instead we find multiple images and codings in which the body is doubled and redoubled." In the postmodern hospital, "bedside is secondary to screenside," and "the image on the screen becomes the 'true' patient, of which the bedridden body is an imperfect replicant, less worthy of attention." [9] After all, why examine "real" bodies in an age when the development of sophisticated electronic imaging systems like x-ray computed tomography and magnetic resonance imaging scanners make it possible to generate "detailed, point-by-point, three dimensional digital models of human anatomy," which can be "processed by computer to yield highly resolved, vivid, colored images of the body from whatever viewpoints are desired and with tissue sectioned or peeled away in whatever fashion"? [10]

Jean Baudrillard argues that under social conditions marked by the pervasive penetration of mass media and other electronic networks of communication, the meanings of hyperreal images must not be sought in their *differentiation from reality*, which would confer representational status on them. On the contrary, he suggests that the space of representation—the distance between sign and referent that grants each an existence independent of the other—has collapsed in societies like ours. Thus the electronically generated sign must be understood in terms of "its 'telescoping' into reality, its short-circuit with reality, and finally, in the implosion of image and reality." [11] This implosion has engendered a crisis around the status of the "real," the definition of which has shifted significantly under contemporary conditions. As Baudrillard has famously put it, "the very definition of the real becomes: that of which it is possible to give an equivalent reproduction . . . ([whereas] classical representation is not equivalence, it is transcription, interpretation, commentary). At the limit of this process of reproductibility, the real is not only what can be reproduced, but that which is always already reproduced. The hyperreal." [12]

Baudrillard has dubbed this condition the "third order of simulation," wherein "reality itself founders in hyperrealism," as everywhere we witness "the meticulous reduplication of the real," typically filtered through multiple levels of reproductive or model-generative media such as photography, videography, and computer simulation. [13] As the proliferation of image networks continues apace, technologically generated signs of the real function as both guarantors of authenticity and destabilizers of our sense of "reality," which becomes mutational. With poetic aplomb, Baudrillard opines that "from medium to medium, the real is volatilized, becoming an allegory of death. But it is also, in a sense, reinforced through its own destruction. It becomes reality for its own sake, the fetishism of the lost object: no longer the object of representation, but the ecstasy of denial and of its own ritual extermination: the hyperreal." [14] Hence the hyperreal scene entails "a proliferation of . . . signs of reality; of second-hand truth, objectivity and authenticity." [15] Because of the manipulability and volatility of technologically generated image environments, we become ever more eager to pin reality down and hold it in place through exquisitely exact(ing) modes of reproduction and enhancement (not just through the perfection of body technologies like x-ray computed tomography and magnetic resonance imaging scanners but equally via, say, televisions with higher resolution, larger pictures, and digitized surround sound). The painstaking reproduction and enhancement of reality that becomes a form of fetishization of the real leads us into the topos of "obscenity," which for Baudrillard entails the technological hypervisibilization of all that can be made visible.

When the difference between "reality" and its "representation" becomes obscure and uncertain, there ensues a frantic overproduction of signs of reality via the technologies of reproduction. It is as if a perpetual "stocktaking of the real" becomes the very basis for contemporary security.[16] The expanding process of hyperreal obscenity involves the technological exhumation of the real in its "fundamental banality" and its "radical authenticity."[17] Its credo is "let everything be rendered in the light of the sign, in the light of a visible energy."[18] Traditional conceptions of "obscenity" identify that which is "hidden, repressed, forbidden, or obscure," whereas hyperreality creates "the obscenity of the visible, of the all-too-visible, of the more-visible-than-the-visible itself. It is the obscenity of what no longer has any secret, of what dissolves completely in information and communication."[19] Its attempts to make the reality of things absolutely manifest engender a surfeit of exactitude and a deceptive facade of excessive referentiality.[20] Hyperreal obscenity magnifies and fetishizes minute details. It both exemplifies and exacerbates the conflation of "reality" and "image" that is characteristic of third-order simulacra. Thus, in a reciprocal movement, technologically reproduced reality signs ease anxieties over the uncertainty of the boundary between reality and representation while simultaneously and paradoxically further disrupting its stability.

This postmodern form of obscenity emerges from the ruins of the modernist will to objectivity, for it would like to expose things to destroy their illusory overtones. It generates a kind of visual terror, however, that is the bastard offspring of the scientific gaze.[21] In obscenity,

> the hallucination of detail predominates—science has . . . accustomed us to this microscopy, the surfeit of reality in microscopic detail . . . this notion of a relentless truth which will never again find its measure in the play of appearances, and which only the sophistication of a technical apparatus can reveal.[22]

The process is exemplified in contemporary hard-core porn, where

> obscenity inflames and consumes its object. It is seen too close up, you see what you have never seen before—your sex, you have never seen it

function so close up, and indeed, happily for you, not at all. It is all too real, too close up to be real. And this is what is fascinating—the excess of reality, the hyperreality of the whole thing. Thus the only phantasm at work in porno, if there is one, is not the phantasm of sex, but that of the real and its disappearance into something other than the real, into the hyperreal. The voyeurism of porno is not sexual voyeurism, but a voyeurism of representation and its loss, an intoxication [vertige] with the loss of the scene and the irruption of the obscene.[23]

Despite its links with scientism, obscenity engenders "fascination," a mode of engagement rooted not in reason or meaning but in spectacle. Fascination is deeply enigmatic, for it "neutralizes meaning through an excess of diffusion." On Baudrillard's account, the contemporary imagistic media fuel a fascination that is "a kind of liquefaction of the sequences of meaning."[24] Baudrillard's writing sometimes suggests that our hyperreal condition is equivalent to the final extinction of meaning, a totalizing assertion that rightly provokes skepticism from his many detractors. Nevertheless, what I find useful in Baudrillard's thinking is the notion that spectacle and fascination loosen the grip of meaning and introduce play into semiotic mechanisms. This facilitates rather than extinguishes struggles over meaning, a consequence that Baudrillard fails to explore but that is central to my analysis.

Like hard-core porn, the Fox Network's tabloid hit *Cops* and ABC's *American Detective* (an imitation of *Cops*) exemplify postmodern media obscenity, where hegemonic meaning and hyperreal fascination contest for dominance. These programs might therefore be seen as the pornographication of law enforcement, whose private parts are apparently exposed (however selectively and deceptively). In Baudrillardian terms, *Cops* and *American Detective* are " 'truth' experiments" that evoke "a kind of thrill of the real, or of an aesthetics of the hyperreal, a thrill of vertiginous and phony exactitude, a thrill of alienation and of magnification, of distortion in scale, of excessive transparency all at the same time."[25] They avow the plenitude of total visibility, as when the camera closely examines the bloody feet and ankles of a still conscious though dazed man who has just jumped from the sixth floor of an apartment building.[26] They present us with the spectacle of an obsessive verification and documentation of the reality of urban police work. Portable cameras reproduce and magnify the minutiae of that milieu.[27] A banal realism cum crude slum naturalism testifies to the realities of law enforcement stripped bare. As Jon Katz suggests, these programs constitute a radical refusal of conventional notions of journalistic detachment:

> The cameras ride with the police in their patrol cars, following the officers and picking up the sounds of jangling keys and handcuffs,

Cops: a victim speaks.

squawking radios and creaking leather as they arrest drunk drivers, rush into vicious bar brawls, quell domestic disputes, chase burglars onto rooftops, arrive at murder and accident scenes, pursue kids in stolen cars at hair-raising speeds, and get punched, kicked, run over, spat upon, stabbed and sometimes shot at by the people they confront.[28]

Because these shows depend on the voluntary participation of the law enforcement agencies whose work they chronicle, their discourse is a cop-centric one. All events are framed by the recurrent monologues given by cops in squad cars en route to their next encounter with a rupture in the social fabric; by voice-overs delivered by cops at various points in the program, which interpret events for viewers; by the on-scene commentary provided by cops at the sites of crimes or disturbances; and by the gazes of the cops that direct the gazes of the cameras. The cops direct the events to which we are given access, assuming the positions of authoritative and controlling figures in the formation of the narrative (as well as in their police work, and these twin modes of control mutually support each other). The spectacle bears all the marks of what Baudrillard might call a generalized substitution of the signs of authority for authority itself, of the signs of power for power itself, produced for the ever present media as an "immense special effect."[29] In an age when social anxieties around issues of security and terror have arguably become our preeminent ones, the simulation of a potent panopticism gains full force. Thus it is neither surprising nor uncharacteristic when Lieutenant William Sieber of the LAPD looks into a *Cops* videocam and instructs the bad guy he imagines is watching that "we don't ever close these files, and we never forget someone. . . . We work cases for years. . . . We know who you are. And we know that you are in New York, or Louisiana, or Boston, or the Midwest. . . . You can run, but you can't hide forever."[30]

A media simulacrum is not a "representation" of some originary "real event," for it collapses the difference between the two. Moreover, it reproduces models that precede it. The signs of effective law enforcement circulated in *Cops* and *American Detective* are based on television's established narrative and generic codes at least as much as they are rooted in the "realities" of urban police work.[31] Such codes or narrative "models" govern the resolution of enigmas, the restoration of order, the actions and development of characters, and so on. Even much of *American Detective*'s ambient sound track is generated from prerecorded models. Debra Seagal, who worked as a "story analyst" on that program's staff, notes that the supervising producer "occupies a dark little room filled with prerecorded sounds of police banter, queer voice-over loops, segments of the *American Detective* theme song, and sound bites of angry drug-busting screams ('Stop! Police! Put your hands up, you motherfucker!')." Moreover, the story analysts regularly compile "stock-footage books" used for embellishment when no on-scene camera has successfully picked up a narratively significant or reality-effect-enhancing ambient sound or image. These books hold "volumes of miscellaneous images containing every conceivable example of guns, drugs, money, scenics, street signs, appliances, and interior house shots."[32] Although the program is based on encounters between "real" cops, "real" criminals, "real" victims, and "real" witnesses, those encounters are no less "fictional" than events in either police dramas or the ten o'clock news. The point at which the "real" ends and the "fictional" begins is simply impossible to determine, and this impossibility is central to the experience of hyperreality.

Seagal's typical workday at *American Detective* entailed scrutinizing twenty to forty hour-long videotapes in order to produce a running log of sounds and images that could be used to create a story. Thus, as she tells it, "by the time our 9 million viewers flip on their tubes, we've reduced fifty or sixty hours of mundane and compromising video into short, action-packed segments of tantalizing, crack-filled, dope-dealing, junkie-busting cop culture." These segments are inserted into a dramatic half-hour format that features the narration of Lieutenant John Bunnell, *American Detective*'s "venerated spokesperson." In 1991 Bunnell was just an ordinary Oregonian narcotics detective. Today, however, "he has a six-figure income, an agent, fans all over the country, and the best voice coach in Hollywood." Bunnell's narration opens each episode of *American Detective*, setting the stage for viewers and describing the challenges confronting the cops. Because he is both a television star and an active lieutenant, he sometimes also participates in the police raids featured on air.[33] The implosion of Bunnell's role into cop-star matches and advances the contemporary implosion of reality and representation into hyperreality and is in turn matched by the imploded roles of some *American Detective* production crew members who "wear badges and carry guns, chasing down suspects even as they film them," and by some officers who "carry videocameras during their operations, simultaneously making arrests and producing their own television shows."[34]

Aaron Doyle has demonstrated that the "reality" seen on *Cops* is an intensively media-processed one that is heavily edited to produce a variety of desired semiotic effects. Media processing shapes not only the *Cops* broadcasts but indeed the very events that unfold before the Minicams, whose presence "redefines . . . situation[s] dramatically."[35] Officer Steve Osawa of the Fremont, California, Police Department notes that being on TV "brings out the ham in the officers," who often "feel they have to fulfill the motion-picture-type image of the police officer."[36] Officers who emulate Hollywood figures in this manner when they appear in front of *Cops* Minicams push the logic of the simulacrum—the perfect copy for which there is no original—yet a step further as they in turn become models for emulation by others, such as an aspiring officer who told Doyle in an interview that he took regular viewing of the program to be a significant part of his training for the force.[37] It isn't only the cops on these shows who play their roles well, though. Every "troubled" or "delinquent" youth, every assault victim, every bystanding witness, every drunken and abusive husband, every long-suffering girlfriend of a career petty thief, every convenience store clerk who has just been robbed gives exactly the performance we (and they) have seen before and come to expect (though it's never been so fascinating, because it's never been so hyperreal). As noted, it is not, then, that *Cops* and *American Detective* are televised representations of "actual" police work; rather, these "actual" encounters between cops, suspects, and civilians begin to reproduce extant media templates. Some arrestees, for instance, have learned from watching the shows that they will be offered the opportunity to enlist as confidential police informants in exchange for judicial lenience. Thus when Bunnell busts one teenager for selling pot, his eyes brighten with recognition as he blurts out, "Hey . . . you're what's-his-name on *American Detective* . . . I watch your show every week! I know exactly what you want me to do!"[38] The recruitment of "confidential" informants on national TV is the kind of paradox that exemplifies a culture of hyperreality.

We know that everybody who steps in front of a *Cops* or *American Detective* videocam is "real," but they play their roles with such dogged intensity that often we can't quite be sure. At times, the cops are just a bit too overconfident, too smug, too arrogant.[39] Victims and witnesses are just a bit too co-operative, too concerned with pleasing the cops, too grateful that the cops are even there. The frenzied criminal lunatics are just a bit too out of control. We sense intuitively that everybody on *Cops* and *American Detective* is playing a role that we (and they) expect them(selves) to play, but they often overplay their roles to just the point where we can no longer be certain—to where they couldn't possibly be acting, because the act is so incredible. The more authentic it gets, the more apparent the artifice, for these characters are no less mediatized than "real."

Cops and *American Detective* are required by law to obscure the faces of ac-cused suspects who will not sign release forms granting broadcasters per-mission to use their likenesses. Nevertheless, it is rare for criminal suspects and others to refuse to sign the releases despite the fact that many—like talk show guests who willingly air their dirty laundry—have been caught in compromising positions.[40] While their psychological motivations are unknowable to us, the willingness of suspects to appear on national tele-vision under conditions that are at best less than flattering and at worst self-incriminating supports Baudrillard's ideas about the increasing pres-sure to render everything visible under the sign of mediatization. Where faces *are* obscured, the reality effect is paradoxically enhanced, so that the urban criminal or "troublemaker" takes on the appearance of a raw datum, an object to be acted on, a social fact. In an age of growing moral panic over urban crime and ineffectual law enforcement, both the signs of threat-ening criminality and the signs of heroically effective cops assume center stage in the mise-en-scène of our social imagination. Key to this is their implicit reassertion of masculinism, which carries deep resonances at a historical juncture marked by a significant backlash against gains made by white middle-class feminism.[41] Cop machismo in the face of an unruly (and equally hypermasculine) criminal threat signifies a continuing need for traditional masculinity at precisely the historical moment wherein there are multiple pressures on that masculinity to reimagine and reconfigure itself.[42]

Images of policing resonate with the popular imagination partly because cops exist at the intersection of several important social contradictions. They literally embody the legitimated authority of the powerful and en-force the regulations that defend their hegemony, though simultaneously they represent blue-collar subjection to dangerously unpredictable situa-tions and miserably threatening working conditions. They have been un-easily gender and race integrated, though they are often made to signify the effectivity and even the necessity of unreconstructed masculinity as well as the fragility of the "thin blue (read: white) line" that stands as a last defense against multicultural urban anarchy. The popularity of *Cops* and *American De-*

tective can thus be linked not only with the imperatives of postmodern hyperreality, as I've suggested here, but also with the intense social struggles and contradictions whose negotiation the programs encourage and facilitate. *Cops* and *American Detective* stage, in a displaced form, some of the key political struggles touched off by Reaganism's backlash against progressive social movements. It is telling that one statistical content analysis of *Cops* and its imitator *Real Stories of the Highway Patrol* found that in comparison with law enforcement agency figures, the TV shows "overrepresent violent crimes, suggesting that the majority of police work involves dangerous violent offenders" and "underrepresent women police officers, especially in supervisory roles." [43] Another quantitative study found that overall rates of arrest depicted on *Cops* are nearly four times higher than those reported by the U.S. Department of Justice's *Uniform Crime Reports*.[44] Together, such findings support the conclusion that in the world of realiTV, stepped-up policing, especially when left mostly to men, is an effective response to multiracial urban disorder.

Running counter to the hegemonic cultural currents that dominate *Cops* and *American Detective* is their resonance with a kind of postmodern fascination that threatens the "critical exigencies" of their messages, for such fascination is "proportional to the disaffection of meaning." [45] Semiosis itself becomes a vulnerable and uncertain process in image-rich, media-saturated societies. Many of the media spectacles that proliferate in such societies open themselves, as Baudrillard observes in another context, to modes of reception that repudiate meaning in favor of digestion "as a form of entertainment, half-sports, half-games . . . at once both fascinating and ludicrous." As popular theaters of the grotesque, such spectacles offer themselves to those who "refuse socialization," who "redirect everything *en bloc* in the spectacular, without requiring any other code, without requiring any meaning." Baudrillard suggests that "we should read in this . . . an offensive practice, a rediversion by excess, an unanalysed but conscious rejection" of meaning.[46] In and of itself, this is neither progressive nor reactionary, neither laudable nor worthy of condemnation.[47] It is, however—despite the often contrary implications of Baudrillard's own analysis—undeniably a product of deeply rooted antinomies between the relatively powerful and the socially weak. This may help to explain a notable historical discontinuity in the reigning discourses of cultural legitimacy as they pertain to television. The dominant critical discourses around TV during the medium's 1950s "Golden Age" prioritized what Lynn Spigel and Henry Jenkins call a "hyperrealist aesthetic," according to which characteristics such as immediacy, liveness, and the "complete simulation of real-life events" constituted the hallmarks of "quality television." [48] Influential East Coast critics thus reserved their highest praise for programming that took advantage of

TV's capacity to perfectly simulate reality and to put viewers on the scene in ways that seemed to allow the audience to participate in the simulation. This is no longer the case. In the age of expanding media tabloidism, so-called reality TV, and especially the "reality-based" cop shows, are widely seen as "the trashiest trash," [49] from the perspective of "legitimate" cultural taste.

Witnessing Hyperreality, or How to Court the Postmodern

Simulation is presently absorbed not with a structure of certainties but with a radical agenda of destabilization. — Michael Sorkin, *Watching Television* [50]

An immense uncertainty is all that remains. The uncertainty at the very root of operational euphoria, resulting from the sophistication of networks of information and communication. . . . No one understands the stake of these techniques any longer. . . . The crucial stake, and the actual one, is the game of uncertainty. Nowhere can we escape it. — Jean Baudrillard, *Xerox and Infinity* [51]

Each week, a voice-over on *Cops* announces that "all suspects are innocent until proven guilty in a court of law." The linkage between law enforcement and judicial judgment provides a segue into another of tabloid television's prominent sites of hyperreality: the docudramatic courtroom programs that reexamine and question the validity of criminal verdicts that have resulted in actual incarcerations. In their implicit recognition and imagistic exploitation of the notion that truth has lost its finality within an image-saturated regime of third-order simulations, programs such as *Final Appeal* and *Trial and Error* do as much to produce reality as to represent it, for their simulatory strategies multiply the truth and subject it to reconfiguration and thus contestation. These mediatized sites for the interrogation and counterproduction of justice are popular substitutes for official courtrooms as venues wherein truth and the various strategies of its production are worked out, struggled over, and socially mobilized.

Final Appeal and *Trial and Error* volatilize truths that have been certified as final by American courts. In these programs, cases on which official judgment has been passed and certified are reopened, reexamined and reproblematized. The resimulation of these cases, their reproduction and recirculation on our television screens, unfreezes the truths that have been made of them and thrusts them into a new field of contestation where their truth is up for grabs. If legal discourse converts complex and multivocal realities into a monovocally singular truth ("the truth"), the broadcast resimulation of courtroom trials in tabloid television reconverts officially certified truths into a discourse of the hyperreal that is "beyond true and false." [52]

Final Appeal and *Trial and Error* thus mobilize simulatory video technologies to question officially certified truths, leaving only an "immense uncertainty" in their wake. Because the truths put in question are those produced by the policing, prosecuting, and judicial apparatuses, there is institutional power at stake. *Final Appeal* and *Trial and Error* combine techniques of simulation with popular skepticism to cast a large shadow of doubt. In doing this, they provide evidence of the power of screen events to displace the primacy of nonmediatized ones.

The power of legal discourse to produce credible pronouncements of "guilt" and "innocence" depends on the theoretical presumption of certainty regarding the division between the real and the fictional—a form of certainty that has been put in crisis by contemporary cultural conditions associated with postmodernity. Nevertheless, the liquidation of such categories as real and unreal, true and untrue, is not yet the accomplished fact that postmodern analyses sometimes suggest it is. Baudrillard suggests that certain "deterrent" powers struggle against the postmodern evacuation of modernist categories. Disneyland, for example, can be understood as a "scenario of deterrence" that recuperates a decrepit reality principle. Although it is a "complex play of illusions and phantasms" that simulates its own reality, Disneyland works hard to convince us that the rest of the United States is real (rather than hyperreal). Indeed, Los Angeles is encircled by "imaginary stations" like Enchanted Village, Magic Mountain, and Marine World that "feed reality, reality-energy, to a town whose mystery is precisely that it is nothing more than a network of endless, unreal circulation." Thus although our cultural condition may be one in which modernist conceptions of truth, reason, morality, and reality are no longer very useful, these concepts themselves have not yet been jettisoned from the discourses through which we articulate a sense of that condition. Scenarios of deterrence enable the perpetuation of such concepts by maintaining or "proving" them "in reverse." [53]

At one level, *Final Appeal* and *Trial and Error* constitute scenarios of deterrence that rescue the truth principle on which the courts rely. (Indeed, from one perspective, tabloid television in general has the "deterrent" meaning effect, for some audiences, of "proving" the authenticity of the "real news.") Consider the "deterrent" power of the words and images that open each edition of *Final Appeal*. As video cameras lead us through a crowded prisonhouse reverberating with the angry taunts of inmates, a voice-over proclaims:

Seven hundred thousand men and women in our nation's prisons. Walk through any cell block, and many will tell you that they are innocent, wrongfully convicted. They are, of course, guilty, and are exactly where they should be. But no system is perfect. Mistakes can happen.

Not often—perhaps one in ten thousand. But if you are that one, the cost is horrific.

This deterrent strategy works to contain the extent to which *Final Appeal* undermines the modernist notion of truth on which courts depend for their social power: a statistical insignificance (one in ten thousand) absorbs the force of a radical epistemological challenge. Ultimately, then, *Final Appeal* reinforces the modernist reality principle by claiming that the problem lies with the way courts sometimes use it rather than with the principle itself. But the imagistic *mode* of the challenge destabilizes the principle to which, rationally, it appeals. This game of destabilization surfaces more forcefully in *Trial and Error*'s opening segment, where a jarring montage of "real" and "simulated" images, juxtaposed, is accompanied by the following monologue:

> "Beyond a reasonable doubt." This is the guardian phrase that empowers juries to protect the innocent in America. But it's difficult for jurors to be "reasonable" when they're not told the whole truth and nothing but the truth. The most conservative estimates say that we wrongfully convict and imprison between six and seven thousand people every year. Two half-brothers were within sixteen hours of being executed when it was discovered that the prosecution's star witness was actually nowhere near the crime scene, and she'd only seen it in a dream. A couple in Southern California was convicted of a murder that never even occurred. The alleged victim was found alive and well and living in San Francisco years later. After police withheld important evidence, Clarence Chance and Benny Powell spent seventeen unjust years in prison for murder. They have finally been freed.

In what "reality" did these crimes occur? *Trial and Error* asks implicitly. In what "reality" were these convictions grounded? *Final Appeal* and *Trial and Error* ultimately question whether any of the institutions of judgment ever operate "beyond a reasonable doubt," and thus whether our institutions of criminality—dependent as they are on the presumption of a sturdy bedrock of objective facts whose existence is certain—ever have a firm foundation in any reality outside of their own evidentiary models and procedural codes. Postmodernist epistemologies would insist on the fictionality of legal truths, which are institutional artifacts that make *a* sense—though not the only possible one—of certain events. *Final Appeal* and *Trial and Error* use images to exploit the constructedness of legally certified truths and to resignify the meanings of criminal convictions.

Although these programs claim, at one level, to offer a "better truth" than the official one, their images operate on another level where any *certainty* of

Courting the postmodern.

the distinction between "true" and "untrue" has collapsed. In an imagistic culture, images develop a degree of relative autonomy as their relationship to a reality beyond themselves becomes attenuated. Baudrillard notes that "events, politics, history, from the moment where they only exist as broadcasts by the media and proliferate, nearly globally, their own reality disappears. In the extreme case the event could just as well not have taken place . . . . They are screen events and no longer authentic events." When events are "mediatized," their relationship to an insular reality dissolves in a rush of imagistic hyperreality. "As Benjamin said of the [mechanically reproduced] work of art, you can never really go back to the source, you can never interrogate an event, a character, a discourse about its degree of original reality." [54] It is not that its originality never existed but that the power of the original is absorbed by the power of simulation in a mediated world (much as the force of mechanical reproduction absorbed the power and "aura" of the original work of art for Benjamin).[55] In the hyperrealized universe of third-order signs, "you can no longer interrogate the reality or unreality, the truth or falsity of something," since the "mediating principle" becomes more powerful than the "reality principle." [56] The imagistic mediating principle absorbs its energy, renders it irrelevant. In an image-saturated society, where media images come increasingly from a diverse array of sources—file footage, computer generation, Hollywood films, "photo ops" (where the "real" event exists solely for the purpose of media image generation), reenactment, and so on—the distinction between "true" and "false" or "real" and "unreal" images becomes difficult to sustain, if not entirely meaningless.

Courts maintain their social power by repressing the constructedness of the truths they produce. For their part, the court TV programs counter judicial fictions with a sort of mediated hyperfictionality. Their resimulation of competing and compelling scenarios questions judicial truths by situating them within a postmodern epistemological frame where meaning is detached from the original contexts of its production. At the same time, their suspicion toward police, courts, prosecutors, and official investigators, which assumes varying degrees of intensity, implicates the powerful manipulations that produce official pronouncements of guilt. The conversion of criminal cases into television images rips the contestation between prosecution and defense truths out of its courtroom context and resituates it in a multitude of television viewing ones. Audience becomes jury as images are put on trial. Consider, for example, the case of Jeffrey MacDonald, aka "the Green Beret Killer," who was sentenced to three consecutive life terms in prison for the murder of his wife and two children. The case was taken up by *Final Appeal* in its premiere on September 18, 1992, not long after the U.S. Supreme Court rejected an appeal from MacDonald for the sixth time. Unable to receive a hearing from the highest court in the land, MacDonald's case was taken before the postmodern court of popular opinion.

Since 1970, when MacDonald's family was brutally murdered, he has maintained that he, his wife, and children were the victims of an attack by mysterious intruders into his home. The prosecution, by contrast, has produced an intricate scenario in which MacDonald, during a banal domestic quarrel, loses control, stabs and bludgeons his wife and children, and then stabs and bludgeons himself to cover his own tracks. *Final Appeal* simulates both versions, using an intricate mix of acted re-creations, retrospective talking-head commentary, presumably original photographic evidence, "found" film footage, and other miscellaneous images. These simulations convey a strong sense of both the plausibility and the partiality of both accounts, the sense in which both truths are simultaneously compelling and fictitious—somehow unable to deliver the goods, to recapture the lost wholeness of events. *Final Appeal*'s simulatory strategy of volatilization rests crucially on the way in which hyperreal media permit easy movement between a variety of discursive modalities while muting if not erasing altogether the distinctions that would position them differently within a modernist epistemological hierarchy of credibility. Thus the program is able to exploit a variety of forms of videographic "evidence" to establish its countertruth that challenges the official courtroom one. Because *Final Appeal* refuses the courtroom's epistemological distinctions between videographic reenactments and "original" photographs of the crime scene, the program is able to produce a variety of articulations that yield a countertruth in support of MacDonald's insistence on his innocence.

In a third segment of the program, after we have been given imagistic re-creations of the cases for and against Dr. MacDonald, we are presented with evidence that has surfaced since the trial and seriously undermines the prosecution's case. We learn of deceit and manipulation by prosecutors driven by a vendetta against MacDonald. We learn of exculpatory evidence hidden in government documents that were unavailable to the defense at the time of the trial. (As we shall see in subsequent chapters, the theme of a government cover-up of "the truth" is a common one in tabloid storytelling.) We learn, most importantly, of an eyewitness account that supports MacDonald's story of an attack by intruders. Although the provider of this account has been dead since 1983, she appears, ironically and appropriately, on a videotape recorded one year before her death. Such testimony would likely be considered inadmissible in a court of law, though in a mediatized venue like tabloid television, a videotaped witness speaking from beyond the grave is as powerful and compelling as any other image. Thus while *Final Appeal* never explicitly repudiates the modernist discourse of "truth," it produces a screen reality that simultaneously counters the official version of things, undermines the dominant mechanisms for the production of hegemonic truth, and shifts the terrain of judgment from an institutional locus to a popular one. Not only are the images swirling around real criminal events placed on trial in tabloid television programs such as *Final Appeal* and *Trial and Error*, then, but so is the very capacity of courts to produce adequate truths. This is consistent with tabloid storytelling's frequent mobilization of popular discourse in ways that question the adequacy of official truths.

Final Appeal's account of the case of Paul Ferrell, broadcast September 25, 1992, provides another example of discursive destabilization at work. Ferrell was convicted of murder in 1989, though the body of the apparent victim has never been found. We learn that he had been having a clandestine love affair with Cathy Ford in early 1988, when she disappeared under mysterious circumstances. Ferrell (now serving a life sentence in prison) and others involved in the events surrounding Ford's disappearance and his conviction provide the commentary that forms the narrative framework for the presentation of screen events. These screen events eclipse the original ones they supposedly reproduce by perfecting and magnifying a number of irretrievable details whose truth or falsity would be impossible to determine. This magnification of detail bears some similarity to the vérité effects generated by *Cops* and *American Detective*. Viewers are allowed to interpret banal microscopic details made portentous through the combined effects of retrospection and simulation. The actors' performances are oddly "authenticated" by the retrospective commentary given by the "real" participants whose roles they play. Frequent intercutting between actor and original interrupts the program's vérité effects and explicitly indicates its staged nature. Moreover, the actors themselves often bear little physical resemblance to the "real" participants, the semiotic effect of which is to implicitly deny the significance of any difference between reality and representation, fact and fiction. That enactment continually calls attention to itself without attendant cognitive disruption illustrates the implosion of barriers between the real and the fictional that is characteristic of postmodern epistemologies. We watch as if TV is not there, though more than ever we are cognizant that we are in the presence of a thoroughly simulated and mediatized event.

Final Appeal mounts a damaging attack on the prosecution's production of the truth of Paul Ferrell's guilt. Sometime after Ford's disappearance, her boyfriend, Darvin Moon, discovered her badly burned truck in the vicinity of Ferrell's trailer home. The proximity of the truck to the trailer immediately casts Ferrell into the spotlight as the prime suspect in a crime scenario. Because of the absence of scorching in the flora surrounding the vehicle, however, some observers believe the truck was burned elsewhere and planted near Ferrell's trailer home. A video-vérité simulation of the discovery of the truck both hyperrealizes the entire spectacle and confirms the alternative theory.

FBI agents investigating Ferrell's trailer find traces of blood under a newly laid carpet and on a wall and ceiling. Laboratory tests show the blood to be that of a woman. DNA tests, however, provide no positive match between the blood found in the trailer and the blood of Cathy Ford. Ferrell tells the camera that the trailer is eight years old, had been previously occupied by others, and may well be stained with blood from a variety of alternative sources. Dan James, Ferrell's appellate attorney, announces that "the blood analysis proved nothing, but the engaging mathematical wizardry that was . . . presented to the jury made that blood look like it was Cathy Ford's blood, when in fact, we have no idea whose blood it" was.

During Ferrell's trial, Tamela Kitzmiller testified for the prosecution, claiming to have received an obscene phone call from a man she took to be the accused. On camera for Final Appeal, however, Kitzmiller recants, claiming that the prosecution convinced her to testify against Ferrell by telling her that he had been involved in a series of murders in Yellowstone Park. "They told me that he was a sicko, and that he needed to be put away," says Kitzmiller. "You know, you have people in an official capacity who are telling you these things as if they're fact." After giving her testimony, Kitzmiller says she waited for prosecutors to produce proof of Ferrell's involvement in the

Yellowstone murders, as they had promised her they would do. This proof never arrived. That it didn't intensifies the skepticism toward officialdom that is a hallmark of tabloid media.

Another prosecution witness, an FBI agent, testified that while giving Ferrell a "hypothetical scenario about Cathy Ford's murder," he had "observed signs of guilt" in Ferrell's "body language." James claims on camera that "this is the first time, *ever*, in the history of American criminal jurisprudence, that this kind of evidence has . . . been allowed to go to a jury." Says Ferrell, "There's no evidence" to show "that I killed or kidnapped Cathy Ford . . . and they know it. And that's why they had to use the body language. That's why he had to make up a complete fabrication of that blood evidence. You know, 'cause he had no evidence against me."

The most damaging testimony against Ferrell came from Kim Nelson, a neighbor. Nelson testified in court that on February 17, 1988, the day of Ford's disappearance, she heard "banging, a gunshot, and a woman's scream" coming from Ferrell's trailer. Nelson tells *Final Appeal*, however, that she really "didn't know nothin' about Paul Ferrell killin' anybody," and that she hadn't seen or heard anything out of the ordinary on the date in question. In voice-over narration accompanying a video simulation of the scene being described, *Final Appeal* host Robert Stack explains that "before the trial," Nelson had "signed a statement typed up by the . . . prosecution team without reading it." Later, prosecutors threatened Nelson with jail time if she didn't follow the signed statement in her courtroom testimony. They also warned that if Nelson didn't help put Ferrell away, she and her children might be his next victims. "So," says Nelson, "I said what was on that paper." In the original trial of Paul Ferrell, then, the power of the written word and of literacy was used against him, but in his popular-media retrial, the power of images and orality strikes back, exploiting the instability of truth in a postmodern culture. Indeed, there is a similarity between the promiscuity of images in a postmodern culture and that of voices in an oral one: in both cases, conditions arise wherein the "truth" sometimes mutates so rapidly that the dominant modernist conceptualization of "truth" seems grossly inadequate to describe it.

We can take this analysis of the destabilizing role played by images in a tabloid culture further. There's a common strategy at work in *Final Appeal*'s reexamination of the damaging testimony given at Ferrell's trial by each of the three witnesses mentioned earlier. It is a strategy that works through the displacement of original events by screen events. In each case, the reenactment of courtroom proceedings, followed by the insertion of new video evidence, demonstrates the untrustworthiness of accounts that were originally persuasive. The retrospective, mediated version of events displaces the primacy of the original, "real" trial, which is shown to have been flawed. Moreover, the new version places the new mediatized evidence on an equal footing with the events of the original trial, destroying the sense of authenticity and authority they gained merely by virtue of their enactment within a "real" courtroom. As the witnesses' testimony is shifted out of its original courtroom context and into that of tabloid television, then, it is made to testify against the legal production of truth rather than against the defendant. It is made to reveal not what went on in "reality" but what went on in the courtroom; it thus questions the supposedly stable relationship between them that enabled the court to claim that it did not *produce* the events in "reality" but merely represented them. The only reality of tabloid television is that of its images, so when courtroom images are "tabloidized," the reality principle dissolves.

Krista Bradford, a former tabloid TV journalist, writes, "I have watched reality become fiction in the edit bays as news footage was intercut with movie scenes and music videos and tarted up with sound effects and music."[57] In her statement, Bradford underscores an important aspect of the postmodern condition: its "reality" is always amenable to reconfiguration through processes of simulation; its truths are never final, stable, or fixed for all times and places. By contrast, they are quite ephemeral, perhaps only authoritative within the local contexts of their production. Most important, Bradford indicates the crucial role television plays in the volatilization of the boundary between the authentic and the inauthentic. Its mediatizing power means that the truth or reality of anything or any event can never be finalized. Rather, it can always be reprocessed. This situation yields both a pessimistic and an optimistic interpretation. On the one hand, it means that truths produced against the power-bloc are never entirely safe from the mediatizing apparatus that, finally, it controls. On the other hand, it means that the power-bloc must find it harder and harder to ground its truths in some fixed notion of *the* real, and that political contestation over truth cannot therefore be brought to an end (as the power-bloc would wish it to be). In the words of Graham Knight, "the real still exists, but it no longer seems to be in place; it is displaced—and replaced—by the expansion of competing sign systems that seek to pin it down from the outside."[58] For Baudrillard, this means that we increasingly inhabit "a sphere, a megasphere where things no longer have a reality principle. Rather a communication principle, a mediatising principle."[59] This is not to say that people in image-saturated societies do not experience something like an empirical reality of their everyday lives but rather to point toward what happens to that empirical reality once it is inserted into the hyperreal play of technologically reproduced and electronically circulated images and, conversely, what happens when the circuits and networks of imagistic circulation become an increasingly large component of lived experience.

Trial and Error and *Final Appeal* provide fuel for the fire of popular skepticism that, at particular times and in particular contexts, turns against the judicial system and refuses its discursive power to produce authoritative truths. The first trial of the officers who beat Rodney King and the urban uprisings that answered its verdict provide one of the most obvious and visible recent examples of this sort of popular skepticism erupting explosively, though there are more ordinary examples of everyday popular skepticism that never achieve the level of spectacularity required to push them into the spotlight of mainstream media. Still, it should be noted that although *Cops* remains a long-running hit for the Fox Network, *Final Appeal* and *Trial and Error* were both short-lived, neither lasting longer than a single television season.[60] We can surmise that *Cops*, with its simulation of law and order in a society whose everyday anxieties revolve increasingly around a variety of forces construed as threats to that order, has greater popular resonance and relevance than either *Final Appeal* or *Trial and Error*. As racial conflict and racism have both grown in the United States, and as the signifiers "crime" and "drugs" have been pressed into service by a white power-bloc eager to recode racist meanings into ostensibly race-neutral discourses,[61] tabloid programming about the disruption and restoration of law and order in our streets has assumed predominance over programming concerned with interrogating the way in which justice is produced in our courtrooms.

And Postmodern Justice for All: The Tabloidization of O.J. Simpson

Nevertheless, tabloidism's concerns with the production of judicial truth were resumed around the decade's most sustained tabloid media event, which involved O.J. Simpson. The African American Simpson, a former football hero, movie actor, and media pitchman, was tried for (and, in 1995, acquitted of) the brutal 1994 stabbing deaths of his ex-wife Nicole and a male friend of hers, Ronald Goldman, both of whom were white. Opinion polls consistently demonstrated a wide gap between U.S. whites, a clear majority of whom accepted the state's "truth" and thus believed firmly in Simpson's guilt, and African Americans, a clear majority of whom *didn't*. As Simpson's trial progressed, this gap grew ever wider. Consequently, Americans argued over the possibility that O.J. was yet another target of a racist police force and a criminal justice system that seems hell-bent on putting as many African American men as it can behind bars. They argued over the validity of scientific evidence that purported to demonstrate with near certainty that O.J.'s blood was present at the crime scene along with that of the murder victims. Such claims as those, rooted in the supposedly "objective" findings of DNA scientists, push whites' emotional buttons by stimulating the widespread white fear of blacks that has been well documented and, at a more implicit ideological level, by tapping into white anxieties about the intermingling of racially different blood. Indeed, one is forced to wonder whether the murders and the investigation and trial of O.J. Simpson would have spawned anything like the kind of high-visibility media event that they did were it not for the racial identities of the victims (and especially of Nicole). Because the white majority in the United States has proven both its intense fear of black men and its relative lack of concern for the fate of black women, we can surmise that had Simpson been accused of murdering, say, his first wife (an African American), the accusation would probably not have provoked the most sustained media event of the decade.[62] This is not, however, to say that this tabloid media event was sustained only by white interest in it, for as we shall see, the case came to have great significance for many African Americans who saw it as a test of the capacity of the *criminal justice system* (a punning phrase that means very differently for blacks and whites) to produce fair outcomes not just for Simpson but for black men in general. For if even a rich and famous black man could not get fair treatment before the law, then what could possibly be done for those struggling with the police and courts under more ordinary circumstances?

The media event provoked by the murders gave rise in turn to a sustained moral panic over media tabloidization,[63] and the outcome of the trial itself engendered a conspicuously racialized and middle-class backlash that was aptly characterized by Alexander Cockburn as "white rage."[64] The line between the moral panic and the backlash is difficult to discern. I would argue that both were fundamentally expressions of anxiety about the troubling multiplicity of perspectives on U.S. society that the Simpson case brought to the fore. Quite tellingly, supermarket tabloids such as the *Globe* and the *Star* were among the most-visible media sites where these perspectives could be readily glimpsed in all their troubling multiplicity. In particular, these publications are notable for the play they gave to explanations of the murders that contradicted the one offered by the LAPD, the criminal prosecutor's office, and a large proportion of the Euro-American population.[65] In this way, the Simpson incident gave rise to tabloid media circulation of a variety of popular counterknowledges and counternarratives that are typically relegated to the margins of, or excluded altogether from, the mainstream press, which is generally much less open to socially delegitimized perspectives than is the tabloid press. This is not to deny the presence of reactionary and racist knowledges in tabloid journalism—clearly they are rife there (as they are throughout U.S. society). In particular, the tabloids were not shy about circulating images and stories depicting the gory murders and detailing the history of O.J.'s propensity to violence in his relationship with Nicole (a reportorial choice that exposes domestic violence, albeit sometimes fetishistically, while reinforcing racial stereotypes, about which I shall have more to say). However, at the same time, many tabloid stories explained the murders and their investigation in ways that implicated the LAPD, the California criminal justice system, and *white* assailants rather than a black man. Such stories clearly went against the grain of the dominant white-power-bearing perspectives on the event. The Simpson case is thus aptly illustrative of the way in which the multivocality and contradictoriness of tabloid journalism often results in a collision between dominant knowledges and a variety of popular counterdiscourses.

The terms "discourse" and "knowledge" deserve some attention here.[66] In my usage, discourse comprises both language and knowledge as they are socially practiced in particular situations. Discourse always carries both the accents and interests—political and material—of its users. It is inevitably power bearing, as it necessarily advances the sociopolitical standing of some discursive communities over and against others. Thus discourse establishes relations of power and control as it determines the ways in which events, objects, and people are inserted into systems of social sense making. The insertion of events and objects into socially established (but contested) ways of making sense of them necessarily entails choosing between the different discourses available to the sense-making agent, for events and objects "in themselves" are incapable of determining which discourses will be brought to bear on (and therefore produce and circulate a sense of) them. The choice between competing discourses is therefore one that *always* has an irreducible political dimension and thus is governed finally by the social interests that benefit from the advancement of this or that way of making sense and not by the "truth" or "nature" of the event or object subjected to this process of sense making.

Discourses operate socially by activating particular systems of knowledge, a word I use to designate one or another coherent way of knowing. This use pluralizes the concept of knowledge and therefore rejects the meanings of the term as it is used within philosophies derived from the Enlightenment. There are many different knowledges in the world. My use of the word "knowledge" thus differs from that of the sciences, which reserve the term to describe things known on the basis of a supposedly accumulative body of "facts" purported to be demonstrably and absolutely "true." The sciences use the concept of knowledge monopolistically to exclude systems of belief that diverge epistemologically from the broad contours of scientific rationalism.[67] From the poststructuralist perspective I adopt here, by contrast, all conceptual systems produce knowledges, which are applied through socially materialized discourses and inevitably apply social power in the process of their materialization. Discourse is thus a product of the relationship between a knowledge and the social circumstances of its particular applications. Different discourses often activate different knowledges and thus produce different "truths," though they do not do so under conditions of equality. Some knowledges are more socially powerful than others, and their social power entails both the power to assert that their own "truths" are "better" than others, and the power to marginalize and repress the "truths" produced by competing knowledges.

Tabloid journalism often proliferates popular knowledges considered woefully inadequate and even disruptive of the solemn responsibilities of the "fourth estate." It often playfully and sometimes earnestly circulates counterdiscourses that question the adequacy of official ones and therefore destabilize officialdom's capacity to produce socially powerful "truths." Perhaps the most socially effective of these official modes of knowledge is scientific rationalism, which has developed a variety of sophisticated strategies for representing its epistemological assumptions and methodological protocols, if not all instances of their application, as if they were beyond question. Tabloid knowledges often express an ambivalent and conflicted incredulity toward scientific rationalism and its power to produce authoritative truths. The flip side of the tabloids' contradictory popular skepticism toward scientific rationalism is the space they create for the investment of belief in alternative ways of knowing. Both this popular skepticism and its corollary production of spaces for belief in alternative knowledges constitute one of a series of focal points for the articulation of both moral panic and backlash.

A useful example of tabloid incredulity toward official knowledges comes from a *Star* story headlined "O.J. Trial Bombshell: I've Found Murder Weapon, Psychic Tells D.A.—and Simpson Didn't Do It." This story undercuts the white majority's "truth" of O.J.'s guilt by invoking a form of knowledge that is as socially marginalized as the black minority's "truth" that proclaims Simpson was framed for the murders. It describes how a well-known psychic named John Monti came to conclude that a gang of three, one woman and two men, rather than O.J. Simpson actually committed the murders. Monti, the story tells us, is famous for solving a well-known New York kidnapping case and for predicting the attempt to assassinate Ronald Reagan in 1981. As well as to the *Star*, Monti has given his elaborately detailed (and seemingly quite plausible) account of the murders (which is based on a "psychic vision" he had "as he stood in the dried blood of the two victims") on Sally Jessy Raphael's eponymous tabloid TV talk show. Lead prosecutor Marcia Clark, however, will (not surprisingly) have nothing to do with Monti. In the view delineated by the tabloid, Clark is so narrowly and rigidly devoted to DNA science that she refuses even to take Monti's phone calls. Monti, for his part, explains that he "doesn't care" about O.J. Simpson, who was, in Monti's words, "a bad husband who beat his wife, but that doesn't mean he should be tried for two murders that he didn't commit."[68] What interests me about Monti's chronicle of the murders is its inclusion in the tabloids (where such stories are typical), its circulation of a "truth" that contests the received (and politically powerful) wisdom, and its role in both reproducing and helping to sustain a form of knowledge that persists as a socially living alternative to the dominant one. Rather than simply excluding the psychic's narrative a priori, the tabloid, unlike the mainstream media, presents the story alongside the knowledge of scientific rationalism, explicitly depicts the antagonistic relationship between the two, and demonstrates their unequal social power to determine which explanations typically come to be treated as true ones.

In the remaining pages of this chapter, I'd like to extend my analysis of the postmodern tabloid media from TV to supermarket print weeklies. The *Globe* and the *Star* were two key print media sites for the circulation of popular discourses concerning the O.J. Simpson affair. While both tabloids presented stories that, as noted, "implicated" O.J. in a variety of (often implicit) ways—sometimes, for example, focusing almost obsessively and with disturbing racial undertones on his violent rage and purportedly voracious sexual appetites—they also did something the mainstream press did not: they took popular counterknowledges around the case *very* seriously. In doing so, they both exploited and exemplified aspects of the postmodern condition discussed in the previous sections of this chapter. In particular, the tabloids' rapid weekly succession of alternative constructions of "the truth" of O.J.'s "guilt" or "innocence"—like *Trial and Error*'s and *Final Appeal*'s successive reenactments of defense and prosecution "truths"—gives their readers an object lesson in postmodern truth making and so gives the lie to claims that either journalistic or judicial truths are discovered rather than produced. The tabloids maximally exploited the ultimate unknowability of exactly what happened on the night of the murders by enacting a profusion of plausible alternative scenarios that collectively demonstrate that in such cases the truth *must be produced* rather than merely "discovered." Their coverage of the Simpson affair thus deserves careful examination here.

A key discursive strategy mobilized by the tabloids is that involving processes of articulation, a concept associated with both the work of Stuart Hall and that of more postmodern theorists such as Gilles Deleuze and Félix Guattari.[69] Hall explains that the concept of articulation exploits the dual meaning associated with the word in British English. There, the term denotes both "language-ing" or "expressing" *and* the construction of a contingent and breakable linkage, as in an "articulated lorry," a truck whose "front (cab) and back (trailer) can, but need not necessarily, be connected to one another."[70] Articulation thus expresses the idea of meanings that come into being through a contingent conjunction of different signifying elements. The process of articulation creates an expressive unity that derives from the specific combination of meaningful elements that are linked to one another in a particular discourse. It complicates older theories of ideology, therefore, by contesting the idea that ideologies are either organically whole or necessarily attached to specific social locations. On the contrary, the theory of articulation proposes that both the elements of an ideological discourse and its connection to particular social formations and political interests can always be broken (disarticulated) and reformed (rearticulated) in a variety of ways.[71]

What I'd like to suggest here, as I have also tried to do in my discussion of *Final Appeal* and *Trial and Error*, is that in a postmodern culture where boundaries between "reality" and "representation" are ever more fluid and, in social practice, increasingly irrelevant, the field of potential articulations and rearticulations undergoes something of an expansion of possibilities and intensities. In their coverage of the O.J. Simpson affair, the *Globe* and the *Star* can be seen as both symptoms and agents of this expansive process. For example, by eliding the differences between "fictional" characters and "real" people, the tabloids were able to articulate bits of both together in ways that expressed different explanations of the murders and their investigation. Thus tabloid stories about star prosecution witness Mark Fuhrman discredit his key role in the investigation of Simpson as well as his devastating courtroom testimony by exploiting the uncertain difference between the "real" cop and the corruptly racist "fictional" police officer character he was helping a Hollywood scriptwriter to create.[72] By the same token, however, another tabloid story deploys seven-year-old movie stills of Simpson *in character* to implicate the actor. The photographs are from a fiction film in which O.J. plays a character who, "in a blind rage," uses "frightening commando knives" to conduct a "bloody one-man war." According to the *Globe*, Simpson "played the part so convincingly" that "he terrified the set photographer." The report moves fluidly between production information about the movie and forensic evidence from the murder scene.[73] Of course, forms of cultural production that combine the "real" and the "fictional" are hardly anything new (an observation that does not render the concept of the postmodern "silly," as some pomophobes would have it). What I call "postmodern" about the current moment is the expanding volume, availability, and promiscuity of images, the growing permeability of boundaries that accompanies this expansion, and the increasing indifference to, and uncertainty regarding, the integrity of epistemological categories that is a symptom of both processes. The concept of postmodernism helps me to name the encroaching qualitative shift in cultural processes that is linked to a quantitative expansion of representational diversity and fragmentation.[74]

Each week, the *Globe* and the *Star* recombined diverse elements of the Simpson story in a way that did not so much produce the emergence of enduring or long-term ideological formations; rather, their ongoing rearticulations of story elements showed the instability or unfixity of both "truths" and signifying practices under postmodern conditions. The tabloids thus expertly demonstrated for their readers that "the truth" of O.J.'s guilt or innocence is a function of the way in which particular evidentiary and narrative elements are articulated to one another and so made to speak. Having said this, though, it is crucial to point out that their stories often spoke to popular suspicions toward the LAPD in particular and contemporary policing practices in general—suspicions that are deeply rooted in the material and social experiences of people of color in the United States. This should warn us against pushing the theory of articulation to the point that it reaches in *some* postmodern thought, where "there is no reason why anything is or isn't potentially articulatable with anything" else.[75] To say that the rapid reconfiguration of "the truth" by weekly supermarket tabloids covering the Simpson affair is expressive of postmodern signification is not, therefore, to say that there are no discernible patterns to either the knowledges they circulate or the social conditions of which they make sense. Because supermarket tabloids target excluded social formations as their primary market, they must therefore mobilize excluded perspectives, many of which are typically granted little if any visibility in the mainstream press. This does not mean that the tabloids give play to all socially marginalized knowledges, for they clearly do not. Their profit motive does, however, push them to include whatever stories their producers think are likely to resonate with readers who have little interest in the mainstream perspectives of the conventional press.[76]

This interest in reaching socially marginalized target markets through appeals to certain forms of excluded perspectives and knowledges is made manifest in some of the predominant styles and tones of voice that are characteristic of the tabloids' coverage of the Simpson affair. For example, the *Globe* and the *Star* appeal often to feelings of alienation and exclusion from the circulation of information. Promises to reveal that which is known and done by the socially powerful—that which takes place behind the scenes, as it were—have a potentially immense resonance with readers who are routinely denied access to information by dint of the very structure of power relations and therefore of communication flows in an unequal society. Consequently the tabloids' reports are often framed in terms of the revelation of various forms of insider information. Indeed, along with the recurrent motif depicting a tragic vision of the California couple (*each* was shown to be obsessive and capable of extreme manipulation of the other, despite the immense bonds of love and devotion that endured between them), this commitment to the liberation of insider information is arguably as close as the *Globe* and *Star* come to the construction of a stable viewpoint that persists over the course of their coverage of the Simpson affair.[77]

This viewpoint takes different forms, however. For example, it supports the former football hero in the *Star's* April 4, 1995, story that ran under the headline "O.J. Couldn't Have Done It." This report articulates a mountain of evidence into a coherent case for the claim that the murders were a consequence of mistaken identity, for the real target of the killers was Nicole Brown Simpson's friend and confidante Faye Resnick. Having made a commitment to its case against O.J., however, the *Star* reports that the "D.A.'s office is now scrambling to try to nail him," despite its awareness of a growing accumulation of evidence that undermines their case—evidence that had been kept from the public but is revealed here by the tabloid.[78] Such stories speak to popular suspicions directed toward the greedily vindictive manipulations of the legal system undertaken by its highest prosecutorial officers.

Inside angles on the Simpson case cut in another direction, however, in *Star's* report on "O.J.'s Life of Luxury behind Bars." This story and others like it speak to class-based resentment of the "special privileges" enjoyed by "America's most pampered prisoner," including better meals and more privacy than others receive in jail, entry to private showers and libraries, and unlimited access to communication technologies such as TVs, VCRs, and private telephone lines, which ordinary inmates are denied.[79] Hence, the tabloids' impulses toward the revelation of secret inside angles drifts in *favor* of O.J Simpson when he is cast as a target of institutional power and *against* him when he is shown to benefit from the privileges bestowed on the wealthy by powerful institutions to the detriment of weaker others. For in their renderings of such stories as these, the tabloids typically express sympathies for the underdogs and the disempowered, whomever they might be in the particular situation at hand.

To take a final example along these lines, Simpson and the LAPD are both cast into the same kettle of rotten fish in an insider's exposé of "O.J.'s Sex and Drug Parties for L.A. Cops." In an interview with the *Star*, a former West Los Angeles Division officer provides a detailed account of the "guys' nights out" frequently attended by him and other policemen, "some of them very high-ranking," at Simpson's Brentwood mansion during the 1980s, where the cops were "treated like kings." The story suggests that the cozy relationship that consequently developed between police operatives and O.J. helped to facilitate the situation that prevailed throughout his relationship with Nicole, during which officers received at least *eight* "911" emergency calls from the latter and yet arrested her partner for spousal battery only *once*. This report thus provides a behind-the-scenes look at the Brentwood boys' club whose decadent and hypocritical ethos contributed immensely to the suffering of Nicole Brown Simpson throughout her marriage to the Juice.[80] This is underlined by the retired officer's revealing descriptions of the ways in which women were objectified at O.J.'s parties. These descriptions resonate tellingly, though not through any intention on the interviewee's part, with the tabloid's points about cops who repeatedly looked the other way when confronted with violent domestic abuse at the Simpson home:

> O.J. said when he was playing with the Buffalo Bills he'd had most of their cheerleaders.
>
> He told me, "They're all gorgeous and great in the sack. I'll get some over to one of my parties — and you're invited."
>
> And sure enough, I turned up for one party at the Rockingham mansion and there were about 20 women there. All gorgeous and sexily dressed.
>
> There were about the same number of guys. Some other ballplayers I didn't recognize, a few Hollywood types, a couple of other cops and two guys who said they were lawyers, but didn't tell me their names.
>
> O.J. was a perfect host. He told me, "Come on in and E-N-J-O-Y." Then he slapped me on the shoulder and said, "Take your pick. Whichever one you want is yours."
>
> I was dazzled by one long-legged brunette who told me she was a dancer. And she certainly looked it. I stuck close to her. There was plenty of booze and coke. It was a status symbol in those days for a host to have cocaine so readily available for party guests.
>
> It was a rich man's plaything and O.J. loved to play.

In this way, the *Star* provides a revelatory glimpse into attitudes toward women shared by both O.J. and members of the LAPD that helps to clarify for readers how violent abuse might have developed within the Simpsons' relationship and been ignored or dismissed by officers like the one quoted. Furthermore, this informant's tales of drug-dealing and drug-doing cops, of going "back on duty with two or three shots of O.J.'s liquor in me," and of Simpson's links with high-ranking police department officials all speak to popular skepticism toward the institutional forces that exert so much control over our lives yet are incapable of controlling their own corruption and hypocrisy — and toward the excesses and privileges of the rich and powerful in general. The story's final sentence, another quote from the former cop, emphasizes its strategy of reader engagement through the revelation of the kinds of insider information that public agencies normally prefer to repress and conceal: "I'm sure my former colleagues will try to discredit me. But I'm telling the absolute truth about O.J. I'd be happy to repeat what I told STAR to police internal investigators — under oath."[81]

The tabloids therefore constantly promise to deliver repressed information to those who resent being kept in the dark about what goes on behind the walls that conceal the activities of the powerful and the privileged. Their desire to expose any inside angles they can generates a kind of fluidly mobile suspicion whose objects and targets may shift radically from story to story and week to week. This leads to a multiplication and dispersion of both perspectives and their political implications. In some reports, it is the corrupt bureaucracies of law enforcement and the criminal justice system whose misdeeds and incompetencies have led to the mishandling of evidence or the formulation of a conspiracy to frame an innocent man that must now be made public. In others, it is the hidden details of Simpson's violently abusive and obsessively jealous attempts to control Nicole that constitute the secret to be unveiled. In some reports, it is the representatives of foreign drug cartels who are indicted for their ruthless terrorization of O.J. and shown to be responsible for the murders of Nicole and Goldman. In still others, it is Nicole who is exposed as an irresponsible and flirtatious "sex addict" who cruelly taunted and manipulated O.J. for years. In all such instances, the tabloids target for interrogation some force that they associate with power exerted unjustly, be it the official power of the state and its agencies, the illegal muscle of drug kingpins, the naked masculine violence and controlling aggression of O.J., or the sexually aggressive and manipulative "feminine wiles" of Nicole.

The glaring instability of their constructions of the "truth" of the matter therefore opens the tabloids' coverage of the Simpson affair to a plurality of alternative explanations that is striking in its contrast with mainstream (read: white) reactions to the murders. The tabloids were unremitting in their willingness to entertain seriously a whole variety of popular counter-knowledges that work, through their skepticism toward the official view, to erode the heavily racialized grooves into which most mainstream thought and coverage of the case had been slotted.[82] Their stories therefore often attacked the LAPD and the prosecutor's case by proffering hidden facts to those who are continually denied access to the truth about what the established institutions and their agents are up to. This appeal was frequently enhanced with claims that the insider information being delivered by the tabloids may never even be heard by the Simpson trial jury because of one or another conspiracy or legal technicality that threatens to corrupt the pursuit of the truth in the courtroom. Like the stories told on *Final Appeal* and *Trial and Error*, these tabloid reports on the Simpson case often work through a process of postmodern articulation that fuses together diverse elements — crime scene pictures, police reports, diary entries, data from official personnel files, testimony from psychics, scientific test results, letters from tabloid readers, movie stills, personal or publicity photos of the Simpsons, and a

Tabloidtruth.

host of other types of evidence—without discriminating between them according to modernist epistemological categories and hierarchies of credibility. It is in this way that the tabloids produced and disseminated popular counternarratives through the assemblage of eclectic arrays of signifying fragments.

The August 2, 1994, edition of the *Globe* provides a useful print media example of the tabloidization of the O.J. Simpson case through the articulation of diverse source elements to produce a unified counternarrative. Inch-high bright-yellow block letters on its front cover promise the story of "How Cops Framed O.J." Alongside these words are pictures of the famous bloody glove, the white Ford Bronco, and Simpson's (undarkened) police mug shot, taken the night of his arrest for the murders of Nicole and Goldman.[83] Above this headline appears a picture of a stiletto knife and a promise to reveal "new clues" concerning "lies and planted evidence." Beneath the headline is an offer of a million-dollar reward. Inside, we learn that the reward will go to the reader who can provide the tabloid with information leading to "the arrest and conviction of the real killer or killers."[84] In connection with this contest, the newspaper's cover announces the publication of "dramatic new evidence from *Globe* readers" on the matter of "who really killed Nicole."[85]

Pages 36 and 37 of the tabloid feature a close-up of Detective Mark Fuhrman under large block letters proclaiming that a "Cop Framed O.J.," and smaller bright-yellow ones stating that the " 'troubled' detective once said he wanted to kill his own wife!" [86] The low-angle half-page picture of Fuhrman is set perfectly adjacent to an equally large blowup of the bloody glove as it lay at the back of Simpson's home; the detective is using a wooden pointer to gesture toward something outside the frame of the photograph. The pointer is cut in half by the shared border between the picture of Fuhrman and that of the glove. The page layout allows the two photos to blend into one that appears to depict an action that both the text of the story and the towering headline looming over this composite image invite us to imagine: it is the "overeager" cop as he leans over to plant the key piece of evidence against Simpson. This composite image thus disarticulates the bloody glove from its associations with O.J. and quite literally rearticulates it to Fuhrman. Moreover, the image not only *illustrates* the accusatory headline to which it is articulated here but also fills the headline with meaning beyond that which it carries semantically and thus makes it "real."

The accompanying story recounts in detail the checkered history of the " 'rogue' cop" Fuhrman and his suspicious role in the investigation of the Goldman and Simpson murders. It draws heavily on Fuhrman's psychiatric

The Globe: planting suspicion.

evaluations, which are articulated with carefully selected quotes from Simpson's legal defense team, from police documents, and from Fuhrman himself, to depict the veteran LAPD officer as a dangerously violent racist who, as one police personnel report had it, spent "the greater portion of time . . . trying to make the 'big arrest.'"[87] The detective's career is shown to be haunted by "a long history of problems on the job," including violent attacks on people of color and the use of excessive physical force to subdue crime suspects. These points serve not only to discredit Fuhrman but also to enhance popular skepticism toward the LAPD's knowledge of the Simpson case by metonymically articulating that case to the ignominious recent history of the department and particularly to the beating of Rodney King. All of this then bolsters the story's claims that Fuhrman, who was (according to "insiders") "furious at being replaced by more senior investigators" at the crime scene, decided to frame O.J. by planting the glove whose subsequent "discovery" would make him the hero of the investigation. The tabloid notes, furthermore, that beyond "the dubious circumstances surrounding Fuhrman's case-building discovery," both incompetence and corruption in the Los Angeles coroner's office may cast further doubt on the evidence against Simpson.[88]

This story of an elaborate frame-up is then articulated to alternative explanations of the murder taken from letters sent to the *Globe* by its readers and placed in a sidebar alongside the Fuhrman report. The Fuhrman exposé and the popular counterexplanations thus work together to undermine both the LAPD's account of the murder and the well-worn cultural narratives concerning the threat of miscegenation and of the black male body that has escaped (white) control that lie just beneath the surface of that account. This is not to say that reactionary racial politics do not enter into the tabloid discourse on the Simpson case. For example, some readers' theories about the murder merely displace the racial threat from African Americans to Latin America. Thus Neil Vinetz writes to the editors of the *Globe* that "the *savage* brutality used to kill Nicole Brown Simpson and Ronald Lyle Goldman has all the earmarks of a Colombian drug cartel assassination." Vinetz explains that O.J. and Nicole were cocaine addicts who had become deeply indebted to Latino drug dealers whose patience ran out. Because the former football star brazenly ignored persistent demands for payment of perhaps as much as $2 million, the dealers "decided to kill Nicole and frame O.J. for the murders."[89] Another *Globe* informant adds that O.J. was forced by drug dealers to witness the execution of his wife and her friend. "He was bound and taken to the murder scene by drug-connected Colombians, who were upset because of his involvement in a drug deal gone bad." Thus, "only after both victims were repeatedly stabbed and slashed to death was O.J. taken from the scene and warned that the same would happen to him and his children if he ever revealed what he had seen."[90] Variations on these accounts of the Colombian connection to the Simpson and Goldman murders enjoyed widespread popular circulation in the wake of the police investigation and the Simpson trial.[91]

It is worth noting in passing that the most *popular* journalistic formats, like tabloid newspapers and television programs, solicit the active participation of their readers and viewers in this fashion far more frequently than do the most highly regarded ones, a phenomenon that usefully serves to focus our attention on one of the significant differences between the discourses of tabloid and serious journalism.[92] Whereas official journalism is founded on the idea of a well-informed professional class whose members bestow their goods on those who lack them, the tabloids often imply a model of dynamic interaction between news workers and readers that produces openings for the participation of the readers in the storytelling process. At least at points, then, the tabloids' information process suspends the communicative authoritarianism embedded in the implicit notion of unilateral truth delivery that underlies the traditional practices of serious journalism. This may help to explain the popularity of tabloids, as well as many readers' sense that the tabloid media have a relevance to their lives that is missing from official journalism.[93] It is arguable, moreover, that the most democratic processes of informing are those that acknowledge readers' and audiences' knowledges and communicative competencies and thus encourage them to participate in the circulation of meanings.[94]

As I have suggested, to see only racialized forces at work in the struggles over *whose* knowledges could muster adequate social power to produce the "final" truth of Simpson's guilt or innocence would, of course, obscure the undeniable significance of gendered meanings on the contested semiotic terrain formed by the bodies of O.J. and Nicole. The murders brought rapid and widespread media coverage of the history of abuse perpetrated against Nicole by O.J. In their wake, the tabloids were, like the rest of the U.S. media, both quick and willing to examine issues related to domestic violence. One way in which they did this was to look to those close to Nicole in order to recover repressed information about her tortured relationship with O.J. John Cohan, a psychic adviser to whom Nicole often turned for help, for example, claims that she was distraught over the way O.J. jealously and obsessively stalked her. Cohan tells the *Star* that according to Nicole, O.J. once stormed into a salon where she was having a facial and accused the handsome man attending to her of "feeling her up." On another occasion, Nicole told Cohan, O.J. secretly followed her car all the way from Los Angeles to Monterey in northern California, where she was going for a quiet weekend with her children and a female friend. She confided in the psychic that during a vicious beating, O.J. once screamed repeatedly that he hoped to break some bones in Nicole's face so she "won't be so pretty."[95] Such tabloid reportage works by purporting to deliver information about the concealed violent excesses that belie the glossy sheen of publicity photos and so is well in keeping with the publications' constant promise to reveal that which has been kept hidden.[96] That the tabloids often turn to the knowledge of psychics, experts who exemplify difference from officialdom, is a symptom of their interest in appealing to readers who are aware that information is perpetually manipulated, massaged, and erased by official sources.

The tabloids dwelled on the emotional ups and downs that seemed to define Nicole and O.J.'s troubled relationship, as viewed through the eyes of their friends and family members. Some, such as Nicole's friends Candace Garvey and Cici Shahian, speak of the guilt they feel for having advised Nicole at various times to follow her heart back to O.J.[97] In an interview with the *Star*, Garvey expresses deep regret for never having recognized the harsh mistreatment Nicole suffered in her relationship with O.J., for as Garvey notes, "He was one of the most happy-go-lucky, charismatic people you could meet and over the years he had been so kind and generous to me."[98] The tabloids' interest in the emotional details of the Simpsons' relationship and in Nicole's connections with those around her enables the papers to examine both the costs borne by some women in the course of their everyday lives with selfishly jealous, violently abusive men and the patterns of concealment and nonrecognition that can enable such costs to remain hidden from even close friends. The stories they tell invite readers to identify with the feelings and perspectives provided by those close to Nicole and thus to make use of these emotional and interpretive resources, perhaps to reinterpret aspects of their own lives. At the same time, these tabloid stories make the issue of domestic violence more publicly visible and therefore susceptible to discussion and placement on agendas for action.

While it is crucial to understand the gendered dynamics of the competing knowledges circulating around the Simpson affair, we need to analyze them in their interactions with the meanings of race, for the two are inextricably intertwined here. The widespread social willingness to address the domestic violence around the Simpson affair stems partly from feminism's continuing efforts to draw attention to the issue. However, this willingness must be viewed with caution, since it was no doubt abetted by the racial identity of Nicole's former husband. It is telling that the public expression of accounts of the Simpson episode derived from the alternative knowledges of people of color (such as those that linked the star's arrest with institutionalized LAPD racism) provoked a power-bloc backlash in a way that highly visible and sustained attention to domestic violence did not. Thus, to cite one example, on a Sunday morning chat show that aired not long after Simpson's arrest (and about which I shall have more to say), there was serious consideration of the domestic violence issues pertinent to the case but no equivalent discussion of the treatment of African Americans by the police and criminal justice systems. This is not to suggest that the U.S. media are bastions of feminism but rather to suggest that the most powerful Americans have shown themselves to be remarkably stubborn in their general refusal to acknowledge just how profoundly their society continues to be shaped in all its dimensions (including its policing and judicial procedures) by white racism. Consequently those who wished to frame the investigation and trial of O.J. in terms of white racism were widely berated, just as when, after the verdict was issued, repentant attorney Robert Shapiro said bitterly of the Simpson legal defense team of which he was a member that "not only did we play the race card, we dealt it from the bottom of the deck."

One of the narrative strategies used repeatedly by the tabloids in their treatment of the Simpsons' relationship involved the juxtaposition of scenes of romantic promise and domestic bliss alongside those of violence and terror. Their recurrent interest in an auspicious Simpson family trip to Cabo San Lucas just ten weeks before Nicole's murder is typical of the tabloids' fascination with this juxtaposition. Several friends who joined Nicole and O.J. on the holiday told the *Star* that they were convinced the two would soon be married again. As Nicole's pal Kris Jenner recalls, "They seemed very much in love. They were so passionate—there was such chemistry between them." [99] Jenner's description of O.J.'s early departure from the other vacationers because of a movie-acting obligation summarizes a great deal about this particular genre of tabloid reports on the Simpsons:

> "They were seated on the patio. Nicole was on O.J.'s lap. She had her arms around his neck and his arms were around her waist. They kissed longingly and lovingly.
> "O.J. then kissed [daughter] Sydney and [son] Justin and told his son, 'Hey Justin, you take care of mommy while I'm gone.' "
> Ten weeks later, Nicole Brown Simpson was dead, left in a pool of blood with her throat viciously slashed and the crumpled, bloody body of waiter friend Ronald Goldman beside her.
> "I'm sickened that I couldn't read more into O.J.'s behavior," says Kris. [100]

This and similar stories are aptly expressive of what I have called the tabloids' *tragic vision* of the Simpson couple. On one level, these stories speak of the fragility of happiness, love, and life itself. On another level, they play to, and encourage white Americans' widespread fear of black men in general, and whites' willingness, in particular, to see in O.J. Simpson what *Star* in another issue and with racially significant phraseology called "the dark side beneath the slick veneer." [101]

Pushing a little further, all of this suggests that, as I've indicated earlier, one powerful dimension of the popular fascination with the Simpson case involves its resonance with deeply rooted historical anxieties around miscegenation, which the tabloids activate and update. The interest they sometimes display in the tragic mix of sexual excitement and danger in the relationship between Nicole and O.J. follows this pathway into the white imagination, where it connects with entrenched desires to *animalize* racial Others. As a friend tells *Star* of Nicole's sexual passions, "She told me she was turned on by the 'animal' [side of] O.J." [102] The tabloids' frequent descriptions of O.J.'s voracious and nonmonogamous sexual appetites as well as the brute force of his physical aggression against Nicole work together to animalize and primitivize him. Consider, for instance, the following excerpts from an October 1994 story:

> Nicole was barely 18 when she met O.J. a year after her graduation from Dana Point High School in Southern California. . . .
>
> By the time Nicole became his second wife in 1985, she was already familiar with the dark side of O.J. — his violent temper, his regular use of cocaine and his rampant womanizing.
>
> Cora Fischman says that Nicole was well aware of the other women.
>
> "But she loved O.J. so much she was able to live with it for years. It was part of her denial." . . .
>
> The final straw for Nicole, after seven years of stormy marriage, was learning that O.J. had shared a string of women with Magic Johnson — who later revealed he was HIV-infected.
>
> Sources tell STAR that Nicole "went ballistic" after being told by girlfriends that O.J. had taken part in orgies at the basketball star's Bel-Air home. . . .
>
> "Nicole, so used to being slapped around by O.J., couldn't believe it when he broke down and cried. He confessed everything to her and said he would change his ways. Then he urged her to get an AIDS test. He told her: 'I'm very worried. I've already been tested.' "
>
> . . . Nicole's close friends talk constantly of her being "dragged down" by O.J.'s appetite for sleaze.
>
> One example was his fascination with wife-swapping and how, early in their marriage, he tried to talk Nicole into joining in a foursome with another famous athlete and his wife. . . .
>
> "Nicole was appalled. She told me: 'It's so sick. Why does O.J. try to cheapen our relationship in this way?' O.J. told Nicole frequently that

one woman wasn't enough for him and he needed sex five times a day, every day." [103]

The tabloids' tragic vision of Nicole and O.J. can thus be seen as a narrative vehicle for the displaced expression of white anxieties about the "uncivilized" and "animalistic" force of racial difference, whose inevitable eruption seems to "drag down" and doom from the outset any and all attempts at a peaceful multiracial coexistence. For if two who loved each other so deeply cannot overcome this problem, goes one logic underwritten by these racist anxieties, then surely neither can an entire society full of racially mixed strangers. Those who think otherwise are simply, to borrow from Fischman's words quoted earlier, in "denial." Ironically, this perspective helps white people deny to themselves that racial problems in the United States are first, foremost, and fundamentally caused by the social, cultural, and political practices of whiteness.

One of the most remarkably subtle examples of the tabloids' invocation of "animalizing" racist discourses comes in a story about Nicole's Akita dog, Kato.[104] The story cites "animal behavior experts" that have deduced O.J.'s guilt from the dog's behavior subsequent to the murders, based on its breed characteristics. The metonymic link between the dog and O.J. that is silently generated by this story works to activate racist meanings associated with genetic determinism. In the contemporary United States, these meanings can only be activated in such a subtle and displaced way because genetic discourse is one form of racism that has been officially discredited. Consider further, along these lines, the Star's description of the "savage" forces that erupted during the beating that provoked Nicole's now famous "911" call, and what happens when such an account is articulated to the tabloids' characteristic suspicion toward officialdom.[105] Although O.J. was arrested as a result of Nicole's report to the police concerning the vicious attack, "he pleaded no contest" and "paid the fine, but didn't perform community service," had counseling only "over the telephone," and thus "got let off lightly" with but a "slap on the wrist." [106] While on the one hand this articulation leads salutarily to the criticism of American courts' apparent refusal to deal adequately with domestic violence, on the other hand, it reinforces the reactionary notion that the legal system needs to be tougher on blacks. So too, in a less direct way, does a story from another issue of the Star that quotes a "clinical hypnotherapist" who claims that "O.J. was 'addicted' to Nicole sexually." The therapist says that "in the end, Nicole cut off O.J.'s supply," and asks rhetorically, "so what does an addict do when he cannot get the thing he craves so desperately?" [107] The discourse of addiction, when it is articulated to race (as it often is), is one that demands a legal crackdown (as we've seen in chapter 1). Moreover, this discourse of addiction works here to "darken" O.J.'s image from the perspectives of whites (for whom, as previously noted, the code word "drugs" has become a potent signifier of racial difference) and so to enhance the story's appeal to cultural anxieties around miscegenation. This appeal is visually heightened by the two-page picture that accompanies the story. It depicts the glowering face of O.J., who stares straight into the camera; set off somewhat behind him, in a space that is visually separated from the one he occupies by an artist's rendering of a lightning bolt that has ripped the photo asunder, is the downcast face of Nicole. Above this image appear the powerful words "Nicole's Dance with Death." [108] It is the perfect picture of what a viewer of D. W. Griffith's racist classic *The Birth of a Nation* once called the "contrast between black villainy and blond innocence." [109]

In light of the intense racism working through such storytelling practices as these, the tabloids' frequent circulation of counterknowledges that challenge the widespread white belief in O.J.'s responsibility for Nicole's murder assumes even greater significance. In one account, it was a distraught admirer of Ron Goldman who committed the murders in a jealous rage after Goldman canceled a scheduled rendezvous with the man in order to meet with Nicole instead.[110] Another implicates an undisclosed close friend of O.J., whom the latter is protecting with his silence.[111] Still another report has it that the murders were committed by three or four mysterious assailants who struck again in Nicole's Brentwood neighborhood less than a year after her demise, this time knifing to death a man who had just returned home from a shopping trip.[112] In all of these reports, the tabloids carefully articulate together elements of evidence that the police and prosecutors either articulate differently or insist are unrelated, such as the two crimes that the *Globe* links to each other, and to a third stabbing, in the last story ("There are too many similarities among the murders to ignore," proclaim private investigators; "You wouldn't really expect the cops to connect the two, would you?" adds one of O.J.'s attorneys).[113] In the first story, police evidence and actual fragments from the transcripts of the deputy coroner's courtroom testimony are woven seamlessly into the tabloid's tale of jealous vengeance. It is moreover among the most interesting of the tabloids' counternarratives in that, in its photographic "reenactment" of the slashings, it visually identifies a Caucasian murderer.[114] Therefore, like other reports of this type, the story inverts the animalizing logic of stories that "darken" O.J. by instead *whitening* the killers of Nicole and Goldman.[115] The following use of uppercase letters in another tabloid story indicates that the *Globe* both recognizes the significance of its claim and wishes to emphasize it: "One insider says the police are now pursuing leads that a WHITE MAN may have been the killer!" [116]

The *Globe* often disarticulates and rearticulates a number of Simpson event elements in a way that reworks the dominant racial logics of the mainstream media. One story, for example, traces the former football star's roots in "rural Arkansas and Louisiana—far from the glamour of Hollywood and the luxury of Brentwood." Whereas dominant white discourses work to disarticulate current race relations from the history that has produced them (conservative whites, for example, continually claim that a variety of antiracist initiatives anachronistically "blame" them for things done by their ancestors), this story, by contrast, generates living links between the racial politics of the present and those of the past. As its author writes, "Like tens of millions of other African-Americans, the fallen football hero's family history is a saga of the struggle to break the chains of slavery and poverty." These words are accompanied by a two-page photo spread centered around Simpson, who is shown from the waist up, bare chested and with his face turned toward the sky; his arms are stretched wide to visually envelop the photographs of both long-dead and still-living relatives, one of whom is standing in a cotton field wearing a T-shirt that reads, "Who framed O.J. Simpson?" The story articulates the personal histories of both O.J.'s rise to stardom and his current predicament with the law to the longer history of his family and its struggles to survive and thrive in a racially unequal society. It thus encourages readers to interpret O.J.'s arrest for murder within the context of an ongoing history of racial oppression, and to interpret his prior successes in light of a history of the hard work and persistence of previous generations of blacks striving to overcome the barriers erected against them. We learn, for example, that O.J.'s great-grandfather Will Potter was "probably the most industrious" of the many people sharecropping the 2,400-acre farm on which the family earned its living, and that Potter's son L. D. "was a star farmer too." This discourse of "stardom" creates a transhistorical link between O.J. Simpson and his tenant farmer progenitors—a link that contests white discourses that seek to disarticulate the race relations of the present from those of the past. Along these lines, the story ends by quoting O.J., who refers here to the small Louisiana community where many of his ancestors lived and labored, and to which he has returned many times throughout his life: "I still need Rodessa and my roots. It may seem like such a dead place to some, but when you're in the middle of New York, Los Angeles or Detroit, Rodessa seems very alive. I need it very badly. I need to get back there to get in touch with myself. I'd like to return again and I'd like to send my children down for a vacation. It's home to me." [117] By calling Rodessa home, Simpson's statement, along with the rest of the story, shows that his struggle to rise from inner-city poverty to success is indissociably part of his family's larger struggle to overcome the legacies of slavery—and so, too, by implication, is his struggle with the LAPD and the California court system.

The *Globe* similarly traces the origins of Detective Mark Fuhrman, though the tale it tells differs decisively from that of the sport and media star descended from slaves and sharecroppers. Like the story of O.J.'s roots, however, this one also connects present with past and in so doing frames the charges against Simpson in racial terms. The Fuhrman story begins by noting that the key prosecution witness "was a raging racist and bully as a youth who never missed a chance to torment and terrify black children." It appears alongside a two-page photo spread that features a large blowup of Fuhrman at age eleven, dressed in blackface and carrying a top hat and cane; this picture is also reproduced on the *Globe*'s front cover. The inset caption reads, "This shocking photo of Mark Fuhrman in blackface reveals the rogue cops' racist views." The story quotes a longtime resident of the Washington town where Fuhrman was raised; the man says of the LAPD cop that "he was a racist kid—no doubt about it. A lot of us figured he'd grow out of it. Now it looks as if maybe he never did." The report goes on to detail a number of specific incidents whereby the "hate-filled Fuhrman tortured his tiny hometown's blacks." [118]

Such stories about O.J.'s roots and Fuhrman's racial hatred prepare us for others about racism closer to Simpson's home, among, for example, his in-laws and even his ex-wife. One *Globe* story reports that Nicole Brown Simpson's sister, Denise Brown, wants so badly to rob O.J. of his parental rights because "she wants Sydney and Justin to be raised in a white community as white children"; she does not "want her niece and nephew to be raised black." O.J. is understandably distraught over this turn of events and fears that if Brown gets her wish, "his children will never know anything about their father's black family. His black roots have always been important to him," explains a friend of Simpson. "He wanted Sydney and Justin to understand gospel music, go to a black church and know his family." The story also reports that according to police sources, even Nicole "once confessed to a friend she did not want to include O.J.'s parents and other members of his family in her photo album—or display their pictures along with her own family portraits in her house." The *Globe* quotes Nicole, who is reported to have said, "I don't want these niggers in my family album." [119] Another *Globe* story reports that onetime "pals" of O.J. from the "posh" suburb where he lives are now, in the wake of the "not guilty" verdict, referring to him as "the Butcher of Brentwood" and treating him "like a leper." After the verdict was issued, more than five thousand people marched in protest through Simpson's neighborhood carrying burning candles and chanting "O.J., get out of L.A." The story quotes a number of angry Brentwood residents who have organized an unofficial campaign to drive Simpson from the (almost exclusively white) community.[120] By emphasizing the terroristic aspects of white racism and underlining links between criminal prosecution and racial *per-*

secution, stories such as these interrogate white anxieties over a perceived African American racial-sexual threat.

If tabloid counterknowledges often undercut racist discourses at the same time that they proclaimed O.J. didn't commit the murders, they sometimes unfortunately *also* activated patriarchal or misogynistic ones in the process. This is no doubt in part because socially disreputable and marginalized knowledges whose truths figure Simpson as a target of LAPD racism can also be made to serve masculinist denials of gendered brutality in their proclamation of his "innocence." Consequently, while tabloid reporting that was more "progressive" along gender lines sometimes reproduced forms of racist narrative, the tabloids' more racially resistant counternarratives often cleared the way for the activation of sexist (and sometimes homophobic) discourses.[121] The June 27, 1995, edition of *Star* provides an illustrative example. There, two stories run side by side, taking up all of pages 36 and 37 and spilling semiotically into each other. The one that takes up slightly less space (about four-fifths of page 36) appears on the left. The other takes up the remaining one-fifth of page 36 and all of page 37, on the right. The story on the left appears under the headline "O.J. Didn't Do It!" and reveals "proof" of Simpson's innocence. The headline over the story on the right announces that "Nicole Seduced O.J.'s Best Pal—under His Nose." The side-by-side placement of these stories generates meaning effects that

The Star: displacing "guilt."

displace connotations of guilt from O.J. onto Nicole Brown Simpson. Thus the story of Nicole's relationship with Marcus Allen, a star NFL running back and close friend of O.J., notes that "she started flirting outrageously with the very eligible young bachelor at a summer barbecue" held in the Simpsons' own backyard before their separation. Alongside the verbal text of the story is a half-page color photo depicting Nicole, in a bathing suit, playfully hoisted on the shoulders of a bare-chested Allen. According to the story, Nicole began a secret affair with Allen after her separation from O.J., despite warnings from a close friend who told Nicole that she was "playing with fire." This is a semiotically loaded warning that suggests Nicole's culpability even as it retains an undercurrent of meanings that silently evoke the threat of violently explosive danger associated with black masculinity in many white discourses.[122]

In this way, the tabloids' coverage of the case against O.J. Simpson sometimes either strategically ignores issues around his history of domestic violence or mitigates the impact of that history through the invocation of parallel narratives whose effect is to "blame the victim" for inciting his rage. To take another example, Star follows one of its retellings of the beating that led to the "911" call with an account of "Nicole's Sexy Spend, Spend Life of Fast Cars, Drugs & Young Men."[123] According to this report, Nicole Brown Simpson "liked to show off her fantastic, hard-won figure in tight-fitting tops and miniskirts." The story also claims that "shopping was her passion," and that each month she spent thousands of dollars she got from O.J. in places like the posh Brentwood Gardens plaza, where she bought her clothes in the smallest sizes available. Furthermore, according to one Santa Monica restaurateur, Nicole "knew how to party. She usually came in from 9 P.M. until 2 A.M. and spent a lot of time drinking shots of her favorite tequila at the bar." A bartender adds that "she was always flirting with different guys. She didn't seem to go for white guys. She gravitated towards big, strong black men." Moreover, according to Rayce Newman, "one of Tinseltown's most notorious dope dealers," Nicole also "dabbled in drugs." Such stories emphasize behaviors that are considered to be "outrageous" from the standpoint of traditional ideas about "proper" (white) femininity, and some highlight the calm and accepting maturity displayed by O.J. when confronted with Nicole's outrageousness, as when, for example, he coolly forgave his close, longtime pal Marcus Allen for betraying their friendship by sleeping with her, and later even generously granted Allen permission to be married in Simpson's own home.[124] One story goes so far as to compare O.J. with the biblical figure Job, a righteous man "whose faith in God was sorely tested by a string of terrible disasters."[125]

Although tabloid stories that vindicate O.J. for the murders speak to (and from) the skeptical knowledges of many people of color, such stories also speak sometimes (albeit differently) to racist white knowledges. There is a way in which, in all this tabloid coverage, Nicole's image oscillates wildly between that of an almost saintly (read: white) tragic figure and that of a rambunctious "bad girl" who did a lot to deserve what she got; it's difficult to avoid the conclusion that the latter figuration is abetted by her boundary-violating sexual associations with black men.[126] In their emphasis on such associations, some tabloid stories appeal to the white racist imagination by "blackening" and so devaluing Nicole (for "blackening" is equivalent to de-valuation in a racist society that consistently idealizes whiteness and dero-gates nonwhites). Indeed, a few of the stories that "blacken" Nicole even reverse the claims found in other reports that emphasize O.J.'s history of abusive behavior: It was *Nicole* who became obsessive and so *stalked* O.J.[127] It was *Nicole* who was "addicted" to sex with *him*.[128] This "blackening" of Nicole from the perspective of the white racist imagination is made com-plete in a set of stories that dwell so fetishistically on either photographs or detailed descriptions of her mutilated body that they seem almost intent on either inviting perverse enjoyment or sending a disciplinary warning to other women who would behave as "inappropriately" as Nicole did.[129] In such stories, the racial and gendered currents of meaning are not at odds with one another (as in some reports) but rather work together in a mutually supportive display of implicitly racist misogyny.

The tabloid media event that the Simpson case was to become, the popu-lar skepticism it would provoke, and the backlash against that skepticism were all vividly foreshadowed at an early stage in their development. One week after the murders, officers seeking to arrest O.J. found themselves in-volved in a now famous slow-speed chase as Simpson's white Ford Bronco led a dozen police vehicles along California motorways without ever exceed-ing the speed limit. The Bronco was driven by O.J.'s boyhood pal and profes-sional football teammate Al Cowlings while Simpson reportedly lay in the backseat holding a loaded pistol to his head. Live video images of the entire chase were beamed across America by news helicopters that hovered con-tinuously above the bizarre entourage; those images were viewed by some 75 million people, more than ever watched even a Super Bowl.[130] By the time of the chase, people had for several days been following news reports that Simpson was under suspicion for the murders. As the chase unfolded, in-creasingly numerous onlookers jockeyed for roadside vantage points. Many of them bellowed cheers or carried large painted signs telling the micro-phones and TV cameras that they backed O.J. A number of commentators viewed the entire spectacle as a quintessential instance of tabloid TV.[131] Along these lines, it is worth noting that Los Angeles suspects fleeing cops now often find themselves pursued by more TV and radio news helicopters than actual police vehicles. The popularity of live coverage of flights from

Onlookers cheer the white Ford Bronco.

the police is so great that in 1999, one LAPD officer launched a service called PursuitWatch, which pages the beepers of subscribers whenever there's a chase in progress on television.[132]

In their cheering support for the fugitive O.J., roadside spectators of the slow-speed chase expressed a popular skepticism similar to that which we've seen in many of the supermarket tabloid stories about the investigation of the murders. As one African American woman would later write to the *Globe* (echoing the opening monologue from *Trial and Error*), "When he was in the Bronco, I was praying for him all the way. I felt that he was just scared of going to prison. He didn't know what to do. There are so many innocent people in prison right now for things they didn't do. He was just frightened when he ran away." [133] Two days after the chase, Health and Human Services Secretary Donna Shalala, Heritage Foundation spokesman and former Bush cabinet member William Bennett, and Harvard Medical School psychiatrist Alvin Poussaint appeared as discussants on the CBS news program *Face the Nation*. If Simpson's roadside supporters foreshadowed something of the popular skepticism that would come to be expressed in the tabloids, the conversation on *Face the Nation* foreshadowed both the white rage that would greet the jury's verdict and the moral panic over media tabloidization that is partially a backlash against popular knowledges that threaten officially entrenched modes of discursive and social authority. For when the topic of discussion turned to the chase, those who stood along the freeway watching, and by extension the broader audience for such tabloidized media events in general, the discussants discursively extended the threat of media tabloidization from the terrain of social representations into that of "law and order":

Moderator: I wondered at the time, as I was watching it, have we somehow gotten into a situation here where we, we see so many pictures on television, we're so bombarded by visual images that perhaps some parts of our society can no longer separate, uh, what's on television from what's real? I mean, these people were not only out cheering on O.J. Simpson, they were putting their own lives at risk! They were forgetting that those cars are real and they can run over you! They were forgetting that he had a gun in the car with real bullets! Let's ask Dr. Poussaint. What, what's your take on this, Doctor?

Poussaint: Well, I think, with, you know, with all the media stories and violence and drama in the movies, that I think that sometimes people do confuse reality with television, and it's all wrapped up in drama and make-believe, and I think that sometimes it doesn't imprint on them how serious it is. But on the other hand, I think they were also out there because some of them really didn't want to believe that, uh, O.J. Simpson could have been involved in such a, a heinous, uh, type of crime. So there was a lot of denial. And I think also what, uh, uh, Donna said, it was somehow sticking it to the police. That somehow in that chase, they were looking at O.J. Simpson as some kind of underdog, uh, who was fleeing the police while they were cheering on. So there was, there was kind of an, an anti-authoritarian attitude, which is also a bit scary. That is, people were, were willing to join in just to, just to fight authority.

Moderator [breaking in over Poussaint's final sentence with astonishment]: Well just, just a minute here! Aren't the police the good guys? "Sticking it to the police"?

Bennett: Well not, not all the time in the movies, and TV.

Poussaint [over Bennett]: Not, not necessarily. In some of our value systems, some, in many cases, police have become the enemy. Now, recently, in Los Angeles, uh, with the Rodney King episode, and so on, the police got a very negative image, uh, during, uh, during that period. So it's, it's not strange that a lot of people, who might feel somewhat negative and see the police as, as tainted themselves, and actually then have an antiauthority, antilaw kind of attitude, more or less cheering on the bad guy from time to time.

Moderator: Bill?

Bennett: Yeah, on the, on the run. On the lam in America. You know, uh, Huck Finn goin' down the raft. On the run. We got a raft, a whole bunch of movies in the last few years of, you know, Kevin Costner or

Clint Eastwood or somebody on the run and bein' chased by the cops and everybody's cheering for that. I think you saw just a little bit of echo of that. But this is the reality problem. This is mistaking appearance and illusion for reality.

This bit of commentary is interesting for its incipient albeit naive and misleading explication of postmodern conditions. The idea of audiences who lack the commentators' ability to distinguish "reality" from media is articulated with a certain nostalgic anxiety over the loss of faith in the LAPD in particular and police authority in general. Especially noteworthy is the delineation of a sense of "reality" that carefully excludes the knowledges of many economically deprived people and people of color who, for a whole variety of what should by now be fairly obvious reasons, refuse the conception of the police as a benign protective agency. Even Poussaint's reference to the Rodney King affair doesn't vindicate these alternative knowledges so much as seek to explain their aberrance in terms of the LAPD's "negative image." Such keywords in his remarks as "denial" and "bad guy" help to illustrate the way in which disparate elements of knowledge about the Simpson case can be articulated together to produce a unified sense of O.J.'s "guilt," which is in turn articulated to the unproblematic sense of "reality" invoked by both Bennett and the moderator. Such disparate elements of knowledge can easily be disarticulated and rearticulated in a fashion that contradicts their patterns of configuration in official discourse, however, as we have seen in some of the tabloid stories discussed earlier. The rearticulation of official truths into popular counternarratives is a process that would culminate in the jury's verdict itself, in the celebration of that verdict by a majority of African Americans, in the moral panic over media coverage of the Simpson case, and in the backlash against the "not guilty" verdict. Moreover, that verdict, its celebration by blacks, and tabloidized coverage of the Simpson case were all articulated together by white discourses that therefore constructed these things as constituent components of the same threatening phenomenon in much the same way as our Sunday morning discussants did with the slow-speed chase, popular films, and the growth of hostility toward the police among some social groups.

Media events that, like the Simpson case, condense some of the most tensely charged and socially central conflicts and crises into their images and narratives often bring about a temporary erasure of some of the differences that ordinarily distinguish "serious" from "tabloid" journalism. Consequently, although tabloids like the Star and Globe gave far less restrained play than the mainstream news to popular counterknowledges that challenged widespread presumptions of O.J.'s guilt, some commentators nevertheless extended the moral panic over coverage of the Simpson affair to the respectable as well as the abject press and thus expressed outrage over a generalized media "tabloidization." Others, along similar lines, attacked what they took to be the media's irrational embrace of popular counter-knowledges of the Simpson affair. Jeffrey Toobin, for example, suggests that in their coverage of the Simpson case, the media in general have *pandered* to people of color by illegitimately suspending their rational skepticism toward the defense team's absurdities. Writing in the *New Yorker*, Toobin decries journalists' refusal to denigrate Johnny Cochran for his decision to adorn the entire defense team with African kente-cloth ties during one day of Mark Fuhrman's infamous testimony. And more broadly, Toobin denounces white reporters covering the trial for ostensibly neglecting to criticize Cochran's inappropriate use of "racial politics" in a court of law. Toobin writes that the defense team's

> *antics* brought hoots from the reporters watching the trial on the closed-circuit feed into the media compound, on the twelfth floor of the courthouse, but when it came to actual reporting on the trial we all turned into a remarkably timorous crew. The reporters were an overwhelmingly white group, and, as far as I could tell, no one ever worried that their treatment of the defense was unduly favorable. Fear of being called racist transcended everything in that newsroom. This extended, I think, even to discussions of the evidence. The safe course for those of us covering the case was to nitpick along with the defense attorneys. . . . Our caution and fear, however, misled. The case against Simpson was simply overwhelming. When we said otherwise, we lied to the audience that trusted us.
>
> By contrast, it would have been no exaggeration to say that the defense's case against the police was absurd.[134]

Here, criticism of the Simpson coverage expresses white anger over the failure of the media to demonstrate appropriate levels of skepticism toward the (putatively) "*absurd*" notion that the LAPD and its officers might *actually* be agents of racism. Toobin's argument rests on an implicit understanding of journalistic (and, moreover, judicial) practice that derives from Enlightenment concepts of rationality and objectivity. These concepts have been central to the dominant Western knowledge regime throughout modernity because they underwrite, constitute, and consolidate white social power. From Toobin's perspective, the aim of good journalism, like that of good science, is to circulate (ostensibly) politically neutral meanings labeled "truths." Such a conception of journalism precludes any consideration of such issues as the way in which "reality" can *always* be made to mean *differently*, the way in which the process of inserting events into this or that way of *knowing them* is *always necessarily political*, and the way in which the mobilization of this or that system of knowledge inevitably serves some social interests over and above others. This is the conception of journalism that is friendliest to the (white) knowledge that characterizes DNA testing as a producer of value-free truths, and most inhospitable to the (black) knowledge that knows that, far from producing politically neutral truths, all manner of scientific knowledges and methods have been deployed ruthlessly and often by U.S. whites against African Americans.[135] The naive objectivism that frequently underwrites the moral panic over media tabloidization also produces the rage of people such as Daryl Orts, who wrote of Simpson to an electronic bulletin board that "with the mountain of evidence against him, the only way to have been found innocent was to use *emotional* and *irrational* testimony.*" Similarly, Michael Coyne wrote of the Simpson trial to the same bulletin board that "this case sounds the death knell of the American justice system. When *rhetoric* so overwhelmingly supersedes *reason* a revolution is required. The DNA evidence alone makes his guilt a virtual certitude. The frame-up theory is so absurd it reflects only the extent of the desperation of the defense. Get me out of this country!" Only from the perspective of white knowledges could one dismiss as "irrational" and "absurd" the idea that U.S. policing is rife with racist practices, including even the manipulation of evidence to produce convictions and incarcerations (a form of police corruption taken very seriously by tabloid TV shows such as *Final Appeal* and *Trial and Error*). Reactions to the verdict by people like Toobin, Orts, and Coyne contrast starkly with that of the *Star*, which in its "O.J.'s Joyful Homecoming" issue published a list of the clues that raise disturbing questions about why the LAPD was so quick to settle on Simpson as its prime and only suspect for the murders.[136]

The threat posed by the "tabloidization" of media in the Simpson case produced interest in, and concern about, the prospect of a tabloidized jury.[137] Early in the screening process, all 304 potential Simpson jurors were asked specifically whether they had received any of their information about DNA evidence from the *Star*, the *Globe*, or the *National Enquirer*.[138] Even before the eruption of the Simpson case in the media, there was anxiety among criminal prosecutors over the growing popularity of tabloid television, which, according to some, has increased the difficulty of securing convictions. California's attorney general Dan Lungren has coined the derisive term "Oprahization" to describe what he thinks is a growing tendency on the part of tabloid television–watching jury members to distrust official accounts of defendants' guilt, to take undue account of defendants' personal histories and social experiences during the evaluation of evidence and deliberations, and to empathize inappropriately with the accused.[139] Los Angeles District Attorney Gil Garcetti has gone so far as to pronounce that the criminal justice system is "on the verge of a crisis of credibility" because of these changes in the sensibilities of jurors.[140] Because of the "Oprahiza-tion" of juries, Lungren wants the state of California to take steps toward "broadening the pool of jurors to include a greater range of society." In effect, Lungren's proposal to "broaden" the jury pool would whiten, gen-trify, and masculinize California juries, as it would interject a higher pro-portion of those whose preference for "serious news" indicates higher edu-cational, cultural, and economic capital. Perhaps because U.S. juries will *always* contain *some* members drawn from relatively disempowered social formations, though, Lungren additionally proposes that judges stress "the importance of values and personal responsibility when they instruct jurors on how to deliberate." [141]

Professional jury consultants—the new knowledge specialists who use social science techniques such as focus group interviewing and statistical analysis to advise trial lawyers on jury selection—consider tabloid talk show watchers to be more distrustful of prosecutors than other jurors, accord-ing to Jo-Ellan Dimitrius, the consultant who counseled Simpson's defense team on the selection of jury members most likely to sympathize with their case.[142] DecisionQuest, a private research and consulting firm that advised the prosecutors in the Simpson case, produced polling data that indicated that "a predilection for the tabloids" was "a reliable predictor of belief in Simpson's innocence." Indeed, of the twelve jurors who produced the "not guilty" verdict in Simpson's criminal trial, according to DecisionQuest's re-search, none read mainstream newspapers regularly, though eight watched "evening television tabloid news, like *Hard Copy*." [143] This should not, of course, be taken to mean that tabloid television "causes" skepticism toward official institutions, knowledges, and social authorities. Rather, the struc-ture of taste that prefers tabloid over "serious" journalism is a product of the social structures that set the interests of popular formations against those of the power-blocs that control the production of official truth in a radically unequal society such as the United States. Thus DecisionQuest found not only that most of the Simpson jurors preferred tabloid over serious news; the firm also found evidence of the jurors' relatively low access to both eco-nomic resources and social power generally: only three of the twelve were home owners, only two were college graduates, ten had no managerial or supervisory responsibilities at work, and five said "they or a family member had personally had a negative experience with law enforcement." Addition-ally, as is more widely known, the jury included only two whites and two men, neither of whom was white.[144]

We should not conclude from the convergence of the jurors' relatively low social status and preference for tabloids that the knowledges possessed by tabloid readers and watchers are *inherently inferior* to those of officialdom and the "quality press." Disreputable popular knowledges are, of course, less socially effective than those that are officially established and that there-fore constitute a powerful regime of truth. The lower social effectivity of popular knowledges is not, however, a product of their inherent inferiority; rather, it stems from officialdom's power to prevent such knowledges from gaining institutional imprimatur, which limits their capacity to contest the regime of truth that discredits them.[145] This limitation can be partially overcome, however, when ordinarily localized dissident voices, perspec-tives, and knowledges gain extended social reach and at least temporarily enhanced visibility and amplification through disreputable media outlets like the tabloids (which are typically far less concerned than the "quality" news about the social legitimacy of the voices and perspectives to which they give play), and through the temporary and partial elision of differences between the "tabloid" and "serious" media that sometimes accompanies crisis events. The Simpson trial was such a social crisis event, not least be-cause it put to the test the white power structure's claims that U.S. policing and legal apparatuses are neither racially biased nor tilted in favor of the middle and upper classes.

We have seen that *Trial and Error*'s and *Final Appeal*'s frequent emphasis on the perspectives of imprisoned convicts over those of officials (police departments, district attorneys, and so on) is partly responsible for the programs' exposure of a myriad of bureaucratic flaws and patterns of cor-ruption. Along similar lines, Louise Mengelkoch has analyzed tabloid cov-erage of the small-town gang rape of a fourteen-year-old girl, Heather Lory, whose father confronted and killed one of his daughter's rapists.[146] Mengel-koch found that because "serious" journalism was both relatively indif-ferent toward the case and, where it did take an interest, primarily con-cerned with *official* accounts of the events at issue (an example of what Stuart Hall calls "the systematic 'over-accessing' of select elite personnel and their 'definition of the situation,' " which is typical of mainstream news and cru-cial to its consistent reproduction of dominant ideologies), the girl was widely accused of lying about the rape and severely ostracized within her community.[147] It was only when tabloid TV programs such as *The Sally Jessy Raphael Show*, *Hard Copy*, and *Donahue* took an interest in the case that the *girl's* perspective gained public circulation and widespread vindication. More-over, her father's case had been characterized by his underresourced public defender as "open and shut" and was well on the way toward being quietly and efficiently processed to produce a very long prison sentence when the tabloid programs began covering the story. Their intense interest led to the revelation of numerous judicial "irregularities" that were, it seems, char-acteristic of "business as usual" in the rural judicial system where they oc-curred, since "certain people and offices were so unused to public scrutiny" of the sort imposed on them by tabloid television.[148] That tabloids often include and amplify voices and popular knowledges that are otherwise excluded from the dominant regime of truth can be seen to account for both their wide circulation among relatively disempowered social formations *and* their rampant demonization by those with easy access to the structure of power and its distributive mechanisms.

Tabloid media often subject the criminal justice system to levels of scrutiny thought to be inappropriately voyeuristic by many mainstream journalists. Tabloidized scrutinization of judicial procedures like that which occurred around the Lory and Simpson cases can, at least partially and temporarily, disturb the regime of truth that stabilizes structures of social inequality by delegitimating and abnormalizing knowledges such as the black one that *knows* that police corruption, racism, and incompetence *do* result in widespread African American incarcerations and executions.[149] Insofar as the amplification of such counterknowledges helps to produce conditions for the possibility of social change, blacks have much to gain from encouraging it—despite the active and ongoing discreditation of popular interest in the trials that occasion such processes of amplification (the Simpson case as media event, for example, was characterized as the "pornographic obsession" of "drooling couch potatoes").[150] However, many African Americans were deeply ambivalent about intense media scrutinization of the Simpson case. Many are extremely suspicious of the recent hypervisibility of black men in U.S. media, a number of whom have served, as George Curry, editor of the black magazine *Emerge*, put it, as "poster children" for various psychosexual pathologies, including Clarence Thomas and sexual harassment, Mike Tyson and date rape, and Michael Jackson and child sexual abuse.[151] Racial difference is culturally constructed as a kind of sexual difference, and there is much evidence to suggest that white anxieties about black masculinity coalesce around a need to monitor and police black male sexuality. So ambivalence and even widespread regret within the African American community over the tabloidized hypervisibilization of O.J. is well-founded, particularly given the case's pronounced resonance with the long history of white fears regarding miscegenation.[152] Nevertheless, many African Americans cared deeply about the case and its outcome—a caring likened by one commentator to "the impulse that made Blacks crowd around radios to follow every punch in a Joe Louis boxing match or that led many Blacks to become diehard Brooklyn Dodger fans after Jackie Robinson broke the baseball color barrier."[153] As another commentator notes, the outcome of the Simpson case was doubly important in light of the way in which a guilty verdict against a "model" African American like O.J. Simpson might provoke whites to "question their ability to judge Black people," a consequence capable of intensifying the racism that already permeates everyday life in the United States.[154] Whereas African Americans therefore had great justification for their suspicions toward the intense interest directed at the Simpson case, saturation media coverage of the trial and its lead-up at least created the conditions, the mechanism, and the possibility for the social amplification of black knowledges about racist police procedures. This possibility is actualized in tabloid stories like the one from the *Globe* that virtually pictures Mark Fuhrman planting the bloody glove beneath a headline that screams that a "Cop Framed O.J."

The discourses of backlash and moral panic generated around the Simpson affair loudly and frequently derided the defense team, the popular media, and the jury for undermining the Enlightenment rationalism used to legitimate and authorize both official journalistic and judicial institutions and procedures. The *Globe* reports, for example, that the notoriously racist former L.A. police chief Darryl Gates "blames the not guilty verdict . . . on the jury's lack of reason." [155] When they are directed at the media, such panic discourses often appeal to the trope of "sensationalism." This trope evokes the concept of intellectually unmediated experiences of the flesh and is widely used to ascribe inferiority to a range of popular cultural discourses and practices, as Pierre Bourdieu has noted.[156] Cultural elites detest "sensationalism" because it undermines the missionary position they compulsively assume toward the people. Jean Baudrillard argues that the primary cultural strategy of officialdom is always "to get some meaning across, to keep the masses within reason," to enforce the constant imperative "to better inform, to better socialise, to raise the cultural level of the masses." Sensationalism and its corollaries, *spectacle* and *fascination*, are sometimes threatening to officialdom, in Baudrillard's view, because they *freeze* messages "in a vacuous ether," causing "a glaciation of meaning." [157] "Rationality" is a controlling strategy of top-down power, but one that founders on sensationalism, as gloomy critics of the Simpson affair have recognized.

The general glaciation of meaning brought about by sensationalism creates opportunities for the colonization of events and the saturation of objects with alternative discourses.[158] So too, by the same logic, do "senseless" acts like terrorism and natural disasters, according to Baudrillard—as does, we might add, a brutal double murder like the one that took place in Brentwood, California, on June 12, 1994. In their defiance of attempts to make sense of them, such events summon a desperate, panicky need to impose meaning.[159] This Baudrillardian perspective offers, I think, some insight into the tabloids' wild profusion of sense-making takes on the murders and their investigation. It is, furthermore, useful for understanding reactions to Simpson's criminal trial and its media coverage on both sides of the racial divide between Euro- and African Americans. Thus while counterhegemonic forces exploited the semiotic opportunities opened by sensationalism, senselessness, spectacle, and fascination, dominant ones decried, bemoaned, and berated them as the dominant forces struggled to reinsert the events into the discursive frames they deemed "rational." Both the white backlash against Simpson's acquittal and the moral panic over media tabloidization thus constitute strategies for the recovery of partially lost and otherwise endangered discursive control over the insertion of contemporary events into this or that way of understanding them. Most immediately, the moral panic over tabloidism promotes the narrow interests of traditional journalistic institutions and practitioners (as we shall see in chapter 3). These interests are closely tied, however, to the more encompassing hegemony of social alliances continuously formed and reformed along multiple axes of power that include but are not limited to those of race, class, and gender. With regard to media coverage of the O.J. Simpson case, white disapproval (such as that expressed by William Bennett on our high-toned Sunday morning chat show) sometimes conflates tabloidization with spectacle, senselessness, fascination, irrationality, irresponsibility, and, ultimately, the "not guilty" verdict itself, all of which are seen as the consequences of a scandalous confusion generated around the boundary between media and "reality" (where "reality" is the name given by the white power-bloc to its truths). Along the way, this disapproval gives powerful expression to the growing white backlash against African Americans' increasingly vocal refusal of Euro-American knowledges and institutions.

3   Bodies of Popular Knowledge:
The High, the Low, and A Current Affair

All these shows are part of a new growth industry. *Washington Post* TV critic Tom Shales has dubbed it "teleporn." It's about psychos and psychics, freaks and geeks, kooks, crooks, and cults. It's about murder and mayhem, drugs and thugs. It's about sob stories and mob exposes. It's about celebrity worship and celebrity desecration. It's about lifestyles of the rich and shameless. It's about peeping through keyholes. It's about a new adage that says that a scandal a day keeps reality at bay. . . . The sleazier, the more shocking and sensational, the better. — Terry Ann Knopf, *Boston Magazine* [1]

I had actually witnessed those daffy story conferences in which the members of our crew pitched suggestions for shows that sounded like outtakes from the Marx Brothers. The rundown, on any given day, would include televangelist spoofs, tales of quadriplegic killers, reports of Satanic teenage murders, cow-mooing contests, Marilyn Monroe bulletins, Elvis sightings — all presented with a kind of wide-eyed exuberance by our goofy staff. They managed to make each farfetched shocker sound like a happy pop of a champagne cork. As the resident grown-up, I always felt like the bomb squad. — Maury Povich, *Current Affairs* [2]

During the late 1980s, tabloid TV displaced the soap opera as television's primary "bad object." Numerous academic and journalistic critics have devoted countless printed pages and endless hours of discussion to the "problem" of tabloid TV. Even Maury Povich, the former anchor of A Current Affair (the Rupert Murdoch Fox Network production that is often cited for pioneering the U.S. tabloid TV news style in the latter half of the 1980s), writes in his autobiography with an odd mixture of enthusiasm and ridicule of the television he helped to define.[3] Povich is distinctly self-conscious about his contradictory attitudes toward the style of news work done at A Current Affair, and he attributes a similar level of reflexive contradictoriness to the program itself, which he describes as "high-spirited and self-deprecating." As its anchorman, Povich frequently "made fun of" A Current Affair's disreputable content by shaking his head and "scowling" on air. "I scared the hell out of the Fox executives and lawyers," Povich reveals, "with my unconcealed opinion about my own show." [4]

A Current Affair is, in the words of David Kamp, "tabloid rethought audio-visually." [5] TV critic Ron Powers has dubbed it "the 60 Minutes of slime." [6] The derision heaped on A Current Affair in particular and tabloid television in general by writers such as Powers and Terry Ann Knopf (quoted in the chapter epigraph) is obviously quite different from the ambivalent mockery that the genre often directs at itself. Even as it parodies his own program, Povich's hyperbolic description of story development at A Current Affair subtly mocks the more earnest offendedness of mainstream journalists such as Knopf and Powers. Mainstream journalism is akin to an official culture, for its authority is enforced through the production of seriousness and reverence. Consequently, it rarely engages in self-parody. Self-parody is, however, an age-old and typical form of popular culture that tabloid television revives in its own way. Mikhail Bakhtin argues that self-parody expresses an oxymoronic impulse to bodily degradation and regeneration, simultaneous death and rebirth.[7] Povich captures something of this contradictory Bakhtinian ethos in his account of the day he read a positive New York Times review describing A Current Affair as "tabloid journalism at its best." Says Povich ironically, "I could have wept. All my life I'd been groping for some clear definition of my style of journalism and now I had it. I was an afternoon tabloid, full of blood and gore and happy mischief. Full of life." [8]

If, for Povich, the Times review nearly inspired tears, his program and the genre it represents have had a reciprocal impact on many serious journalists. "Serious" journalism establishes its respectable cultural identity in part by working hard to distinguish itself from its socially low counterpart, tabloidism (despite the fact that serious journalism's commercial imperative sometimes requires that it emulate this debased other).[9] Official journalism therefore defines the concept of tabloid television on its own terms and for its own (derogatory) purposes. (Tabloid television, a popular form with considerably less social authority than official journalism, does not produce similarly disparaging accounts of the serious news, though tabloidism often mobilizes the weaker power of parody against its socially respectable counterpart, as we shall see.) The construction of a cultural hierarchy that distinguishes "serious" journalism from disreputable tabloidism is an important example of the more general process whereby dominant social taste formations elevate themselves culturally and exclude "others" from apparent worthiness. The creation of an exclusive and inegalitarian sphere of "respectable" middle-class culture always depends on the production of hierarchies that differentiate between "legitimate" and "vulgar" tastes.

This chapter begins by examining the construction of "respectable" tastes and sensibilities within the discourses circulating around tabloid media. As recent cultural studies scholarship has demonstrated that the practices and symbology of the body are key sites for the construction of cultural tastes and hierarchies, I pay particular attention to representations of bodies in both images and verbal discourse. I then analyze some of the ways in which disreputable bodily forms work through tabloid television to evoke counterknowledges and to unsettle cultural classifications, for popular culture always does more than provide the low-Other against which the respectable attempts to distinguish itself. Tabloid discourses actively transgress official journalism's criteria for seriousness and legitimacy and so create spaces within which popular ways of knowing can flourish. Such criteria are agents of what Michel Foucault calls "power/knowledge," for they keep the production of truth within carefully circumscribed boundaries that delimit a cultural topography over which the socially privileged exert maximal control. Power/knowledge is a concept that parallels both Bakhtin's understanding of "seriousness" as a technique of officialdom and Baudrillard's notion of "meaning" as an instrumentality mobilized by the "enlightened" against the "mass." Conversely, officialdom is met head-on by the subversive laughter of grotesque realism, and meaning is contested by the absorptive power of the "mass" that prefers spectacle. Spectacle, fascination, grotesquery, and laughter, then, are elements of a countervailing popular force that challenges dominant notions of respectability. Of these, it is perhaps *laughter* whose historical significance is most often underestimated; "laughter is the joker in the pack of time" and "a vital source of social renewal" that "stops us taking it all too seriously" and "makes the game a game again."[10]

Responding Seriously to Tabloid Culture

The tabloid media regularly provoke disgust and revilement for their wanton violation of the established canons of journalistic judgment, a phenomenon that reveals the threat they pose to controlling cultural "standards." In its reactions to the expansion of tabloid media, respectable journalism indirectly expresses fear and loathing for those in the lower ranks of social hierarchies; by characterizing tabloid television as "trash," socially legitimated tastemakers therefore carry out a generalized cultural police action. This is nothing new: the production of jeremiads against both tabloid media and their audiences extends at least as far back as the 1920s, when Aben Kandel wrote that tabloids serve "lurid" and "insipid" "pap" to a population of "mentally helpless" "addicts" made up of "shop-girls, stenographers, housewives, lower theatrical folk, laborers, and—what is most serious—school children."[11]

Within this revulsive strain of antitabloidism, the phenomenon is often described as a contagion that proliferates the cultural deficiencies of the vulgar mass for whom "media trash" stands metonymically in these accounts. Tabloid television's cancerous spread incites surgical strikes issued from the pens and mouths of discriminating cultural diagnosticians, cultivated arbiters of taste and seriousness. A battery of discursive artillery reinforced with sexual and medical metaphors targets this pathogenic intruder on the body social. Thus, for example, "the tabloid disease has been spreading across television like an ugly fungus," writes *Los Angeles Times* critic Howard Rosenberg.[12] "The tabloid virus, previously confined to the fringes of syndication, is gradually infecting prime-time network programming," echo a group of mainstream journalists in *Newsweek* magazine.[13] This notion of tabloidism as cultural contagion resonates interestingly with Jane Shattuc's experience when she tried to survey people about tabloid talk shows at a world-class research hospital in Boston. She found that male doctors in particular were especially disdainful of the programs and typically pointed out quickly that "they listened only to classical music at home." When asked anyway if they ever watched, they often shook their heads, grimaced, and answered, "Not if I can help it." As Shattuc notes, "talk shows appeared to be some plague they preferred to avoid."[14]

A *New Republic* diatribe entitled "The Idiot Culture," by Carl Bernstein, describes some of the symptoms of infectious tabloidism: in our "sleazoid info-tainment culture," the "lines between Oprah and Phil and Geraldo and Diane and even Ted, between the *New York Post* and *Newsday*, are too often indistinguishable."[15] Such diagnoses evoke conservative fears for the sort of disruption of cultural boundaries that is usually associated with postmodernism and multiculturalism. Critics such as Bernstein are the border police of the fading cultural aristocracy who correctly recognize that the stability of traditional categories is necessary to the maintenance of established forms of social authority. His concern for what he takes to be a vanishing distinction between Oprah Winfrey, who empathetically plums the emotional depths of women's everyday lives, and Ted Koppel, whose demeanor exemplifies the belief that detached objectivity is the proper route to true knowledge, resonates with anxieties over the multicultural and feminist relativization of scientific rationalism and other modern forms of white and masculine cultural authority. The alleged disappearance of the difference between Winfrey and Koppel is considered dangerous because it threatens to reorder a system of cultural classifications that has often sought to exclude the voices of ordinary women from the domain of that which is considered important.

Bernstein writes that "in this new culture of journalistic titillation, . . . the lurid and the loopy are more important than real news. . . . For the first time in our history the weird and the stupid and the coarse are becoming our cultural norm." [16] Bernstein's language here is revealing: dominant social formations pay close attention to the boundaries that circumscribe and regulate the contents of the "normal," a cultural category that is widely used to express the difference between socially legitimated and disruptive ways of knowing and behaving. The disregard for this boundary displayed by tabloid media that treat the marginal as if it were central predictably draws the ire of mainstream journalists. By inserting the abnormal into the space usually occupied by the socially central, the tabloid media invert the values of the "quality press." It should thus come as no surprise to find that they are often seen to be dangerously pathogenic.[17]

The rhetorical strategies brought to bear on tabloid media often demonize their audiences as they inscribe class distinction. "Trash TV is nothing more than cultural junk food," affirms a large group of *Glamour* magazine's readers. "Those of us with tastes above the lowest common denominator have to demand a higher standard."[18] Pierre Bourdieu makes the useful point that the use of gustatory metaphors to describe cultural consumption in general effectively naturalizes class distinctions, for "the dual meaning of the word 'taste' . . . serves to justify the illusion" that differently valued and unequally distributed cultural capacities and preferences are spontaneously generated by their possessors.[19] The repudiation of tabloid television on grounds of superior taste makes a public display of supposedly ascendant cultural competency and thus reinscribes social distinction. The metaphor of junk food here is particularly revealing, given the role that diet plays in the inscription of class distinction on bodies. In 1980s and 1990s U.S. culture, the eradication of all fat from one's diet has become a preeminent marker of middle-class status. (A friend who owns a café in a very mixed-class neighborhood in a small Midwestern city observes that class position is an almost flawless predictor of which of her patrons will order doughnuts and which will order bagels—without cream cheese.) For the middle classes, "junk food" invariably signifies "fat" (whether in its embodied or dietary form). Calls for the eradication of media "junk food" such as "trash TV" amount to a kind of cultural liposuction that would like to eliminate unsightly social differences.

Some critics raise more conventionally political issues in response to the rise of tabloid television, though their analyses are typically informed by both liberal theory and middle-class ideas about taste and "seriousness." The new forms of television "news-entertainment" are "insidious," say Ian Mitroff and Warren Bennis in *The Unreality Industry*.[20] Their "banality" lulls us "silently and seductively into collective dumbness."[21] Mike Drew, a TV and radio critic for the *Milwaukee Journal*, defines tabloid television as "sensationalized trivia, pandering to a craving for amusement and voyeurism instead of providing the facts needed for good citizenship."[22] Common criticisms of tabloid media find an unholy alliance between commercially interested broadcasters and the prurient interests of audiences. Invariably, the "masses" are cast as irredeemable asses. Mitroff claims that "most people don't know or care what they're watching as long as it moves and there's color." Alvin Boskoff, a sociologist at Emory University, writes similarly that "only a small fraction of people who use the media are interested in what we would call significant, vital issues." Boskoff claims that tabloid television has exacerbated this situation in unprecedented ways and that its audiences have therefore lost the capacity to "distinguish between the trivial and the important."[23] Similarly, Daniel Schorr offers a disparaging diagnosis of ostensible audience dysfunctionality:

> I believe that a blurred sense of reality is a disease that makes it hard to react to real events, real problems. . . . I wonder whether this contributes to the low voter turnout at the polls, the low response to census-takers and the growing number of people who don't file income tax returns. . . . Couch potatoes, wake up. The poverty and potholes are real and won't go away by themselves. The deficit is not a simulation.[24]

Concerns for the putative unsophistication of tabloid media audiences and the commercially successful programs that "pander" to them lead to increasingly vocal pronouncements that reinscribe a distinction between the kinds of journalism deemed necessary for the survival of democracy and the tabloid journalism many viewers often prefer. At least one comprehensive academic survey of television news viewers has found empirical evidence of a vast gulf between popular tastes and professional journalistic practices. According to the surveyors, when network newscasts include the kinds of stories that reporters considered to be "good journalism," they rate most poorly with audiences. By contrast, audience approval ratings soar when television newscasts include stories that professional journalists consider to be "sensationalistic."[25] Boskoff's claim that most TV audiences are incapable of distinguishing triviality from seriousness offers one way to interpret these findings, though it is obvious that such an explanation has profoundly antidemocratic implications. I don't wish to argue that existing forms of tabloid media are, in and of themselves, capable of generating a level of public discourse adequate to the maintenance of democratic social institutions (a claim that would merely invert the antitabloid ones put forth by authors such as Boskoff, Mitroff, and Bernstein). The point I do wish to make is that the "defense" of democracy advanced in these explicitly political antitabloid diatribes masks a discursive power that seeks (however unintentionally) to control public life by delegitimating popular tastes and marginalizing those who possess them. Like other forms of imperializing power, it strives to monopolize the authority to determine the seriousness and therefore the worthiness of various journalistic tastes and practices.

Consider, for example, the opinion of Peter M. Herford, director of the Benton Fellowships in Journalism at the University of Chicago, who thinks that the development of interactive television technologies to give audiences some control over news content would be "disastrous." In Herford's rather establishmentarian view, "letting the public vote on what it wants to hear about in news broadcasts eliminates . . . the opportunity to tell an audience what it needs to know." [26] Like panic over the generic hybridity of tabloid television ("is it 'news' or 'entertainment'?"), professional journalists' fears regarding the democratization of control over news style and content are fueled by the disintegration of boundaries. They therefore seek to reinforce distinctions between a benign paternalistic elite and a pedocratic audience.[27] Richard Campbell usefully explains along these lines that "television's ability to cut across class, racial, and gender borders threatens both liberal and conservative elites and their hierarchical hold on what constitutes knowledge and virtue," so that television news has become an increasingly crucial field of struggle over questions of taste and seriousness. "Elites, after all, gain their status by making sure that most people and most things are categorized below them." [28]

The tabloid media are often excessive, emotive, antiscientific, unsubtle, crude, and "tasteless." Characteristics such as these, which might describe a wide range of popular cultural artifacts, invite both the productive vitality of audiences and the disparagement of elites to work on them.[29] There is nevertheless something curious about the intensity with which critics of the tabloid media focus on the object of their attacks. Peter Stallybrass and Allon White speak helpfully to this issue in their analysis of mechanisms for the production and maintenance of cultural distinctions between "respectable" social formations ("the high") and abject ones ("the low").[30] Because the high imagines itself to be that which it imagines the low is not, the high becomes dependent on the figure of the low for the successful production and maintenance of the high's own identity. Thus the abject, whose social power is negligible, becomes symbolically central, and the high invests an apparently inordinate amount of energy in its demonization of the low. The simultaneity of the high's dependence on, and repudiation of, the low generates a complex play of disgust and desire for the abject within "respectable" culture (as televangelist Jimmy Swaggart's fateful attraction to the lure of prostitution suggests). This in turn produces an intense anxiety that continually refocuses attention on the danger posed by the low, and especially by its apparent capacity to slither over the border that separates low from high and thereby contaminate the latter—an anxiety that is very much in evidence throughout the journalistic and even academic criticisms of tabloid media.

The crucial role played by the low in the symbolic formation of high identity therefore reveals much about the process by which critics demonize the low-Other of tabloid television. Television newscasts exist, in part, to produce a semiofficial sense of our national cultural identity. It is therefore unsurprising when respectable commentators pronounce that shows like A Current Affair are "vile" and declare that the stakes in the war against tabloid television are nothing less than the determination of "what kind of people . . . we want to be."[31] The vilification of tabloid television is part of a struggle to control which of "us" will be admitted into the category of "we people." The exertion of control over public culture requires some means of controlling both the social legitimation and delegitimation of different identities and the determination of what the category "news" will be made to include and to exclude. Consequently there is much at stake in the demonization of both television tabloidism and the "vulgar" audience to whom it "panders." Exclusionary politics begin with the cultural demarcation of high from low. Moral panic over the popularity of tabloid media thus appeals to constructions of U.S. national identity built on the presumption of a consensus formed around Eurocentric, masculine, educated middle-class tastes and a monolithic sense of what counts as "real news" while it infantilizes and vulgarizes audiences who enjoy "tabloid trash."

Despite the binary structure that their key terms imply, Stallybrass and White suggest that relationships between the high and low are generally quite fluid and contradictory (as has also been noted by theorists of postmodernity). Their ideas help to illuminate not only the strange intensity with which critics vilify the tabloid media but also those boundary-crossing excursions often associated with tabloid media consumption and known under the sign of "slumming." "Slumming" can be understood as a form of cultural tourism that performs a number of operations for its practitioners. It reinforces high tastes and identity formations by directly contrasting them with culturally excluded ones. It also enhances the sense of willful mobility that is one mark of status and privilege. To use Bourdieu's terms, slumming moves one conspicuously beyond the boundaries of one's cultural habitus in a manner that enables mobility itself to serve as a constitutive parameter of that very habitus. Cultural mobility both displays and extends social capacities and visual powers. When it is expressed as tabloid slumming, the cultural mobility of upscale consumers can serve to produce a sense of pleasurable diversion from the pressing demands of everyday obligations. As one commentator puts it with regard to tabloid newspapers:

Tabloidworld! It's . . . a parallel universe . . . a warp in space-time . . . a portal between our humdrum world and the next dimension, where evidently all hell is breaking loose. . . . For years I shunned the tabloids stacked by the supermarket register for being as tawdry and lurid as a state fair's midway, and just as alluring. I didn't want anyone to see me peeking into those neon-lit pages, like a farm boy goggling at the midway's hootchy-kootchy tent. Then, at a Barbados resort, I met a Boston electronics firm's high-voltage president, who told me his secret for relaxing after a turbocharged day in the corporate cockpit. "It's a fire in the fireplace, a glass of vintage Chablis from the wine cellar and a stack of tabloids!" he said. "Zip! You're in another world!" [32]

How to understand the illicit allure that marks this author's relationship to the journalistic equivalent of the midway hootchy-kootchy tent? Stallybrass and White draw our attention to the recurrent patterns of disgust and desire that typify encounters between the socially privileged and the culturally abject:

the "top" attempts to reject and eliminate the "bottom" for reasons of prestige and status, only to discover . . . that the top includes that low symbolically, as a primary eroticized constituent of its own fantasy life. The result is a mobile, conflictual fusion of power, fear and desire in the construction of subjectivity: a psychological dependence upon precisely those Others which are being rigorously opposed and excluded at the social level. [33]

Or as the journalist Howard Kurtz notes in the *Washington Post*, the public denunciation of tabloidized journalism "contains the seeds of its own contradiction," for "the same public that complains about saturation coverage" of events like the O.J. Simpson case is also "devouring that coverage in record numbers." Kurtz concludes that "millions of news consumers seem drawn to the very thing they claim to detest." [34]

Consequently, while the serious respondents to tabloid culture generally view the phenomenon as debased, impure, and unworthy of attention, they nevertheless (and paradoxically) grant it much. Indeed, even their indignant, shocked, and disgusted reactions against dirty tabloid indecency often take on their own sensationalistic and prurient overtones. Such overtones expose the conflictual fusion of revulsion and attraction that motivates the serious response to tabloid media styles and sensibilities, as is illustrated by the following luridly melodramatic tale of innocence betrayed and violated:

We appear to be witnessing . . . a conceivably irreversible muddying of the standards of television journalism. Once . . . TV news came in three distinct forms: the high-toned network newscasts, their more homey, yet still respectable, local cousins and the documentary off-shoots of both. Now this pristine structure has been invaded by a new kind of journalistic sensibility with its own audience-grabbing philosophy. The seasoned insights of a Peter Jennings, the crinkly-voiced credibility of a Tom Brokaw, are being gradually drowned out by . . . the "news punks": brash, showbizzy hucksters bent on pandering to the most basic urges of the broadest possible constituency with a product as down-and-dirty as the censors will stomach.[35]

Bodies, Tastes, and Tabloids

Taste classifies, and it classifies the classifier. Social subjects, classified by their clas-sifications, distinguish themselves by the distinctions they make. . . . The denial of lower, coarse, vulgar, venal, servile—in a word natural—enjoyment, which constitutes the sacred sphere of culture, implies an affirmation of the superiority of those who can be satisfied with the sublimated, refined, disinterested, gratuitous, distinguished pleasures forever closed to the profane. That is why art and cultural consumption are predisposed, consciously and deliberately or not, to fulfill a social function of legitimating social dif-ferences. —Pierre Bourdieu, Distinction [36]

Despite the instability of distinctions between the high and the low, there persist numerous cultural practices that work continually to reinscribe them. Those that endow human bodies with social meaning are among the most important. The body is a terrain on which distinctions between taste and tastelessness are constructed and played out. It is a social theater for the enactment and display of superior or inferior judgment. For social distinc-tions to sustain operable and efficient systems of hierarchy and discrimi-nation, they must seem to emanate from a source that is more stable than society itself. Because the human body is a site where the social and the natural intersect, corporeal practices and discourses often work to natural-ize sociocultural differences. The *embodiment* of taste allows people to be-lieve that the superiority or inferiority it signifies is anchored firmly in the solid bedrock of the natural. Hence people frequently invoke body images to convey the judgments of taste necessary for the production of social dis-tinction. Cult cinema hero John Waters writes, "I'm convinced that typical *Enquirer* readers . . . are physically unattractive, badly dressed . . . and over-weight. Especially overweight."[37]

Newspaper editor Geneva Overholser, commenting on "talk show sen-sationalism," says, "I find most of this about as appealing as I find a loud drunk." [38] This analogy by way of the figure of an excessive and socially un-disciplined body both naturalizes Overholser's deep revulsion and enables those of her listeners with similar tastes to share the experience of its visceral force. However, there is more going on here than the mere invocation of a powerful image. In their analysis of the relationship between bodily form and sociocultural hierarchy, Stallybrass and White argue that the distinction between "classical" and "grotesque" bodies is of prime significance because it is foundational for the elaboration of all our distinctions between the high-respectable and the low-abject. Fatness, loudness, and intoxication are forms of grotesquery that ground a system of cultural classifications and provoke revulsion, regulation, and the imposition of discipline. At the same time, however, they are historically linked to celebration, protest, and rebellion. [39] As Stallybrass and White observe, "the grotesque physical body is invoked both defensively and offensively because it is . . . fundamentally constitutive of the categorical sets through which we live and make sense of the world." [40]

In his cultural analysis of corporeal forms, Michel de Certeau writes of the way in which bodies are "machined" so that they "spell out" the logic of a social order. [41] The media are among the machines through which bodies are processed in this way. They inscribe norms on the body and so make both the norms and the bodies legible to all. Consider, for example, the primary body in television news, that of the anchor. The body of the anchor occupies the epistemological center of the news and plays a significant role in the establishment of its social credibility. This differentiates TV news from traditional journalistic print media, which established their authority through the use of language that connotes "objectivity." Serious print journalism therefore developed an extensive set of textual conventions that produced an illusion of political neutrality by erasing or at least minimizing the presence of an authorial subject and so appearing to emanate as if directly from an objective reality. The regime of the television personality thus inaugurates a break with the epistemology of the serious newspaper, for the presence of the anchor's body disturbs the objectivist model developed for print journalism. [42] The social authority of broadcast news depends on the body of its central subject, the anchorperson. [43]

The body of the sober anchor is a node through which the serious truths of the day are dispersed. Like the classical body, emblematic as it is of transcendent bourgeois individualism, the network news anchor is elevated and detached from the commonality and its social context. The news anchor emulates the repression of physicality that makes of the classical body a kind of disembodied presence, and so the anchor's body is subdued, and its physical energies are wholly displaced into facial representations of cognition. As Robert Stam observes, the news anchor is a paragon of minimalism.

Through the enactment of a kind of "studied expressionlessness," network news anchors' "faces become empty icons."[44] The minimization of the anchor's body and the camera's emphasis on the iconography of his (gender deliberate) bland yet intense facial expressions combine to televisually encode the Western cultural hierarchy that maps corporeal space so that the head is privileged (expressing the social dominance of the contemplative sphere of elite culture) and the lower bodily strata are reviled, demonized, and renounced as polluted. The aptly tagged "talking head" thus visually indicates the official news's renunciation of the body's earthy materiality, a renunciation that is also expressed through "respectable" television journalism's claims to rise above "sensationalism." For "sensationalism" is a metaphor that works to distinguish the bourgeois from the popular by invoking the concept of purely fleshy and therefore intellectually unmediated experience.

The serious news distills and condenses the materiality of its knowledge-anchoring bodies into images that symbolize their abstracted intellectual essences and thus prefers to represent them from the neck up. When the news does admit entire bodies into its representational repertoire, it must discipline them strenuously. On the *McNeil/Lehrer News Hour*, for example, the disciplinarity of the subdued body extends from the muted and normalized sartorial language of the blue suit to the rigid postures assumed by conversants in their orderly arranged armchairs. At their most undisciplined moments, the proceedings "degenerate" into an absurdly repressed and muted flurry of gesturing arms and raised voices, and even this troubles some commentators, who interpret such "fireworks" as corruptions of the orderly quest after journalistic truth. This is indeed a far cry from the "chaotic" indiscipline often generated on the tabloid talk shows, where the spectacle of bodies and voices pushed beyond the limits of tasteful restraint is a frequent consequence of the inclusion of those lower orders that are routinely excluded from serious shows—and ironically, therefore, from participating in the circulation of the truths deemed most necessary for the realization of democracy (see chapter 5).

Margaret Morse argues that the social authority of television network news is rooted not so much in its promise of "objectivity" as in its anchors' displays of various subjective attributes that create a sense of their sincerity, credibility, and even godlike omniscience. Their "zero-degree of deviation from the norm" suits them for a place at the center of news discourse.[45] Moreover, the anchors' embodiment of nondeviation from norms helps reciprocally to constrain the possible range of knowledges that might be expected or allowed to constitute the category of "news." The news anchor's body is properly stationed within the system of norms and dominant discourses that constitutes U.S. culture's mainstream sense of "reality" and thus works to hold its relations of power and resource allocation in place. The official news attempts to extend the disciplinary control it exerts over the anchor's body and speech to control those of its viewers as well: it aims finally to station bodies in front of their television screens and to produce a *believing* consciousness within each viewer's body. The figure of the sober anchor might therefore be understood as a kind of disciplinary relay station that combines adherence to social codes of normality with the cultural authority of the classical body and thus underwrites the status of serious news as an agent of normalizing knowledge/power. In this way, other knowledges and social realities are marginalized or excluded altogether, as are the voices of those who live on the margins of society and consume its cultural "trash." The institutionalization of discourses that systematically exclude popular tastes and knowledges is crucial to the reproduction of a public realm on which most socially subordinated groups are encouraged not to tread.

Gerald Stone, executive producer of both *A Current Affair* and the Fox Network's tabloid-style *Reporters*, observes that most establishment journalists are "university-educated, East Coast-based . . . snobs whose peer-group status depends on distancing themselves as far as possible from the smell and grime of the police beat." [46] Here Stone designates some important characteristics of the respectable cultural habitus. The first of these is *distance*, which Bourdieu identifies as a primary marker of elite cultural status.[47] Distantiated detachment in all matters of consumption is the cultural manifestation of a socially privileged distance from material necessity. This privileged habit of distantiation finds its parallel in the transcendence that the classical body must continually strive to display, particularly in relation to two key cultural pollutants named by Stone: *dirt* and *odor*. The point resonates with Bernstein's panicked account of the "idiot culture" spawned by tabloid media, in which he decries "a social discourse that we—the press, the media, the politicians, and the people—are turning into a sewer." [48] The pungent image of the sewer has played no small historical role in expressing the dangers of contamination posed by the lower classes to the transcendent purity of the classical body, its distance from vulgarity, and its clarification of the boundary between high and low. The sewer inaugurates a metonymic chain running through the lower bodily strata, the city's lower spaces, and the lower populations who inhabit them. But again there is fascination, indeed desire, fused with the high's disgust for the low, as even the abject sewer is imbued with special powers of revelation. Victor Hugo wrote of a humble stratum of truth, a vulgar sincerity lurking in the city's lower alimentary canal:

> Every foulness of civilization, fallen into disuse, sinks into the *ditch of truth* wherein ends the huge social down-slide, to be swallowed, but

to spread. No false appearances, no white-washing, is possible; filth strips off its shirt in utter starkness, all illusions and mirages scattered, nothing left except what is, showing the ugly face of what ends.[49]

The sewer's power to reveal the "ultimate truth of the social" is rooted in its "melodramatic coercion of extreme opposites into close intimacy," for it commingles the lofty and the vulgar within a common disordered space that implodes the differences between them.[50] This is a characteristic shared between the sewer and the scandalous, postmodern discourses of tabloid media. The sewer's implosion of the difference between high and low is considered revelatory, as Hugo's fascination with its symbolic power indicates. The sincerity of the sewer's filth produces a starkness of truth that is simultaneously abject and powerful. It fascinates and disgusts at once. The socially powerful strive to distinguish and distance themselves from its starkness through the production of loftier truths. But this is no simple task in light of the special powers of revelation associated with the glaring realities of the sewer, so it is a project that is, through a kind of anxious overcompensation, often paranoically overdone. There is a trace of anxiousness in the denunciations of tabloid media issued from the mouths of defenders of the serious tradition. This anxious pose is evident in Bernstein's critique of tabloid culture and of the "sewer" that is this "talk-show nation." Steeped as it supposedly is in the "idiocy" of "gossip" (that most insistently feminized of discursive forms) and chained to "the ever descending lowest common denominator" (a middle-class code phrase for nonbourgeois tastes), our troubles can be vanquished only through the triumph of "real journalism," whose seriousness Bernstein reveres and champions.[51]

Bernstein scathingly labels gossip "the lowest form of news."[52] Yet the "gossipy" feel of many tabloid media forms implicitly questions what some feminist critics call the "male-stream" values embodied in the "hard-nosed" knowledges associated with Western patriarchal rationalism and empiricism. Furthermore, it provokes the formation of an orally productive culture of gossip, especially among the women who consume these media.[53] Gossip is a boundary-blurring cultural form that erases the difference between participants and spectators. It is also a common medium for the circulation of popular knowledge even though it is often deemed to be trivial, feminine, and inferior. Patricia Mellencamp notes that gossip, like the unofficial culture of grotesque realism, is "sanctioned but potentially transgressive" and "historically tied to a negative image of the body—old, wrinkled, and female."[54] Gossip is often used to produce solidarity and intimacy among the socially subordinated, to interrogate elite privilege, and to engender forms of expression that violate strictures ordinarily imposed by the rules of social propriety.[55] Some social formations have produced cultures rooted in "gossip" because it is neither easily monitored nor controlled and constrained from above (which partly accounts for its disreputability). Rumor, a type of unofficial knowledge grounded in orality and closely related to gossip, can also be used to refuse dominant knowledges.[56] Gossip and rumor are very old forms that are both nevertheless quite well suited to postmodern conditions. Their slipperiness and instability match contemporary manifestations of uncertainty and debate over epistemological foundations and the nature of "truth." Their social dispersion and constant mutation lend them a distinctive plurivocality that differentiates them from those monological discourses produced by one or another officialdom as a way of controlling multiplicity.

Irony and Irreverence

It could have happened to you or me, but it happened to Maury Povich. He was an anchorman and a journalist. He wanted to be taken seriously. But for nearly twenty years his career lurched along, never quite taking off. Then, one day, he got a call from Aussieborn media mogul and Twentieth Century Fox owner Rupert Murdoch. He wanted Maury Povich for his new show. Povich couldn't guess the consequences. Neither he nor the news itself was ever the same again.

... What follows is the story of a man who shocked the nation, then was vilified and reviled. ... He became ... Maury Povich, killer of Western culture. —Maura Sheehy, *Manhattan, Inc.*[57]

Television's tabloid-style newscasts surely have their talking heads; Maury Povich is among the best known of the bunch. Povich, "a protean talent who looks by turns horny, sentimental, cool, and distraught," is most memorable for his renunciation of the conventional anchor's stoical enactment of the cultural authority associated with the classical body.[58] "I had a small cult following who appreciated my television style," writes Povich in an autobiographical account of his professional days before *A Current Affair.* However, he says of the instability of his turbulent career in mainstream journalism, most audiences found his trademark "raised eyebrows and ... attitude of amused and tolerant skepticism" to be too "subversive" for network news.[59] Povich found, in *A Current Affair,* the perfect vehicle for the expression of his less-than-sober style. "I thought we were some bastard version of the six o'clock news, gussied up with smoke and a synthesizer," he writes with an air of self-parody (103). "I wanted to be Lenny Bruce as anchorman: stream-of-consciousness stories hitting some deep, shocking nerve of truth and recognition" (100).

According to Bakhtin, popular culture is distinguished by its carnivalistic embrace of bad taste, offensiveness to officialdom, comic verbal compositions, vulgar language, ritualistic degradation and parody, emphasis on laughter, and excessiveness of all forms, but especially of the body.[60] Such characteristics are typical of the tabloid media. The carnivalesque results from an explosively antagonistic collision between the elevated culture of officialdom and the lowly regarded cultures of the people. Tabloid media derive much of their energy from the juxtaposition of journalism, that most solemn of television's social responsibilities, and disreputable popular tastes for melodrama, scandal, sexual intrigue, parody, and stories about paranormal phenomena. The carnivalesque is based on forms of exaggeration and play that testify "to the power of the 'low' to insist upon its rights to a place in the culture."[61] It typically inverts normal patterns of social life and involves "the peculiar logic of the 'inside out,'" where "travesties, humiliations, profanations," and "comic crownings and uncrownings" take place.[62] Although weakened and diminished in modernity, the carnivalesque nevertheless persists in fertilizing various spheres of cultural life.[63] The historical diminution of the carnivalesque is a result of its abjection, regulation, and constriction by officialdom. However narrowed and weakened, though, it retains disruptive elements whose effects are indexed partly by the extent to which they offend those with "legitimate" and therefore socially powerful tastes.

The Lenny Bruce persona that Povich strives to create indicates the importance of laughter and transgression for A Current Affair. The stream of consciousness he seeks in his presentational style deviates markedly from the norms of mainstream news work. Whereas the script(ure)s of the teleprompter reflect the propriety and seriousness of official language, "stream of consciousness" suggests an affinity with the unfinished, in-process style of carnivalesque speech. The "shocking nerve of truth" Povich strives to pique recalls Hugo's description of the stark "sincerity" of the sewer, that "ditch of truth," that "conscience of the town" where "there is darkness . . . but no secrets."[64] Indeed, Povich writes of himself and his Current Affair cohorts, a band of "toothless, street-fighting Aussies," that

> we were bound together by an undiminished and happy zest for vulgar truth. No comforting euphemisms, no sappy evasions—life, in all its messy incarnations was, for us, endlessly fascinating. Somewhere along the line, each of us had been thwarted by those careful guardians of taste and style known in the industry as "the suits."[65]

The image of television journalism's officialdom conveyed through the phrase "the suits" is as class marked and disembodied as the "talking head." By contrast, Povich's interjection of physicality, of the body principle (how-

The faces of Maury Povich.

ever subtle and contained) into his delivery of the news contests the disembodied transcendence of the sober anchorman. A repertoire of trademark smirks and facial contortions, waggish expressions, and excessive
vocal modulations introduced irony, skepticism, and downright disbelief,
surprise, or even stupefaction into Povich's presentation of tabloid stories.
Although in practice the differences between his physical style and those
of more mainstream newsreaders often appear minor (Povich isn't Lenny

Bruce, nor is his commentary actually stream of consciousness—though he has been dubbed "Mr. Tabloid" by the producers of A Current Affair), both the subtle differences themselves and Povich's autobiographical descriptions of them indicate a deeply ironized orientation. Indeed, the subtlety of the differences indicates not their insignificance but rather the rigidity and vigor with which the norms of news delivery are enforced—otherwise they could not be so easily transgressed and parodied. Philip Weiss observes that

> Povich ends each show with a leer and the line, "Until next time, America," as though the show had been a dinner-time quickie with the viewer, and the rubber-faced lewdness his role calls for, the alacrity with which he moves through a half dozen expressions and voices (from furry soft to wired and mean) is a motility reminiscent of the veteran porn star.[66]

Weiss's invocation of the figure of the "veteran porn star" here is revealing. Its insistent abjection of Povich suggests the extent to which his style of news performance threatens mainstream journalistic norms of taste and seriousness.

Unlike the disdainful jeering directed at Povich by establishment journalists, the laughter that Povich evokes on the air is at once mocking, derisive, triumphant, and ambivalent. In carnivalesque style, "it asserts and denies, it buries and revives." [67] Television critic Ron Powers mistakes A Current Affair for a slickly cynical denunciation of the low and the socially weak. "Rupert Murdoch's vision of American life is . . . marinated in morbid contempt for the common man . . . [and] condescending cruelty," Powers writes.[68] He fails to detect any popular voices in the discourse of A Current Affair, nor does he find there any of the socially regenerative power associated with carnivalesque laughter; he locates only the show's powers of degradation. This is largely due, however, to his own high-minded contempt for popular tastes: audiences that support A Current Affair's putative portrayal of "proletarian life in its most prurient, puerile terms" by tuning in are summarily dismissed (in derogatory tones that are uncannily like those that he accuses Murdoch of propagating) as an unfortunate and enduring fact of life in the United States (190).

Powers's high-bourgeois cultural habitus prevents him from recognizing the close connections between grotesque realism and popular tastes. He writes contemptuously of the "mountebanks, Tammyfayes, buffoons and monsters" that inhabit the world of A Current Affair. "The locus of identification must be with" Povich, announces Powers. Advancing the abjection of the feminine and the feminization of the abject, Powers sees Povich providing "the legitimizing counterweight of authority" necessary to offset the "surrealism" of a news program produced for "career matrons who put on their faces while riding the commuter bus" (185, 187).[69] Quoting George Orwell, Powers accuses Murdoch's *A Current Affair* of appropriating a "Sancho Panza view of life" (one rooted in the perspective of the "unofficial self," the "little fat man in all of us" whose voice is that of "the belly protesting against the soul") but omitting the "underlying smile of affirmation" for Sancho Panza that Orwell found admirable (but with which Powers himself seems uncomfortable).[70] Powers fails to understand that Povich's delivery is deeply ambivalent, infused with simultaneous bemusement, mockery, and affirmation. Sheehy, by contrast, claims that the "sheepish looks, groans and glares" that punctuate Povich's on-air reactions produce a sense of leveling communality, an awareness that "we're in it together."[71] Povich does indeed provide a point of potential viewer identification that the disembodied anchor disavows.[72] However, Povich's performance is part of a far more complex system of identificatory possibilities than Powers discerns.

Povich's mode of performance enacts the very clash of officialdom's constipated seriousness with the disruptive antidisciplinarity of popular taste that is the mise-en-scène of the carnivalesque. "I was," Povich writes in his autobiography, "embarrassed by the gaudy nature of some of the stories we were programming for *A Current Affair*."

> Over the years I had learned to express my personal opinion about stories by tossing the audience a set of signals: a lift of my eyebrow, a wag of my head, the raising and lowering of my voice . . . I could deliver on-air reviews. Nobody could take all that stuff straight. I could lift the curse off UFO encounters with my eyebrow. I could issue wry disclaimers for the stories about the effects of nude beaches and the cavorting at a *Soldier of Fortune Magazine* convention.[73]

By using facial expressions to represent skeptical or mock disapproval of the strange and bizarre, by laughing at the absurdity of stories that would never find a place in the serious news, Povich fed off the disjuncture between respectable and popular tastes and enacted a leveling and incredulous burlesque of mainstream journalism's attempts to garner credibility. His parodically ambiguous and ambiguously parodic performance of official disesteem enabled *A Current Affair*'s producers to "show anything at all," Povich writes, "from high-priced hookers to lowdown scams." Says he, "they had an automatic disclaimer—me." Povich claims that this plurivocal ironization of television news played to both popular tastes and more "respectable" audiences' fascination with the abject. *A Current Affair* "covered both sides," says Povich. "The ones who wanted all the gore and glitz and the ones who wanted to express the higher sensibilities—but still wanted to watch" (101). The elite could thus train its desirous gaze on the abject and at the same time, by interpreting Povich's demeanor as an expression of disapproval to identify with, affirm the sense of superior taste and self-entitlement that enables and enhances access to many forms of social power and privilege.

Povich nevertheless made it difficult to sustain such an interpretation for long, for he relished iconoclasm and interjected irony at every turn. "Some shows go to the edge," he once said on air. "We take it one step further: we *are* the abyss" (190; italics mine). Povich scorned the pretensions of the quality press. He thus billed his program as a "daily fix of silliness, irony, and tub-thumping anger" infused with "an odor of disrespect for authority" (172–73). His bête noire was the sedate and dignified anchor, disembodied figure of authority, dispenser of the official truth. "Somehow the notion had come about that news was church business and had to be uttered with ponderous and humorless reverence," Povich writes. "Instead news was a circus delivered by clowns and dancing bears and should be taken with a lot of serious skepticism" (214). A *Current Affair* thus took frequent aim at the serious business of fourth-estate journalism. For example, when Ted Koppel, the host of ABC's news program *Nightline*, borrowed footage of Malcolm Forbes's seventieth birthday party in Monaco from a *Current Affair* satellite feed, A *Current Affair* countered with a report expressing "make-believe shock" over mainstream journalism's emulation of the tabloid newscast. Povich explains that "we had a phony grade school teacher, who said Koppel was jealous of me, and a phony dean of a journalism school, who said our rivalry went far back, and was not surprising since Koppel had once tried to change his name to 'Ted Povich' " (195). A fitting reversal of newscasting's crown prince and clown prince, the gag unveiled a journalistic world turned upside down. If one of the hallmarks of the official news is the way in which its discursive operations tend to work toward producing an earnestly credulous audience-subject, the brilliance of Povich's A *Current Affair* lies in the ongoing joke that it makes of the credibility and the seriousness of the professional journalistic establishment.[74]

The pomposity and credibility of professional journalists were not the only targets in A *Current Affair*'s sights. The program's leveling impulses were directed at other realms of officialdom and elite social circles as well. In late 1988, for example, while Mikhail Gorbachev was visiting New York, the program made Donald Trump the object of its ridicule. The man responsible was reporter Gordon Elliott, an Australian import and "world class prankster" who was "globally famous for his improbably public antics." Says Povich of Elliott, "when he sniffed the odor of disrespect for authority that permeated our every waking moment" at A *Current Affair*, "he knew that he had arrived at his true spiritual destination."[75] Povich describes how Elliott had learned of the "shattering disappointment" that had stricken Trump's "skyscraper ego" when Gorbachev canceled a scheduled visit to Trump's opulent and self-importantly titled palace, Trump Tower, that vertical signifier of capitalist and phallic power. Trump and Gorbachev had met once before at a Reagan White House dinner, and "the Donald" had apparently taken great satisfaction from the idea of consorting with statesmen. Elliott decided that Trump ought not to be disappointed by the cancellation, so Elliott contacted Ronald V. Knapp, a rubber salesman who once won a Gorbachev look-alike contest. Knapp was properly accoutered with an artificial purple birthmark and placed inside a stretch limousine trailed by a parade of cars simulating an entourage of dignitaries. For good measure, Elliott put "a few knockout models" in Knapp's limo on the premise that "sex always pays off in a story." Trump was notified of his impending appointment with destiny.

The makeshift parade of mock dignitaries proceeded down Fifth Avenue at lunchtime, causing great fuss and commotion as shoppers and passersby yelled "Hey, Gorby!" eliciting waves, smiles, and Russian-accented hellos from Knapp. In the meantime, Trump, perched high above the city at the top of his office tower, was prepared by aides for the historic rendezvous. Public relations advisers counseled Trump that he should be waiting outside the building when Gorbachev arrived, so he rushed to the street and pushed his way through a bogus security detail to reach Knapp. "Good to see you again," said Trump, flashing a smile. Although Trump's previous encounter with Gorbachev had been "an official blur," he now acted as though he and the Soviet premier had been close pals since childhood. Trump was, therefore, "blushing, caught up in the bigness of the moment," when he noticed the women in the back of the limousine. As Povich tells it, "something whispered to him that the head of all the Russias would not travel openly around New York City with two very conspicuous bimbos in the backseat. Not if he had a fiery wife like Raisa." Trump, who did not like being duped, later issued formal statements denying that he had fallen for the ruse. The Current Affair videotape, however, belies Trump's denials with its documentation of the wan expression that gradually overtook his appearance, signaling his queasy recognition of what was unfolding around him.[76]

Such pranks were more than mere "silliness." They were part of a concerted assault on power, pretension, and pomposity that motivated some of the best of the tabloid news work done at A Current Affair.[77] They appeal to a popular distrust of all that is high, an inclination toward leveling that, in the Trump story, literally brings the lofty down to ground level.[78] Trump is summoned from high atop his tower to the grubby street, where in the whirl of a media circus, he is ritually chastised for his hubris amid a pulsing throng of celebrants. The broadcast circulation of these images enables an enormous audience to participate in this ritualistic uncrowning of a princely ass, in a carnivalistic spectacle whose logic undermines the seriousness of officialdom by disrupting its hierarchization of high and low. Bakhtin's elucidation of the carnivalesque is aptly descriptive of this media pranksterism, which initiated a kind of "free and familiar contact among people" who are otherwise separated by the "impenetrable hierarchical barriers" that constitute the social geography of everyday life in the contemporary United States. A *Current Affair's* tricksterism here "brings together, unifies, weds, and combines the sacred with the profane, the lofty with the low, the great with the insignificant, the wise with the stupid," and therefore ritualistically degrades all within officialdom that is ceremoniously self-inflating.[79]

What's more, A *Current Affair's* media pranksterism here mockingly burlesques the contemporary genre of political spectacle known as the "photo op." An "artificially" spectacular televisual incident like this could occur only in a society traversed by electronic communication systems that have regularized the production of media events such as those that this one imitates and parodies. The media spectacle staged between Trump and A *Current Affair's* faux Gorby implodes, however temporarily, all distinctions between not only the high and the low but also the authentic and the inauthentic. As a parody of the highly conventionalized "photo ops" that, in contemporary society, motivate mediatized meetings between social power brokers whose faces have been turned into electronic icons, this mock event's popular skepticism implicitly questions the seriousness and "authenticity" of all such media events.

The Trump story is typical of the kind of news that commentators routinely bemoan—as they have for at least eight decades [80]—because it is seen to exemplify a process whereby the "good" of solemn and serious official journalism is driven out by the "bad" of "news as entertainment." [81] This lament about the depredation of serious news has become so commonplace that it now constitutes a critically uninspected foundation of middle-class and elite "common sense" about popular journalism.[82] Its weakness is that it not only neglects the diversity of tabloid media content but furthermore assumes that journalistic forms that "entertain" are innately vapid, insignificant, and unworthy of investigation in their own right. It simply begs the question: what meaning effects are generated by these disgustingly entertaining media? [83] With regard to journalistic story selection and placement, the lament *assumes* that some events are *inherently* more worthy of attention than others. But the criteria that underlie such judgments are, of course, socially produced and so necessarily bound up with the dynamics of class, race, gender, age, and so on. When the "significant" happens to converge so neatly, as it consistently does, from the perspective of the lament, with the official spheres of party politics, the government, business, the military, and the mainstream scientific community, one might be forgiven for suspecting that the categories of "seriousness" and "significance" are produced through a politics of knowledge that silently but actively promotes dominant class, gender, and race interests. This is not, of course, to suggest that these spheres of officialdom are in any way unimportant or unworthy of attention, but rather to challenge the exclusion of other domains from the realm of what matters. Evidence that the popular imagination has re-directed its activities away from areas where elite opinion leaders believe it ought to focus should be seen as a symptom of the extent to which the people recognize how severely limited their agency is within the realm of officialdom — constructed and controlled as it has been by the power-bloc — and as a clue that suggests that there are far more interesting things going on in the arenas of "news as entertainment" than the lament is capable of grasping.[84] Indeed, although the tabloid media do venture into the realm of "serious" public life, they often do so with playful, parodic, and campy irreverence, as stories like the one lampooning Trump and Gorbachev dem-onstrate. It is perhaps their playfully populist skepticism, which treats the serious business of journalism as if it were a circus, that more than anything else provokes the indignant lament over the success of tabloid media.

A *Current Affair*'s irreverence is enhanced and abetted by its devotion to the construction of a recycling station for popular sounds and images. Such stations are increasingly numerous in a media culture that, according to one strand of postmodern theory, constitutes "a Leviathan-like lattice work of programmes, circuits, pulses, which functions merely to process and re-cycle the 'events' produced (excreted) within itself."[85] This trend is evident in A *Current Affair*'s heavy use of the aural and visual detritus of the media age, including old and somewhat newer Hollywood film footage, music videos both earnest and parodic, and the plundered sound and image tracks of sit-coms, fictional television dramas, and game shows. Such detritus is strewn throughout the program's renderings of the day's events in a fashion that collapses temporal and epistemological distinctions as well as generic pro-gramming categories. The memorabilia of our film, television, and popular musical heritage thus encrust the news stories with interpretive activators resurrected from the sound and image banks that are the primary reposi-tories of popular-cultural capital in the contemporary era. Hollywood Cold War film footage, for example, saturates A *Current Affair*'s 1989 coverage of the fall of the Berlin Wall; documentary images of Jerry Lee Lewis and his teenybopper bride, along with the strains of his music and Chuck Berry's "You Never Can Tell" ("It was a teenage wedding and the ol' folks wished 'em well"), fill a 1989 report about a girl who was unfairly expelled from a suburban Chicago Catholic high school for getting married; Julie Brown's campy music video "The Homecoming Queen's Got a Gun" ("Everybody run!") accompanies the story about a "pistol-packin' beauty queen" who was arrested on weapons charges after her appearance in the 1989 Miss

America pageant. A *Current Affair* seeks the outrageous and reports it outrageously, when and where it can find it; when it can't, it seeks to spin the more mundane in outrageous ways, and the sounds and images that the show borrows from the history of entertainment media help it to do this.

In this way, current events are reprocessed through the popular memory that has crystallized around the artifacts of the classical and contemporary Hollywood, rock, and network television industrial complexes. Frank P. Tomasulo observes that postmodernity entails an increasing reliance on electronic and cinematic evidence for depicting and understanding historical events, so that "our concepts of historical referentiality (what happened), epistemology (how we know it happened), and historical memory (how we interpret it and what it means to us) are now determined primarily by media imagery." [86] I'm suggesting here that A *Current Affair* adds another turn of the representational screw to this logic of postmodern events, for it deploys our cultural sound-and-image-history in order to construct interpretive frames that collectively constitute a popular alternative to the discourses of serious journalism as a way to make sense of the day's happenings. When, for example, A *Current Affair* uses *Brady Bunch* footage and music to embellish its 1990 account of an escaped Boston convict who eluded his jailors by taking to a rooftop and refusing to come down until they could name all the fictional children in the quintessential seventies sitcom family, it not only invites laughter at the inept prison officials who were unable to produce a satisfactory answer despite hours of effort (and laughter *with* this prisoner's mockery of those officials and the bureaucracy they represent); as a kind of secondary semiotic and metonymic effect, it also suggests the laughability of all news and invites skepticism toward serious journalism's self-serving and disingenuous attempts to differentiate itself from show business "entertainment." A *Current Affair*'s playfully explicit indifference to boundaries between "news" and "entertainment" thus gives the lie to the serious news and exposes its hypocrisy. Speaking to the same sensibility that underlies A *Current Affair*'s playful use of popular cultural sounds and imagery to frame and interpret the day's events, another emblematic figure of television tabloidism, Geraldo Rivera, notes that the "line between news and entertainment" is a "corporate distinction—esoteric and arbitrary—based on budgets and the perceived purity of broadcast journalism." [87]

Laughingly skeptical irony and campy irreverence do not, however, exhaust the stylistic range of A *Current Affair*, whose image-recycling apparatus also underwrites tones of populist indignation that permeate what we might call the "investigative tabloidism" that the program often undertakes. As I intend this term, investigative tabloidism (like its mainstream journalistic counterpart) assumes a morally motivated and self-consciously adversarial stance that evokes outrage at the violation of commonsense values and the victimization of ordinary people and particularly of the socially weak and "innocent."[88] If the investigative impulse forms a point of intersection between tabloid television and mainstream news, the differences between its "high" and "low" forms are, like many other differences between tabloid and "quality" journalism, ones of emphasis and degree more than of kind. Because of mainstream investigative journalists' commitment to what Theodore Glasser and James Ettema call a "culture of objectivity," such journalists perform a set of complex rhetorical gymnastics to disguise the moralistic purposiveness of their work and to convince themselves, their audiences, and their critics that what they routinely make are *news* judgments rooted in a universe of objective facts rather than *moral* ones grounded in (and working to reproduce or reconstruct) concepts of "right" and "wrong."[89] As *A Current Affair* and other tabloid media don't inhabit the same culture of objectivity that authorizes the middle-class press's claims to legitimacy and credibility, they don't share the same imperative to negotiate with such great care the contradiction between the indignantly adversarial stance associated with investigative journalism's implicit aspirations to "moral custodianship" and, on the other hand, the need to appear objective and morally disengaged.[90] This often leads tabloidism's investigative journalistic forms in the direction of melodrama, toward a heightened sense of moral outrage, an emphasis on affect and an apparent lack of concern for creating impressions of detached objectivity of the sort that are so central to the "respectable" investigative press's sense of its own mission.

Along these lines, Jack Katz has found that the more educational, cultural, and economic capital a particular newspaper's readers hold, the more that paper will decline to use invective and execration in favor of "what are conventionally regarded as emotionally neutral, technical terms, in particular the formally non-prejudicial, officially constrained language of courts and lawyers." Whereas in a moderately sized headline, for example, the *New York Times* describes as "bribery" the illegal payments from GTE-Sylvania executives to corrupt state transit officials in order to protect shipments of substandard lightbulbs, the tabloid *Daily News*, by contrast, reports the same incident in large front-page type that reads, "*Subway Bulb Gyp.*"[91] The everyday language of *A Current Affair*, like that of other tabloid newscasts such as *Hard Copy* and Geraldo Rivera's *Now It Can Be Told*, similarly evokes populist indignation often. In, for instance, its 1989 story about a sadistic small-town police and animal control officer alleged to have shot at, and even swerved his car to hit, "beloved" local pets, *A Current Affair* refers repeatedly to the "Rambo dogcatcher" whose "trigger finger got him in hot water," and whose propensity for "taking aim" at gentle canines has left "heartbroken" one teenage boy whose "teddy bear" of a black lab was killed by the cruel

cop. In a 1989 report on Manuel Noriega, *A Current Affair* claims to expose the
U.S. government's "dirty little secret": that "the midget madman obsessed
by macho muscle" regularly "threw orgies" for willing and corrupt U.S. officials and made "sex tapes" of the events to serve as his "insurance policies."
In a 1992 story about a rifle company worker fired after twenty-two years
of service for allegedly stealing thirty-five cents, *A Current Affair* indicts the
"snipering" bosses who "let [the former employee] have it with both bar-
rels" and who have seen to it that his "whole future may be shot," as he lost
his medical insurance along with his income and was subsequently denied
unemployment benefits.

The differences of tone and sensibility that distinguish investigative tabloidism from the investigative journalism of the more "respectable" press
correspond well with Bourdieu's delineations of popular and bourgeois
taste. From the perspective of bourgeois taste, excessiveness, emotionality,
exaggerated expressiveness, and insufficiently ambiguous moral contrasts
—defining characteristics of the melodramatic imagination—are sure
signs of "vulgarity" and "unsophistication."[92] Among the key markers of
bourgeois distinction, therefore, are formality, polite restraint, and forms
of linguistic technicality and abstraction that indicate detachment and sani-
tize through euphemism.[93] These traits stand in stark contrast to the exaggerated language, excessive affect, and moral indignation that melodramatic investigative tabloidism evokes. Such characteristics as the latter can
be seen to constitute the emotive flip side or the affective inverse of *A Current Affair's* laughing aspect. Like tabloidism's laughingly irreverent skepticism, its excessive melodramatic affect and populist indignation violate at
once the proprieties of middle-class etiquette and the conventions of "respectable" journalism that are inevitably shaped by those proprieties to one
degree or another.

Bourdieu observes that the coldly "impeccable formalism" that is the
hallmark of "bourgeois politeness," but is rejected within proletarian culture, serves both as a mark of social distinction and as "a permanent
warning against the temptation of familiarity."[94] This is a warning that
A Current Affair breaches freely time and again by affording its viewers the
opportunity to enter into a kind of affective communion with its featured
subjects—a characteristic that unites this program with the tabloid talk
shows, which similarly often feature working-class and lower-middle-class
people, and especially women, sharing their emotional tribulations, tragedies, and victories with an audience of sympathetic strangers. Like cinematic melodrama, *A Current Affair* inscribes emotions upon the surfaces of
bodies through the use of intense facial close-ups (along with actual Hollywood film footage) in its stories (including, in the "Rambo dogcatcher"
report, long close-ups of both the heartbroken boy and the happily gentle

Labrador retriever whose life was needlessly cut short). In this way, the program enhances the excessive affect generated by its verbal language and removes the ethos of its news work yet one step further from the sanitizing, rationalistic detachment of the "respectable" press.

Consider, for example, the 1989 report on the murder of a young former homecoming queen from Wisconsin by her onetime classmate, who is the current county "dairy princess." In the studio interview granted to *A Current Affair* by the victim's sister, the program's lingering videographic emphasis on the cracking voice, tear-stained face, and intense emotionality of its interviewee clearly tugs—scandalously, some would say—at "respectable" journalism's mask of detached rationality. The belittlement of such emotionalism as that which often characterizes *A Current Affair*'s tabloid news work can never be class or gender neutral; it serves to produce social distinction, just as the popular taste for such affectively engaged material is the product of particular class and gender locations. The criticism of popular melodrama—in journalistic or other forms—on the grounds that it is "emotionally manipulative" of its audience silently reproduces and reinforces the Enlightenment-derived and patriarchal privileging of "rationality" over affect and, furthermore, necessarily depends on the implicit invocation of cultural consumers that are imagined to be either more vulnerable to "manipulation" or less discriminating than the critic. It is telling that the critique of "emotionally manipulative" culture is generally exclusive to encounters between bourgeois critical discourse and the terrain of the popular, for this reveals the significant extent to which elite habits of thought are committed to imagining popular and media cultures as sites of ceaseless manipulation, and to envisioning their "ordinary" participants and audiences as the helplessly manipulated.[95]

Its melodramatic tendencies lend to *A Current Affair* a capacity for moral earnestness and traditionalism that uneasily counterbalances its ironic overtones and laughing popular skepticism. In a 1993 story on "Hollywood madam" Heidi Fleiss and her cohort of beautiful young providers of sexual services to the stars, for example, reporter Steve Dunleavy's unique flair for moralistic heavy-handedness angles the piece toward conventional riffs about contrite but tragically fallen women who "sold their bodies" for material riches. However, amid all the overt moralization and sermonizing about innocence lost, what is perhaps most interesting about the story is that like other tabloid media forms, it opens a small space for voices and perspectives that typically command little respect or attention in middle-class culture. Consequently Fleiss and her "number one girl," Brandi McClain, use their *Current Affair* airtime to raise some significant issues not often addressed in mainstream media outside of tabloid television. Indeed, one of the most significant things about the kinds of "shocking" and "scandalous" events that are the very stuff of tabloidism is that it is precisely the media activity to which such events give rise that often leads to the amplification and increased circulation of voices and perspectives that were of course previously socially present but constrained to operate at lower levels and within more narrowly circumscribed spheres. Tabloid media attention can cut such voices and perspectives loose and make it possible for them to achieve levels of publicity previously denied them.

Reflecting, for example, on her treatment by the LAPD and the court system, Fleiss says that she feels as if she's being operated on by ten unlicensed surgeons, while the rich and powerful men who were the backbone of her (highly lucrative) business are free to go about their lives as if nothing had happened. She thus links her feelings of disempowerment—here, through the use of a medical metaphor (albeit from a very different perspective than the one from which such metaphors are invoked to pathologize tabloid tastes)—to her treatment at the hands of the law enforcement and justice systems rather than to her work in the sex industry. McClain supports Fleiss's assessment of the Hollywood "boys' club" that has learned to stick together to protect its own. She wonders aloud, forcefully and articulately, how it can be that the women in her business are subjected to prosecution while the men involved, without whose demand there would have been no service, nevertheless walk free. McClain contradicts the frequent dehumanization of sex workers in patriarchal culture by asserting that her friend Fleiss is a "good person" with a "good heart." Snickering cynically and openly about certain of her clients, McClain displaces onto them some of the energy that typically leads to the treatment of women in the sex industries as objects of disdain or ridicule; here, those rich and powerful men become the butt of her jokes: the Hollywood producer who has an "extensive collection of rubber goods" and foolishly thinks he's fooling them when he disingenuously "promises every girl a part in his movie"; the rock star who makes similarly transparent and inflated pledges; the movie hero who asks all the women to dress up like cheerleaders and pretend they have a game the next day. The amplification and increased social circulation of such voices and perspectives as Fleiss's and McClain's, having been activated by the media event that is the occasion for their newfound high audibility—and insofar as they are able to engage the interests and imaginations of television audiences—stimulate new struggles over meaning in the trenches of everyday life.

The tone of McClain's jokes is typical of the laughingly mocking but also frequently indignant cynicism with regard to power, bureaucracy, and, incidentally, Hollywood that permeates many of the stories told on A Current Affair. While on the program power may be embodied in political, organizational, or bureaucratic forms (including the U.S. or foreign federal, state, or local governments and their agents or agencies, political parties, and businesses — especially those associated with the entertainment industries), power is also examined closely and often in its familial, domestic aspect and with regard to interpersonal relationships generally, which are typically shown to be characterized by the "dark plottings" that preoccupy the melodramatic imagination.[96] Interpersonal power is embodied, for example, in the figure of a corrupt "video voyeur" in A Current Affair's 1989 story about Mike Gibbons, who "secretly recorded his love sessions with three separate women" and showed the videotapes to several of his friends. The report focuses on the anger and sense of violation experienced by "Ann," "Amy," and "Linda," who appear on camera but in shadows. After the melodramatic tradition, A Current Affair here complicates notions of the woman-as-victim by showing that the three "weren't about to let [Gibbons] get away with it," so they "got together, got mad, and got even."[97] To do so, however, they had to overcome the failings of the California criminal code, which contained no provision whereby Gibbons might be held responsible for his inexcusable actions. They therefore encouraged an enthusiastic prosecutor to offer the courts a clever interpretation of "eavesdropping" laws designed to protect "confidential information." Gibbons was found guilty, and "now," says reporter Robin Dorian, "the bed he will be sleeping in could be behind bars." Footage of James Spader's award-winning sleazy character from Hollywood's Sex Lies and Videotape (Steven Soderbergh, 1989) — a film that, as one reviewer puts it, takes "a philosophical look at the hidden agendas that undermine relationships" — is used to embellish and frame our interpretations of the events covered in the Gibbons story.[98]

The 1989 story of one embattled Texas family, the Sylvesters, also well illustrates the way in which A Current Affair uses melodramatic conventions and pop cultural allusion to examine issues around interpersonal or domestic victimization in contexts structured by combinations of individual malevolence and bureaucratic corruption, ineptitude, or indifference to the fates of ordinary but noble people. Pat and Butch Sylvester and their two daughters claim to be under constant threat from the "monstrous" boy they adopted seventeen years earlier. A Current Affair embellishes the story with hauntingly gothic music and images of the demonic Damien from The Omen (Richard Donner, 1976), Freddy Krueger from A Nightmare on Elm Street (Wes Craven, 1984), and the hockey-masked Jason from Halloween (John Carpenter, 1978). By the age of eight, Toby was conducting animal sacrifices. According to Pat, the young boy with "dark, cutting eyes" got a "high or rush" from the blood. Before long, he was making death threats toward his siblings and parents. According to sister Terri Sylvester, "He's talked about how he's going to do it. He's talked about stabbing us." Apparently, the "bad seed" Toby's propensity for violent emotional outbursts led him to conduct a "reign of terror" over the other family members after he learned that he was adopted. Pat says that " 'adoption' was a very open term in our house. You know, we explained to him that we picked him, he was a chosen baby; we didn't want him to think he was an accident, or a mistake." Nevertheless, "He was, uh, very angry, hostile, unpredictable, violent." Toby increasingly blamed Pat and Butch Sylvester for his natural mother's decision to give him up for adoption. Sometimes his anger and hostility drove him to "bite out chunks" of his sister's flesh.

The Sylvesters' anguish was not relieved when they turned to the agencies of the State of Texas. Reporter David Lee Miller explains that when they realized the boy's "behavior was out of control, the Sylvesters sought professional help and committed Toby to the children's psychiatric unit here at the Austin State Hospital. But after two months, he was released as an outpatient, and each day he grew bigger, stronger, and more frightening." Although the Sylvesters legally terminated their parental obligations when Toby was fourteen, their modest finances (Butch is a mailman) have been crippled by the costs of his psychiatric care, court-appointed attorneys, and child support payments for which the State of Texas continues to hold them responsible, despite the fact that it has taken over day-to-day care. Finally, Pat and Butch have discovered Department of Human Services records that indicate that important facts about the boy's history were concealed from the Sylvesters when they adopted him in 1972. Toby's birth mother suffered from debilitating mental illnesses, and his natural father allegedly beat to death one of her other children. None of this was revealed to the Sylvesters during the adoption process even though, as a Texas Department of Human Services memo plainly states, Pat and Butch had made clear to the agency that they were only willing to adopt a child with "no major emotional disturbances."

Now, although Toby no longer lives with them, he continues to make death threats against Pat and Butch by telephone. Because they've been unable to sell their home, the Sylvesters feel that the State of Texas should pay for their relocation to a place where they will be safely out of Toby's reach. The story's criticism of state deceit and irresponsibility is punctuated by low-angled images of the large, alienating, coldly bureaucratic headquarters of the Texas Department of Human Services (whose agents refuse to talk to A Current Affair), which are contrasted directly and starkly with the warm familiarity of a humble, small-town, single-family ranch home that has lately, however, become a chamber of horrors. Even so, "despite the seventeen years of hell, at times, Pat and Butch still think of the little boy they so badly wanted to be their son and the family that might have been." Pat's final comment is worth quoting at length, as it conveys so much of the flavor of this domestic melodrama:

It's only been the past year that I can really talk without crying. I mean it, it's, it hurts. Sometimes, especially around his birthday, I want to hold him. I want to get that smell back. Like when I used to bath him, and I'd pick him up, you know, and here was this sweet, powdery baby that you could kinda' snuggle up to you. You know, I just, some days I just wanna touch him so bad I can hardly see straight. But that fear, that threat, that pain, the physical pain—not just the emotional pain but the physical pain—always comes back. Somewhere deep down in him there's a monster.

As Pat Sylvester speaks her final sentence, the camera slowly zooms in on an old family photograph, in to an ultratight, extreme close-up of the penetrating eyes of a small boy who wears a mischievous smile—a smile that seems, in retrospect, to conceal beneath an otherwise innocent-appearing exterior the seeds of "dark plottings." In this regard, the shot functions as a perfect metaphor for the family unit as it is constructed in many of A Current Affair's populist tales of domestic malevolence and bureaucratic deception. As Phillip Weiss notes, in A Current Affair, the family is an "unstable unit" that is "full of lies."[99] Robin Wood has argued that in their representation of the family as a monstrosity, seventies horror films like Texas Chainsaw Massacre (Tobe Hooper, 1974) and The Hills Have Eyes (Wes Craven, 1978) ultimately critique both patriarchal bourgeois domesticity and capitalism.[100] Although A Current Affair does not represent familial relationships with the same level of starkness that Wood lauds in these films, it nevertheless, in the Sylvester story and many others, suggests—partly through the incorporation of actual footage from contemporary 1970s and 1980s horror movie classics (and in counterpoint to Reagan-Bushism's imaginary vision of blissful domesticity)—that the domestic sphere is a deeply dangerous and unsettled realm. Through the regular display of horrific domestic melodramas, A Current Affair thus "make[s] the familial strange."[101] The defamiliarization of the family in tabloid television as elsewhere in popular culture, helps nurture and sustain suspicions toward the right-wing domestic imaginary—suspicions of the sort that erupted explosively in 1992 in the form of a massive grassroots backlash against the Republican Party's miserably failed "family values" campaign.

However, the story of the Sylvesters also illustrates an important element of A Current Affair's tabloidist "project" that is evocative of what Stallybrass and White call "displaced abjection," which they characterize as an aspect of the carnivalesque, though the concept seems equally applicable to A Current Affair's melodramatic forms (which, as I have suggested, after all can be seen as the emotive flip side or the reverse affective charge of the program's carnivalistic impulses). The links the Sylvester story creates, albeit indirectly, between psychological illness and monstrous evil serve implicitly to demonize people with mental disabilities and to reify both "normality" and "abnormality." This effect is enhanced by the fact that, presumably because his whereabouts are unknown (despite his occasional phone calls to Pat and Butch), Toby's voice and perspective are not presented in the story while those of other Sylvester family members are. We are therefore unable to judge, for example, whether and to what degree Toby's apparent emotional and behavioral problems may stem from feelings of alienation from the other family members, perhaps spawned by mistreatment, owing to his adopted status. If one hallmark of tabloid media is that they often create more space for the voices, perspectives, and knowledges of the socially weak than their mainstream journalistic counterpart, the way in which they do so leads, in the Sylvester story, to a kind of displaced abjection. Stallybrass and White explain that "displaced abjection" designates the way in which the "nostalgia" and "uncritical populism" of the carnivalesque can lead it at times toward the abuse and demonization of the weakest social groups, "those who 'don't belong.' "[102] In the case at hand, the critique of power (embodied in the state bureaucracy) on behalf of the socially weak (here, the working-class Sylvester family) might be said to loop around along a kind of elliptical boomerang trajectory whereby its energy is multiplied and ultimately discharged in the face of the *even socially weaker*: Toby. Consequently, while on one very real and significant level this story blames corrupt bureaucratic authority for the destruction of an ordinary U.S. working-class family, its critique along these lines is undercut by the way in which it ultimately targets an even more fundamental nemesis: the psychological abnormality that has bred such a "monster" as Toby.

The melodramatic imagination is right at home in a text that is as postmodern as *A Current Affair*. In his widely influential study of melodrama, Peter Brooks ties the form to the emergence of modern Western society in the wake of the French Revolution and the disruption of traditional modes of authority, especially those associated with the church.[103] Brooks sees the moral clarification performed by melodrama's stark bifurcation of good and evil to be reassuring in a new age where everything is in motion and up for grabs. In a 1988 essay, Lynne Joyrich rehistoricizes melodrama for postmodern times. If for Brooks melodrama is a sense-making system that perpetuates moral and epistemological certitudes in the wake of their modern disruption, for Joyrich the form now "engulfs" TV, interjecting and inflating the stakes of morality and reality in response to the simulacral weightlessness of postmodern hyperreality. As she puts it, "in a simulated society which typically stages reality in order to 'prove' its existence, melodrama offers a way to assert the 'actual' drama of life. . . . Its hyperbole and emotional heightening correspond to the difficulty of naming the reality it strives to locate."[104] Seen from this perspective, the melodramatic excesses of *A Current Affair* and other tabloid media forms (including especially the daytime talk shows, where melodrama is heightened perhaps in direct proportion to the elevation of pervasive and increasing uncertainties about the "reality" of guests) serve a function that parallels the "reality-based" cop shows' overproduction of signs of the real (to which I have pointed in chapters 1 and 2). Indeed, the way in which *A Current Affair* makes heavy use of recycled popular-cultural sound and image tracks in its narration of the day's events only exacerbates the logic whereby the hyperreal implosion of any categorical boundary between "reality" and "representation" calls forth a kind of postmodern melodrama capable of reasserting, in Joyrich's terms, the " 'actual' drama of life." The close but somewhat contradictory connection between *A Current Affair*'s tones of melodramatic populism and its ironic use of stylistic bricolage can thus be linked at the most fundamental level to postmodern problematics of the image.

Gender Trouble: Disturbing Norms, Unsettling Histories

We're a show about people who wouldn't make the network news.

—Maureen O'Boyle, *A Current Affair* anchor [105]

Tabloid television is often taken to task for ostensibly ignoring issues around party politics and government policy making. What the tabloid media may lack in attention to the official political system, however, they make up for with their intense interest in the gender politics of everyday life. Consequently, among the most interesting of *A Current Affair*'s preoccupations emerge in its stories of gender nonconformity. Whereas, as I've suggested earlier, tabloid television news work may (like all journalistic discourse) sometimes reify notions of "normality" and "abnormality," because of the combination of its irreverent irony and its emphasis on phenomena that exceed the boundaries of the normal, *A Current Affair*'s styles of reportage often perform an inverse operation that disturbs and unsettles norms, particularly those that have to do with cultural constructions of gender. Consider, as a case in point, the 1989 report about Billy Tipton, a well-known jazz saxophone player and pianist. During the course of his sixty-year-long career, Tipton performed with the likes of Duke Ellington and Frank Sinatra. According to *A Current Affair*, he was also a "family man." Together, he and Kitty Oakes, his wife of nearly twenty years, adopted and raised three sons. Billy even served as a scoutmaster.

Billy Tipton died in 1989 at the age of seventy-four. Near the end of his life, although he suffered from a bleeding ulcer, Billy refused to visit a doctor. He died in the arms of his son, Billy Tipton Jr. Moments after his death, the younger Billy learned, from a paramedic, the secret that had kept his father from seeking medical attention for his deteriorating condition: Billy Tipton Sr. was a *woman*. Before his death, none of the other family members—including Kitty—were aware of Tipton's "anatomical sex."[106] When they married, Billy told Kitty that he was "unable to be as a normal man" because of injuries he had sustained in a car accident. In all their years together, the couple never had sex. Says Kitty, "It didn't matter, because he gave me . . . a warmth, and a love, and a caring and support. . . . This is what I got." Throughout their marriage, they slept in separate rooms. Nevertheless, Oakes proclaims without equivocation that Billy Tipton "*was the perfect husband every woman dreams of.*"

The family is one of the primary sites for the operationalization of norms. In the Billy Tipton story, however, family norms are violated. One might argue that tabloid television's emphasis on nonconformity to norms works to strengthen the system of social disciplines and punishments to which those who deviate are regularly subjected. Graham Knight, for example, observes that tabloid journalism's "fascination" with "the threat of menace inscribed in those outside the boundaries of the normal" is tied to mechanisms by which power strives "to differentiate, divide, and exclude in order to produce relations of dependency, inequality, control."[107] Like all hegemonies, though, a normalizing one is never finalized but is instead always in process and so constantly subjected to interrogation, negotiation, and contestation. Because norms are necessarily and profoundly unstable, and because tabloid television devotes so much energy to their detailed examination, it rarely reproduces them in any kind of straightforward way. On the contrary, it regularly invites viewers to question the validation of some gendered practices as "normal" and the invalidation of others as "abnormal" (which is not to deny that some viewers undoubtedly make a conservative sense of many tabloid stories and so read them in a way that affirms established gender norms).

One way in which the tabloid media approach norms is to question their capacity to account adequately for the wide range of ways in which people experience and understand their lives in the late-twentieth-century United States—a point that emerges repeatedly in the October 1993 "Am I Normal?" edition of *Oprah*. The sheer volume of tabloid media images of gender nonconformity seems to render the very idea of the "normal" inadequate, incredible, and beside the point. Viewers whose identities and experiences engender an acute awareness of the mismatch between social norms and various aspects of their own lives have a particularly powerful incentive to produce counternormalizing meanings from tabloid television's images of nonconformity and marginal normality. The tabloid media's special interest in stories that outstrip the explanatory power of norms implies the failure of norms to represent the complexity of social experience and so creates opportunities to refuse norms altogether. In the Billy Tipton story, Kitty Oakes refuses patriarchal norms that govern the relationship between marital intimacy and sexuality and thus refutes the judgment that her "deceptive" and "abnormal" marriage of twenty years was a failure. In her humorously ironic characterization of Tipton as "the perfect husband every woman dreams of," Oakes implicitly criticizes normal patriarchal domesticity. The story of Billy and Kitty denaturalizes conventional patriarchal relationships, challenges heteronormativity, and suggests that, as the saying goes, the best man for the job may be a woman. Both the humor and the seriousness of Oakes's "perfect husband" remark assuredly strike a resounding chord for a good many viewers. Her refusal of normalizing judgments is thus likely to be pleasurable for at least some audience members who are similarly aware of the inadequacy of patriarchal norms. Tabloid television's abundant displays of "deviance" do not therefore necessarily reinforce norms. On the contrary, they often volatilize the "reality" of norms and implode the difference between the normal and the abnormal, just as television's copiousness of images destabilizes the boundary between reality and representation.

A *Current Affair*'s story about Tipton's lifelong performance of masculinity thus questions regulatory norms that are produced and enforced at the sites of gender and sexuality. Judith Butler argues that the regulatory functions of conventional gender identity are concealed by the notion that gender is determined by one's psychic interior, when it is in fact produced by "public and social discourse" that its subjects enact bodily through various forms of performativity.[108] Liberal philosophical and political discourse supports this concealment by maintaining a dichotomous separation between "individual" (interior) psychic space and "social" (exterior) public space.[109] However, certain forms of cultural practice can draw attention to various forces of control, concealment, and normalization. By foregrounding gender as a mode of performativity, cross-dressing, for example, "fully subverts the distinction between inner and outer . . . space and effectively mocks" the idea that gender is expressive of an interior psychic essence, as well as the very "notion of a true gender identity." As Butler puts it, "*in imitating gender, drag implicitly reveals the imitative structure of gender itself—as well as its contingency.*"[110]

Billy Tipton's lifelong "masquerade" of masculinity, as it was dubbed by A *Current Affair* reporter Mike Watkiss, was not quite the same as drag. It did not, in itself, mobilize the sort of disruptive, gender-troubling counter-performativity of which Butler writes, for the simple reason that it didn't foreground itself *as a performance*. In the narrativization of Billy Tipton's life, however, A *Current Affair* does foreground performativity. For example, the elaborate use of puns (which are typical of tabloid television's polyvocally playful discourse) around the concepts of "performance" and "composition" foregrounds linguistic undecidability and, by extension, the very indeterminacy of Billy Tipton's sexual and gender identity (which necessarily questions the postulation that each subject has a "true" and stable gender identity). Thus the story focuses repeatedly on the convergence of Tipton's career as a musical composer and performer with his lifelong performance in the role of a man. "Billy Tipton was . . . something of a legend," proclaims Watkiss's narration.

> He was great on piano. He was tremendous on sax. Billy backed up Sinatra. He played with the Duke. . . . Yet for all his many accomplishments, Billy Tipton will probably best be remembered for his ability to act. Because, you see, Billy Tipton was actually a woman, a jazzy gender bender who, for nearly sixty years, turned the entire world into a stage while composing for herself a brand-new life as Mr. Billy Tipton.

This reportorial narration is spoken over numerous documentary images of a very masculine Billy Tipton, who is pictured variously with fellow musicians, alone at his piano, and standing alongside his wife, their baby on his arm. Immediately following Watkiss's opening remarks, we cut to a close-up of Kitty Oakes, who says that Billy "was the perfect husband every woman dreams of." These images and this testimony play on the artifice inherent in Tipton's "performance" or self-"composition," underscoring h/er credibility in the role. It is precisely the credibility of h/er performance as a man that renders incredible the idea that s/he possessed a "natural" gender. The *Current Affair* story trades heavily on the shock experienced by Tipton's wife and children when they learned h/er secret and invites television viewers to identify with the family members' extreme surprise and disbelief. This disbelief implicitly reinforces the credibility of Tipton's masculinity and also, therefore, the incredibility of the concept of natural gender identity. Says Billy Tipton Jr., regarding the jolting discovery:

> One of the paramedics turned to me and asked . . . if my dad had had a sex change at any time in his life. And I became outraged at this. At first it was a, it was a great shock . . . I could not believe that this had happened. But it was only moments later that I told myself, I said, "Hey, this, nothing's changed." No matter what he was, I loved him just the way he was.

Watkiss observes that "it seems Billy's deception was the perfect composition." Accompanying Watkiss's observation is a still image that emphasizes the performativity of Tipton's enactment of masculinity. In the image, Billy, dressed in masculine clothes, stands on a stage, in front of a

Billy Tipton: family man.

curtain, alongside a television screen. Both he and the screen face the camera. Tipton is pointing at the image on the screen, which contains three men in costume (one of whom is wearing an obviously fake mustache). These men are also on a stage, in front of a curtain. Their exaggerated gestures signify that they are in character, performing. Alongside the television screen sit two more men, one of whom is watching the television while the other watches Tipton. This virtual *en abime* suggests the equivalence of Tipton's gender/performance[111] with the act performed by the characters pictured on the television screen near which s/he stands. Although it is but one of many photographic images used in the story, we might say that this *en abime*, with its emphasis on performativity, is paradigmatic of the rhetorical strategy brought to bear on Billy Tipton's life by *A Current Affair.* By demonstrating that h/er life as "Mr. Billy Tipton" was purely performative—that even h/er wife of twenty years knew h/er *only through h/er performance* of the (culturally constituted) attributes of masculinity—the story implicitly questions the postulation that Tipton had a preexisting gender identity against which we might measure h/er "act" or h/er masculine attributes.

In the Tipton story, we find a popular-cultural example of deconstructive sensibilities that are often associated almost exclusively with academic theory. At the same time, however, this story contains traces of the same normalizing assumptions that it questions. In the Tipton story, there are at least two different subtextual discourses competing for dominance and for truth effects. The first entails the idea that Billy Tipton's gender identity was purely performative and therefore questions normalizing assumptions about the "truth" of gender identity in general.[112] The second suggests, contradictorily, that Tipton had betrayed h/er "true self" with h/er "deceptive" masquerade. Thus Watkiss notes that "almost everyone close to Billy seems to think the masquerade started as Billy's way of breaking into the male-dominated world of music." From this perspective, Tipton's lifelong performance was little more than "a way for a talented young woman to be taken seriously in a place where women weren't always welcome, especially sixty years ago." To be sure, this explanation criticizes patriarchal power, as the following exchange between Watkiss and Oakes demonstrates:

> *Oakes:* Society has said, "Women: you're not smart enough, you're not strong enough, you don't have the talent. We are going to block you out of the male world."
> *Watkiss:* And Billy Tipton proved them wrong.
> *Oakes (gleefully):* That's right!

At the same time, however, this perspective mitigates and undermines Tipton's implicit challenge to conventional assumptions about gender identity by suggesting that "inside" was a "real woman" who sacrificed her *true self* for her music.

Nevertheless, the gender trouble stirred up by the Tipton story is not entirely calmed by the suggestion that Tipton's performance was nothing more than a deception necessitated by the music industry's exclusion of women from its ranks. It remains to be answered why Tipton continued the performance (if its purpose was purely instrumental) for decades after h/er career was established. And it remains to be known why Tipton would embrace h/er role so completely. Moreover, most of the photographic evidence and personal testimony presented in the story suggests uncannily that Tipton was immensely happy as a "man." Finally, Tipton's own son posits that the sex discrimination hypothesis cannot in itself adequately resolve the issue of Billy's gender/performance, and that the elder Tipton should therefore "have left something behind" to explain. Thus the story's more normalizing subtext, which implies that Tipton sacrificed her *true* gender identity for career opportunities, is not fully capable of silencing the norm-disturbing possibility that it equally proposes: that gender identity is nothing more than a performative and regulatory social fiction.

The norm disruption that lies at the heart of many tabloid stories can be understood as a product of multiplicity, dispersion, and multivocality. A quick detour through Michel Foucault's famous critique of "the historian's history" will provide some insight into these characteristics of tabloid discourse.[113] Foucault argues that this historian's history "metaphysically" locates the dominant sense of the present in the origins of the past.

It violently "dissolves" the multiplicities of the past into "an ideal continuity—as a teleological movement or a natural process." [114] Events and objects nevertheless remain multiple and disparate, however, and thus retain their capacity for resignification through insertion into different discursive practices (despite historians' attempts to discipline this unruly potential by producing coherent and unified narrative discourses).

Following Nietzsche, Foucault opposes "genealogy" to "history." Whereas "history" depicts the current regime as the inevitable expression of an unbroken continuity rooted in "human nature" and a presumptively teleological social evolution, genealogy, by contrast, foregrounds discontinuities and contradictions that are maleficently muted in conventional historical narratives. Genealogy thus stresses incommensurability and seeks to restore the forgotten multiplicities, repressed heterogeneities, and erased alterities of the past to expand the possibilities of the present and the potentialities of the future (which the historian's history narrows or closes down). Genealogy "introduces discontinuity into our very being—as it divides our emotions, dramatizes our instincts, multiplies our body and sets it against itself." It negates similarity and uniformity and rejects even the principle of the self's identity with itself. It has three privileged modalities: (1) "parody," which revives "the buffoonery of history" whereby the ponderous and venerated truths of the historian are subjected to the genealogist's laughter; (2) "dissociation," which multiplies and disperses identities that history strives to fix and singularize; and (3) the "sacrifice" of the contemplative subject, which is "directed against truth" and seeks to destroy orthodoxies. Genealogy teaches one how to "laugh at the solemnities of the origin." It is "history in the form of a concerted carnival." [115]

As we shall see in the next chapter, tabloid media often foreground contradiction and discontinuity in this very way. Their signifying practices multiply, disperse, and destabilize the self. They provoke a laughter that undermines the solemnities of the origin. A case in point that I shall discuss here is *A Current Affair*'s 1989 presentation of the story of Charles McGuire, for his is an unruly body that resonates with undisciplined meanings and overspills the identity that is socially assigned to it. We are informed that McGuire, who is running for a seat on the Houston City Council during an election year fraught with "mudslinging and scandal," may be "Houston's perfect candidate," as "she's a gal with nothing to hide." Wearing a bright red dress that matches the color of his lipstick and beaming with confidence, McGuire poses a rhetorical question: "What're they gonna find on me? . . . If I get elected as a transvestite, then what're they gonna say next?" Over the falsetto voice of Frankie Valle singing his pop single "Walk like a Man," we see shots of McGuire's lower body and then full figure, wearing the same red dress as s/he ascends the steps to Houston's City Hall. A reporter's voice-over observes that Charles/Catherine McGuire is a "Texas Tootsie walking a fine line in the land where men are men and, in this case, so is the woman."

"Born Charles McGuire, this cowboy made a name for himself as a football star in high school," then moved on to Texas A&M "to rough it out in the prestigious corps." As the image track cuts from a shot of marching military men superimposed over a still photo of Charles in uniform to an extreme close-up of perfume bottles on a makeup table where Catherine applies lipstick in a mirror, we are told, however, that "all that macho upbringing couldn't suppress his secret desire." Although "Catherine McGuire is a self-made man who built an empire in road construction," he prefers "to accessorize his hard hat with high heels." A camera pans to follow a bulldozer backing across a construction site and comes on Charles wearing his bright red dress as he confers with a burly worker. Later he displays a black sequined gown and comments that "it takes a real man to wear this dress. See, it slits up both sides."

Charles speaks candidly about the "rough road" he has traveled as a "cross-dressing candidate." The "first question everybody asks me is which restroom do I use. And, uh, usually I say, 'If you was dressed like this, which restroom would you use?' " Says A Current Affair's reporter Robin Dorian, "Don't let the outfit fool you. Charles, aka Catherine McGuire, has the muscle, and legs, to stand his ground in this political battle." And stand his ground he does, as we see images of a smartly dressed drag queen passing out campaign buttons to Houston voters and hear Lou Reed's "Take a Walk on the Wild Side" on the sound track. Charles "turned a head or two in Washington, D.C.," we learn, when he "attended President Bush's inaugural ball." But "now he's got his own agenda." To wit: "We've been through some hard times, and now all we want to do is get it built back up. And if it takes a guy in a dress to do it, I don't think the voters of Houston care."

Although news discourse often comes closer to resembling the historian's history than Foucault's genealogy, it is striking that this Current Affair story makes no attempt to discipline the contradictions embodied in the figure of Charles/Catherine McGuire into yielding up a monovocal narrative. Rather, it places contradiction and discontinuity in the foreground. Charles McGuire's origins in the homosocial worlds of Texas high school football and the A&M military corps are not found to contain the essential truth of his identity. Instead, the normality of his youth (he was even voted "most popular" at his high school) is presented as simply discontinuous with the marginality of his desire to cross-dress, which is now central to his identity. When McGuire comments that "it takes a real man to wear this dress," he sharpens the rupture that divides him from himself. His comment invites laughter at the solemnities of masculinity implied in his own

Catherine McGuire on the job.

Charles/Catherine McGuire: engendering contradiction.

Charles/Catherine McGuire on the campaign trail.

"macho" origins. In the *Current Affair* story, McGuire's identity is dispersed across the domains of the masculine and the feminine, volatilizing and relativizing both.

The story introduces discontinuity into McGuire's very being, multiplying his body and setting it against itself. The contradictions between masculinity and femininity that McGuire literally embodies are neither smoothed out nor papered over. The juxtaposition of images of the football star Charles with those of Catherine having her hair done brings them into stark opposition. The image of Charles wearing a bright red dress to his construction job is powerfully contradictory as well. To see the drag queen confer with a husky, male, blue-collar subordinate inverts ordinary power relations within a patriarchal regime whose reproduction depends on normalization. Indeed, the very premise of a story about a political candidate openly flaunting his own difference represents a cultural inversion of no small proportions, for U.S. electoral politics, especially in the age of electronic reproduction, entail the simulation of a kind of hypernormality (consider the Gipper's traditionally chivalrous masculinity, or the hallucinatory "family values" of the Bush and Quayle administration).[116] While normal U.S. electoral politics requires that candidates search for the skeletons in their opponents' closets, McGuire invites Americans to admire the dresses he keeps in his. Thus the McGuire story parodies electoral campaigning in a media culture in much the same way as *A Current Affair*'s ritualistic uncrowning of Donald Trump implicitly lampoons the artificiality of officially staged photo ops.

The 1989 story of Jeffrey/Sarah Luiz brings *A Current Affair*'s concern for gender nonconformity together with its interest in melodramatic tales of personal victimization at the hands of an impassive bureaucratic authority. If the report on Charles/Catherine McGuire playfully foregrounds and heightens our sense of the discontinuities of the self, the story of Jeffrey/Sarah melodramatically associates identity dispersion with melancholic suffering. Whereas Charles/Catherine celebrates h/is difference from other candidates for public office, Jeffrey agonizes over the fact that a tightfisted insurance company has blocked h/im from h/is lifelong dream of becoming Sarah. H/is family is highly supportive of h/is decision to have gender reassignment surgery, as h/is mother and sister explain on camera. The insurance company, however, is not, and their refusal to pay for h/is operation has left Jeffrey/Sarah floundering in a "transsexual twilight zone." H/is three years of estrogen treatments have given h/im a distinctly feminine voice and appearance, but doctors say that s/he can no longer take the hormones without undergoing the surgery—surgery that s/he can't afford. Says Luiz, "I'm like a woman on top and a man on the bottom. It's like odd, I mean I get flipped out every time I, you know, take my clothes off. It's so bizarre." S/he explains that "this isn't a place I ever wanted to be stuck in. I mean, I didn't set out to become a half-and-half person. I meant to become a woman, physically, to match my inside. But now I've been left trapped in this and gone through so much pain."

Whereas the stories of Billy Tipton and Charles/Catherine McGuire, each in its own way, subvert conventional gender categories, that of Jeffrey/Sarah Luiz highlights the disorienting dysphoria that can accompany the destabilization and dissolution of established identity moorings. Jeffrey/Sarah combats this dysphoria by invoking the reassuring solidities of essentialism in a way that clarifies more than it clouds the gender picture. "I've always felt like a woman in a man's body," s/he notes. A *Current Affair*'s reporter adds that Jeffrey/Sarah is only "trying to correct a mistake he says Mother Nature made," an observation whose very language reinscribes the traditional connotative association between femininity and the natural along with the idea of innate gender. But the reinscription of these sense-making solidities is itself troubled by the boundary-disturbing unconventionality of Jeffrey/Sarah's transgendered status, which is not easily contained by even the discourses of essentialism, especially given A *Current Affair*'s tabloidist emphasis on the liminal zone in which its subject finds h/imself trapped; for h/is insurance company's stinginess has locked h/im in a kind of prolonged antigendered stasis—"a nightmare no-man's land which she can't escape: half man, half woman." Consequently the story's appeal to a form of gender essentialism is considerably complicated by its subject's predicament and by its sympathetic support for Jeffrey/Sarah's desire to exert some measure of control over the performance of h/is own gender identity.

The inversions, transgressions of normality, and celebrations of contradiction that characterize many of A *Current Affair*'s gender-troubling stories are the apex of tabloid television, "quality" journalism's disreputable Other. Tabloid television's playfully ironic discourse starkly opposes the monovocality and seriousness of much mainstream journalism. Allon White writes that "seriousness always has more to do with power than with content. The authority to designate what is to be taken seriously (and the authority to enforce reverential solemnity in certain contexts) is a way of creating and maintaining power." [117] The solemnity of official news underwrites the power-bloc's attempts to monopolize the production of truth as well as the power to designate what shall count as significant issues. The playful irreverence and contradictoriness of tabloid television should be interpreted not as signs of its journalistic inferiority but rather as evidence of the countervailing powers of the popular.

4   Fantastic Populism: A Walk on the Wild
Side of Tabloid Culture

Each society has its own régime of truth: the types of discourse accepted as true, the
mechanisms that make it possible to distinguish between truth and error. —Alan Sheridan, *Michel Foucault: The Will to Truth*[1]

Asampling of the U.S. supermarket tabloids *Weekly World News* and
Sun reveals a diverse body of fantastic reportage. In 1991, for example, the
Weekly World News writes that a vintage World War II Messerschmitt airplane
has been strafing tourists as they bask in the sun along the edge of the Ber-
muda Triangle (a "time warp travel expert" claims to have knowledge of
a dozen similar cases); that "the ghostly apparition of a beautiful young
girl" has been "terrorizing three fraternity brothers at George Mason University" by spanking them while they sleep; and that four Spanish monks
have captured Satan himself, whom they describe as "having fiery red eyes,
long, pointy fingernails," and very bad breath.[2] The *Sun*, meanwhile, reports that extremely sensitive microphones "placed around the grounds at
Graceland, Elvis Presley's Memphis mansion," have recorded "melancholy
musical medleys by the King—performed from beyond the grave"; that the
$1.5 billion Hubble telescope has photographed an invasion force of more
than forty alien warships headed toward Earth; and that "President Bush
is constantly protected by invisible bodyguards" whose presence has been
discovered by a twenty-three-year-old college student using infrared photography.[3]

These stories are "fantastic" in the sense that they are imbued with an
aura of otherworldly incredibility, from the perspective of mainstream
thought and belief. Popular culture has a long historical association with
the fantastic, which is the "other" of the regime of truth established with
the modernization of Western societies and the Westernization of modern
societies. Their "otherness" largely constitutes the "unbelievability" of fantastic tabloid knowledges, which are often labeled "superstitious" and are
primitivized and juvenilized in a variety of other ways. Fantastic knowledges
can be understood as *evasive* ones, for they evade the explanatory powers of
official truths that serve to extend the *social* power of dominant interests and
alliances. Under postmodern conditions, the expansion of media networks
and the fragmentation of knowledge in general enable the fantastic ways

of knowing that modernity has sought to eviscerate to instead thrive and multiply.

The *Weekly World News* and the *Sun* are journalism's ghettos of deviant knowledge, and there is evidence to support the assumption that they circulate most heavily among socially ghettoized readers — people who are marginalized by the intersecting effects of class, race, ethnicity, gender, age, and educational distribution.[4] As I have noted in previous chapters, the differences between conventional and tabloid journalism are sometimes quite fuzzy.[5] In this chapter, however, I will analyze some forms of fantastic storytelling that bring differences between tabloid and mainstream journalism into perhaps their sharpest focus. As fantastic tabloidism sharpens these differences, it also challenges both the substantive contents of conventional journalism and the stance toward knowledge on which it relies.[6]

Pierre Bourdieu's major work on taste demonstrates that the social legitimacy accorded to cultural objects deemed legitimate and the social power of the people who value and consume them are mutually constitutive.[7] Bourdieu gives the name "cultural capital" to the most legitimated tastes and discursive competencies, the bulk of which are, like economic capital, possessed by the socially powerful and privileged.[8] John Fiske, however, proposes a distinction between "official" and "popular" forms of cultural capital that is missing from Bourdieu's theory.[9] Official cultural capital comprises tastes and competencies that are privileged and promoted by cultural institutions such as schools and art galleries. By contrast, popular cultural capital is made up of tastes and competencies produced outside of, and often against, official cultural institutions.[10] Fiske thus suggests that analysts of popular culture should extend Bourdieu's work to include forms of "popular-cultural capital" that can be used to advance the interests of disempowered social formations.[11] The convergence of the fantastic tabloids' patterns of circulation with their dismissal or derogation by official arbiters of taste and judgment suggests that the tabloids are an important source of popular-cultural capital.

Fantastic Tabloids as Menippean Satire

Madness makes men look at the world with different eyes, not dimmed by "normal," that is by commonplace ideas and judgments. In folk grotesque, madness is a gay parody of official reason, of the narrow seriousness of official "truth." It is a "festive" madness. —
Mikhail Bakhtin, *Rabelais and His World*[12]

In his major work on Dostoevsky, Bakhtin developed a theory of what he called "menippean satire," which encompasses a group of "seriocomic" literary and dramatic genres running from antiquity into the twentieth century. Although his work on the menippea is less well known than his theories of the carnivalesque, it is not unrelated to them. More important for our concerns, it provides a productive framework for the analysis of fantastic supermarket tabloidism. Menippean satire is both flexible and mobile, as it permeates a number of different genres.[13] It forms a series of counterpoints to the official cultures that work institutionally to manage heterogeneity. Official truths strive to iron out contradiction and drown out alternative voices. Official cultures immerse people in symbols, rituals, and practices that stabilize social order. They seek to "absolutize a given condition of existence" (127). By contrast, the menippean perspective emphasizes perpetual renewal as it "transports" people to alternative imaginary spaces. It carries otherworldly accents and images of a "life that has left its normal rut, almost a 'world turned inside out' " (163). It resonates with a laughter "directed toward . . . a shift of authorities and truths, a shift of world orders. . . . This is . . . a laughter that contains a whole outlook on the world" (127). It resists easy incorporation into the official sense of the world. Menippean satire parodically and irreverently juxtaposes elements of official or learned discourse with scandalously common forms of speech and thought. It thrives on the grotesque. It exaggerates wildly. It produces exceedingly fantastic tales that defamiliarize the normal order of things. The menippea makes a mockery of socially legitimated cultural forms by bringing them into contact with the absurd and the outlandish, the disreputable and the base. That menippean satire parodies the discourses of official culture does not mean it simplistically negates or "nakedly rejects" them, however. Rather, the menippea exposes what Bakhtin calls the "laughing aspects" of official discourse ("everything has its parody, that is, its laughing aspect," although official cultures typically repress this "laughing aspect"). Menippean satire operates like "an entire system of crooked mirrors, elongating, diminishing, distorting in various directions and to various degrees" (127).

Bakhtin's thinking here bears some relationship to Michel Foucault's analyses of discursive power in the modern age.[14] Foucault has demonstrated that the operations of power in the modern Western world depend on the production of both well-disciplined subjects and well-disciplined knowledges. His concept of "power/knowledge" specifies the integrated social production of discourse, knowledge, discipline, and power. Consequently the connection between the disciplined production of discourse and the discursive production of social discipline is intimate. Bakhtin's theorization of social *indiscipline* may therefore be usefully read as a correlate to Foucault's theorization of discipline. Bakhtin stresses the undisciplined nature of the carnivalesque in general and the discursive indisciplinarity of menippean satire in particular. Its "experimental fantasticality" produces decentered perspectives.[15] Philip Holland writes that "to any vision of a completed system of truth, the menippea suggests some element outside the system."[16] When official knowledge collides with its laughing aspect "there is a weakening of its one-sided rhetorical seriousness, its rationality, its singular meaning, its dogmatism."[17]

Because tabloids are texts, it is useful to compare some of the textual characteristics of menippean satire with those of supermarket tabloids. Menippean satire features a "three-planed construction" involving heaven, earth, and hell, between which characters and events move freely. The menippea produces an "organic combination . . . of the free fantastic, the symbolic" and the "mystical-religious," all conveyed with a pervasive air of "crude slum naturalism." This "slum naturalism" anchors the disorienting fantasticality of menippean rhetoric in the gritty realities of everyday life, for the menippea is concerned with "the adventures of an idea or a truth" in its movement through the world. Moreover, the slum naturalism of fantastic menippeanism suggests a certain affinity with postmodern culture, for it implodes distinctions between the ordinary and the incredible, thus combining categories that are held apart by modernist epistemologies. Finally, the menippea contains overtones of "philosophical universalism" and "a capacity to contemplate the world on the broadest possible scale" (though "complex and extensive modes of argumentation" fall away). What remains are "naked 'ultimate questions' with an ethical and practical bias."[18]

This is familiar tabloid terrain. Consider, for example, the *Weekly World News* front-page story for August 20, 1991. Under the headline "Guardian Angel Michael Landon Appears to 8 People!" a full two-page photograph features a larger-than-life Landon gazing benevolently at the reader. Opposite Landon's image is the smaller figure of his former schoolteacher, Rita Moll, who looks up toward the heavens. The background is composed of fluffy white clouds against a gray sky. Inset print tells the story of how Landon came to the frail and aged Moll in the middle of the night and cured her of stomach cancer. On the following two pages are pictures of seven other ordinary people from across the United States, along with their respective stories of how Landon intervened in their troubled lives. An adjacent photograph pictures Landon in white robes, his head surrounded by an angelic aura. The "slum naturalism" of the stories (and pictures) of the blessed eight provides the backdrop for each of their miraculous testimonials. The passage of the concrete embodiment of mystico-religious wonder through the everyday world is chronicled in the stories of Landon's contact with his eight beneficiaries.[19] It is notable that this story collapses at least three distinct "realities" into a single fantastic simulacrum: that of the "real" Michael Landon, who had recently died of cancer; that of his most popular fictional TV character, Jonathan Smith (a guardian angel who returned to Earth each week to help people in need in the series *Highway to Heaven*); and that of Moll and the other "ordinary folks" in whose troubled lives Landon/Smith intervened. Such postmodern implosions help to facilitate the contemporary menippean imagination.

Menippean characters often experience "unusual, abnormal moral and psychic states." In menippean narratives, "insanity of all sorts," "split personality," and "unrestrained daydreaming" rupture the unity of stable identities so that "the possibilities of another . . . life are revealed."[20] The fragmentation of identity in menippean satire can be seen to undermine the process whereby language and other representational systems work to position people stably within both semiotic and social structures, for the menippea emphasizes moments when such positionings break down. It should come as no surprise that narratives about unstable, fragmented, and undisciplined selves are culturally popular, for they metonymically evoke an imagined breakdown of the orders that strive to constitute selves as well-disciplined and unified subjects held in social stasis.

A host of tabloid stories feature radical identity shifts, personality doublings, multiple selves, outbreaks of insanity, and cross-species hybridizations (involving people and animals, animals and animals, people and aliens, animals and aliens, and even aliens and inanimate objects).[21] For example, David Burton (1991) writes in the *Weekly World News* that Catherine Chevalier, a top psychic, can split herself into two people in order to go to different places at the same time. Chevalier says that anybody is capable of performing this feat.[22] This story raises obvious, appealing possibilities for evading everyday structures of surveillance and discipline, imposed workplace obligations, and so forth. Many similar tabloid stories imagine radically unstable, fragmented, and incoherent identities and forms of consciousness. A related subset foregrounds the noncoincidence of aberrant or exceptional individuals with their expected social roles and capacities. One, for example, features a sweet seventy-four-year-old woman who is a successful trainer of professional boxers. Another highlights a sightless man who uses x-ray vision to "see" cancer and other diseases before doctors can.[23] For those who don't feel comfortably aligned with the reigning sense of normality, the tabloids' excessive parade of unusual and exceptional characters can be both pleasurable and empowering.[24] Salient examples from the tabloids include recurrent stories of gender transformation, for instance, "Sex-Change Dad Is Now Son's 2nd Mom," which appeared in the *Sun*. This is a story about a husband and father whose "heart wasn't in" his masculinity, so he became a woman. She still lives with her wife and son, though both adults "are like sisters now," each dating other men.[25] Stories like this foreground the instability and alterability of socially constituted identities.

Menippean situations are often organized around "scandal scenes," eccentricities, inappropriate speech and performance, and "all sorts of violations of the . . . established norms of behavior and etiquette." The menippea questions the dominant cultural order by violating or inverting the norms, mores, and systems of etiquette that work to hold it in place. "Scandals and eccentricities destroy the . . . wholeness of the world, they make a breach in the stable, normal ('seemly') course of human affairs and events."[26] Instances of eccentric or inappropriate behavior reported in tabloid stories include things such as transgressions of "appropriate" maternal conduct and "useless" dispositions of economic capital.[27] Menippean scandal scenes often challenge official representations of the powerful. Tabloid examples include a *Weekly World News* report that "George Washington Grew Pot" and a *Sun* story revealing that former U.S. presidents Van Buren, Buchanan, and Arthur were closeted gays.[28]

In fantastic tabloidism, the organic fusion of diverse menippean elements produces a horrifically scandalous textual amalgam that violates all the norms of official journalism. Legitimate journalism carefully disciplines its discourse, enabling some knowledges to exert their powers through its texts while excluding the possibility of others even being spoken of.[29] In "real news," categories such as "science" and "religion," "economics" and "foreign affairs," "politics" and "entertainment," "reality" and "fantasy" are separated by rigid boundaries. The fantastic tabloids rigorously deny the integrity of official epistemological categories, though. Science and religion, for example, might be inextricably intertwined. Thus, according to one tabloid report, Soviet geologists were astonished when an oil drill dug through the gates of hell, releasing a "terrifying winged creature" and enabling the scientists to hear the screams of the damned through the shaft in the ground.[30] Through displacements and a kind of metonymy, stories like this implicitly criticize entrenched forms of power/knowledge by expressing and speaking to popular anxieties about the ecological fallout and other human consequences associated with the galloping will to technological mastery over nature; this will to technomastery is driven by an antidemocratic scientific priesthood that, intentionally or not, by virtue of the specialized complexity of its knowledges, excludes ordinary people from participating in its decision-making processes and everyday practices.[31]

In menippean tabloidism, then, the categories that structure socially dominant knowledges, including mainstream science and official journalism, interpenetrate and play promiscuously off one another. Earthly political machinations might be bound up with the activities of aliens from outer space or figures from the worlds of sport and entertainment. Nor must official proclamations of death bring an end to one's political career in this life. Thus various reports in the *Weekly World News* have George Bush receiving

Apocalyptic cover/age.

One for the (se)X-Files.

important advice from professional wrestler "Nature Boy" Ric Flair, former president John F. Kennedy, and an unnamed space alien captured in 1990 by the CIA.[32] A small photograph of the same alien, though now shaking hands with Bill Clinton, appears in the upper-right corner of the *Weekly World News* for June 7, 1994. The headline on this issue announces that "Twelve U.S. Senators Are Space Aliens!" Among the twelve senators pictured on the cover are John Glenn, Sam Nunn, and Orrin Hatch. Reports such as these laughingly fuel popular suspicions of officialdom's representations of its own doings and buttress a skeptical belief in the idea that *they*—the officials—*never* tell *us* the full story. The suspicion that governs the informational regions of a popular-cultural economy expresses displaced resentment over the capture and control of key areas of public life by dominant social formations. The menippean elements of supermarket tabloids thus suit them well for circulation within a system of popular-cultural capital.

The Unsolved Mysteries of Everyday Life

When convention and science offer us no answers, might we not finally turn to the fantastic as a plausibility?—FBI special agent Fox Mulder, *The X-Files*[33]

The critical analysis of tabloids must do more than inventory their textual characteristics. It must read texts against the contexts of their popular consumption and so open questions about their "situational thrust." It must seek to recuperate the progressive potential of texts even when it is repressed and "half-denied" within the texts themselves. It must recover the critical aspects of popular texts by amplifying the voices of opposition that may be muffled within them.[34] Fantastic tabloid texts do address specific relations of power that are operationalized in the cultures of everyday life. They do this in ways that create and circulate a menippean sense of the world. This initiates what we might call rhetorics of transformation that imaginatively deform many of the forces that shape the contours of daily life. Fantastic tabloid rhetorics produce skewed perspectives that interrogate the normal order of things. They do not monologically criticize existing social relations, for they thwart monologism of all sorts. They are rife with gaps, excesses, and contradictions that are difficult to resolve into singularities. Fantastic tabloid texts can be made to mean in a variety of different ways. Some of these ways underwrite dominating modalities of social power while others question or challenge them.

Gender power is central to the dynamics of everyday life. Fantastic tabloids frequently transfigure gender conventions and relations in interesting ways. In the September 12, 1989, edition of the *Sun*, for example, Dr. Bruno Grosse tells the story of Martin Camacho, who was "transformed" into a woman when he was struck by a bolt of lightning. Grosse writes that "the high-voltage jolt permanently altered . . . Camacho's genetic structure, causing female hormones to take control of his body! . . . 'Sometimes I wish I could die,' cries Martin. 'But I figure living life as a woman is better than living no life at all. Still, it's turned my entire world upside down.' "[35]

The *Sun* story explains that following the "tragedy," Camacho was fired from his job as a golf course groundskeeper and forced to accept employment as a department store cashier. Camacho is literally jolted out of his place within the gender system and repositioned in relation to its everyday mechanisms of power. This story, like so much fantastic tabloidism, is premised on the occurrence of a spectacular event that disorders the orderly and disrupts the contours of the socially constituted self. In one way, the Camacho story affirms an essentialist understanding of gender (it takes a fantastic and aberrant event to alter one's gendered identity; there is a bipolarity of gender positions). On another level, however, the story interrogates and defamiliarizes essentialist conceptions of gender. By imagining a world where gender positions are anything but inert, the story questions the stability of the boundary between the masculine and the feminine. It thus participates in an oxymoronic logic "in which everything is pregnant with its opposite." This is an alternative popular logic based on "nonexclusive opposites and permanent contradiction which transgresses the monologic true-or-false thinking that is typical of Western rationalism."[36]

The Camacho story paints a concrete image of the contingency, reversibility, and ruthlessness of gender power. Sexist voices are surely present here, as in the characterization of the transformation as a bizarre "tragedy" mysteriously visited upon Camacho. Nevertheless, the Camacho story resonates with voices of oppositionality as well. The rhetoric of "female hormones . . . tak[ing] control of [Camacho's] body" lends itself to alternative readings. A reading aligned with patriarchal power might emphasize the "inherent" danger or putative aberrance of femininity. Audiences reading against patriarchy, however, can take pleasure in the symbolic imagery of rebellion (the "female . . . taking control") and in the reversal of fortune that subjects Camacho ("the macho"?) to the effects of gendered power. The counterpatriarchal pleasures provided by the Camacho story arise from the force of its imaginative and fantastic transformation of the normal order of things—for "normal" names the discursive territory colonized and reproduced by dominant knowledges and practices (see chapter 5). The Grosse story struggles to bring its readers into a nonthreatening position of comfortable sympathy with Camacho and his wife, whose marriage has been thoroughly disrupted by the fateful lightning strike. Nevertheless, this attempt to impose a patriarchal closure on the story's imaginative possibilities ultimately fails to silence the oppositional voices it evokes.

The fantastic discourse of supermarket tabloids often taps the utopian impulse that constitutes menippean satire as a "countermodel of cultural production and desire." [37] Popular utopianism ought not to be hastily dismissed, for it typically contains the germ of a critical perspective on the current order as it works to imagine a better one.[38] It can thus at least lubricate the mechanisms of progressive social change. Henry Jenkins, for example, has traced the utopian impulses that energize the activities of a mostly female fan community whose members produce and circulate their own romance novels and music videos set in the diegetic world of *Star Trek*. His work demonstrates how fantastic texts facilitate the pleasurable imagination of alternative worlds while their critical impulses interrogate and defamiliarize the lived realities of this one. Jenkins writes that "for some women, trapped within low paying jobs or within the socially isolated sphere of the homemaker, . . . to enter fandom is to escape from the mundane into the marvelous." [39] At the same time, however, these fans crucially reorient the original *Star Trek* programs to make them reflect and engage "traditional feminine and contemporary feminist concerns, . . . sexuality and gender politics, . . . religion, family, marriage, and romance." [40] The texts that these fans generate are thus generically fantastic yet ordered around issues linked to the gender relations the fans experience in their everyday lives.

Tabloid texts are often similarly oriented around interactions between the mundane and the marvelous. For example, in April 1990 the *Weekly World News* told the story of a household washer that turned into a time machine:

> Patty Kearns loaded sheets in her new washer but that's not what came out.
>
> When the machine finished rinsing she opened the lid and found a coat like the ones George Washington and other American colonists wore over 200 years ago—in the 1700s!
>
> "This is insane," said the 26-year-old woman from Seattle. "I know I put sheets in the washer and I know I pulled this old coat out.
>
> "There's no way this could be a practical joke because I live alone and have two German shepherds that I keep in the house.
>
> "They won't let anybody in when I'm here alone so I don't know what to think. A friend of mine says my washer must have a 'time warp cycle.' And I'm beginning to think she's right."
>
> A historian has seen the colonial-style coat that Miss Kearns found in her washer and confirms that it is authentic.
>
> He seriously doubts that anybody is playing a joke on the woman because the coat is in near-perfect condition and worth a fortune.
>
> "I could sell it to a private collector or museum today for $25,000-plus," said the expert. "I'd give anything to know where it came from."

Miss Kearns has yet to decide what she'll do with the coat but says she's inclined to sell it. Meanwhile, university experts and paranormal researchers have contacted the woman about studying her washer.

They believe there is "a very real chance" that it transported the coat through time from the 18th century to the present.

"It could have something to do with radio waves generated by the motor or peculiar vibrations that occur when the washer is running," said one expert. "Then again, the coat may have been transported through a time portal. They're very rare but when they do open time has no meaning.

"The past can become the present and vice versa. And if that's what happened here, then someone in the 18th century has this woman's sheets.

"Only hard research and a thorough study of this washing machine will tell us exactly what went on. It should be an exciting piece of research." [41]

This story transforms the workaday world of mundane housework into a fantastic realm where washing machines come equipped with a "time warp cycle." Domestic machinery produces interesting and mysterious events, and even potential profits, rather than sheer drudgery (often done in the service of others). It's no coincidence that fantastic tabloid discourse quite frequently revolves around the magical transformation of the most ordinary objects and experiences (fantastic stories involving office machinery are also common). The popular fantastic evokes "the possibility of a completely different life." Bakhtin's analysis of the role of dreams in menippean narrative is relevant here. "The life seen in the dream makes ordinary life seem strange, forces one to understand and evaluate ordinary life in a new way (in the light of another glimpsed possibility)." [42] Here we have a "dream" wherein a domestic machine produces potentially staggering profits for its operator. There is thus the trace of a utopian principle that the reader is invited to contrast to the more ordinary experience of housework.

The Kearns story (like the Camacho one) is also striking for the multiplicity of readings it bears. It exemplifies the general "producerliness" of fantastic tabloids.[43] Producerly texts are incomplete, full of gaps, contradictions, and open questions. They challenge readers to produce coherence, fill in gaps, resolve contradictions, answer questions left open. The producerliness of fantastic tabloids is situated not only at the level of individual stories but also in the often contradictory relations between different stories. The fantastic tabloids' evasion of the explanatory power of dominant knowledge formations contributes crucially to their producerliness. It enables them to resist the exclusion of imaginative possibilities and thus to

avoid the imposition of closure. The tabloid's refusal to provide any definitive answer to the washing machine mystery opens the story for popular discussion and completion by its readers. Its producerliness leaves the Kearns
story open to a variety of different readings. For some readers, the Kearns
report undoubtedly evokes skeptical rejection (as tabloid stories often do).
Others will find scientific jargon about "radio waves" typical of the way experts try to produce convincing explanations of events they don't understand any better than ordinary people do. Still others will feel confirmed
in their belief that there's a rational and scientific explanation for everything (despite the extent to which tabloids, in general, make it very difficult to accept such a viewpoint without equivocation).[44] In any case, the
story is typical of fantastic tabloidism in that its producerliness makes it
ideal for circulation within a system of oral popular culture. This points
toward an important contrast between official and popular-cultural economies. The legitimated knowledges that circulate as official cultural capital—textbook science and mainstream journalism, for example—can be
exchanged for socioeconomic advancement: better grades in schools and
universities and higher-paying jobs. The knowledges that circulate within a
system of popular-cultural capital do not offer opportunities for socioeconomic advancement but do facilitate entry into the oral cultures of everyday
life (partly because they are well suited to the interrogation of those official knowledge systems that play a key role in the reproduction of the social
order).[45]

Fantastic tabloid stories sometimes express dystopian rather than utopian impulses. A useful example appears under the 1989 *National Examiner*
headline "Brain Surgeon Turns Patients into Helpless Robots." Ted Corners reports that Dr. William T. Z. Brezniko of Novoseltsikov, Bulgaria, has
been inserting "remote control computer chips into his patients' brains
during surgery." By "using his home computer as a remote control unit"
and "programming his patients to do everything he says," Brezniko has
created a small cadre of personal slaves that cater to his every whim. The
story includes details about Brezniko's abuses of specific patients. A beautiful woman has been "programmed" to give him sex whenever he wants
it. A stockbroker has been programmed to make money for Brezniko. A
"homemaker and mother of four" has been programmed "to go to Dr. Brezniko's house each morning to clean and do laundry," and to "[cook] for the
Brezniko's—without pay."[46] These fantastic case histories use technology
and the conventions of science fiction to defamiliarize ordinary social relations. Thus, for instance, the stories of the beautiful woman and the homemaker depict patriarchal social arrangements not as natural and desirable
but rather in terms of greedy and manipulative masculine technopower.

Like the others we've seen, the Brezniko story is packed with contradictory meanings. If we consider the historical appearance of this story near the end of the Cold War, for example, we can see that Brezniko's name, the location of the events in an Eastern bloc country, and the obvious associations between mind control and the meanings that capitalism assigns to communism all suggest a reading that is comfortably aligned with U.S. officialdom. Consequently many readers might well make a communist demon of Brezniko. However, the Brezniko story resonates as well with popular suspicions and resentments of the medical establishment (and its practices) in particular and of the rich and powerful in general. Consider, for example, the stockbroker whom Brezniko technologically manipulates to his own economic advantage. For some Americans reading during the decade of Michael Milken and Ivan Boesky, the image of a rich and powerful man controlling the stock exchange would activate class meanings powerful enough to erase the effects of the story's pro-capitalist anticommunism. Will economically deprived readers necessarily care whether or not Bulgaria even has stockbrokers, if the figures in the story can be made to serve their suspicions of greedy rich folk? The story also encourages a more general class antagonism toward Brezniko by foregrounding the antagonistic relationship between high culture and popular tastes. In a paragraph about Staslav Koslan, a Novoseltsikov radio station owner, Corners writes that "before Dr. Brezniko operated on Koslan's brain to remove a small tumor, his radio station played only pop and rock. Now the station plays two hours of Dr. Brezniko's favorite classical selections every day between noon and 2 p.m., which is the time Dr. Brezniko likes to listen to the radio. The station's listening audience is shrinking, but Koslan stubbornly sticks to the new format." [47] In this way, the story's expression of class resentment—*their* tastes undemocratically control *our* radio!—works against the grain of the official Cold War reading it might otherwise be made to support.

I've argued that the fantastic tabloids generate a menippean discourse that inverts and interrogates various forms of cultural authority that work to constitute a controlling officialdom. This is crucial to their role as circulators of capital within a popular-cultural economy. I've also argued that these tabloids do not simply negate or reject official knowledges but bring them into contact with their "laughing aspects" and thus make them appear strange and unfamiliar. The fantastic tabloids produce a semiotic terrain on which the power-bearing aspects of dominant discourse are unable to function smoothly. Hegemonically accented discourses do appear within the fantastic tabloids, but they are caught up in the tabloids' system of "crooked mirrors."

What results? Discursive power is up for grabs in the anything-goes world of the fantastic tabloids. A wide range of knowledges compete for control over the meanings of events, including popular knowledges that are generally discredited and excluded altogether from mainstream journalism. The power to exclude such knowledges from the realm of legitimate information is one of the key powers of officialdom. It is an important way of exerting control over the meanings of social reality, and thus over the people who inhabit it. In fantastic tabloids, the socially legitimated and power-bearing discourses of officialdom are challenged by weaker disreputable ones that defamiliarize normal social relations and thus create space for the imagination of different ones. Of course, the cultural processes of textual production and consumption are completed only when texts are taken up by real readers and inserted into their actual social relations. Therefore, it is useful to examine the social relations that join real readers to one another and to the tabloid texts they choose to consume.

Despite the tabloids' significant popularity, surprisingly little scholarship has examined tabloid readers or the protocols of tabloid reading—though this becomes less surprising when one considers the incredibly low cultural esteem in which the publications are held. Not surprisingly, their producers rely far more heavily on the immediate data provided by weekly sales figures than on the scant reader research and demographic analysis they've actually done.[48] In the realm of academic research, there have been scattered quantitative studies, though such approaches are incapable of providing much insight into the cultural dynamics of tabloid reception.[49] More productive is the approach taken by S. Elizabeth Bird, who has used qualitative empirical methods informed by ethnographic theory to analyze readers' experiences and understandings of tabloid discourse. Bird's analysis is based on 114 letters she received from tabloid readers in response to a solicitation placed in the *National Examiner*. Seventy-seven of the letters came from women, thirty-two from men, and one from an organization. Bird notes that "the responses ranged from scrawled, barely legible notes to neatly typed, carefully presented letters." [50] Of the 114 letter writers, Bird chose 16 to participate in follow-up interviews.

Bird found extensive evidence of "a class-based feeling of powerlessness and alienation from the mainstream" that was generally shared by the 114 writers whose letters she received (125). She writes that "regular [tabloid] readers share some common experiences, defined at least in part by class and a subsequent feeling of alienation from dominant ways of thinking" (138). Bird is careful to nuance her use of "class" in the analysis of tabloid reading—almost, in fact, to the point of self-contradiction: "The frustration felt by tabloid readers does not stem from their position in some kind of under class," for "most tabloid readers actually seem to be positioned such that they are fairly well educated and interested in the world around them." Nevertheless, she notes that in general, tabloid readers "perceive themselves as unable to do anything significant about events" (132). Bird finds that weekly supermarket tabloids are regularly read by people of very different ages, interests, and racial or ethnic identities. Beyond shared feelings of alienation from the culturally dominant, she ascribes no singular motivation or monolithic reading strategy to tabloid devotees. This accords well with Stuart Hall's view that culture is organized not around "objective" boundaries between discrete classes but rather around the more fluidly mobile "us" versus "them" divisions that loosely constitute social relations between the variety of alliances that comprise the people and the power-bloc.

Bird further observes that from the viewpoints of regular tabloid readers, the weekly newspapers "are seen as an alternative, a way of knowing about the world that is not offered in other media." She writes that "the tabloid is the one forum where, in addition to stories that could be found elsewhere, the whole gamut of nonmainstream, nonrational ways of seeing the world is offered." But she takes care to note that different readers do different things with these alternative knowledges, including "picking and choosing" according to their existing beliefs and interests (137–38). The multiplicity of reader orientations, interests, and reading strategies brought to bear on the tabloids indicates the popular heterogeneity that the official culture's strategies of homogenization are up against. It also helps to explain the producerliness and the polysemy of the fantastic tabloids: to serve varied interests and beliefs, they must be amenable to the production of alternative readings. Finally, it supports a theory of tabloidism as a circulator of popular-cultural capital. Tabloid stories are used discriminatingly by different segments of the people to extend and refine existing tastes, interests, and knowledges.[51] Some readers are particularly interested in UFO-related stories, for example, like the man who records their details, along with those of his own direct sightings, in a log that he uses for correspondence with a UFO study group in Canada (146). Bird found that each of the sixteen tabloid readers she interviewed professed belief in one or more forms of paranormal phenomena such as reincarnation, near-death experiences, numerology, astrology, ESP, alien visitations of Earth, and others (119). Such popular, occulted knowledges persist despite (or perhaps because of) their constant disavowal and marginalization by the truth-producing institutions of the official culture. That the official culture continually strives to discipline popular knowledge indicates the antagonistic and power-laden nature of the relationship between the people and the power-bloc. That repressed popular knowledges nevertheless persist demonstrates the people's power to retain forms of cultural capital that resists the discursive disciplinarity of officialdom.

Although Bird found evidence of a tendency among her respondents toward a type of social conservatism that she characterizes as " 'traditional,' 'family-oriented,' religious, and patriotic in a nostalgic, flag-waving sense," she also found ample evidence of tabloid readers' deeply felt antagonisms toward the powerful institutions of the official culture. Many tabloid readers believe that "the government—'they' up in Washington—has its own agenda and is conspiring against the people." This popular skepticism is also extended to the mainstream media, big business, and establishment scientists who, like the government, are strongly suspected by many tabloid readers to be "hiding information from the American people." Bird quotes from a letter whose overt racism is described as uncharacteristic of the entire sample, but whose apparent contradictoriness, in conventional political terms, expresses the sort of mixed politics she ascribes to her respondents. She describes the letter, written by a fifty-eight-year-old woman, as a "thirteen-page tirade of personal and political grievances" and includes the following excerpt in her book:

> Our Gov't is rotten for letting in all these Damn Foreigners and giving them jobs and saying to hell with the Americans who voted them in. I think Pres. Ronald Reagan is a Tyrant Mad Man who loves killing our young Servicemen. I say impeach the bastard!!! . . . I haven't been able to get a job! First the Blacks took them all. Now the Gov't is! Our nation is in a mess. Only Jesus's 2nd Coming can help America! God Bless America, Again. . . . I am still laughing at how we Bombed Hiroshima and Nagasaki and put those Japs in their place. I think our Pres. is crazy for sending Millions and Millions of dollars to the Contras so they can shoot some farmer in a field. (129–130)

Bakhtin uses the term "heteroglossia" to denote the transection of competing voices and conflicting discourses within society, its popular texts, and the minds of their readers. A conflictual heteroglossia pervades the pages of the tabloids as well as the speech and writing of Bird's respondents. Heteroglossia presumes contradiction. It enables the figure of the lightning-stricken Camacho to demonstrate that masculinity simultaneously excludes and contains aspects of the feminine. By the same token, the heteroglossia of the letter just quoted brings together a strange and conflictive mix of racist working-class reactionaryism and potentially progressive anti-Reaganism. It shows, for example, how, in a fashion that is similar to the dynamics of the Brezniko story that I've discussed, an apparent class affiliation with Nicaraguan farmers can undermine this writer's potential sympathy for Reaganism's racist populism. The ill-formed, incoherent, and multivalent mélange of political impulses expressed in this letter should be subjected to a symptomatic analysis. It is a symptom of the absence of an adequate oppositional agency in U.S. political life that might serve as an articulating force, helping to facilitate the fusion of such diverse dissident energies into an effectively expressive populist resistance that does not depend on the racism to which this author appeals.[52] It is a symptom of the need for a radical populist cultural politics that seeks, on the heteroglossic terrain of the popular, to disarticulate legitimate discontents from the discourses of racism and rearticulate them with those of democratic social and economic justice. The heteroglossia that is characteristic of tabloid culture should be understood in terms of the political possibilities it creates.

Bird characterizes supermarket tabloids as "supremely relativistic." She notes, in addition, that "few if any" of her respondents "believe everything in the tabloids." Bird explains that "the message of tabloids," however, "is that anything is potentially believable" and that "all things are possible" (207). She seems to miss the crucial point that the corollary of the tabloid "message" that "anything is potentially believable" is that anything is also potentially *unbelievable.* The power to disbelieve officialdom is necessary (though in itself insufficient) for political opposition. Although the fantastic tabloids may fail to fuse diverse and displaced expressions of popular resentment regarding the alienation and social subordination of the people into a coherent resistive political discourse, their ongoing and heteroglossic provocation of laughing skepticism toward dominant systems of knowledge at least helps to sharpen and sustain what I'd like to call the *empleasuring* popular power to refuse official truths.

In her concluding chapter, Bird asks whether we should "accept and even celebrate the 'divergent rationality' of readers" who believe in the possibility that fantastic tabloid stories are true. "Espousing many aspects of the 'divergent rationality' of the tabloids *simply ensures that proponents advertise their subordinate class to the world,*" she answers (207; italics mine). I think that this conclusion is fundamentally wrong: popular culture is grossly oversimplified if it is reduced to something that does nothing but produce negative distinctions vis-à-vis the socially dominant. The discriminating process of accumulating and using some forms of tabloidist knowledge and skeptically rejecting others fills a "cultural lack" for those deprived of official cultural capital and provides self-esteem and a form of social prestige recognized at least by one's peers, if not by the socially privileged and powerful.[53] Furthermore, the "divergent rationality" of fantastic tabloids, *by its very existence*—which must constantly be fought for and actively maintained, since there is nothing to guarantee that existence in advance—challenges powerbloc control over the *procedures* whereby certain knowledges are legitimated and truth is thus produced. The growth of tabloidism during the Reaganite eighties suggests that as the gap between the powerful and the weak expanded, so too did the popular need for cultural practices that enabled the people to produce ways of knowing that did not depend on, and even antagonized, those who tried to monopolize control over the power of authoritative judgment.

Usually, TV is afraid of the borders of human conduct. We're not going to be. We will examine the outer edge of reality television.—Mark B. von Monsky, executive producer, *Hard Copy* [54]

It is not easy to be a real scientist when multiplying media (the Internet, television channels like Fox and the Discovery Channel, pseudoscientific publications like OMNI and *Discover*) are bestowing an aura of informational legitimacy on dowsing rods, creationism, encounters with extraterrestrial life, extrasensory perception, the existence of angels and ghosts, and other occult and New Age phenomena.—Alan Shapiro, *Ctheory: Theory, Technology, and Culture* [55]

Tabloid television has no *precise* equivalent of the fantastic supermarket tabloids. There are institutional differences between the commercial print and broadcast media that help to ensure differences between the sorts of fantastic tabloidism that each produces. Bird argues persuasively that supermarket tabloids succeed because they strike a "responsive chord" with their readers. She explains that supermarket tabloids differ from most media products in that they rely more heavily on direct sales revenues and less heavily on money from advertisers (since most advertisers see tabloid readers as "undesirable targets"). As a result, there is "an unusually close fit between the world view portrayed in the papers and that of their readers." [56] Indeed, whereas TV programmers often kowtow to the whims of advertisers, things in fantastic supermarket tabloidland seem to work the other way around: advertisers write copy and design ads to match the unconventionality and sheer wackiness of the newspapers' stories themselves in order to connect with the readers whose sensibilities those particular narratives reach. [57]

Therefore, just as the fantastic tabloid newspapers' journalistic discourses parody those of the "respectable" press, and their science reports and general epistemological stances transgress and parody the doctrines and dogmas of scientific rationalism, so do their advertisements parody and indeed make a mockery of dominant ideologies concerning the nature of success, achievement, and acquisition in capitalist societies. Far from trumpeting the right-wing mantra that hard work, ingenuity, and good old-fashioned stick-to-it-iveness are the true and only means to whatever successes one's heart desires, the fantastic tabloids' advertisements depict a world where, as in the one implied by the rumor that Proctor and Gamble's CEO got where he is by selling his soul to Satan (see chapter 1), wealth and power obtain through anything *but* plucky devotion to the Protestant ethic.

Consequently the road to fortune that is mapped out in tabloid advertising is strewn with "miracle dolls" wielding magic wands, lucky "Golden Clovers," Haitian "hypnotic power beads," powerful talismans, magical amulets, luck-enhancing soaps, bath crystals, perfumes, dusting powders and number books, and a slew of psychic guides and helpers: Indian psychics, personal psychic advisers, tarot readers, "premiere psychic astrologers," clairvoyants, psychic spiritualists, and "celebrity psychics." All of these are promoted as requisites to that which the official ideology and its cultural institutions claim are the consequences only of individual merit, effort, and commitment, but which tabloid readers know are as unequally distributed as all social goods: fulfilling work, love, and money. In this way, fantastic supermarket tabloid advertising undercuts the Horatio Alger myth so deeply embedded in the belief systems disseminated by the power-bloc.[58] It speaks to, and provides grist for the mill of, a popular distrust of official ideologies regarding the reasons for success, happiness, emotional well-being, and even good health.

The "fit" between the "world views" portrayed on television, to use Bird's terms, and those of most TV audiences is not necessarily as close as the fit between tabloid newspapers and their readers. With the decline of network television's centralized oligopolistic structure and the emergence of a "new multichannel marketplace" in the age of cable and satellite delivery systems, however, the medium has developed strategies for catering to a wider variety of social taste formations than it once could. Under these new conditions, TV programmers are less apt to think in terms of the "mass audience" implied by Fordist production models and so more likely to conceptualize their viewerships in post-Fordist terms as a fragmented set of niche markets. Nevertheless, programmers still seek, insofar as it is possible, to garner both a "mass" audience and, within that, the kinds of "quality demographics" that appeal to advertisers.[59] Thus one observer writes that despite post-Fordist production trends, many television industry executives have continued to resist narrowcasting in favor of persistent attempts "to reach the big, broad network audiences."[60] This tendency is sustained because powerful advertisers would rather buy expensive prime-time air spots than place their ads during syndicated programs to reach a narrowly targeted audience fragment. Marketing executive Barry Kaplan explains that although the latter strategy is cheaper than the former, it is also thought to be less cost-effective, as fewer viewers actually see narrowcast commercials, and of those who do, many encounter the same advertisements unnecessarily and perhaps annoyingly often.[61] Consequently, despite an increasing awareness of television audience fragmentation in the age of the multichannel universe, there is still a high premium placed on programming aimed at the broadest possible viewership. This, coupled with higher production costs than those associated with fantastic supermarket tabloids such as the *Weekly World News* and the *Sun*, tends to produce a "mainstreaming" effect in television programming, whereby the most socially marginal discourses are either pulled toward TV's discursive center or pushed outward to the fringes of the programming day (where they have a difficult time reaching a large audience).

To be sure, television's discursive mainstream or center has moved down-market as the networks have lost portions of their more demographically desirable audience to satellite and cable programming as well as the "VCR revolution." The increased visibility of tabloid television genres is one manifestation of this downmarketing strategy. Moreover, the demand for non-mainstream, unofficial, tabloidized media forms has been nourished by recent trends toward dislocation of the new technical and managerial middle classes that were created and thrived from roughly the end of World War II until the mid- to late 1980s, when they were hit hard by the first shock waves of global economic restructuring and then corporate downsizing and the increasing casualization of the professional workforce. These conjunctural forces enhance the extent to which we can see it as far from coincidental that tabloid television took off when it did, during the latter half of the eighties. In a fascinating analysis along these lines, John Langer argues that tabloid perspectives have been "unhitched" from their previous moorings and are now "free floating" throughout the television universe. Consequently, for "an increasingly subordinated fragment of the new [post–World War II] middle class," the "lived reality of sedimentation and dislocation is given the opportunity to find its circumstantial and conjunctural moment 'articulated' to the kinds of vicissitudes which reach across the narratives assembled by reality programming."[62] Despite this diffusion of tabloidism, however, there is certainly justification for the view that whereas "mainstream" or official television journalism has in recent years been increasingly tabloidized, so too have many programs in the tabloid genre been mainstreamed or normalized.[63] This normalization or dampening of discursive extremes may indeed be a sign that tabloid television is learning to converse with recently dislocated fractions of the "new" postwar middle classes whose class-cultural matrices are thus currently defined by a shifting composite of "respectable" but increasingly alienated, subaltern predilections and orientations.

There are further manifestations of difference between print and television tabloids that relate more closely to the formal properties of the two media themselves than to the institutional sources of disparity I have noted. Television's multiple perceptual channels endow it with a semiotic richness that print media obviously lack. Television's capacity for moving-image, voice-over, graphical, musical, and performative signification enable it to produce hyperrealistic effects that point up by contrast the relative semiotic poverty of the supermarket tabloids. This might help to explain why the print tabloids are more inclined toward "wild stories" than are most tabloid television programs.[64] What the fantastic tabloid newspapers lack by comparison in signifying channels and raw semiotic resources (the *Weekly World News* doesn't even have color print), they more than compensate for with their excessive "wildness." The print tabloids have learned to make loud noise without the synthesizers and borrowed Hollywood sound tracks of tabloid TV news programs (such as *A Current Affair*). They've learned to cause a ruckus without the help of the tabloid talk shows' physically rowdy and vocal studio audiences (see chapter 5). The supermarket tabloids have learned to grab our attention without benefit of the hyperrealism of *Cops* and *American Detective*, and without recourse to the grippingly melodramatic filmed reenactments of *America's Most Wanted*. The fantastic tabloids have learned to express laughter and irony and parodic popular skepticism without Maury Povich's plastically expressive face and "Lenny Bruce as anchorman" performativity.

Along with what I have called their semiotic richness, tabloid television formats often exploit the sense of participatory immediacy on which the medium bases many of its appeals to audiences. Jane Feuer has argued that "as television in fact becomes less and less a 'live' medium in the sense of an equivalence between time of event and time of transmission, the medium in its own practices seems to insist more and more upon an ideology of the live, the immediate, the direct, the spontaneous, the real."[65] I take Feuer's point to be an important one, even though I have found postmodern accounts of hyperreality to be more productive than ideology theory for analyzing the connection between tabloid television and the medium's strong and arguably growing tendency to produce and exploit effects of liveness and immediacy.[66] These effects of liveness and immediacy generated through the medium of television enhance and heighten the sense of participatory inclusiveness that is characteristic, albeit to a lesser degree, of tabloid journalism in its print forms.[67] "Phone in now and you can help catch the killer/help solve this mystery/join in the discussion and help our guests resolve their relationship problems." Perhaps because of its relatively greater interest in generating effects of on-the-scene liveness and direct audience participation, tabloid television correspondingly underemphasizes the fantastic "wildness" present in much of the print tabloid discourse that we've looked at in this chapter.

Such qualifications notwithstanding, television clearly has its domains of the fantastic. These are not confined solely to the "trashy" realm of tabloid TV journalism, for many of the same topics covered in fantastic supermarket tabloids are, it seems, just as likely to be found in some of the more

respectable quarters of television fiction, including the relatively prestigious Fox Network drama *The X-Files*. Interestingly, whereas *The X-Files* extends supermarket tabloid skepticism toward both the federal government
and the mainstream scientific establishment, the show does not seem to
evoke the same volume of either condescending groans or dismissive laughter often hurled at tabloid media. Although it has done programs about
vampires, werewolves, satanic minions, demonic possession, alien abductions, government conspiracies and cover-ups, mad scientists, secret military adventures and weapons tested on unwitting U.S. citizens, genetic experimentation and human cloning, telekinesis, ESP, malevolent forms of
artificial intelligence, reincarnation, unknown organisms created by or re-
acting against man's affronts to the ecosphere, hauntings, body swapping,
voodoo spells, and a host of other paranormal phenomena, *The X-Files* has
nevertheless garnered a sheen of respectability and been recognized with
the oft sought after appellation "quality television" that is denied the TV
tabloids. Perhaps its explicitly fictional status rescues it from the sneers
that routinely greet culture texts that explore similar issues under the guise
of a journalistic format. *The X-Files* nevertheless shares the skeptical sensibilities of fantastic tabloidism. Several commentators have pointed out
that the *X-Files* slogan suggests a rather traditional stance with regard to
at least the existence and theoretical obtainability of a singular truth—*the*
truth. Jimmie L. Reeves, Mark C. Rodgers, and Michael Epstein argue, for
example, that the show's slogan, " 'the truth is out there,' runs counter
to postmodernism's doctrine of disbelief." [68] Leaving aside the issue of
whether "postmodernism" is a "doctrine of disbelief," I'd like merely to
point out that commentators such as these typically fail to notice that the
pun contained playfully within the *X-Files* slogan significantly modifies its
meaning. To declare something at once "true" and "*out there*," as if in left
field, is (as in fantastic tabloidism) to embrace the self-contradictory stance
of simultaneous belief and disbelief in the very truth that is thus declared.
It is to put "the truth" in quotation marks. It is to persist in refusing the
closure that more conventional notions of "the truth" impose in social practice, if not at the level of official doctrine.[69] In fantastic tabloidworld, belief in the truth can only ever be skeptical, tentative, provisional, uncertain,
and ultimately self-negating—because boy, is this "truth" ever *out there!* The
massive popularity of *The X-Files* and the production of copies like *Millennium*
testify to the idea that skeptically suspicious tabloid perspectives have indeed become unhitched from their previous moorings and now float freely
and pervasively throughout our media universe.

Wildly "out there" truths can be found on television beyond the realm
of dramatic fiction formats in tabloid newscasts such as *A Current Affair*

and *Hard Copy* as well as on the daytime talk shows, but probably the best examples come from other programs that, like both *The X-Files* and the fantastic newspapers discussed earlier, specialize particularly in stories about phenomena considered "mysterious" or "inexplicable" from the perspectives of socially dominant knowledge systems. Explanation is a primary form of cultural colonization, and phenomena that evade explanation and colonization by "legitimate" knowledges invite popular productivity. Stories of such paranormal phenomena, including hauntings, vampirism, werewolves, psychic activity, visitations by extraterrestrial beings, miraculous cures, out-of-body experiences, mysterious crop circles, and demonic possession, are found regularly on N BC's *The Other Side*, Fox's *Encounters* and *Sightings* (which was canceled by the network after two seasons but has found a second life in syndication, where it is carried by 205 stations), ABC's *Unsolved Mysteries* (to a lesser degree), and the syndicated *The Extraordinary* (found on only 56 stations).[70] Sometimes such stories challenge the very epistemological principles that underlie scientific rationalism, and at other times they merely question the contents of that which has been officially certified "true" without explicitly challenging the implicit assumptions that guide the process of its certification. In either case, stories that express popular skepticism toward the official truth more or less explicitly criticize the social formations whose interests are best served by its circulation. In telling these stories, the tabloid programs typically emphasize voices of popular experience and knowledge that are effectively marginalized or spoken *for*, if not excluded altogether, in mainstream television news and information formats. I shall discuss five specific examples of fantastic tabloid TV storytelling, and I shall pay particular attention to those popular and "ordinary" voices this narrative genre admits into its discursive repertoire.

Stories about the extraterrestrial are common in tabloid television. A typical example comes from a 1990 edition of *Unsolved Mysteries* that examined the military investigation of a mysterious flying object that crashed near the little town of Kecksburg, Pennsylvania. In the words of Robert Stack, the program's host and narrator, "In 1965 a tiny town in Pennsylvania was invaded. First from the sky, and then by the U.S. military. Some residents claim that a UFO crashed, and the government covered it up." This narration emphasizes the social antagonism between the residents of the small, rural Pennsylvania village and the institutions of the military, which are construed as the instruments of an invasion force. Tabloid knowledge deals often with themes of "invasion." This is probably no coincidence, since the histories of most socially subordinated groups are full of struggles against multifarious colonizing or otherwise invasive forces; themes of invasion thus have high popular resonance.

Throughout this tabloid UFO story, reenactments of events narrated from the perspectives of Kecksburg townspeople and on-camera interviews with local residents about their memories of the incident now twenty-five years past are set against U.S. Navy reports concerning the mysterious object that lit up the Pennsylvania sky before falling to Earth near a modest country farmhouse. Through a process of imagistic rearticulation similar to those discussed in chapter 2, these ordinary voices are assembled to produce a local knowledge of the Kecksburg event that defies the military's truth. Unsolved Mysteries' filmic interpretations of these everyday oral accounts weave them into a new discourse that circulates, however, well beyond the local context of their original production. Although the circulation and social effectivity of localizing forms of knowledge are often confined to the production of a "communal identity" for the members of a particular locale, Unsolved Mysteries thus uses images to carry the Kecksburg townsfolk's local knowledges to other communities that share the Pennsylvania villagers' antagonistic relationship to the U.S. military and its versions of the truth.[71] Part of the significance of fantastic tabloid television therefore lies in its imagistic amplification of local popular knowledges.

The story opens with a specially produced filmic image of an orange fireball hurtling through the sky at relatively slow speeds along a low trajectory. Interspersed with this is a series of reenactments of the activities of various local eyewitnesses on the day of the event, along with their present-day remembrances of the incident. These local narrators were all children at the time, and each describes his feelings of wonderment on witnessing the descent of an object the likes of which he had never seen before. The owner of a farm located a half mile from the woods in which the mysterious object crash-landed then describes receiving phone calls from government agencies interested in locating and recovering the thing. An official from the U.S. Navy instructed her to "watch the area" and report "anything strange" that might develop. Within fifteen minutes, she says, the Pennsylvania State Police delivered two unidentified men wearing civilian clothes and equipped with a Geiger counter to the perimeter of her property, from which they set out to search for the object.

By nightfall, a number of search teams composed primarily of volunteer firemen had been organized under the supervision of the state police. The searchers were told that an airplane had gone down in the area. One of the search teams riding in a police cruiser came upon a promontory overlooking a bright light flashing rhythmically in a hidden ravine below. In the words of a fireman who was on the scene:

It, uh, wasn't searchers down in the woods with flashlights or anything. It was a, a real bright blue. Real bright, like a, uh, electric welder.

The, uh, the flashes seemed to be *timed*, at what intervals I don't know. But it was a timed thing. It, uh, it wasn't like flashbulbs, or anything like that.

This scene is recreated in a filmic simulation that accompanies the fireman's narration, which informs us that on discovering the bright blue light, the Pennsylvania State Police closed all roads surrounding the ravine, effectively blocking public access to the area.

Somewhat later, while teams of searchers traveling on foot scoured the woods circumjacent to the trench containing the mysterious object, a group of volunteer firemen happened on a sight that each would remember for the rest of his life. One of the firemen describes the discovery:

Here was this humongous metal object, half-buried in the ground. . . . To me, the object looked exactly like a fresh acorn that you pick off of a tree. There was no wings. There was no motors. There was no pro-pellers. There was no identification whatsoever that would identify it as a aircraft that I would know. There was a bumper on the bottom part of it. On that bumper there was what I call, it looked to me like the ancient Egyptian hieroglyphics. It was markings like stars and shapes and figures and circles and lines, and what it was, I don't know. To this day I've never seen anything like it. I've studied the ancient Incas, I've studied the Aztec Indians, I've studied the Egyptians. I've looked at pictures of Russian writing. I've looked at pictures of Polish writ-ing. I've looked at pictures of Hebrew writing. Nothing. Nothing that resembles it. Chinese writing: no.

As the firemen moved closer to the mysterious object, however, a small mili-tary entourage arrived and instructed them that the area had been placed under quarantine, and that all civilians were to leave at once.

Meanwhile the little village of Kecksburg swarmed with military person-nel, who established a "command center" in the volunteer fire department and commandeered a farmhouse near the ravine. All civilian movement within the area was severely restricted. Nevertheless, various townspeople witnessed some of the military's secretive undertakings. One eyewitness who was part of a crowd lining a narrow road overlooking military opera-tions reports that just before being ordered to disperse by an officer on duty, the people watched four men in "moon suits" carry a large wooden crate into the forest surrounding the gorge. The crate was clearly too small to hold the mysterious thing itself, but large enough, notes Robert Stack, to con-tain "someone or something inside the object that the military wanted to remove." Some time later, others watched as a flatbed military truck sped away from the Kecksburg area carrying a large covered article on its trailer.

Footage presumably produced by *Unsolved Mysteries* suggests that the hidden object was the acorn-shaped metallic craft found in the ravine by searching firemen.

We are then presented with the findings of a local UFO researcher who has spent ten years trying to unravel this mystery. Through his research, Stan Gordon has amassed evidence that eliminates the possibility that the object was either a meteorite or some sort of space debris. He has determined, however, that "whatever came down in Kecksburg that night is of high importance to the military agencies." Included among the agencies that placed requests for information regarding the incident are the Houston Space Center, NORAD, the Air Force Command Post, the Pentagon, and the Office for Emergency Planning. Nevertheless, "the most mysterious thing about the whole case," Gordon says, "is that after twenty-five years, the government still refuses to give *us* any actual information on what occurred" (italics mine).

Official military reports do acknowledge that recovery operations were undertaken near Kecksburg. However, they suggest that the fallen object was a meteorite and insist that all operations were terminated at 2:00 A.M. on the morning following the crash, after hours of fruitless searching.[72] Among *Unsolved Mysteries*'s last words on the Kecksburg incident are those of local eyewitnesses, on which so much of this case against the official truth is built. Says one man who observed some of the secret operations in Kecksburg on December 9, 1965, "The military's idea of finding nothing is completely false. There was something down in that ravine that night. There was something that glowed an awful bright light. And they took something out of there that night." Says another, whose voice is inflected with passion and anger:

> The official reports that the military and the government put out, as far as I'm concerned, are a bunch of bull. If this thing was a meteorite, then why didn't they just bring it out and say, "Here it is." Let the reporters take pictures of it, let the firemen see it, let the people in this area see it. Why the big mystery?

Through its articulations of suspicion toward official truths that construe the Kecksburg incident as a benign search for a crashed airplane, *Unsolved Mysteries* exposes the invasive techniques imposed on a locale and the bodies of its occupants to limit and control popular access to information. Although the eyewitness accounts and interpretations of the Kecksburg townsfolk have been systematically discredited by the government and excluded from its version of the truth, the program assembles fragments of their popular discourse into a countertruth that powerfully questions and undermines the military one. The discursive colonization of popular experi-

Sightings.

ence, a powerful strategy of social control, is thus obstructed through the inversion of the system of prioritization that places the speech of ordinary folks in a subordinate relation to that of officials and experts. This inversion underscores tabloid television's role as a circulator of popular-cultural capital as it works to align its audiences with the skepticism and suspicion that popular knowledge directs against the controlling strategies of official institutions whose procedures for producing truth are shown to be profoundly antidemocratic.

We find a similar critique of dominant knowledge/power at work in a story about alien abductions that appeared on the Fox Network program *Sightings.* Here popular suspicion implicates forms of imperializing expert knowledge that dismissively construe individual accounts of abduction phenomena as the products of physiological disorders and media-induced psychopathologies. Such storytelling is typical of *Sightings*, which always encourages its audience to treat the popular fantastic seriously.[73] In telling its story about people who claim to have been abducted by extraterrestrial aliens, *Sightings* centers on the accounts of events given by abductees themselves, who appear to be otherwise "ordinary" people. Their abductors, however, are far from ordinary. Some are described as "creatures with oversized heads and dark, almond-shaped, protruding eyes." Others, we are told, are "insectlike" or "reptilian" beings with clawlike hands and rude dispositions. Still others are thought to be human-alien "hybrids" bred from encounters with previous abductees. One of the most striking aspects of the abduction phenomenon, according to the report, is that thousands of people have now come forward in one way or another to reveal, independently, very similar stories of having been taken from their beds during the middle of the night and experimented on sexually or surgically in labs located aboard UFOs. Most of the abductees report having undergone multiple abductions, sometimes beginning in early childhood and continuing through old age. One longtime follower of the abduction reports claims that in almost all cases there is some sort of reproductive issue involved.

The *Sightings* report pits the marginalized discourse of the abductees against the dominant ones of scientific rationalism and skeptical empiricism. By emphasizing the abductees' knowledges of the abductions and thus decentering normally prioritized voices of scientific expertise that implicitly prioritize normality, *Sightings* makes these dominant discourses appear to be somewhat inexplicably held minority beliefs. As it does this, the program frames the contestation between alternative accounts of the abduction reports as a struggle over who will rightfully speak for those who report having been abducted. Various corporeal discourses are located at the center of this struggle, as control over one's own body is equated with control over the production of its truth. In this struggle, the abductees are caught between two colonizing forces: one that they understand to have sexually and surgically violated their bodies, another that exerts its power over them by producing dismissive accounts of their experiences, accounts widely designated more truthful than their own. These dismissive, socially empowered truths of scientific rationalism are expressed in the story by the editor of a scientific journal who claims that the abduction reports are nothing but the result of a "popular myth" generated by "talk shows" (thus constituting a sort of media-induced mass hysteria) and a doctor who specializes in sleep disorders who asserts that the phenomena can be adequately explained as the consequences of "hypnogogic hallucinations" brought on by narcolepsy. Such pathologizing diagnoses work to secure social control by justifying and helping to sustain the disciplinary power that is continuously mobilized by official knowledges and institutions. These diagnoses are, however, as noted earlier, marginalized and explicitly challenged within the *Sightings* story.

Like the official explanation of the Kecksburg event, scientific dismissals of the alien abduction phenomenon are made to appear *incredible* alongside the first-person narrative reports given by the abductees themselves, which are accompanied by ample images of various aliens, enactments of abductions, and other visual "evidence." The status of these images is different from that of video footage used in mainstream newscasts, among the primary functions of which is the production of truth effects that serve as guarantors of the actuality of events and therefore of the empirical factuality of the news reports. Indeed, the authority of the serious news is

The image of an alien visitation.

enhanced by the way in which conventional journalistic video footage generates a semiotic effect that Charlotte Brunsdon and David Morley call "being-thereness," which enables viewers to experience events as if through "direct perception."[74] By contrast, the *Sightings* footage of aliens is used primarily to engage viewers' imaginations and to enhance the pleasure, identified by Bird in her study of tabloid readers, of treating these stories "*as if* they are true." Bird notes that by "taking an 'as if' stance" in their gossip about tabloids, readers "play with the ideas and possibilities" embedded in the papers.[75] A key difference between televisual and print tabloids, then, is that the hyperrealism of TV's semiotically rich sound and image tracks pushes the perceptual capacities of the "as if" to levels unattainable through newsprint and combines them with the pleasures of "being-thereness" in a way that facilitates even greater enjoyment. By combining the pleasures of the "as if" with those of "being-thereness" in this way, *Sightings'* visualizations of abduction scenarios question the normal differentiation of the truth effects generated by the socially empowered discourses of scientific rationalists from those produced by the discourses of the abductees themselves. Both are made to appear equally bizarre and equally credible, as the brusque and condescending dismissals of abductee self-reports are set alongside detailed personal testimonials that are visually enhanced by images of alien intruders creeping into bedrooms during the small hours of the night.

Despite this imagistic elision of the *discursive* difference between firsthand memories of abduction and condescending scientific dismissals of those memories, *Sightings* highlights the different *social* positions occupied by its interlocutors. These are expressed as the differences between alternative epistemologies. Whereas the scientific dismissals of abduction phenomena are spoken from the perspective of a normalizing "universal reason," the abductees' accounts are embedded in the particularity of embodied experiences:

> They opened my back. I knew my back was open 'cause I could feel, it was almost as though a slit had been drawn down my back and across to the side and they had opened a flap of, of flesh and, and tissue.

> The most humiliating thing that happened to me is they put a cylindrical sort of thing over my genitals, and it made me have an orgasm in a second. And I really feel like I'm one of those few men who knows what a woman feels like if she, when she's raped.

> I've been on a table and I've seen something removed from my body that I will call a "fetus." The baby was so small I couldn't believe that it could live on its own. I remember putting my finger in the arch of its foot. I was afraid to look at the face. I was afraid to see what it looked like.

The difference between the scientists' knowledges of abductions and those of the abductees is, as in the Kecksburg story, a difference between imperializing and localizing powers. The discourse of scientific rationalism seeks to extend its social power by expanding the range of phenomena it can authoritatively explain, which requires it to negate the accounts produced by the abductees. By contrast, the discourse of the abductees seeks to defend its terrain against a pincerlike double incursion: on the one hand, their felt experiences of violation by aliens; on the other, their deprivation of social legitimacy by scientists. The terrain they defend against this double incursion entails the most localized of social sites: the body, and its power to produce speech. What I think is most important in this defense of the body and its speech, from the perspective of cultural analysis, is not so much the empiricist truth of whether the abductions actually occurred as the power play between competing discourses, which has significant social and political repercussions.[76] The right to speak and be heard, the right to be taken seriously, and the position from which one is consigned to speak are all crucial elements in the disposition of social power. The power of scientific rationalism undergirds the truths it produces, and its control over truth guarantees its social power. By extending itself over as many events as it can manage, it exerts an exclusionary control over the production of legitimate speech, marginalizing the voices that defy its narrow logics.

It is a telling point that the abductees' stories emphasize issues of bodily control and invasion. In a disciplinary society, among the main channels of power are the microphysical controls that are exerted over individual bodies in virtually every social context. Issues of bodily control, violation, and victimization are key territories of political struggle in societies such as the late-twentieth-century United States, for the body is where political control and structural social power take hold of individuals and become concrete. It is the site where social individuals comply with or resist the system of norms and powers that ultimately advantage some and disadvantage others.[77] Running subtextually throughout these stories of alien abduction, then, are politically significant issues that have been recoded through the popular fantastic. At the most obvious level, we encounter meanings about some of the ways in which power takes hold of women's bodies in patriarchal societies—thus the *Sightings* report is rife with imagery and language around issues of rape, reproductive choice, and sexual consent. Such images resonate loudly in tabloid television because they occupy a prominent position in the popular imagination. They are symptomatic of the same conjunctural social forces that have made sexual harassment central to the gender politics of everyday life in recent years. They are symptomatic of the extent to which, in contemporary U.S. society, the pro-choice T-shirt that proclaims, "My body is a battleground," tellingly indicates both the key terrain and some of the stakes of cultural struggles between competing knowledges. The men of science in the *Sightings* story attempt to speak for the bodies of abductees in much the same way as the "scientific" discourses of "post-abortion syndrome" seek to speak for women who have terminated pregnancies.[78] This story can thus be seen as a continuation in another register of the corporeal struggles over power and control that are engaged around issues of reproductive rights. Moreover, the voices of the abductees resonate in a displaced way, with the struggle to be heard and to be taken seriously that was waged during the early 1990s by people such as Anita Hill and the female officers and other women who went public with their stories of sexual harassment at the U.S. Navy's Tailhook convention.

But this story is also symptomatic of anxieties about the maintenance of cultural boundaries and purity in a world increasingly marked by composite cultures, cross-fertilization, and hybridity. Such anxieties have moved toward the center of the U.S. social imagination as the hegemonic narratives of containment that were the hallmark of Cold War culture have given way to postmodern dispersion.[79] The recent proliferation of alien abduction reports can be understood as a response to the breakdown of such narratives of containment and as an expression of increasing uncertainty over boundaries. As Jodi Dean notes, widespread belief in the abduction phenomenon presumes "an understanding of the world, of reality, as amorphous and permeable."[80] This way of understanding the world both supports and is supported by the recession of the Cold War (with its rigidly immobile "iron curtain" metaphors) as a politically orienting schema and the concomitant loss of *focus* on the U.S.S.R. as an external enemy. As the Islamic world has become the primary target for the Western projection of evil impulses and vilification, anxieties about racial difference in general have intensified and thus taken up some of the slack produced by the partial conversion, in the U.S. cultural imagination, of the U.S.S.R. from communist foe to potential market.

This intensification of cultural anxieties about racial difference provides some important clues with regard to the recent hypervisibility of tabloid knowledges about alien abduction phenomena. A comparison between some of the Cold War aliens of 1950s U.S. cinema and the post–Cold War aliens of *Sightings*'s abduction narratives is instructive along these lines. Michael Rogin has shown how fifties SF films such as *The Thing*, *Invasion of the Body Snatchers*, and *Them!* work through a set of cultural anxieties about communism, matriarchy, and the conformist pressures of mass society, all of which overlay and mutually recode one another within these movies. In each film, a more or less explicitly feminized alien entity mobilizes its reproductive mechanisms toward massifying, deindividuating, socially homogenizing ends. These Cold War aliens threaten to "replace individual identities (identity as difference) with identities identical and out of control."[81] The aliens of *Sightings*, on the other hand, are physically androgynous sexual predators who violate the boundary between the masculine and the feminine as well as between the public and the private. The fifties films "evoke the nightmare of uncontrolled female generativity."[82] By contrast, narratives about the nineties abductors, whose difference is said to be inscribed in corporeal surfaces and racialized phenotypes (such as the "almond-shaped eyes" and "oversized heads" attributed by abductees to common species of alien invaders), can be seen to express displaced anxieties about a racially inflected sexual threat that is (perhaps) less "savage" and less racially specific than, but nevertheless not unrelated to, the one we've encountered in both *America's Most Wanted* and the O.J. Simpson case. If the fifties SF films reveal anxieties about U.S. cultural massification (as well as communism and matriarchy), tabloid abduction narratives express, among other things, anxiety about multiculturalism in the United States. In addition to issues of sexual predation, the aliens' stealthy nocturnal incursions into terrestrial bedrooms resonate in a displaced way with concerns about the control of both borders and terrorism—for these abductees feel nothing if not terrorized, trespassed against, and violated. In their own way, these abduction narratives thus recapitulate struggles over the policing of national geographic and identity boundaries in an age of stepped-up culture wars, accelerated transnational mobility, and enhanced agitation for tighter controls on immigration and for the development of new strategies to combat terrorism.

As in the *Unsolved Mysteries* story about Kecksburg, Pennsylvania, *Sightings* sometimes explores the government's role in covering up information about extraterrestrial aliens and technologies. Immediately following the alien abduction story previously discussed, *Sightings* offered a report suggesting a government cover-up of activities at a secret military installation in the Nevada desert. Host Tim White's narration bridging the separate stories illustrates how *Sightings* opens a space in its viewers' imaginations for the possibility of government involvement in the abductions. Says White at the end of the abduction story and leading into the story about the secret military installation:

> Even some of the most skeptical members of the psychiatric profession agree that the abduction phenomenon is not a hoax, that the causes for these stories are to be found not in alien spacecraft, but right here on Earth.
>
> When we return, *Sightings* finds evidence that at least *some* UFO encounters may be the result of top secret experiments the government doesn't want you to know about.

This transitional narration suggests the possibility of a link between the alien abduction phenomenon and the government's involvement in secret research projects that, according to one commentator, constitutes a "cosmic Watergate." The possibility of such a link is never explicitly spoken, for it doesn't need to be. Nonetheless, it is clearly present as an alternative to the idea that *alien species* are responsible for the systematic abduction of ordinary Americans. Its credibility as a way of explaining abduction reports owes much to the existence of widespread popular knowledges about events like the U.S. government's years of (now discredited) denial that Agent Orange is toxic to humans and its involvement in numerous experiments on people who were made to unwittingly ingest radioactive materials. (The government's involvement in this unconscionable research finally gained widespread public circulation, along with other formerly repressed information about the activities of the Atomic Energy Commission during the Cold War, thanks to the Clinton administration's release of documents that had been kept classified during the preceding presidencies.)

This story is organized around the idea that many UFO sightings probably involve top secret military aircraft that "the government doesn't want *you* to know about." At the story's core is a mysterious military installation hidden away in a system of hills and deep desert valleys near Groom Lake, Nevada. Dubbed "Area 51" by UFOlogists, the installation has become a center of popular theorizing about government involvement in the disposition of captured alien technologies. Says one researcher, "In the Nevada desert, we have things that would make George Lucas envious. We have things out there that are . . . literally out of this world." Here tabloid television's hyperreal implosion of discursive categories enables Sightings to use popular science fiction as a basis on which to challenge the government's public definition of "reality." Nevertheless, military and other government officials persist in their strenuous denial of even the presence of an installation in Southwestern Nevada. As the researcher puts it, "One of the problems associated with Groom Lake is the fact that it is a place that does not officially exist."

Sightings displays grainy black-and-white photos taken with a telephoto lens of large buildings and towers tucked away in a series of desert foothills as "proof" of the reality of Area 51. Images of structures with doors thought to measure two hundred by four hundred feet are presented with narration suggesting that you could "put anything in there." Interspersed with these photos are eyewitness accounts given by ordinary people and amateur video footage of recent UFO sightings in the Southwestern United States, all of which combine, as in the Kecksburg and abduction stories, to provoke popular skepticism against socially powerful knowledges. Sightings even presents video footage of a "federal official" who "insisted on hiding his identity." He appears in a grainy, green-bathed videotape wearing a disguise reminiscent of the Kecksburg "moon suits." His voice, like his body, is also disguised, technologically modulated to prevent identification. The semiotic effect of this disguise imputes an alienness to the informant that suggests, as in the Kecksburg story, a positional equivalence between aggressive extraterrestrial beings and invasive government agents that makes perfect sense from the perspective of popular knowledge. According to the anonymous witness:

> Area 51 is the most highly secured installation in this country. It's guarded both over the air and on the ground by elite Air Force Security Police and Department of Energy Special Response Teams. They are heavily armed, and their total mission is to keep people off this installation. . . . If someone came to me and said there's just absolutely nothing that secret, and they decided they were going to hike into Area 51, I think that could be the biggest and perhaps the last mistake they are going to make in their life.

Michael DiGregorio, editor in chief of Far Out Magazine, adds that Area 51 "is an ideal place for top secret, highly classified military projects, to re-

Area 51.

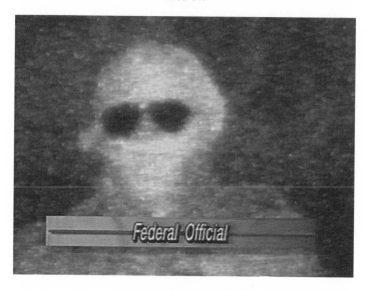

Federal official or alien?

fine them, to take them to the next level. . . . You have deep, deep desert valleys, high mountain ranges to camouflage and mask these things when they fly." Says DiGregorio, "The military is the top dog here in Nevada. No doubt about it, they run the show." He asks what might be behind the high-level military secrecy and heavily armed security surrounding Area 51. "Are these people still locked into a Cold War mentality? Is that the point here? Or are they really hiding something that's, that's *totally alien*? Is, is this *otherworldly technology* that's being applied to Air Force 'black projects?' " (the UFOlogists' name for these top secret research programs). These comments foreground the nexus of discursive and technological powers that lie at the heart of hegemony. Popular knowledge is well aware that power-bloc lies, secrecy, and officially established truths are used to conceal and facilitate the mobilization of imperializing technologies, like the military ones housed in Area 51. Suspicious and skeptical popular knowledges, despite their pathologization in the bourgeois imagination as "paranoiac conspiracy theories," are key discursive formations for the expression of resentment against hegemonic attempts to monopolize access to social power.

Approximately two years after the appearance of this story about Area 51, *Sightings* broadcast a report entitled "Patterns of Denial," which also explored links between secret military weapons development in the Nevada desert and the institutional concealment of captured alien technologies. Says White in this second Area 51 story, "Despite high-level leaks about top secret aircraft testing here, . . . the Pentagon continues to issue their standard denials—even to Congress." DiGregorio adds that "the military has established a pattern of denial concerning these aircraft, beginning in the late fifties and continuing to this day." White then provides the following narration over a procession of historical photographs of military aircraft on the image track:

> The pattern of denial started with the U-2. In the fifties, sightings of strange cigar-shaped craft were followed by leaks about a new spy plane code-named "U-2." The military denied the existence of any such plane—until Francis Gary Powers was shot down over Russia in a U-2. The pattern continued in the 1960s, with the SR-71 Blackbird. In the seventies and eighties, with the Stealth Fighter and the Stealth Bomber. And now, in the nineties, it's happening again. There are new sightings of disk-shaped craft, new leaks suggesting the discovery of an antigravity device. And the same old denials.

Sightings thus articulates these incidents into a long history of military deceit regarding the development and mobilization of weaponry. The political implications of the counterknowledge that results are obvious and significant: that patterns of denial regarding the military deployment of extraterrestrial technology enable powerful institutions to avoid public accountability and possibly facilitate the physical abduction of ordinary people for purposes of secret experiments of the sort that have been conducted on U.S. citizens by their government's agencies for decades. That such countertruths are sometimes able to defy repression and produce widespread public acceptance leading to official admissions of guilt and conspiracy is evidence of the power of popular culture to influence the course of history. Often, only tabloid media, of all our society's news and information sources, accord such repressed countertruths a level of credibility. George Knapp, an investigative journalist who appears in the "Patterns of Denial" report, conveys something of the tabloid attitude toward marginalized popular beliefs that are often dismissed without serious consideration:

> There's a certain conceit, I think, among journalists that, well, if it's real, if it's true, we can get it, because Washington, the government, the Pentagon, they all leak like a sieve. Well, that may be the attitude in journalism, but if you ask military folks, they will tell you that secrets can be kept. Secrets *are* kept. . . . I think there's a strong possibility that we have recovered some sort of alien technology and are trying to incorporate that into military programs.

Popular knowledges and the tabloid media have consequently become quite adept at filling the knowledge vacuums created by official silence. Skeptical tabloid storytelling and the production of suspicious popular knowledges are strategic interventions into the epistemic void produced by official refusals to confirm or deny. Against well-established patterns of deceit and disavowal, the tabloid media produce their own accounts that not only challenge what few positive statements officials have offered but also fill the surrounding void with unlicensed forms of popular knowledge assembled from a patchwork of ordinary voices, shadowy figures, anonymous sources, and experts in heretical sciences such as UFOlogy.

The last of my televisual examples, another story from *Sightings*, implicates racial power exerted through government institutions and demonstrates that fantastic tabloidism does not always view difference with unambiguous suspicion (as it seems to do in some alien abduction reports). This time the unlikely culprit is not the U.S. military but rather the New Jersey Department of Transportation. Soon after they began excavations for New Jersey Highway 55 near Deptford Township, several workers were overheard in a bar discussing a number of Native American artifacts they had unearthed at the construction site. Rumors about the artifacts spread quickly and caught the attention of a local historian, who subsequently petitioned the Department of Transportation for access to the site but was denied. Unable to stop the construction project through legal channels, the historian went to Chief Wayandaga, shaman for the Eastern Delaware Nation. Wayandaga also petitioned the Department of Transportation, noting that "to us, our ancestors are sacred. And anything that is connected with our ancestors, the whole area, to us, is sacred. And we do not defile it in any way. And we don't want anyone else to defile it." Wayandaga explains, however, that

> they just laughed at me. So I raised my hands to the heavens and I prayed to the Great Spirit and I prayed to my ancestors. Then, all these things happened. . . . The winds came up and blew vehicles off the road with . . . their workers in them and I think that at that particular day there were fifteen who died as a result of it. It was not that I wanted the people to die. It was that I wanted the site to be left alone.

In the months following Chief Wayandaga's prayer, there were an inordinate number of "mysterious" accidents at the construction site. *Sightings* host Tim White describes some of them, noting that "the sheer number of tragedies seemed to be more than coincidence." Nevertheless, the New Jersey Department of Transportation (unsurprisingly) "denies that there was anything unusual about the deaths and injuries that have occurred." To admit otherwise would validate the Native American knowledge about the tragedies at the construction site and the sacredness of the grounds on which it is located. Therefore the government agency mobilizes empiricism and scientific rationalism against the socially weaker discourses used to challenge its actions. Scientific rationalism, of course, has no concept of the "sacred," nor of the spiritual protection of territorial rights, so that, from its perspective, Native American claims on the burial ground are *senseless*. The *Sightings* report, however, questions the truth put forth by the Department of Transportation.

One of the central issues in the case is the department's insistence on the scientific "unprovability" of Wayandaga's claims for the existence of a burial ground at the site of Highway 55. In support of the state's position, a project coordinator appears on camera with a variety of artifacts that have been unearthed there and subsequently cataloged with anthropological precision. They date, he tells us, from as early as 6000 B.C. The bureaucrat observes that the soil at the construction site is "fairly acidic," so that "organic remains" will "not last very long" there—"two, three hundred years tops before they completely disintegrate into the soil." Because one could therefore *expect* to find no physical evidence of burial, the government department claims it has invalidated the Delaware Nation's petition a priori. As the project coordinator pronounces, "The bones are no longer there. The descendants are no longer there. *We do not know* if somebody was buried there or not." Hence the scientific evidence provides no grounds for halting the construction project.

By contrast with the supposedly "objective" scientific discourse used to support the Transportation Department's disposition of the contested lands, Chief Wayandaga's knowledge is based on an *explicitly interested* under- standing of the lived practices of the Native American settlement that once existed on the construction site. He describes his argument with a govern- ment official: "I said, 'Well even if there's no bones left, that still was a burial site.' 'So how do you know?' [he asked]. I said, 'How do I know?' I said, 'These are my ancestors, that's how I know.'" Wayandaga continues, "If there was a village, then within a hundred yards in one direction or the other, there would have to be a burial site. Because, after all, they didn't have horses. They didn't have any other means of transportation. So they had to carry the body." Nevertheless, the Department of Transportation agent per- sists in his insistence that without scientifically valid evidence, we cannot infer the existence of a burial ground on the site now occupied by Highway 55. In its presentation of the conflict, *Sightings* intercuts between footage of the project coordinator and the chief to emphasize the contradictoriness of their respective arguments and the imbalance of power that exists between them, and to provoke audience antipathy toward the bureaucrat. Signifi- cantly, his image is shot from an unusually low camera angle and marked by videographic effects that bathe half his face and body in a harsh, bright light while shrouding the other half in shadow, all of which accentuates the "us versus them" framework within which *Sightings* represents the antago- nistically arrayed forces of hegemony and counterhegemony.

In this story, then, we have an excellent illustration of scientific ratio- nalism operating in its social role as a denier of popular knowledges. As such, it is mobilized to advance dominant interests that seek to extend their reach over ever more people's lives. The Department of Transporta- tion's Eurocentric scientism invalidates the Native American way of know- ing, which uses prayer to the Great Spirit, concepts of the sacred, and an intimate understanding of ancestral ways to contest imperialization. Were the department to admit that the mysterious deaths at the construction site may have occurred through the intervention of the Great Spirit, as Chief Wayandaga claims, the department's continued extension of power over the lands of New Jersey would be seriously threatened, for it could no longer ignore the voices of those who have different ideas about how vari- ous grounds ought to be treated. Consequently the highway department dismisses the inordinately high number of deaths at the construction site by calling them a "coincidence," a word used by scientific rationalism to deny the significance of an event. All of this demonstrates that the New Jer- sey Department of Transportation's control over the contested lands near Deptford Township is not exerted only through physical machinery. It is operationalized not only through bulldozers and cement mixers, for to clear

Chief Wayandaga.

DAVID MUDGE
NJ DOT Project Coordinator

The face of a New Jersey highwayman.

the land for its highways, the government also needs the discursive power of an epistemology that enables it to dismiss Native American knowledges as "silly superstitions."

The discursive power of scientific rationalism, like all of the power-bloc's social powers, is never absolute. Its capacity to adequately explain and thus to control the lives of the people is constantly taken to task in tabloid culture. The popular fantastic of tabloid television, like the menippean discourse of fantastic supermarket tabloids, is an important arena wherein the explanatory powers of official knowledge are questioned and often refused. Although the fantastic popular knowledges often circulated in tabloid television are, to be sure, socially weaker than those produced by the cultural forces of the power-bloc, they are far from insignificant. While they do not articulate a coherent critical vision of the current sociopolitical order, they do embody some of the disruptive forces that emanate from marginalized social positions. Moreover, they help to produce and sustain a living, popular antagonism toward hegemonic institutions and ways of knowing.

Because the discursive power to establish truth is central to the strategies of social domination, we ought not to trivialize popular skepticism toward official systems of knowledge. The production of counterknowledges and countertruths matters because it supports the existence of culturally decolonized spaces. Rather than dismissing fantastic tabloid media as agents of mystification and depoliticization, we must begin to listen more attentively to the voices and stories to which tabloidism accords a level of credibility that has long been denied by serious journalism and the official culture of which it is a part. Tabloid culture, in its fantastic forms, often works to resignify the meanings of events in ways that provoke popular suspicions, some progressive and some reactionary. Some fantastic tabloid stories encourage and enhance repressed and displaced cultural anxieties about racial difference. Others, by contrast, ease the way toward the formation of some types of interracial popular alliances. What new alliances become possible when the white population of a small Pennsylvania town begins to share a perspective that has long been familiar to colonized peoples: that aliens are coming (and that the government and its military organizations are up to no good)? I wonder what sense the Kecksburg townsfolk might have made of the *Sightings* report on Chief Wayandaga's battle against the New Jersey government, or what meanings the members of the Delaware Nation might have taken from the suggestion that the United States Army is abducting white U.S. citizens for use as subjects in biological research projects. I doubt they would be surprised. Perhaps they would be pleased by the prospect of a political alliance with an unlikely social formation that is similarly resentful of the profoundly antidemocratic institutions that control so many sectors of U.S. society.

5 Normalization and Its Discontents: The Conflictual Space of Daytime Talk Shows

During the daytime, the talk shows round up the dregs of the Earth for the daily sleaze-letting. Kids watch—in the summer, or after school. Thanks to talk TV, my kid knows more about birth control than a pharmacist. Think of what they absorb about our cultural values from women with breasts the size of ocean liners, housewives who moonlight as prostitutes, and crack addicts who sell their babies. —Joy Overbeck, TV Guide [1]

The people on these shows are an emotional vanguard, blowing the lid off the idea that America is anything like the place Ronald Reagan pretended to live in. —Elayne Rapping, The Progressive [2]

It seems only fair to start by telling you, in a nutshell, what I really think of talk shows. As gayman, I think they're a wretched little place, emptied of so much wisdom and filled, thank God, with inadvertent camp, but they're the place most enthusiastically afforded us—a measure of our cultural value. We are taking, and are being given, much more pub-lic media space now, but only because talk shows forged a path in there, and we had best understand what we can from the wretched little space where we were once honored guests. —Joshua Gamson, Freaks Talk Back: Tabloid Talk Shows and Sexual Nonconformity [3]

In October 1995 a moralistic senator from Connecticut, Joseph Lieber-man, joined forces with the self-anointed secretary of civic virtue and former Reagan and Bush administration official William Bennett to host a press conference denouncing U.S. daytime TV talk shows as sites of "moral rot" and "cultural pollution." [4] Although Bennett captured media attention by outing businesses that advertise on talk shows, it was Lieberman who came surprisingly close to theoretical prescience when he observed that the pro-grams unsettle distinctions between the perverse and the normal. [5] Day-time talk shows, staples of the new tabloid media, do indeed thrive on contestation over the difference between normal and abnormal. They in-vite the participation of people whose voices are often excluded from U.S. commercial media discourse, such as sex workers, ordinary women, blue- and pink-collar laborers, the homeless, the HIV positive, people living with AIDS, youths, gay men, lesbians, the transgendered, people with unconventional body shapes and sizes, alien abductees, convicted criminals, prison inmates, and other socially marginalized "abnormals." Says Elayne Rapping of the daytime talk shows, "There is something exhilarating about watching people who are usually invisible—because of class, race, gender, status—having their say and, often, being wholly disrespectful to their 'betters.' "[6]

If Reaganism entailed a widespread cultural repression of voices and identities representing social difference, Reaganism's repressed others returned with a vengeance on TV's tabloid talk shows, whose numbers grew impressively from the mid- to late 1980s and exploded spectacularly during the early nineties. By widening both the sense of social distance and the power gap between the haves and the have-nots, and by stepping up the surveillance and policing of alterity, twelve years of Reagan-Bushism intensified already bitter conflicts around social difference.[7] The oft-noted intense conflictuality of U.S. daytime TV talk shows is symptomatic of social conflicts that escalated sharply during the Reagan decade and the Bush years. But it is also symptomatic of an expanding rupture in the longer historical trajectory that Michel Foucault has delineated in his genealogies of "normalization."[8] "Normalization" refers to the mechanisms and objectives of certain regulatory practices made possible and dominant by the development of the modern human sciences and their attendant forms of expert knowledge. In this chapter, I will develop an analysis of U.S. daytime talk shows that draws on Foucault's ideas but also attempts to indicate their ultimate inadequacy for understanding a phenomenon of tabloid culture such as this one. The inadequacy of Foucault's work for understanding talk shows stems largely from its basis in the comparatively homogeneous societies of early modern Europe, which lacked, for example, racial conflicts on the level of those characteristic of both the Reaganist United States and the *Ricki Lake* show.

Norms R Us

The existence of a whole set of techniques and institutions for measuring, supervising and correcting the abnormal brings into play . . . all the mechanisms of power . . . disposed around the abnormal individual, to brand him and to alter him.—Michel Foucault, *Discipline and Punish*[9]

I begin with a brief discussion of the concept of normalization, since the issue of norms (and the abnormal) is necessary for an adequate understanding of daytime talk shows. Modern knowledge practices that derive from the scientific epistemologies of the Enlightenment are ultimately responsible for the construction and social centrality of the concept of the "normal."[10] "Normality" is a product of power-bearing prescription combined with the medicalization of social identities and differences. Knowledge practices that center the "normal" and marginalize its others constitute a field of power that is immensely significant. The medicalization of social difference has led to the institutionalization of a regime of truth based on normalizing practices that work to sustain asymmetrical and power-laden relations between the "normal" and the "abnormal" (subjecting the latter, for example, to social stigmatization and treatment). Normalization is thus central to both the mobilization of power and the stabilization of order within Western societies. Commentators such as Mark Philp therefore claim that an obsession with creating "a normal and healthy population" lies at the very heart of modern social control.[11]

As Western societies modernized, most of the corporeal marks that had traditionally indicated privilege, status, and affiliation were displaced by "a whole range of degrees of normality."[12] If premodern social control was exerted predominantly through the spectacular imposition of the sheer force of the sovereign on the bodies of certain transgressive subjects, industrial society required more efficient means of regulating its citizens. Power had to invent new ways to ensure that its effects would circulate "through progressively finer channels, gaining access to individuals themselves, to their bodies, their gestures and all their daily actions."[13] Contemporary democracies rely on institutional techniques of normalization to facilitate the surveillance and regulation of social differences. In one sense, normalization imposes homogeneity. But at the same time, it individuates by enabling the measurement of gaps between the normal and the abnormal along a variety of different axes. Consequently, in societies based on formal legal equality, norms become culturally central, since they introduce and regulate all shades of individual difference within the context of a compulsory level of homogeneity.[14]

Normalization entails the marginalization not only of particular individuals but also of particular aspects of the individual self, physical and psychological dimensions of our lives that we police, suppress, and deny because of the possibility of subjection to normalizing judgments.[15] The very notion of one's "self" is always already a fictive construct that systematically selects some aspects of experience, being, desire, and so forth for inclusion as elements of one's "identity" and excludes others with equal systematicity. Philp notes that the human sciences' "normalising and subjecting attempts to define some single, cohesive human condition" have made us into "divided selves, treating sanity, health and conformity to social mores as components of our 'real selves,' and repudiating as foreign to us our diseases, irrationalities and delinquencies."[16]

Foucault notes that psychiatry and the other human sciences have always been closely allied with various social policy-making and policing functions.[17] Therefore they usually intervene in situations that are seen to threaten the maintenance of "public order," including those where crime disrupts the systematic maldistribution of material resources and security, where sexual practices transgress reproductive exigencies and regulatory mores, and where racial differences question the ostensible universality of European reason. The knowledges developed in response to Enlightenment philosophy's "demands for a rational order of governance . . . founded on reason and norms of human functioning" have thus led to the social dispersion of normalizing discourses and practices.[18] Although prisons, hospitals, factories, military barracks, and schools are not exactly microcosms of contemporary Western societies, such institutions nevertheless serve as laboratories for the development of socially generalizable techniques of observation and power-bearing, normalizing judgment: the repetitive exercise, the examination and panopticism, to name just a few from the Foucauldian panoply of disciplinary practices. But what also gets socially generalized is the very idea of normalizing judgment—the belief that normality is an essential component of social health. Former social scientist and longstanding U.S. senator Daniel Patrick Moynihan, for example, has come to symbolize the centrality of normalizing knowledges in modern social policy making, which Christopher Lasch has termed "the medicalization of politics."[19] On a Sunday morning chat show appearance in 1994, to choose a convenient example, Moynihan complains characteristically that Americans are "getting used to a lot of deviancy, taking it for granted." He opines that contemporary disturbances of the boundary between "normal" and "abnormal" lie at the heart of American social degeneracy and will likely "destroy" the human species.[20] Moynihan's discourse normalizes the elaboration of a political regime on the foundations of the human sciences, an undertaking that is fraught with risks and inconstancies.

Within the contemporary regime of social power, as Foucault has put it, "the judges of normality are present everywhere." Thus we are now in "the society of the teacher-judge, the doctor-judge, the educator-judge, the 'social worker'-judge," and, we might add, the talk-show-host-judge. "It is on them that the universal reign of the normative is based." Foucault avers that "each individual, wherever he may find himself, subjects to it his body, his gestures, his behavior, his aptitudes, his achievements."[21] We must question this assertion, however. In postmodern culture, any clear and categorical sense of the difference between "normal" and "abnormal" has been rendered volatile and incredible. This owes partly to the fact that many people who are frequently targeted by normalizing judgments have begun to produce a variety of resistive counterdiscourses. The consequent multidiscursivity of key sites of cultural productivity within U.S. society has generally destabilized a number of normalizing discourses by unmasking the power that had once been hidden beneath such designations as "reason," "truth," and "science." Multidiscursivity is a product of struggles to assert that marginalized social differences have a right to exist beyond a society's margins, despite the attempts of dominant knowledges to silence, speak for, and even eliminate alterity. Tabloid talk shows are among the primary sites of multidiscursivity within U.S. media culture. This is not to say that talk shows are utopian spaces of discursive democracy. Multidiscursivity takes place within a context of unequal social relations and is therefore best illuminated not by theories of democracy but rather by ones of power, domination, and resistance, for it is usually driven by antagonism and inflected with hostility.[22] While relations between competing discourses in talk shows are fraught with hostilities and inequalities, the genre is nevertheless one of the most significant arenas in contemporary media where socially weak and marginalized formations compete with stronger ones for the power to advance their own sociopolitical interests.

Talk shows are frequently dismissed as the electronic descendants of nineteenth- and early-twentieth-century circus sideshows. Neil Postman and Steve Powers, for example, revive this cliché in their glib characterization of the talk show genre as "nothing more than a highly profitable freak show" that "serves as a diversion from the urgent issues of the day." [23] Such a view is not only naively simplistic but also demeaning to those whose persecution, deprivation, and social marginalization consign them to virtual invisibility in most commercial media programming besides talk shows. This particular brand of social invisibility is especially debilitating in societies such as the United States where, increasingly, the most significant sociopolitical struggles are waged in and through the media. Laura Grindstaff, a scholar who worked for more than a year behind the scenes at two tabloid talk shows, observes that the genre is crucially shaped by the socially generalized silence that surrounds the sorts of people and issues to which these programs give voice, "since the more excluded a group or topic has been, the more likely it is to appear on a daytime talk show." [24] Marginalized social formations learned quickly to capitalize on the media space that talk shows readily afford them.

Cultural conservatives like Postman and Powers are not the only critics of TV talk shows. Some on the Left, like Elayne Rapping, argue that whatever media presence the oppressed, subordinated, and socially excluded might gain from participation in talk shows is largely irrelevant, for commercial television inevitably contains the threat they pose to dominant ideologies. However, although their sponsors, producers, and hosts may try to control the circulation of meanings in talk shows, favoring and reinforc-

ing those that are most ideologically acceptable and condemning or marginalizing those that aren't, the popularity of these programs owes at least
in part to the fact that both guests and audiences continuously threaten
to break free from the control that producers seek desperately to secure.[25]
If, as structuralist Marxists assert, media ideology creates compliant subjectivities and, as poststructuralists claim, techniques of social discipline
produce docile bodies, neither power works very effectively in talk shows,
where both bodies and subjectivities display a remarkable range of capacities. Indeed, the discursive practices of talk show participants suggest that
the concept of "subjectivity" is inadequate in this context, for it implies
"subjection to" and thus passivity. Instead, we must think of talk show participants as discursive (and therefore social) *agents*—not the "free agents" of
liberal pluralism but rather the relatively socially weak and disempowered
agents who nevertheless possess both a sense of their own sociopolitical
interests and the capacity to assert and defend them in a variety of creative
ways.

Norms Aren't Us

The resignification of norms is . . . a function of their inefficacy, and so the question of

subversion, of working the weakness in the norm, becomes a matter of inhabiting the

practices of its rearticulation. —Judith Butler, *Bodies That Matter: On the Discursive Limits of*

"Sex" [26]

Throughout modernity, various forms of scientific knowledge have been instrumental in the production and social mobilization of norms. Although
the very concept of the "scientific" contains within itself the grandiose
promise of knowledge that is detached from and unanswerable to power,
the "human sciences" are nevertheless responsible for producing an ever
expanding web of disciplinary specialists who in fact operationalize controlling power at a multitude of new points of application.[27] In light of this,
one of the most remarkable things about the cultural space created by the
tabloid talk shows is that within it, the hierarchy of knowledge that subor-
dinates "ordinary" ways of knowing to those of the credentialed scientific
expert is frequently turned on its head. Thus, although the analytical perspectives of scholars and other outside experts are often included in the programs, they don't seem to count for as much as the first-person voices of
direct experience that are the typical objects of expert analysis.[28] This gives
the programs a unique structure of feeling: sometimes antagonistic, sometimes defensive, sometimes celebratory, sometimes all of these by turns,
the first-person ethos of the talk shows defies the power-bearing detach-

ment of scientistic experts. Although ordinary epistemological hierarchies are not always inverted in the talk shows, the power of dominant discourses is nevertheless often weakened there by multidiscursive dilution and contestation over meanings. This creates opportunities for insurgency by discursive guerrillas who are quick to capitalize on any openings they can find.

Tabloid talk show guests are often subjected to a variety of normalizing judgments proffered by panelists and audience members alike. For example, when *Donahue* featured men and women involved in games of sexual domination and submission, numerous studio audience members and telephone callers complained about the "sickness" and "abnormality" of the guests, their practices, and their desires. Among the guests were two men who wore leather masks throughout the program to conceal their identities (because of widespread bigotry), one amateur and two professional dominatrixes (garbed in studded leather), a maker of "fetish films," and a psychiatrist whose knowledge of the practices of sexual domination was that of a relatively sympathetic outsider. This episode of *Donahue*, like many tabloid talk shows, was very much involved in the negotiation of issues around gender, performance, identity, and difference—areas where norms work hard to insinuate order. Practices of sexual domination are theoretically and politically significant precisely because they disturb the order that norms work to stabilize. If the production and enforcement of norms are as central to the mobilization of power in contemporary society as I believe they are, then the evasion and interrogation of norms are far from insignificant. Indeed, they must be recast as indispensable powers whereby the socially weak undermine controlling mechanisms for the identification and disciplining of social differences.

When Donahue's audience and Donahue himself spoke from a normalizing perspective, his guests were quick to produce alternative accounts of their own sexual identities. For instance, one man from the audience says, "I was curious if the women can look back in their past and point to any dysfunctional relationships with family members that caused them to . . . get great pleasure from [sexual domination]." This comment implicitly postulates the "dysfunctionality" of the guests' sexual practices by positing their origin in a "dysfunctional" cause and is interesting for at least two reasons.[29] First, it raises the question of whether many men would posit the "dysfunctionality" or abnormality of *masculine* sexual domination vis-à-vis women. Second, it is significant that the question is posed not directly *to* the women, in the second person, but rather in the clinical, diagnostic third-person form, for normalizing power depends on the exclusion of "abnormal" perspectives from the realm of "truth." Nevertheless, in response, Mistress Jacqueline, a professional dominatrix, denies the dysfunctionality of "the [S/M] scene" and asserts its positive benefits, thereby shifting "dysfunctionality" *from* her practices and relocating it within the very norms that marginalize them:

> I was never really told that I could do anything much in my life. I was supposed to do the usual: get married, go to college, become a school-teacher, blah, blah, blah. I did all that, and then I went on, I got my master's degree in clinical psychology. But I had a lot of stuff in me that wasn't expressed, and there was a point in my life where I decided to go out and *explore*, and explore some of my own fantasies and secrets. And through this scene, I've actually developed a great deal of self-esteem.

Implicit in Mistress Jacqueline's response is a critique of the prohibitive and regulatory function of norms, which she associates with lifelong feelings of constraint and disempowerment. For her, norms of femininity (which she calls "the usual") kept her from exploring different avenues of self-expression, pleasure, and empowerment, which she has found as a professional dominatrix. Moreover, her career has been enormously lucrative while providing her with a sense of self-esteem she had previously been denied. The spillover of self-esteem and empowerment from her sexual games into her everyday life undoubtedly relates to the way in which those games enact rituals of inversion that place men in an entirely submissive relationship to women. We see spillover effects when, for example, after Donahue expresses an attitude toward Mistress Jacqueline's work with which she takes exception and then repeatedly gets her name wrong, she assertively upbraids him while playfully feigning a kick in his direction with the pointed toe of her black leather boot.

S/M is a tellingly typical topic for talk shows and so is worth thinking about in some detail. These games of power/pleasure/pain uncannily embody the cultural inversions characteristic of the carnivalesque, along with its ritualistic juxtapositions of degradation and regeneration, disgust and desire, of which Mikhail Bakhtin has so eloquently written. Anne McClintock's analysis of S/M evokes this connection with carnivalistic motifs: "The paradox and scandal of S/M is its flagrant exposure in the form of a spectacle of the conceptual and political limits of the liberal ideal of the autonomous individual." [30] In the *Donahue* episode, we are treated to videotapes of Mistress Jacqueline as she enacts this spectacle with a client—footage that would undoubtedly be considered too "tasteless," "weird," and "titillating" for mainstream journalism. McClintock suggests that the outrage and ridicule with which S/M is often met in contemporary mainstream culture is a product of its provocative recognition and display of the artificiality and reversibility of power relations. [31] Princess Pamela Payne, another professional dominatrix on the program, supports the view of S/M as a ritualistic inversion of power dynamics, noting that "a lot of the guys that come to see

Mistress Jacqueline and client.

me, the clientele, they're blue-collar and white-collar workers. They fired somebody that day. They want to be disciplined for doing that. You know, they want to be put back in their place." The guests on the program stress repeatedly that many participants in the S/M scene are otherwise "normal" appearing men, some of whom occupy relatively powerful positions in their ordinary lives. (Indeed, Mistress Jacqueline describes one of the leather-masked men on the panel, a regular client who says he "belongs" to her, as "the most influential of people.") The importance of anonymity to the otherwise socially powerful men involved in the S/M scene demonstrates the centrality of norms as controllers of access to power. Moreover, it underlines the significance of S/M as a power inverter: not only do the domina-trixes gain power over their clients at the level of sexual play, but they equally gain control over their clients' anonymity and thus over their reputations. Mistress Anne makes the point nicely: "When I'm playing domination, I always believe that I should wear more clothes than the submissive, that part of their being submissive is the fact that the man is naked and exposed."

Mistress Jacqueline's newfound self-esteem stems not only from the ritu-als of inversion involved in the sexual games themselves but also from the confidence and financial independence that she has achieved as the owner of her own enterprise (which includes publications, an alternative thera-peutic practice, and a telephone chat line designed to help people inter-ested in the scene to meet one another). Moreover, the very defiance enacted through her refusal of norms seems to have equipped Mistress Jacqueline with a sense of pride, spirit, and confidence that is reflected, for example, in her easy use of humor to deflect the abuse leveled at her by an angry telephone caller to the *Donahue* show. This caller (a woman) announces, "I think that this is a form of brutality." Referring to Mistress Jacqueline, the woman continues, "and I think, for the *pig* . . . with the long hair, who has two thousand clients, . . . this is a form of prostitution. . . . Any man who'd like to get beat up by a woman has some serious mental problems."[32] To these remarks, Mistress Jacqueline responds in a disarmingly parodic manner: (laughing) "Excuse me, I'm not into *verbal humiliation*, darling." It is illustrative of the social inclusiveness of tabloid talk show dialogue that after the call criticizing Mistress Jacqueline's business as "a form of prostitution," a twenty-seven-year-old woman telephoned *Donahue* to express a different viewpoint: "I'm a prostitute in New York City, and I don't think there's anything wrong, you know, with what these women do." Mistress Jacqueline thanked the caller for her support, adding, "and I don't think there's anything wrong with what you do, either."

In their *strict* insistence on payment, women who perform commercial S/M (and, indeed, other sex workers as well) enact a theatrical spectacle that highlights the unnaturalness of unpaid domestic and sexual labor.[33] Not surprisingly, middle-class culture typically erases the voices of both the prostitute and the dominatrix. Indeed, normalizing judgmentality tries to shame them into silence. They often refuse to be silenced, however, and the talk show is one of few sites within media culture where their refusals can be vocalized. The social demonization of all sex workers is a form of normalizing power. The commodification of sex by women—and particularly the commercialization of "deviant" practices—violates regulatory fictions regarding what can properly be construed as labor. Indeed, McClintock argues that sex workers are socially demonized because they demand money for services that men expect to receive for free. "Prostitutes screw the system, dangerously interfering in the male distribution of property, power, and profit." Sex work that is not under the tight control of male pimps, legislators, police officers, and judges "differs from most women's work," McClintock argues, "in that it is far better paid, has flexible working hours, and gives women considerable economic independence from men." She quotes a prostitute who told her that "it's the stigma that hurts, not the sex. The sex is easy. Facing the world's hate is what breaks me down." McClintock concludes that "the whore stigma," a particularly virulent mode of masculinist judgmentality, "disciplines all women," for "the license to despise a prostitute is a license to despise any woman who takes sex, money and mobility into her hands." Thus "empowering whores empowers all women, and educating men to respect prostitutes educates men to respect all women."[34] TV talk shows are an arena of discursive contestation where sex workers can fight back against the whore stigma that is used as a technique of normalization that targets women in general.

By producing a resistant counterdiscourse in dialogue with the normalizing one expressed by many audience members, talk show guests often work to educate others to better understand and respect their differences. They may challenge elements of language, for example, and assert terms that they prefer over those often used against them. Thus Mistress Jacqueline admonishes her audience, "Could we not use the word 'beat-up,' because we, we prefer . . . saying 'spanked' or 'whipped' or 'tied up.' We're not beating anybody up." Mistress Jacqueline continues, asserting that the S/M scene is, among other things,

> about mutual consensuality. All of us up here [onstage] are into this scene in a very, very responsible way. We talk about things up front . . . We don't coerce anybody. It's all about mutual enjoyment. It's about having fun. And it's really a very intimate relationship, because you're expressing to people your innermost selves. . . . It's not about pain, it's about pleasure/pain. It's about expressing little things about yourself. A lot of the people that I see like to cross-dress, for instance.

Such a strategy reconfigures dominant modes of sense making and thus produces a new sense of what it means to practice S/M. This reconfiguration indicates that the normal and the abnormal do not exist in a stable and exclusive relation to each other. The difference between the two is not, therefore, a categorical one but rather a relative, fluidly mobile, and dynamic one that requires constant negotiation and renegotiation. Talk shows constitute sites of negotiation between normalizing and norm-interrogating discourses whose powers are mobilized through various articulations of one's own social identity. Christine Gledhill usefully explains that "the term 'negotiation' implies the holding together of opposite sides in an ongoing process of give-and-take," where meaning "arises out of a struggle . . . between competing frames of reference, motivation and experience."[35] Mistress Jacqueline's rearticulation of the S/M scene entails a complex set of negotiations between conventional and marginalized sexual practices and identities.

The resignification of norms thus necessarily involves practices of identity negotiation. The term "identity negotiation" requires a complex conceptualization of social identity that avoids the assumption that identities are fixed before their entry into discursive processes. Identity is instead always in process. It is constantly reconfigured through the negotiations that discursive struggles engender. Consequently, talk shows are best understood not as spaces where already fixed identities come into collision.

Rather, they are sites where different actors negotiate the articulation of their own identity formations. Such articulations of identity are rarely pure, for they shift between different discursive formations. The members of the S/M scene, for example, refer throughout the Donahue program to the "normality" of their childhoods, their daily lives, their previous marriages, and so forth. They even justify their practices using some of the same concepts and formulations that have historically been mobilized against "perversities" such as S/M. Mistress Jacqueline's explanation of her work in explicitly therapeutic terms, for example, suggests an area of negotiation between the discourse of S/M and those of the normalizing human sciences. This point of negotiation evokes what Foucault calls "the tactical polyvalence of discourse." Foucault observes that the same discourse may be mobilized in the service of alternative, even mutually opposed, strategic aims.[36] That the marginalized discourse of S/M negotiates actively with more normalizing ones should not, therefore, lead to the conclusion that the latter have effectively incorporated its difference into their regime of truth, thereby domesticating the political threat that difference poses. The S/M practitioners repeatedly set their dissatisfaction with what they experience as a stifling and bland sexual normality against the pleasures they experience in the S/M scene. Clearly at stake in all this (and quite contradictorily, for the men especially) is the power to produce a sense of identity over which each participant has more control and from which he or she derives more pleasure than is possible in their "normal" lives.

Negotiation is, of course, a two-way process. Apropos of this, the S/M practitioners' discourse seems to exert some power against the normalizing judgments bespoken in several audience members' comments. Some audience members even expressed an interest in the S/M scene that seemed previously to have been either absent or successfully shamed into silence but that developed over the hour-long course of the show. Perhaps through the process of negotiating with counternormalizing discourses, some audience members were encouraged to police themselves less vigilantly for problematic regions of abnormality. In such instances, the discursive space of the tabloid talk shows is significant for the way in which it allows for the persuasion of our self-policing faculties to lower their guard from time to time, if only temporarily. Interestingly, along these lines, the first audience member to speak during this episode of Donahue prefaced her question by nervously asking the host, "What's a nice Catholic Ohio girl doing at a show like this?" Near the end of the hour, by contrast, Donahue spoke with a telephone caller who began, "I'm a librarian from Iowa, and I wanted to ask Miss Anne [the amateur dominatrix on the panel who is an out-of-work librarian] if she felt a contradiction, like in her personality and what not. I, I'm interested in this, but I'm, I'm scared." Confronting and accepting the existence of significant internal contradiction may violate the most normalizing under-standings of the self, but it is crucial to the process of identity negotiation. Consequently, the following exchange ensued:

> *Mistress Anne:* If you can tell somebody to put a book back on the shelf and put their chair back in the place quietly, then you're aggressive enough to make a good dominant.
> *Donahue:* You would like to be a dominatrix?
> *Caller:* Yes, I would.
> *Donahue:* And you would like to be a dominant over men.
> *Caller:* Yes . . .
> *Donahue:* Are you in a relationship with a male person now?
> *Caller:* Yes, yes, I am.
> *Donahue:* Have you, do you have the courage to talk to him about this?
> *Caller:* I don't think so. I'd like to.
> *Carter Stevens (panelist and fetish-film maker):* Then do it! That's the big, that's the biggest problem, is people are afraid to talk about this!
> *Donahue:* I bet they are.
> *Mistress Jacqueline:* Tell him to watch this show. Tell him to turn it on right now.

This exchange speaks to the way in which the enforcement of silence functions as a powerful normalizing instrumentality. There is a coincidental linguistic similarity between the words "science" and "silence," but there is also an important if usually neglected connection between the concepts they signify, for in social practice, science has a way of systematically in-ducing effects of silence on some individuals and populations at particular times in specific places. In his or her claims to objectivity and rationality, the scientific expert purports to rise above contingency and politics. Cindy Patton notes that this move legitimates the sciences' role in the social con-struction of boundaries between the normal and its other.[37] The inscription of such boundaries consigns the other to a publicly observed silence, the suspension of which is encouraged only under specifically prescribed con-ditions involving carefully controlled incitements to speak (about which I shall have more to say). Scientists routinely speak diagnostically of those who defy conformity. Despite claims to objectivity, diagnostic discourse always serves a controlling function that either silences or marginalizes the voices of diagnosed subjects by subsuming them within its own explana-tions.

Talk shows create spaces wherein the diagnosed can boldly express their refusal of such diagnostic discourses and audience members can heretically join in support of their dissident voices. Consider alien abductees, to take an example that is somewhat (though not entirely) removed from the issue

of sexual normality. Alien abductees think of "going public" as a coura-
geously sacrificial act of good citizenship made in the interest of community awareness and safety—courageous because, as abductees well know,
from mainstream perspectives they appear to be irrational and unscien-
tific.[38] The talk shows, of course, are perfect arenas for the expression of
defiance against all manner of expert knowledges and scientific orthodoxies
in the name of firsthand experience and emotional authority. When alien
abductees appeared on the *Ricki Lake* show, they were met, predictably, with
an outpouring of ridicule and condemnation. But they also found sympathy and support from a minority in the audience who encouraged the abductees to continue speaking of their painful experiences despite dismissal
and trivialization by those who cling dogmatically to an official truth that
rigidly denies outright the validity of their personal narratives.[39] Like alien
abductees, sexual nonconformists are expected to remain silent in mainstream U.S. culture. "Silence," Patton writes: "the never spoken, the yet to
set itself into language, . . . madness, the unrepresentable, the space of that
which is not to be represented, the closet."[40] For almost three centuries,
the human sciences have spoken of sex and sexuality as "public health"
issues, a hegemonic deployment of discursive forces that has produced various closets designed to ensure the silence of those consigned there. Nevertheless, the tabloid talk shows constitute a media space that time and again
disrupts various enforced silences.

Foucault asserts that "the rallying point for the counterattack" against
the regulatory deployment of modern notions of normal sexuality ought
to be "bodies and pleasures."[41] By this, he may mean nothing more (and
nothing less) than the social mobilization of differences that question the
capacity of norms to account for the multiplicity of pleasure-bearing practices through which many people produce a sense of self that partially
evades hegemonic incorporation. The guests on the S/M episode of *Donahue*
speak on behalf of nothing so passionately and unashamedly as the insistent
claims of bodies and pleasures, against massive discursive deployments of
the forces of normalization and "healthy sexuality." Judith Butler objects
that Foucault's defense of bodies and pleasures violates his own arguments
against essentialism (the problematic idea that there is a "prediscursive libidinal multiplicity" or a " 'multiplicity of pleasures' in *itself* which is not
the effect of any specific discourse/power exchange") and sexual liberationism (the problematic idea that "by saying yes to sex we say no to power").[42]
We need not assume, however, that bodies and pleasures are either natural or essential (and therefore amenable to "liberation") to recognize that
the multiplication of sexual identities and practices visible in popular culture troubles the established regime of heteronormativity by confounding
its binarisms and "exposing its fundamental unnaturalness."[43] The tabloid

talk show universe is, perhaps, the foremost popular cultural site for the expression of libidinal multiplicity, where socially marginalized bodies, pleasures, and knowledges proliferate.[44] This proliferation cannot but rework the discourses that determine the terrain of the culturally intelligible and acceptable.

Bodies That Speak

Jerry Springer. Once the talk show host was mayor of Cincinnati. Now he's mayor of Sodom. . . . On Springer's show, men learn their girlfriends are actually boys; wives learn their husbands are sleeping with their sisters or ex-wives or both; women learn that their 13-year-old daughters are strippers or their 60-year-old mothers are whores. — David Plotz, Slate[45]

In her analysis of Oprah Winfrey, Gloria-Jean Masciarotte observes that nowhere on television is the individuation of bodies and selves so thoroughly displaced by the spectacle of a collective, talking body as in the daytime talk shows. Masciarotte writes that "the television talk show recoordinates voice and body through the use of visual and aural spectacle. The television talk show participants all perform; there is no naturalized speaker." The openness and indisciplinarity of the tabloid talk shows contribute to the production of a space where norms may be questioned openly, where ordinary distinctions between participant and spectator break down, where the sociality of the body is emphasized over its individuality. Masciarotte writes that "the talk show I is only defined when it too participates. In the publicity of the talk show the constitutive gestures of the individual body are extended from the private to the social as both are traversed by the voice."[46] This engenders a multivocal dispersion of discursive power.

Rapping echoes these themes in her observation that the tabloid talk show's structure "approaches the nonhierarchical. The host is still the star, of course. But in terms of authority, she or he is far from central."[47] Like tabloid newscasts such as A Current Affair, the daytime talk shows decenter the figure of the perfectly stationed talking head, exemplified by the conventional news anchor (see chapter 3). Whereas the authoritative talking-head anchor of the normalizing news speaks official truths, commands reverence, and projects a sense of objectivism and distance between himself and his audience, the body of the tabloid talk show host is materially rooted in the collective body of the audience, and his or her voice enjoys neither special privilege with regard to the articulation of truth nor any objectivized detachment from the issues under discussion. The talk show host is part of a collective body defined by the speech that circulates between its members, a dialogical body whose voices often ring with greater frankness and familiarity than is typical of public discourse in middle-class culture. Not surprisingly, socially central voices frequently disparage the talk shows not only for their "superficiality" and "trashiness" but for being "chaotic" and "anarchic," for not following the rules of etiquette, civility, and order said to be required for "legitimate" public discussion. For example, one mainstream journalist writes that "it's hardly a secret that talk shows aren't serious," but new evidence may show that "they're worse than just mindless entertainment"; indeed, they may be "crippling" their audiences' communicative capacities, because they show people "talking at each other, not to each other, interrupting each other constantly, and rarely listening at length to what others have to say."[48] Similarly, psychologist Robert Simmerman complains that talk shows are particularly dangerous to children, whose "sense of civility" is said to be eroded by the programs.[49]

Of course, the rules of "civility" and "politeness" imposed on "legitimate" public dialogue have, in practice, a controlling and exclusionary effect that hierarchically limits the range of topics considered appropriate, the manner in which those topics will be treated, the types of voices that will be admitted into the dialogue, and the number of interlocutors seen to be acceptable. Rapping provides a useful example that illustrates the difference between "polite" dialogue and talk show "anarchy," whose loose discursive controls allow marginalized voices to interrupt and challenge dominant knowledges. She describes an episode of *Donahue* that dealt with eating disorders, noting that the host had apparently failed to grasp that this was both a significant feminist issue and a matter of life and death for many women. However, by trivializing the issue, Donahue provoked a passionate and conflictual rebellion against his authority by the program's studio audience, home viewers of the live broadcast who participated by telephone, and the guests themselves, actresses who had recently appeared in a film about women and weight consciousness entitled *Eating*.

Like the dominatrixes who appeared on *Donahue* to discuss the S/M scene, these women resisted the authority of their host's masculinist judgmentality. Consequently, women telephoned the program with stories of how their weight had made them suicidal. Others rebuked Donahue for treating the topic frivolously. Still others provided information about support groups and feminist counseling services. As the refusal of trivialization gathered momentum, "one by one, those downstage and then those on stage—the celebrities—rose to tell their stories of bulimia, anorexia, self-loathing, many with tears streaming down their faces."[50] Rapping observes that the "respectable" journalist Ted Koppel would probably never permit such a scene to take place. Instead, several well-credentialed and mostly white male experts would answer "*his* questions about what medical and academic professions know about eating disorders." No audience would participate, there would be little if any dialogue between guests, and no shouting, tears, or other "excessive" emotional involvement with the issue would be allowed, for the middle-class masculinism of the established news brings with it a strong tendency to discount personal styles that don't legitimate and authorize themselves by manufacturing connotations of detached rationality. Furthermore, such excesses are much more easily managed within the established conventions of the "respectable" chat show, whose structure enables the host to quickly regain control and restore order if confronted with unruly guests.[51]

This kind of control is difficult to establish in the tabloid talk shows, which temporarily suspend hierarchies and therefore permit forms of communication that are ordinarily prohibited by both media and more generalized conventions of social interaction. Daytime talk shows engender a frankness and freedom of expression that obliterates the social distance between participants and liberates them from the strictures of "decency" and "etiquette." [52] People speak with perfect strangers about the most intimate or painful or degrading details of their lives. Controls that ordinarily constrain public discourse are loosened. Men with fetishistic desires and their dominatrix mistresses talk openly about their sexual games. Women employed in the sex industries discuss their working conditions and the relationship between their work and their "ordinary" lives. Gay and lesbian teenagers explain their experiences of everyday persecution to straight folks in the studio audience and those watching at home. And so on. Moreover, talk show familiarity tellingly encompasses not only the relations between guests and audience members but also those between viewers and hosts. Oprah Winfrey notes the intimacy with which strangers greet her in public.[53] It is difficult to imagine Dan Rather, Peter Jennings, or Ted Koppel being similarly received.

In a seminal essay, Paolo Carpignano and his colleagues argue that the talk shows' erosion of any physical separation between audiences and hosts works to deprive the latter of their "spatial authority" and is symptomatic of a more general postmodern crisis of representation that has disrupted the contours of the modernist political spectacle in the age of television.[54] The (sometimes frenetic) circulation of the host's body through the audience, where it travels as freely as the interlocutors' voices, encourages the extension of talk show discourse to encompass the physicality of the collective audience-body. We can interpret the paradigmatic image of Phil Donahue running full speed through television studio aisles, carrying a microphone to individuals wishing to be heard, for example, as an index of the tabloid talk shows' subordination of the host function to that of the collective audience-body; it suggests, as well, the host's almost organic connection with the audience and difference from the stationed news anchor, whose body we scarcely know at all. Indeed, the bodies of tabloid talk show hosts are often subsumed as members of a body of popular knowledge. Consider the supermarket tabloids' and television audiences' fascination with the oscillatory growth and shrinkage of Oprah Winfrey's body. Or the oft-replayed image of Phil Donahue wearing a skirt and panty hose for a program about cross-dressing. Or the indelible image of Geraldo Rivera's nose, which was broken during an on-air confrontation with skinhead guests and subsequently swelled to protuberant proportions. Television's talk tabloids create a participatory forum, and the body of the talk show host is a fully materialized and participatory body.

Not only is the talk show body participatory; it is also a site of struggle. Talk shows showcase bodies that defy discipline and transgress limits: fat and elderly strippers, transsexual teens, cross-dressers, and many others. There is a close connection between bodily and discursive forms of transgression or indiscipline. Indeed, because the body is an inevitably signifying entity, bodily indiscipline is itself a form of discursivity that both facilitates and provokes others (such as vocal outbursts). Unleashing the body endangers constraints that secure silence and thus help to maintain social order and so inequality. In talk shows, the temporary suspension of some constraints ordinarily imposed on bodies both provokes and sustains disruptive voices that are normally silenced in public discourse. When the voices of alterity are kept publicly silent, norms can maintain relative invisibility, the modality in which, like secret police, they operate most effectively. When they are driven out into the open and forced to express themselves explicitly, norms become subject to challenge, interrogation, criticism, and therefore change.

These processes, whereby the power ordinarily exerted through norms is undermined and thrown up for grabs, are central to the dynamics of bodies and speech on the tabloid talk shows. For purposes of illustration and elaboration, let's consider a 1995 episode of the *Ricki Lake* show entitled "I'm Gay, You're Gay—but You Give Gays a Bad Name!" As the title suggests, this installment is devoted to conflict between gay men (and, to a lesser extent, between lesbians) over what counts as appropriate public behavior. Featured as guests are two pairs of white gay male friends (Rick and Reid, and Brian and Eric), two black gay male cousins (Stacy and Timmie), and a black lesbian couple (Tonia and Nikki). Also included as a panel of expert commentators are three comedians dubbed the "Funny Gay Males." The audience is a mostly young and multiracial mix of men and women. The central area of contention for the guys onstage is clustered around issues of public display, openness, flamboyance, and flirtation. For the two women, it concerns Nikki's propensity to dress like a man and Tonia's wish that Nikki would foreground her feminine features.

On the surface, this program could easily and neatly be fit into our most commonplace stereotypes about the talk show genre: that it exploits people of difference in its sensationalistic appeals to the normalizing voyeurism of an audience bent only on demolishing the hapless guests. Indeed, Jaffe Cohen, one of the "Funny Gay Males," invokes precisely this stereotype in a subsequent discussion of his appearance on the "I'm Gay, You're Gay" program. Cohen writes that the talk shows can be disastrous for gay men, who are "invariably asked to flame so fiercely that they all but incinerate the audience." Consequently his confidence was none too inspired when, on his way to the taping, he caught his first glimpse of the studio audience waiting to enter the building, a group of "boisterous kids" who "looked too wild to appreciate anything more mature than the finals of the World Wrestling Federation." [55] Nevertheless, a closer look at this program reveals that far from a stereotyped circus culminating in the ritual massacre of unfortunate guests, what unfolds is actually a fascinating discussion of some complex issues concerning sexual identity and performativity, homophobia and violence, difference *within* the gay and lesbian communities, and the uncertainty and messiness of distinctions between the straight and gay/lesbian worlds, between straight and gay/lesbian desire. Rather than the gay participants being asked invariably to flame fiercely for an audience of gapers, flamboyance (and the issues that surround it) is made the very topic of discussion and debate. When Brian, who is gay, explicitly criticizes the very flamboyance that Cohen suggests the talk shows naturalize (by ostensibly demanding it of all their gay guests), he forces us to question Cohen's assertion. (Brian doesn't like the way flamboyant gays "flaunt themselves" as if they're "all that, a little bit more and then some.") But this is not to suggest that flamboyant gays are either demonized or ridiculed on this program. On the contrary, at the center of the multipronged conflict that unfolds within this episode, impelling and animating its development all along, are the proudly and pleasurably defiant bodies of flamboyance.

These are *bodies that speak*, as when twenty-year-old Eric struts onstage, brimming over with attitude, enunciating corporeally, and announces that "I am one hundred percent queer," "I came out when I was fourteen and a half," and "I have *been* out *since* I was fourteen and a half!" or when Timmie, in Cohen's words, "flounces" into the fray "wearing his windbreaker like a feather boa" and flirting with the audience "like Pearl Bailey on speed." [56] Rick and Stacy, in response, articulate their fears for the safety of their more outrageously expressive friends. Rick, for example, talks of the dangers of flamboyance in a Southern redneck town like the one where he and Reid live.

In a friendly, animated, and Southern-accented voice, Rick says, "I'll be the first one to tell ya, I can be a big ol' sissy too, but not in those places. . . . You don't do that. You will get killed. And he don't only endanger himself, but me, also." Ricki suggests, however, that maybe Reid is just demonstrating that he is "comfortable with who he is and his sexuality," to which Rick replies, "Yeah, he's comfortable with that and I don't have no problem. But there's places that you can carry on that extreme. Not out in public. Not in a town like where we're from." Says Stacy, too, of his cousin Timmie and the risks his flamboyance engenders, "He'll just be buried before I will be." All of this touches off a discussion that is remarkable for its inclusion of topics rarely encountered on commercial television outside of tabloid talk shows. Stacy and Rick speak, for example, about how Timmie and Reid like to go in drag and hit on straight men. For Rick and Stacy, this is a dangerous practice that can only lead to disastrous consequences, but Reid and Timmie hint, to the contrary, that a surprising number of straight-identified men are neither deceived nor put off by their advances, an idea that suggests the fluidity of sexual desires and practices and the instability of sexual identifications. As Timmie puts it, "I think guys know it. I mean, you're in drag, half way through dinner, guys, you *have to* know it." If ideas about the fluidity of sexual identity are by now widespread on the terrain of academic gender theory, it is in tabloid talk shows where they find some of the most nourishing popular-cultural soil in which to thrive.[57]

From this discussion of flamboyance, the emergence of issues such as homophobia and gay bashing is, particularly in a popular media forum, a far from trivial matter. It creates opportunities for the intervention of voices that are not often heard within the mainstream of public culture, such as that of Cohen, who says on air of Timmie's and Reid's flirtations with straight men, "I just think it's a shame that we live in a world where that kind of flirting could get you killed. I just think it's a shame that the world still has people that get so bent out of shape by that. . . . That type of flirting could engender a lot of anger on the part of certain types of straight men, so you have to be really careful." That the tabloid talk shows create a space for such voices as this one forms a counterpoint to the hue and cry against the genre in the wake of the widely discussed (so-called) "Jenny Jones" murder. Scott Amedure was murdered by Jonathan Schmitz for revealing his secret attraction to Schmitz during a *Jenny Jones Show* taping in March 1995. On the one hand, *Jenny Jones* had failed to consider the important issue raised here by Cohen. However, what was perhaps most striking about the wave of public reaction against the program (which had, after all, dared to treat gay desire with the same celebratory overtones normally reserved for straight sexuality) was the relative paucity of voices targeting instead the homophobia that was both responsible for the murder and deeply inscribed in American culture as a whole—and especially in American culture outside of talk shows, since in the programs, as Gamson points out, it is usually homophobic bigotry, rather than homosexuality, that is treated as a "freakish" phenomenon.[58]

Gamson's point is indeed borne out when on the "I'm Gay, You're Gay" show, a straight woman expresses surprise (which is tinged with hostility and, it seems, a bit of unacknowledged disappointment) at the fact that the kiss Reid blew to a stranger in a nearby car in his redneck Southern town wasn't answered with a gun blast to Reid's head. This surprise-tinged-with-disappointment is met by angry objections from Ricki and icy silence from most of the audience (albeit giggles—of astonishment?—from a few there and extra-loud clapping from one). Such reactions as this woman's are well outside the mainstream of apparent studio audience sentiment, which is generally cautiously supportive of the flamboyant panelists at the "I'm Gay, You're Gay" program. Thus another straight woman says to Timmie, "You and Reid, I'm with you all. Go on and flaunt your stuff, just be careful what you doin'. 'Cause what you doin' ain't no different than what a woman may do when she put on her little skirt and her makeup and run out to the night-clubs, OK?" The supportive concern couched in this comment, made by a black woman, bespeaks a knowing empathy for the vulnerability imposed by the violence that often ensues when the relatively socially weak—whether people of color (and especially, in the United States, black men), women in general, or gay men—dare to publicly express their own sexuality, desires, or sexual agency. Or as another black woman from the audience says, her face etched with deep concern, "To each his own. You know, it's not what you do, it's how you do it. 'Cause New York is crazy and you'll definitely get hurt. Be careful." "Craziness," for this woman, is thus associated not with the panelists' expressive flamboyance but with those who would harm them for it. Periodic camera shots of faces in the audience testify to how respectfully this group listens to the panelists onstage, and how willing they are to engage intently with their issues. As one woman in the audience says to Brian (who has just been complaining about Eric's flamboyance despite Eric's objection that, just as there are different types of heterosexuals, so are there different types of gay people), "I just think it's a matter of respect. You have to respect everybody. Right now, he wants to be respected for who he is, OK? And you have to give him that respect."

But there is more to the prevailing moods here than a general sense of respect and engagement. There is also an all-pervasive sense of fun in which most of those present seem to participate. This audience, their host, the "Funny Gay Males," and the other onstage guests seem to do an awful lot of good-natured kidding, smiling, and laughing. It is as if the periods of seriousness and sustained conflict are suspended in, and punctuated by, an

Timmie: backfield in motion.

ethos of shared revelry. When, for instance, an older-than-the-average *Ricki* audience member asks nervously and with sincere naïveté how these panelists learned that they were gay and indeed how, in general, a person can tell if he or she is gay, Ricki asks back, with a dash of irony, "Are you still questioning your own sexuality, ma'am?" Lake's remark is significant for both its implicit assertion that sexual uncertainty and ambiguity do not occur only in "others" and for the apparently friendly laughter it provokes from all (including the sincere questioner herself), which seems to drain the tension from the ensuing discussion by panelists of their early recognition of their own sexual feelings—a topic that, when raised between straight and gay people in many contemporary contexts, evokes fear, loathing, anxiety, and violence rather than relative comfort and good-natured amusement. An index of the relative comfort that prevails here is the way in which, after several panelists have responded to the older woman's query, the next audience participant attempts to play matchmaker for the guests, suggesting that although he's not sure whether they're "into interracial relationships," Timmie and Reid would make "a helluva couple." But the ethos of shared revelry that permeates this *Ricki Lake* show is perhaps best encapsulated in the moment when Timmie, who had been talking with his cousin Stacy about how much fun they have dancing together, jumps from his seat at the urgings of the audience and performs an outrageously tail-shaking, gyrating, upbeat erotic dance while the gallery whoops, cheers, laughs, and howls over strains of piped-in club music.

Timmie's ecstatically provocative dance and the gallery's response to it are instantly suggestive of something that is operating along and in concert with the pervasive sense of fun here, and which is far more interesting than the cautious support expressed by participants in this particular but typical *Ricki Lake* show session. Amid all the playful banter and fun self-expression (the guests' strutting, dancing, camping it up, and wriggling provocatively), there's something like the artifice of flirtation going on between the gay men onstage and many presumably straight members of the audience. When Timmie and Reid insist that their dates in drag with straight men aren't really fooling anybody, when Timmie and Stacy allude to the girlfriends of men with whom Timmie has slept, and indeed when Nikki announces happily that Tonia's child's appellation for Nikki is "Mommy-Daddy," one feels that this talk show space is open to the disruption of certain sacred boundaries. Consider the moment when a young, presumably straight-identified, clean-cut, short-cropped man rises to deliver what this audience takes to be perhaps the best relationship insight of the day. Says the close-cropped man to the flamboyant members of the panel, "We've been talkin' how straight people can give straight people a bad name, and gay people give gay people a bad name. It's that, unfortunately since homosexuality is less accepted than heterosexuality, your actions are more closely scrutinized and magnified, and it's just givin' these guys a little extra baggage that they really don't need." When Ricki asks Timmie for a response, Timmie's outrageously funny reply to this handsome young man—who has just suggested, in effect, that Timmie should tone it down a bit—is "Name and number?" As the audience erupts with laughter and the close-cropped man, bright red, smiles shyly, Timmie says, "Now you see? You see? He was not offended." (When he has just finished his outrageous dance, however, Ricki points out smilingly to Timmie and with reference to the close-cropped man, "I gotta say that was terrific. But you know what? It's still not gonna win you a date with him up there!" All laugh even harder.)

This kind of laughingly flirtatious banter between self-styled queens and straight guys in the audience enacts the sort of playful negotiation that undercuts heterosexist fear and loathing of gay and lesbian sexualities. (And in this it is very much like what we saw in the audience reaction to *Donahue*'s S/M episode.) It is precisely this ethos of playful experimentation with flirtation, I think, that facilitates the moment when another man from the audience says of Eric, smilingly, "I'm straight, but if he told me I got a nice package, he'd get my attention." It is within such a context that audience members can conclude, as several here do in their on-air remarks, that gay men don't do any harm to straight people by hitting on them, and that if they're comfortable with themselves, straight men shouldn't get upset when gays approach them. As the program comes finally to an end, the audience and guests jump to their feet and dance together (chanting, "Go

Ricki!" in time to theme music). Cohen is led to conclude, in his retro-spective ruminations about the show, that "those kids, who had looked so threatening on my way into the building, were actually far less homophobic than they appeared. In fact, I was nothing less than astounded as, one by one, they gave the thumbs up sign to the young queens onstage." [59]

We should not underestimate the significance of what happens on pro-grams like this one, the presence of which, within the confines of a commer-cial media universe whose homophobia is well established, is really nothing short of amazing. Its significance is enhanced by television's propensity to provoke discussion among not only studio audience members but those at home as well, for as many media scholars have shown, television is an extremely important part of the oral cultures of everyday life.[60] Moreover, most forms of tabloidism create a space for the interrogation of socially authoritative knowledges that are generally treated with deference in the media outside of tabloids, and this will to irreverence, which is particu-larly marked in tabloid talk shows, is especially encouraging of discussion among those whose voices are typically silenced at just that moment when authority-bearing discourses enter the fray.[61] In her study of the audiences for tabloid talk shows, Jane Shattuc finds that women extend the discus-sions that take place on these programs into their own lived environments to generate conversations and on-line confabulations "about how their per-sonal experiences intertwine with politics on issues such as abortion and welfare."[62] S. Elizabeth Bird similarly finds that women who read super-market tabloids expropriate the contents of the newspapers into the soci-ality of their everyday life worlds and use them "as focal points for discus-sion and gossip" and "as springboards for sharing opinions about their lives."[63] In light of findings such as these, it is safe to assume that a good number of viewer discussions unfold around significant issues of sexual and gender politics including some or all of those raised by the panelists and studio audience analyzed here (homophobia, desire across sexualities and identities, sexual ambiguity and uncertainty, and so on). We can easily imag-ine such conversations working to bring these issues into contact with the specific life conditions and experiences of the diverse audiences that make up "the community of talk show viewers," defined, as Shattuc suggests it is, "by citizenship and the right to speak out."[64]

What happens on the aptly titled "I'm Gay, You're Gay" program speaks, I think, of the importance of the kind of relaxation of embodied and discur-sive constraints that tabloid talk shows routinely facilitate. On these pro-grams, it is far from unusual to see gays and lesbians talking openly about their sexual experiences and identities and indeed, throughout the 1990s, as Gamson notes, often within episodes that integrate straight and les-bi-gay identified sexualities under the discussion of topics such as "I Love Someone I Can't Have" (*Jerry Springer*), "I Saw You on Geraldo and Just Had to Meet You" (*Geraldo*), "Is There Life after a Career in Porn?" (*Donahue*), and "Surprise! I'm Hooking You Up" (*Ricki Lake*). Gamson suggests, therefore, that "talk shows are among the few places where right-wing paranoia about the liberal media is not so far off."[65] This point seems all the more apposite in light of the admittedly somewhat didactic titles that are broadcast at the start of several segments of the "I'm Gay, You're Gay" show. These titles seem designed to counteract conservative stereotypes and heterocentric ignorance, as well as to confound any sense of clear and categorical difference between straight and gay identities:

> True or False: AIDS is spreading most rapidly among homosexuals?
> Answer: False: Women are the fastest growing group of people with AIDS.
> True or False: All gay men are promiscuous?
> Answer: False: Promiscuity has nothing to do with sexuality.[66]
> True or False: All drag queens are gay men?
> Answer: False: Many drag queens and female impersonators are heterosexual.
> True or False: All gay men are florists, fashion designers, or nurses?
> Answer: False: Gay men work in all capacities in all professions, just like everybody else.

In the United States, whiteness, like heterosexuality, is a normalized and normalizing category.[67] Appropriately, on the talk shows, the body sometimes becomes a site of spectacular struggle over hegemonic meanings of racial difference. Another *Ricki Lake* show example, this one from a February 1994 edition that explored the topic of blacks who resent other blacks' complaints about racism, will serve to illustrate my point. Included among the guests is Ken Hamlin, a conservative African American who hosts a call-in radio show in Denver, Colorado. Throughout the program, Hamlin berates other black guests and audience members for their insistence that white racism has had a significant impact on their lives and ought to be combated. Against complaints that blacks are routinely subjected to unacceptable levels of scrutiny and surveillance by white shop owners who suspect that all African Americans are thieves, for example, Hamlin says, "Whenever I go to Bloomingdale's and somebody follows me [around the store], you know what I assume?" That "they're there to help me," he continues, answering his own question, "because I never leave home without the card." Then, bounding out of his chair and waving an American Express Gold Card at the audience, he announces, "America works! Wise up! America works!"

Hamlin's Gold Card and regular visits to Bloomingdale's are apparently alien to the experiences of most folks in the audience, and they try to tell him so. But when an audience member rises up and says to Hamlin, "I think you need to come off your bourgeoisie attitude," he erupts, telling her, "Young lady, . . . you're not even thinking for yourself," and "I knew that word before you were born." Hamlin arrogantly refuses to let the woman finish her comment. Such appeals to the dominating power of age-based social authority are not well suited to a youth-oriented forum like the *Ricki Lake* show, however. Consequently the melee that ensues aptly illustrates the way in which, within the conflictual space of the tabloid talk shows, authority is established and perhaps held temporarily, only to be destabilized or overturned by competing voices. It illustrates, as well, that the conflictuality of talk shows is very much a product of the wider social conflicts that are at stake within them. Significantly, despite Hamlin's attempts to use his age and economic achievements to authorize his claim that racial inequality is a product of black deficiency rather than white power, the studio audience (which is multiracial but mostly nonwhite) reacts loudly and bodily to his provocations. Thus once he has shouted down the woman that questioned his bourgeois attitudes, the camera focuses on several rows of black women seated near the back of the room, who immediately jump to their feet and begin a chant punctuated by rhythmic gestures toward the door. The image is one of bodies in motion—highly charged, mobilized, energized, and disruptive bodies unified in a moment of empowering refusal. The smiles on the faces of these women whose bodies sway together in a collective and irreverent dance express the pleasure they find in defeating Hamlin's attempt to control the production of truth and meaning in that small television studio on this day. The cynical critique that characterizes talk tabloids as "inauthentic" spectacles that serve only the economic motives of their producers and sponsors at the expense of "real debate" about "real issues" typically neglects the fact that these programs serve a popular demand to see and hear bodies and voices that have been undisciplined and turned loose in spaces that can justifiably be understood as microcosms of a conflict-ridden society.

Discipline is a norm enforcer. Discipline is social power applied to bodies. The refusal of disciplined comportment is a refusal of social power by those whom it targets. The refusal of discipline embodied in the audience's physical reaction against Hamlin should be seen not as "chaos" but rather as a refusal of the power borne in his dismissive attitude toward their knowledges of racism. It seems not to be his indifference to the rules of conversational etiquette that provokes this audience to rise up so much as his attempt to elevate himself over them. He becomes the representative of controlling forces they encounter daily, by their own accounts, in the concrete form of white loathing and haughtiness. Hamlin's well-heeled condescension toward the audience, ostentatious brandishment of an American Express Gold Card,

Hamlin flashes the gold.

Crowd to Hamlin: you ain't all that!

and almost apologetic attitude about white racism seem to come all too close to white power for this audience to take sitting down. Their refusal of disciplinary power extends from "inappropriate" physical displays to the production of counterdiscourses against the dominant ideological explanation of black poverty, which says that in the United States, people of color are limited only by the extent of their (ostensibly "underdeveloped") desires to succeed.[68] Thus the same audience member who characterizes Hamlin's attitude as "bourgeois" also tells him later that "if you're going to pass judgment on us, what I'm trying to say to you is, your money is not going to matter. You're still a black man, and they're still going to take your money away from you." Such a perspective speaks directly from the lived experience of a society where whites profit immensely by tenaciously retaining ownership of the businesses that blacks patronize and the buildings in which they live.

Another black guest talks of how her black husband and a white man were both killed in the same Washington, D.C., neighborhood during the same week, and though it took the police department only a few days to find the white man's killer, nobody was ever arrested for her husband's murder. This guest, identified only as Victoria, rebels against the official (white) truth by attributing the nonarrest to institutional racism.[69] She passionately refutes Hamlin's cure for urban violence against nonwhites, which holds that blacks and Hispanics who live in high-crime areas should move to better neighborhoods, where they won't be at risk. An exchange ensues, the conspicuous intensity of which is fueled by key contemporary struggles over racism and racial inequality. Says Victoria, "You know what, Mr. Ken? You are a well-trained house-nigger," which draws enormous applause from the audience. She continues, "You're sitting here waving this American Express card. . . . You're worse than my four and five year old. My son gets a toy, 'Ha, ha, I got it and you don't.' " Not intimidated by Hamlin's condescension, Victoria proclaims, "You know what, I'm proud! Black, proud, and I'm standing up and I'm speaking my mind to you!" Victoria's refusal of Ken's explanation of her troubles speaks powerfully of racially inflected social deprivation. Says Victoria, in response to Ken's suggestion that she and her husband were personally responsible for putting themselves at risk by choosing to live in a dangerous neighborhood:

> I came from Job Corps. Eighteen years old. Pregnant. Nowhere to go. The only thing there was for me was a homeless shelter for pregnant women. On top of that, I got on the Tenant Assistance Program in Washington, D.C. I didn't have a choice of whether I wanted to go live on "the Hill," in the Capitol!

Like the regular presence of gay and lesbian voices on talk shows, the importance of such witnesses to the black American experience as these should not be discounted. Their inclusion within the genre has grown steadily throughout the 1990s.[70] Jane Shattuc writes that "race is woven into the fabric of [tabloid talk] programs through the color of guests, audience members and hosts," and that "the shows are major arenas for disadvantaged African-Americans to enunciate their anger at a white system."[71] In the words of Mark Schone, after *Ricki Lake*'s appearance in 1993, tabloid talk shows became "the MacNeill/Lehrer of the hip-hop nation."[72] Like some other tabloid media, talk shows are better than the official news at attracting a young, urban, multiracial, *disenfranchised* audience. That theirs is a socially marginalized and alienated audience is underlined by the *Ricki Lake* staff's decision to place metal detectors at the studio entrance (" 'If you have any guns or knives on you,' says a *Ricki* underling, 'give them to us now, and we'll give them back at the end of the show' ").[73] Former New Kid on the Block turned talk show host Mark Walberg recognizes the racially encoded message that underlies conservative attacks on the tabloid talk shows: "When Bill Bennett talks about 'the dark side of life,' he means that in more than one way." [74] Seen in this light, the conservative "pro-family" crusade against these programs is not just classist in its disgust for the "trailer trash" often associated with the genre, not just sexist in its trivialization of the "women's issues" and voices that have always occupied the center of the talk show universe, and not just homophobic in its revilement of the sexual nonconformists who have long been "honored guests" in this corner of TV land.[75] Its combination of classism, sexism, homophobia, and white racism must be situated within the larger backlash against the set of social interventions often grouped under the designation of "multiculturalism," of which the talk shows are a popular media form. Their spectacular display of the dispossessed, of racial difference, and of socially marginalized sexual identities is a potent reminder of the very problems that were created and exacerbated by William Bennett during his public career as executor of Reaganite education, drug, and cultural policy. Schone makes the point nicely in this characterization of Bennett: "As a freelance foe of talk shows, he's suppressing the proof of his negligence in the name of good taste." [76]

In a sophisticated and compelling essay, Janice Peck analyzes a thirteen-episode antiracism series that ran on *Oprah* during 1992.[77] Peck demonstrates how an interplay between the mutually supportive discourses of liberalism, therapeutic psychologism, and Protestantism develops within the *Oprah* series and works to reproduce inferentially racist assumptions under the cover of antiracist intentions.[78] The central problem Peck identifies is that these three discursive sets inherently favor a variety of *individualistic* explanations of racist phenomena and therefore militate against the discussants' abilities to formulate the causes and consequences of racism in *social* terms. This problem is exacerbated, Peck claims, by Winfrey's desire to avoid threatening or alienating her white viewers and the show's need to be perceived as advertiser friendly. Nevertheless, Peck mentions several examples of voices in the programs that work against the grain to disarticulate racism from its culturally forged links with individualistic discourses and rearticulate it with more socially oriented ones.

The individuating tendencies that Peck analyzes with great acuity are not unique to talk shows but endemic to U.S. culture as a whole. Nevertheless, because of the talk shows' general willingness to include the voices of the socially marginalized (whose social agency therefore necessarily shapes and imprints the genre to one degree or another), the programs are among the notably few sites in media culture where such tendencies are, however infrequently, challenged, disrupted, or otherwise put in question. The frequency of such challenges and disruptions has increased with the success of *Ricki Lake*, which has striven since its inception to reach a young, urban, and multiracial audience that is quite different from the core supporters that *Oprah* courts. Consequently the edition of *Ricki Lake* on intra–African American debates about white racism brings us a number of voices that frame the issue in social rather than individual terms. Indeed, despite Hamlin's attempts to assert an individualistic explanation of both racism and economic success, the audience and four of the five other guests consistently refocus the issue on social dynamics and the importance of solidarity among nonwhite communities.

Joe, a black stand-up comedian, explains, for example, how pervasive the effects of racism are in his life, noting that he has to be "on guard at all times," because "you don't know where racism may come from; you don't know *who* is racist." Joe argues that because of things they learn from social institutions like the mainstream media, white folks persistently treat him as if he were a threat. Joe berates Hamlin for long since detaching himself from the Bedford Stuyvesant neighborhood that Hamlin fled as a young man. Joe and Hamlin are soon joined onstage by another African American, Lawrence Otis Graham, and a white woman identified only as Michelle. Graham has written a book called *The Best Companies for Minorities* and has documented, through extensive research, some of the structural, social, and economic dimensions of contemporary racism, which he relates to the audience along with some personal anecdotes. For instance, over the course of two years, Graham surveyed seven hundred corporations and found only eighty-five whose recruitment and promotion practices he could call nonracist and nonsexist. He notes, additionally, that during the last U.S. recession, whites gained 70,000 jobs, Hispanics gained 60,000 jobs, and Asians gained 50,000 jobs—yet blacks lost 60,000 jobs. Finally, he talks about his experience of having left his law practice to go "undercover" as a waiter at a country club that boasts a former U.S. president among its members yet denies entry to blacks, Jews, women, Asians, and Hispanics, despite the fact that their financial profiles and credentials are often similar to those of the club's white affiliates. Moreover, the "upstanding" staff and enrollees at the club have designated the dorm where black employees live "the monkey house."

Such voices as these compellingly fuse the macro, structural, systemic dimensions of U.S. racism with those of painfully personal lived experience. Consequently it comes as no surprise when Ricki asks Michelle if she's "living in a dream world" after Michelle has asserted that nobody should ever claim their race or gender as an "excuse" for having been denied a job and that having a "positive attitude" toward the future will solve the problem of racism. Michelle's dreamy vision of race relations contrasts starkly with the brief sketch of U.S. history given by the last guest to join the others, Ophira. Says Ophira:

> I hear a lot of people talking about, that, you know, "white people and black people have the same chances in this country," and "white people can experience racism." Well, that is a myth. . . . This country was founded by white people standing on the backs of Africans and Native Americans. You know, for four hundred years we've ensured a privilege . . . that everyone with white skin is, you know, benefiting from today. . . . I'm a Jewish woman and I know that my experience in this country has been—while it hasn't been culturally white, . . . I have experienced white skin privilege. Jewish people came to this country by choice, not by force, as did all other ethnic groups besides Africans. So we have an advantage, instantly.

When Michelle responds to Ophira that "if you start teachin' the kids of today about being together, not teaching 'em to hate each other," Ophira interrupts with the observation that "you can't be together, we can't be equal, until we all have equal opportunity and treatment in this country." This discursive framing of racism as a social rather than an individualistic phenomenon is continued in the titles that, like those from the "I'm Gay, You're Gay" episode, occur at the beginning (and ending) of several segments. One states that "there are NO African-American governors, and only ONE African-American senator in the U.S." Another reads that "currently, there is not a single African-American CEO among the nation's 500 largest industrial corporations." A third title announces that "62% of our studio audience said that society holds African-Americans back from success." A fourth title qualifies this finding by noting that "60% of the Caucasians in our audience said African-Americans complain too much about racism"—though the next screen puts this racialized judgment into perspective: "26% of African-Americans feel the same."

For its part, the studio audience supports the voices from the stage that are working to promote an understanding of racism as something more than the idiosyncratic tendency of certain bad individuals. One woman in the audience, for example, who reacts angrily to Hamlin's perspective offers a comment that, like those of several guests, connects racism with the economic system, its job markets, and the hiring practices that take place there. Says she:

THERE ARE NO
AFRICAN-AMERICAN
GOVERNORS, AND ONLY
ONE AFRICAN-AMERICAN
SENATOR IN THE U.S.

-THE JOINT CENTER FOR
POLITICAL AND ECONOMIC
STUDIES

CURRENTLY, THERE
IS NOT A SINGLE
AFRICAN-AMERICAN CEO
AMONG THE NATION'S
500 LARGEST INDUSTRIAL
CORPORTIONS.

-BLACK ENTERPRISE
MAGAZINE

Ricki: **down for the truth.**

Now you say to forget racism . . . Mr. Ken . . . and just go on. . . .
You think it's that easy. This black brother right here [Lawrence Otis
Graham] had to go out and write a book, what companies us black
people can go to, to find jobs. Until they get that little question off the,
the employment applications — "what ethnic group are you in . . . ?" —
racism is *not* going to be over with. We bump into it *every day!* OK? *Every
day!* And your Amex card cannot get it off the application, OK?

Normalization and Its Discontents 215

The audience erupts in support. In this way, they join the onstage guests in a demonstration of black resentment of the economic deprivation that is so racially inflected in the United States, and of the racism that is sustained in part through economic means and measures.

With regard to these issues around the intersection of race and class, the difference between studio audience reaction to Ken Hamlin and Lawrence Otis Graham is indeed a telling and interesting one. Both men are designer suited—solidly upper middle class in a way that contrasts markedly with the more casual and "ordinary" appearance of most studio audience members. Yet whereas Hamlin provokes what is no doubt a class-driven anger and vitriol with his American Express Gold Card (to which, by the end of the show, several guests and audience members have tellingly made reference) and his tales of the friendly and helpful staff at Bloomingdale's, Graham's mention in passing of having graduated from Princeton and Harvard law school is met with warm, enthusiastic, and supportive applause. For whereas Hamlin departed Bedford Stuy without looking back, Graham has devoted much of his professional energy to exposing the racism of affluent whites and attacking barriers that work against the social and economic interests of *all* black folks. Many in this audience seem to identify with Graham's encounters with racism as an "undercover" waiter, and with his complaint that even when dressed in a suit, in midtown Manhattan, he can't get a taxi to stop for him. Such a complaint works here to forge racial solidarities *across* class lines while by contrast "Mr. Ken," as several take to calling him, *exaggerates his class position as a way to deny race*—and the studio audience knows it well. In their contrasting reactions to Graham and Hamlin, the audience highlights the importance to them of the strength of community ties and the imperative to always remember them. The audience's reaction underlines its collective recognition of the way in which racism is *rooted in sociality* and points to their awareness that so too must be any effective attempt to counter racism. Thus while they resent Hamlin's race-denying class pretensions, the audience is proud and supportive of Graham, who hasn't allowed his own personal success to wipe from his memory his brothers and sisters who've not fared as well as he. If, as Peck suggests, the talk show studio audience functions as an "identificatory bridge" between home viewers and the topic under discussion, then the at-home audience for this program is encouraged to identify with the contemplation of racism as a fully social rather than an individualistic phenomenon—and one with deeply felt consequences at that.[79]

The tabloid talk shows grant the voices of ordinary experience a pride of place that derives from, but greatly exceeds, mainstream journalism's traditional vox pop elements. Moreover, these programs are distinguished by their openness both to socially marginalized topics (such as alien abduction and sexual bondage) and to socially excluded voices (such as those of gays, lesbians, and young African Americans). They can thus be characterized as multivocal sites of hegemonic struggle where *alterity* regularly asserts its right to exist and to shamelessly occupy a place in the culture. This is not to mistake talk shows for utopian discursive democracies. They do not incarnate the Habermasian "ideal speech situation." The power dynamics that constitute the discursive space of the talk shows are better understood in Foucauldian terms. Foucault notes that the exertion of power always implies the presence of points of resistance that must not be deterministically understood as the underlying supports of a system that is perpetually self-reproducing. These multiple sites of resistance that are dispersed throughout the networks of power relations are capable of "inflaming certain points of the body, certain moments in life, certain types of behavior." Such inflammations of the body social are mobile and transitory, though they produce cleavages that fracture the unities of discourse and identity and reconfigure social formations, cutting up and remolding individuals themselves.[80] The assertion of their right to difference by the practitioners of domination and submission, however carefully negotiated, and the expression of interest in the S/M scene by home and studio audience members who might otherwise have remained silent constitute an everyday example of the sorts of shifting cleavages and fractured unities that furrow across individuals themselves and contribute to the reconfiguration of their very identities.[81] Similarly, Gamson notes that when daytime talk shows address the issue of the difference between different sexual orientations, identity tends heavily toward extreme instability and uncertainty: "Husbands are suddenly leaving their wives for other men, wives are declaring their desire to sleep with women, friends are turning friends gay, people are turning from gay to straight, and so on. You cannot really tell who is what; people are boundary jumping all over the place, as though heterosexuality can leave the body whenever it wants."[82]

It is ironic to find such forces at work in a format that is as confessional as the talk shows are, for in Foucault's view, it is precisely through the practices of confession that controlling power makes alterity accessible to surveillance and thus to subjection by normalizing judgment. Stephen Schiff argues that talk show watchers take part in "confession and self-sacrifice, through surrogates who present themselves on the altar to undergo public chastisement for our edification."[83] Talk shows can indeed be seen to support Foucault's claim that "we have . . . become a singularly confessing society," that "the confession has spread its effects far and wide," that "Western man [sic] has become a confessing animal."[84] The talk shows' interlocutors *do* "tell all" in the presence of viewers numbering in the millions. Ultimately, though, the relations of power characteristic of the talk show differ significantly from those of the Foucauldian confession. Foucault writes that "one does not confess without the presence (or virtual presence) of a partner who is not simply the interlocutor but the authority who requires the confession, prescribes and appreciates it, and intervenes in order to judge, punish, forgive, console, and reconcile."[85] Such authority, however, rarely goes unquestioned or unchallenged in the tabloid talk shows, whose interlocutors are not typically disciplined into penitence. More often, they actively negotiate normalizing judgmentality in a variety of ways that are not so much liberating as contestatory and expansive. Whereas the Foucauldian confessional is a site for the affirmation and enforcement of dominating truths and normalizing judgments, talk shows characteristically engender a mutability of truths and identities, a multiplicity of voices, the transgression of norms, and the spontaneous eruption of forces that emanate from society's excluded formations. Thus there is a significant level of discursive volatility built into the tabloid talk shows that outstrips the explanatory power of the theory of confessional normalization.

People often ask what would ever motivate others to discuss embarrassingly intimate details of their personal lives on globally syndicated TV. The Foucauldian concept of confessional culture provides a partial but ultimately unsatisfying answer to this question. Equally important, as I've suggested here, is the way in which tabloid talk shows make it possible for some, who are not often accorded such opportunities, to loudly lay claim to media space. In a society that seeks systematically either to silence or to manage the speech of those disempowered through the dynamics of "normality" and "abnormality," race, class, ethnicity, sexual orientation, gender, age, and criminalization, the talk shows provide socially subordinated and marginalized people with the rare chance both to make themselves publicly heard and, *significantly*, to exert at least some small measure of control over the process. Consequently what is often referred to as talk show "exploitation" is a highly complex, unstable, and reversible phenomenon: as media producers exploit marginalized populations for profit and professional advantage, so have the socially disenfranchised become adept at exploiting talk shows and their production staffs to gain access to media space.[86] But I want to suggest, too, that the *will to television* that motivates people in their quests after media space in talk show world is symptomatic of hyperreal cultural conditions and the increasing allure of the electronically mediated in relation to that which has not been processed through TV.

Tabloid talk shows are not, of course, spontaneous eruptions of popular discourse (though their interlocutors do sometimes erupt with great spontaneity). They are, by contrast, "staged" media events whose conflictuality and popularity are products of both their mediatized orchestration and the "real" social struggles they mediate. In this sense, talk shows are emblematic of the implosion of "reality" and "representation" that is a defining characteristic of hyperreality. Theorists of the hyperreal argue that the changing relationship between the non–electronically mediated and the imagistically mediatized should be understood not as the replacement of "reality" by a media-induced "falseness" or "artificiality" but as a mutation of our sense of "the real" that entails a postmodern implosion of the modernist categories of "reality" and "representation." Perhaps the concept of hyperreality can help us to better understand the urge that compels thousands to cross the boundary between nonmediated and mediatized spheres of experience—a boundary whose trace is still active in our social imagination despite the current rapidity of its ongoing erasure. As Patricia Joyner Priest observes, "self-disclosure on television is a clear example of boundary permeability."[87] People are now married on talk shows, conduct domestic disputes there, and finalize divorces before a live studio audience. The woman who told Michael Moore's TV Nation that she wished to confront her sister Rolanda about significant family issues but would feel confident enough to do so only in front of a talk show audience displays an attitude that is emblematic of the extent to which mediatized (hyper)realities have decentered non–electronically mediated ones, as well as the degree to which, as Baudrillard might put it, the models generated on television are increasingly important templates according to which we conduct our "real" lives and relationships. This woman noted further (and not without a touch of televisually savvy irony) that she constantly evaluates each experience of her everyday life for its suitability as a talk show topic.[88]

A 1994 edition of The Jerry Springer Show presents us with an exemplary media en abime that poses the problem of hyperreality on at least two separate but intertwined levels. The program features "guests . . . who say they're tired of their mates pressuring them to be more like the actresses they watch in porn movies." This leads Springer to question whether the videated reality of adult entertainment is interfering dangerously in the "real" reality of his guests' relationships, since the men in the featured couples "are starting to concentrate on the films" more "than on who they're in bed with."[89] Guests and audience members argue with each other as the program explores a variety of significant issues at the core of contemporary sexual politics. The "normality" of porn fandom is scrutinized and interrogated, as are the unsatisfying limitations imposed by prevailing conventions of "normal" sexual practice. Two porn actresses come on the show to discuss how many of their own fans, men and women alike, have told them their work has greatly enhanced the fans' own sexual relationships. Women argue over the body images presented in pornography, as one panelist, for example, notes that she couldn't possibly compete with the media images that have captured her husband's imagination unless a wealthy benefactor were to provide her with liposuction, breast implants, and a nose job. Individuals and couples raise issues about the strain that incompatible sexual tastes can produce within relationships. Several women discuss men's tendencies to make selfish and insensitive sexual demands of their lovers. Individuals onstage and in the audience debate whether porn acting is "degrading" to *all* women despite the financial and sexual independence and sense of self-esteem and control it enables *some* to achieve. All these issues arise out of Springer's concerns about the disturbance of "real" sex by mediatized porn.

However, perhaps the most interesting thing about this show, with regard to the question of hyperreality, is the status of the four guests around which it is built. The episode opens with Heather describing how her boyfriend Eric's devotion to porn videos is destroying their relationship, since he is constantly comparing her to his favorite porn stars and asking her to do things he has seen performed on videotape but that she finds distasteful. Heather's friend Robin, who is also onstage, describes Eric's unfairness and insensitivity and discusses how she has to comfort Heather whenever she becomes distraught over Eric's perverse sexual desires and their effects on her relationship with him. Then from stage right comes Heather's brother Todd, who charges toward Eric, pointing at his face and calling him "a sick, twisted, perverted bitch." Todd joins the first three guests onstage, adding his voice to their accounts of the destructive impact Eric's porn addiction has had on his relationship with Heather. The four remain there throughout the entire program, during which they are joined by the two porn stars, a brother and sister fighting about the brother's taste in pornography, and two straight couples, three of whose members enjoy porn and are trying to convince the fourth to join them in group sex.

Unbeknownst to Springer, his staff, and his audience, Heather, Eric, Robin, and Todd, around whom much of the program's conflict revolves, are not in fact "actually" embroiled in a controversy over pornography. Heather and Eric are not even involved in a romance. On the contrary, all four panelists are University of Wisconsin undergraduates who have concocted an elaborate ruse. They invented their story after a friend of Heather's, as a practical joke, phoned Springer's production staff in response to an on-air call for potential guests to appear on a future show about pornography. Heather's friend reported that "my boyfriend's a porno addict, and wants me to get into it, and it's ruining our relationship." She also told them her name was Heather Stoneman, and gave them Heather's actual phone number in case they should pursue the call further.[90] Soon the staff of the *Springer Show* was calling the "real" Heather "at least five times a day." Heather quickly recruited confederates, who began developing characters. Eric's was particularly demanding, since the first-year college student was unfamiliar with the classics of adult entertainment. Hence he had to "study his new role as a pornographic connoisseur" to convince Springer's staff of his authenticity.[91] Heather, for her part, told the television producers that Eric wanted her to "perform pornographic activities, like sex with horses and other crazy shit." [92] Before long, Heather received word from the executive producer that she, Eric, Robin, and Todd had been chosen to be the focus of the upcoming pornography program.

Although all talk show guests are coached through rehearsals by production staffs striving for maximal dramatic impact, the four university students would require some special preparation. Therefore, Heather's neighbors "began holding 'Springer tests' where they would ask Eric and Heather questions Jerry might use." These sessions helped Eric prepare for a surprise phone call that came a few days before the show. It was from Springer's staff, who wanted to know the names of Eric's favorite porn stars. In addition, the staff wanted to see photographic evidence that would authenticate Eric and Heather's three-year relationship. On short notice, the "couple" had to stage a series of snapshots, which were quickly processed by a one-hour developer and sent to Springer's offices via an express delivery service. The production staff of *The Jerry Springer Show* was at last satisfied with the identities of its soon-to-be stars. Once taping of the show began, the four confederates were so compelling and convincing that they remained on camera throughout the entire program, while several presumably "authentic" porn buffs flown from Oklahoma to Chicago (where the program is produced) weren't even allowed to take the stage. Indeed, Springer's producers were so pleased with Heather and the others that they asked her if she had any friends who had appeared in *Playboy* and might be available for a future appearance on the talk show.[93]

This story illustrates a number of important points about the hyperreality of tabloid talk shows. In the age of electronic images, events increasingly defy any finalizing anchorage in a reality that exists independently of its mediatization. Even the relationship between Heather and Eric could be photographically resignified—and at hyperspeed, thanks to one-hour processing and express delivery—to suit the wishes of the *Springer Show* producers. This is not to say that the couple's television performance was "inauthentic" but rather to redefine its authenticity in terms of its mediatization: Heather and Eric successfully embodied or figured a number of serious and significant issues capable of capturing the imaginations and the attention of the studio audience and, presumably, of many viewers at home as well. Were this not so, the program would not have generated the impassioned debates it provoked. Guests such as these are compelling because they deliver something like what Gamson usefully calls "truths told in lies." [94] In tabloid TV, such truths rely on the real-seemingness that the medium is capable of conferring on the figures that it mediates—a real-

"Truths told in lies."

seemingness that both produces and is produced by the mutation of our sense of the real within a regime of hyperreality. Heather and Eric can thus be seen as quintessentially hyperreal media figures whose authenticity is more a function of their mediatized real-seemingness than anything else. To characterize their mediatized figures as "fake" or "untrue" is ultimately pointless, for the only "truth" to which we finally have recourse in such situations is the unstable one of mediatization itself.

The sort of performance given by Heather and Eric may indeed be a common occurrence on daytime talk television, as numerous observers have noted.[95] Ultimately there is no way of knowing how many tabloid talk show guests have "concocted" their identities in the manner of Heather and Eric. It makes little sense, though, to characterize these programs as "inauthentic," as many consequently have. It seems equally senseless to distinguish categorically between "real" guests and "fakes" such as the four described here, for like other "reality-based" television forms, talk shows depend on a certain media role playing that is demanded of everybody involved in their production. Through this process of media role playing, both one's "real" sense of identity and a variety of socially powerful norms are made available for destabilization, contestation, negotiation, and resignification. Like "truth," the volatility of norms—which is ultimately a consequence of ongoing social contestation—is enhanced by the hyperreal implosion of any categorical distinction between "reality" and "representation."

In his concluding remarks on the episode featuring Heather, Eric, and their friends, Jerry Springer tries heroically to reinscribe the troubled distinction between "reality" and its mediatized image, evincing an implicit awareness of the crisis of representation that lies at the heart of the hyper-real experience:

> This is not about the marital evils of adult films. Let us just assume that in a free society, grown-ups are permitted in the privacy of their homes to view films that sexually arouse them, expand their willingness to engage in erotic experimentation, or to simply feed their fantasies. . . . But . . . if these movies are interfering with your relationship, if they bother your lover, if they become the focus of your attention and imagination rather than the person enveloped in your arms, then it's time to turn the VCR *off* and your lover *on* with your undivided attention and passion. Love is never a *movie.*

For Springer, his panelists, his audiences, and all of us, however, the line between "reality" and its mediatized "representations" has been profoundly disturbed by our transmutation into a culture of hyperreality. It will not be so easily reinstantiated as Springer suggests that it might.

Post-script

Jerry Springer entered the hyperreal spotlight once again in 1998. During that year, his program's popularity skyrocketed in conjunction with a massive increase in the number of violent confrontations between guests on the show. Consequently Springer's ratings surpassed even those of *Oprah,* a feat no other talk show had accomplished in ten years. Senator Lieberman responded by renewing his attacks on talk shows and calling Springer's the "closest thing to pornography on broadcast television." [96] One of Springer's competitors took a different critical tack. At the beginning of the 1998–1999 television season, talk show host Sally Jessy Raphael grabbed headlines by complaining that audiences' belief in the reality of the genre had been damaged by Springer's program.[97] Her concern was that like professional wrestling, the *Springer* show was seen by many viewers as artificial and choreographed, a development that she feared was rapidly destroying the "credibility" of *all* talk shows.

Raphael's anxieties over the *Springer* show and her response to those anxieties are symptomatic of hyperreal cultural conditions. To prove the "reality" of her own program, Raphael and her producers decided that in the future, most shows would contain footage of the backstage production process, such as video clips of staff debates about whether to go ahead with the making of particular episodes that have been proposed and, if so, which guests should be included or excluded. Raphael suggests that her motivation for the inclusion of footage of backstage happenings is rooted partly in the special priority that is assigned to events that are processed through the visual media of the electronic age, which she explains in personal terms: "I've been in this business since I was a kid and I realized that almost all the important things in my life were on camera." The hyperbolic flourish that Raphael expresses in the following rhetorical question overstates, but not by much, the disturbance of the ontological certainty of bodies and the epistemological grounds for identity that others have associated with post-modernity: "Do you really exist when that camera goes dark?" she asks. Consequently Raphael assigned camera operators to begin *nonstop taping* of everything done by her program's staff and guests each working day. She had decided this was necessary to her project of authentication. As Raphael puts it, "What you can't do is script this stuff, because then it becomes unreal." [98] Death to the script. In a calculated gesture toward hyperreality, Raphael's show would go *post-script*.

There is high postmodern irony in the idea that the inclusion of video footage of backstage events can serve to *authenticate* both Raphael's program and the talk show genre more broadly.[99] It is doubly ironic that Raphael's inspiration for this move came from two "fictional" media products, *The Truman Show* (Peter Weir, 1998), a film about a man whose entire life is, unbeknownst to him, lived within the confines of a globally popular soap opera that is broadcast live for twenty-four hours each day, and *The Larry Sanders Show*, the HBO weekly series about the production of a celebrity talk show. Only under conditions of media image saturation could it make sense for Raphael to respond to the crisis of representation that is generated by such conditions—a crisis that entails a fundamental uncertainty about the difference between "representation" and "reality"—by generating and circulating *different* images that will supposedly resolve this crisis and restore the categorical distinctions whose disruption it has brought about. In hyperreality, images authenticate images according to a logic that turns on itself and spirals toward implosion.

6 Conclusion: Cultural Struggle, the New News, and the Politics of Popularity in the Age of Jesse "the Body" Ventura

In place of the Old News, something dramatic is evolving, a new culture of information, a hybrid New News—dazzling, adolescent, irresponsible, fearless, frightening and powerful. The New News is a heady concoction, part Hollywood film and TV movie, part pop music and pop art, mixed with popular culture and celebrity magazines, tabloid telecasts, cable and home video. —Jon Katz, *Rolling Stone* [1]

I think they might conclude that some millennium virus gripped the United States, and everyone decided to participate in a tabloid culture. —Stanley Kutler, *Wisconsin State Journal Online* [2]

I think what we're seeing here is an example of the culture for whom daytime talk shows and tabloid headlines have become a reality against which they measure their lives. —FBI special agent Dana Scully, *The X-Files* [3]

On the morning of Sunday, August 31, 1997, the Mercedes-Benz S-280 carrying Princess Diana and her lover Dodi Fayed rammed into a concrete abutment on a Paris roadway, killing the car's high-profile occupants. By one report, the automobile's speedometer was frozen on impact at 122 miles per hour (in a 30 mph zone).[4] This event would occasion a remarkable outpouring of media criticism operating on at least two levels. In the first instance, widespread outrage was directed at the swarm of motorcycle-borne paparazzi that chased the Mercedes in hot pursuit of salable photographs of "the face that launched a thousand tabloids." [5] This outrage led to a generalized condemnation of tabloid photographers from a variety of quarters. On the day after the accident, for example, newspaper photographers on the streets of Paris and London were taunted and "cursed as assassins" by passersby and mourners.[6] Columnists and other journalistic commentators everywhere castigated the "ruthless junkies, who supply the tabloids, the rest of the media and the public with the photos they—we—all simultaneously seem to crave and denounce," for hounding and harassing the princess literally to her death.[7] Celebrities such as Tom Cruise, Elizabeth Taylor, and Madonna went public with their own firsthand tales of hot pursuit by paparazzi in search of tabloid images.[8] As one observer said in summary of this first wave of reactions to the deaths, "you would think that the Paris-based paparazzi unquestionably ran Diana's car off the road in an accident uncomplicated by excessive speed or the near-stupor of the driver," whose blood alcohol level on impact was estimated at three or four times the French legal limit.[9] Especially in light of such circumstances, that so many were so willing to focus blame for Diana's death on the tabloids is symptomatic of widespread anxieties over media tabloidization.

As in the O.J. Simpson affair, the second phase of this postcrash news criticism included media self-flagellation and hand-wringing over the massive amount of journalistic attention paid to both the event and, paradoxically, the assessment of its coverage. The Diana event was seen as an uncontrollable tabloidized media juggernaut; in the words of Howard Kurtz, writing between the death of the princess and her memorial ceremony, the media response was "an O.J.-like wave that swamps all else in its path, building on itself as it roars" onward.[10] A Wall Street Journal editorial implied that the tabloidized media coverage of Diana's death was symptomatic of cultural pathology, for "normal" people would be "grossed out and sickened" by this purportedly journalistic reduction of "human tragedy . . . to cheap melodrama."[11] Columnist Jonathan Yardley treated the event as an occasion to lament the "arrant nonsense" that proclaims that the respectable press and the tabloids are of a piece with each other. This might seem to have been an odd choice on Yardley's part, given that his characterization of this viewpoint as "arrant nonsense" came in conjuncture with what was precisely a high-water mark for the blurring of distinctions between mainstream and tabloid journalism. But his decision appears less strange when we consider that it is exactly this blurring of boundaries that provokes the anxiety that motivates Yardley to plead for the "establishment press" to rise above the abject tabloid media and prove this nonsense wrong, at this most desperate hour "when all of us have been tarred with the brush of Diana's paparazzi and the publications that disseminate their work."[12]

Like the words of FBI special agent Scully quoted at the beginning of this chapter (which were, ironically enough, uttered on a TV show often accused of perpetuating popular tabloidist beliefs), these twin waves of world reaction to the events surrounding the death of Princess Diana serve as a potent reminder that anxieties over the "tabloidization" of media have become central to the diagnostics of contemporary culture—so much so, I believe, that they constitute a full-fledged moral panic. To be sure, concerns over the media's news and information operations are significant and justified. Democracies do require open flows of information and commentary. What is troubling, however, is the extent to which anxieties over media tabloidization both obscure the more progressive aspects of the tabloid media (which I have chosen to emphasize at a number of points throughout this book, not least because the simplistic derogation of tabloid culture has become the reigning "commonsense" position in the contemporary United States) and lend themselves to the validation of cultural hierarchies that silence many of those to whom the tabloid media have learned to speak.

Tabloid media matter because they constitute an important site of ongoing cultural politics. Cultural politics involve struggles over meaning that produce our understandings of ourselves, our "others," and the place of ourselves and our others in the world. The meanings produced through the insertion of events and identities into this or that way of knowing form the basis on which all other political activities rest. Under postmodern conditions, that basis is not so much a stable bedrock as a volatile swirl of images and words amenable to constant contestation and resimulation. Postmodernist theories assert that truth is not determined by the events or "reality" of which that truth speaks and that the production of truth is a kind of work that is always imbricated within various operations of social power. This is not to say that all truth claims are equivalent. There is a material world beyond discourse and beyond the swirl of electronic images that occupy such a central place in a mediatized culture. The futility of attempts to treat both the world and human events as things that can be known on their own terms does not mean that these "realities" can simply be made to mean anything at all. Any "reality" can, however, always be inserted into a multiplicity of different knowledge games, with the consequence that the alternative truths they are capable of yielding necessarily support different sociopolitical interests. What is important, then, is to develop ways of understanding the role that power plays in determining which knowledges come to be treated as true and whose do not.

Among the hallmarks of tabloidism is that it creates media space for the circulation of alternative knowledges as it caters to the disreputable tastes of alienated and relatively disempowered social formations. At its worst, tabloidism (like official journalistic forms) surely features the hegemonic and normalizing voices of racism, sexism, and homophobia. At its best, however, it multiplies and amplifies the heterogeneous voices and viewpoints in circulation in contemporary culture, giving rein to many that are typically excluded from the dominant regime of truth through the dynamics of race, class, gender, age, and sexuality. The shrill and revulsive response to tabloid media from "respectable" journalism and other elite social quarters indicates the extent to which their popularity threatens officialdom's power to regulate the discursive procedures through which we make sense of society and of ourselves. "Serious" journalism is far more concerned with controlling, organizing, and ordering the hierarchy of voices it admits into its discursive repertoire than is tabloid news, whose contents are driven by ratings and circulation. In a tabloid media space such as that created by the daytime talk shows, for example, a conflictual ethos and loose discursive controls mean that hegemonic, normalizing, and authoritarian voices rarely go uncontested.

Tabloid knowledges originate from, and flow back into, different spheres of social experience. In the long term, the capacity of popular knowledge to seep fluidly across different domains of everyday life has inevitably political consequences, though these are generally indirect and furthermore cannot be adequately foreseen or predicted. Nevertheless, from time to time signs do arise that indicate the impact of popular skepticism in one institutional arena or another. We've seen that Dan Lungren, California's attorney general, has coined the term "Oprahization" to describe changes in U.S. juries that many prosecutors feel have increased the difficulty of securing criminal convictions. (Says Lungren, "people have become so set on the *Oprah* view, [that] they bring that into the jury box with them.") [13] Thus talk show watchers are widely considered by prosecutors and professional jury consultants to be more likely than others to distrust official accounts of "the truth." (We've seen, for instance, that Los Angeles District Attorney Gil Garcetti has pronounced the criminal justice system to be "on the verge of a crisis of credibility" because of these perceived changes in the sensibilities of jurors.) [14]

One significant consequence of these perceptions is that defense attorneys have become more willing to produce arguments that would once have seemed exotic in an American court of law. For example, when Daimion Osby (an eighteen-year-old black resident of Forth Worth, Texas) shot and killed two men for threatening him over a gambling debt, defense attorney Bill Lane argued that his client's behavior could only be made sense of in terms of an "urban survival syndrome" caused partly by living in "one of Fort Worth's most dangerous neighborhoods." [15] The availability of, and willingness to offer, such a defense are conjuncturally linked with the contemporary growth of a tabloid culture replete with images of urban disorder (such as those circulated in *Cops* and *America's Most Wanted*) and shot through with the mediatized voices of everyday experience (like those found in the daytime talk shows). Perceptions of an "Oprahization" of juries can thus be seen to account for a certain adventurousness among defense attorneys. "Oprahization" can also be linked conjuncturally with a certain openness among juries themselves. This is not to support the kind of naive causal argument suggested by prosecutors like Lungren and Garcetti. However, history does not throw up a random series of accidents but rather presents events that are conjuncturally related to one another.[16] The popularity of talk tabloids as sites for struggling over and working through issues such as racism and its pervasive consequences for the everyday lives of people of color (see chapter 5) can be linked conjuncturally with, for example, the outcome of a survey of eight hundred people undertaken by the *National Law Journal* that found that 68 percent of blacks and 45 percent of whites felt that an attorney could present a compelling trial defense for a black man charged with murder on the grounds that he was driven by fury resulting from long-term everyday subjection to racism.¹⁷

What I have been calling our contemporary "tabloid culture" is a product of the social amplification of a variety of popular knowledges that in one way or another question the capacity of more official ones to produce the authoritative truth of the experience of living in the contemporary United States. Of course, the popular production of "extreme" knowledges that refuse and interrogate manifestations of the official truth is nothing new. Cultural historian Carlo Ginzburg, for example, has given us the riveting tale of an Italian miller named Menocchio, whose fantastically alternative cosmology was so threatening to the Roman Church that he was put to death in 1599 for refusing to relinquish his views.¹⁸ The production of heretical counterknowledges may indeed be seen as a constitutive trait of popular culture generally. Nor is tabloid journalism itself a new phenomenon. Nevertheless, during the last decades of the twentieth century, it has developed new forms, permeated others, and thus achieved an enhanced and expansive presence in our current media environment. That environment is the product of a society whose modernist certitudes have been called into question and where the competition between alternative knowledges is arguably hotter than at any time since the onset of modernity; it is symptomatic of the extent to which, as Jodi Dean puts it, "we have moved from consensus reality to virtual reality." ¹⁹ Tabloid media thus express the growth of cultural multivocality that is a consequence of both postmodernity and struggles over multiculturalism. The demonization of tabloid media by spokespeople for what Jon Katz calls "the Old News" and by the well educated in general is evidence of the social forces working to reinscribe and police certain boundaries that have been reconfigured by both multiculturalism and postmodernity, including those between "serious" and "frivolous," "high" and "low," "truth" and "fiction," "normal" and "abnormal," "order" and "disorder," "taste" and "tastelessness," "reason" and "emotion," the "hard" and the "soft." The fixation of such categories throughout Western modernity has been part of a cultural politics working to hold a complex system of hegemonic dominations in place.

During the 1994 U.S. senatorial elections, Florida Democrat Hugh Rodham (the brother of Hillary Rodham Clinton) was contested in the primaries by a former radio talk show host who believes that the federal government has been covering up its involvement with UFOs and captured alien technologies. A poll conducted during the same year found that Americans between the ages of eighteen and thirty-four are more likely to believe in UFOs than in their government's promises to provide them with Social Security benefits when they retire.[20] In 1998 Bill Clinton's popularity ratings shot astonishingly and unexpectedly through the roof after Hillary appeared on morning TV and dismissed allegations of serious presidential misdeeds as products of a "vast right-wing conspiracy."[21] Each week on the X-Files, Fox Mulder uncovers a new clue to the elaborate latticework of dark plottings that conjoin the plans of an invasive alien species with the covert activities of a shadow government that, like the one exposed during congressional investigations of the Reagan administration, has formed at the highest levels of the U.S. intelligence and military communities and is implicated in such significant historical events as the assassinations of JFK and Martin Luther King Jr. Such examples as these are symptomatic of the growing significance of tabloid counterknowledges that question the benignity and undermine the social effectivity of a range of official truths.

The expansion of Internet culture displays further symptoms of the same conditions that have led to the explosion of tabloid media. Like the supermarket tabloids discussed in chapter 2, the Internet was one of the very few media sites where reports challenging the orthodox (white) knowledge of O.J. Simpson's guilt could be readily accessed. And just as world reaction to Princess Diana's death was symptomatic of a growing moral panic over media tabloidization, so Internet activity around that incident can be seen as a symptom of the spread of popular tabloidist knowledges along the frontiers of cyberspatial culture. Within hours of the crash that claimed the life of the former Princess of Wales, the Internet was awash in heretical tales of conspiracy about the racistly vindictive British royal family, said to have engineered the fatal collision in order to avert the prospect of a marriage between the mother of the future king of England and an Arab. On the Internet, conjecture abounds around the Masonic flag Buzz Aldrin is said to have planted on the moon. People read and write of pyramids on Mars that were spotted by NASA probes but covered up by the federal government. The potential exposure of a hidden chamber containing the ark of the covenant is given as the real reason for Arab distress over the restoration of the Western Wall Tunnel in Jerusalem.[22] Like those instituted by the tabloid talk shows but even more so, the discursive spaces inaugurated through the mediation of the Internet are ones in which the stability of the modernist bases for epistemological and social authority and the criteria for the designation of expertise are subject to particularly high levels of ongoing challenge and disruption. This stems primarily from the fact that, as Mark Poster observes, "the 'magic' of the Internet is that it . . . radically decentralizes . . . the apparatuses of cultural production" by putting "cultural acts" and "symbolizations in all forms" in the hands of more users than any other technology for the broad dissemination of meanings.[23] The Internet is thus particularly susceptible to the creation of media terrains for the formulation and circulation of alternative popular knowledges.[24] These dynamics of contestation between competing knowledge formations are bound up with the postmodern cultural conditions that I have emphasized throughout this book. At a time when much of what we know is a product of electronic images generated by technologies that are under the control of powerful others, there is nothing particularly implausible about the idea that those others might choose to manipulate what we know. Our knowledge of the surface of Mars, to continue an earlier example, is largely a product of the images generated by government apparatuses; there is thus nothing at all "crazy" about the idea that it is entirely within the power of the government to manipulate our knowledge of Mars for whatever reasons it may have. That the Internet would emerge as an important site for the extension and expansion of heretical popular tabloidist knowledges is thus not surprising either, for it is a countertechnology that powerful others, despite their best efforts, have not yet learned to control (at least insofar as we know).

There are at least two misunderstandings that I wish not to provoke by claiming that the recent expansion of tabloid media can be linked to both postmodernity and struggles over multiculturalism. The first is the idea that tabloid television "reflects" or "mirrors" the changes occurring in the society of which it is a part. It is a fundamental assumption of structuralist, poststructuralist, and postmodernist media theory that there is no meaning-bearing "reality" for television to "reflect," though each of these theories deals with this claim differently. For structuralism, "reality" cannot be known, and therefore understood, until it is inserted into a system of signs (a "language"), none of which simply "refer" to something outside the system. Rather, the constituent components of the system work in concert to produce the meanings—the "identities"—of "things" in "reality," according to the internal codes that give those components their systematicity. Foucauldian poststructuralism, in turn, entails the recognition that such systems of meaning as language are inextricably imbricated within the operations of social power and are continually struggled over by competing sociocultural interests. By shifting structuralism's central problematic from that of "language" to "discourse," poststructuralism both designates the multiplicity of sense-making modalities that exist within any particular language system and also indicates that its object of analysis (discourse) is in itself a real, material, power-bearing entity rather than an idealist construct.[25] Finally, postmodernism (under the sway of the concepts "hyperreality" and "simulation," as I have used the term) extends poststructuralism's revision of structural linguistic theory to account for the implosive character of meaning production in an image-saturated society and emphasizes the imagistic volatility and increasing instability of our notions of "truth" and "reality." Like its theoretical antecedents, postmodernism eliminates the possibility of media "reflecting" or "distorting" an independent reality and emphasizes the interpenetration of media with our identities and experiences to the point at which it becomes exceedingly difficult, if not impossible, to disentangle them. Thus, as I have argued throughout this book, the media are part and parcel of the ongoing struggle over the social production of meanings that constitute our "reality" and shape the distribution of power within it. Indeed, it can be said with increasing justification that in this electronically networked society, media processes are the primary site of struggle over the power of discourse to constitute meaning in ways that variously serve some sociopolitical interests over and against others.

I equally hope that the suggestion that the explosion of tabloid media can be linked to struggles over multiculturalism is not taken to imply that the "New News" provides "equal representation" to all of the voices competing to be heard within the din that multidiscursivity necessarily entails. Tabloid media are not a discursive democracy wherein all the voices in society contest one another on equal grounds. The current high visibility of tabloid media demands to be understood not in terms of liberal pluralism but rather in terms of power and of the procedures whereby socially weak and strong voices and knowledges contest one another from dominant and subordinated positions. As Stuart Hall reminds us, popular cultures are never whole and coherent but are instead shot through with cleavages and contradictions. Certain elements of tabloid media embody the power of social forces working against multiculturalism, as I have suggested is the case with some forms of masculinist "reality-based" law enforcement programming. By the same token, as I argue in chapter 5, the struggle over normality that erupted in tabloid talk shows throughout the eighties and into the nineties was produced in part by Reaganism's polarizing social strategies and repression of voices speaking from positions of difference. Following Graham Knight's evocative phrase, tabloid media can productively be understood as a site of "scenarios and strategies clashing and cloning in a panic-stricken agonism of manoeuvre and advantage."[26] At each point where dominating power confronts its "counterstroke," its "underside," its "limit," the weak power on which it runs aground forms the "motivation" for new developments within its own networks of domination, which in turn provokes the emergence of new resistive strategies.[27]

I do not intend the term "multiculturalism" only in its racial and ethnic senses. It is meant equally to cover the increasing audibility within the popular news and information media of voices and types of knowledge that had formerly been more effectively marginalized through the dynamics of class, age, and gender. The proliferation of tabloid TV programming, for example, challenges traditional journalism's narrowly constricted vision of what is allowed to count as a "public issue." This constriction is a product of official journalism's heavy investment in the knowledges, concerns, and values of the well-educated white masculine middle-aged middle classes. As Elayne Rapping notes, "when TV emerged as the dominant cultural form, it presented to us a middle-aged, middle-class, white-male image of authority," for television was, in a sense, "developed to put a reassuring, controlling facade over the structural fault lines of American life."[28] In television news, this image of authority is perhaps best embodied in the figure of the anchorman, whose "voice is grave, resonant with the burden of transmitting serious matters," and whose proper arenas of knowledge—"White House communication strategies, leaks from State Department sources, leading economic indicators"—are remote enough from the popular cultures of everyday life to match the transcendent distance evoked in his comportment.[29] Appropriately, tabloid television disturbs not only the figure of the traditional anchorman, as I have argued in chapters 3 and 5, but equally the definitions of truth, seriousness, and authority that he embodies.

The current proliferation of tabloid media is part of a more widespread expansion of mechanisms by which various ways of knowing what it means to live in U.S. society are produced and circulated. Journalists have not been the last to take note of this. Katz, a journalist, points to the growth of an alternative "information culture" that circumvents the traditional journalistic establishment. Thus, for example, African American rappers N.W.A. warned listeners about the dangerous Los Angeles Police Department in "Fuck Tha Police" fully two years before mainstream journalism's recognition of LAPD brutality after the beating of Rodney King. Similarly, just before Martin Luther King's birthday in 1992, Public Enemy drew attention to his broken dreams of racial harmony in a furious video that imagined the assassination of state government officials in Arizona, at that time the only state in the union that refused to recognize the holiday commemorating the life of the slain black leader. In Washington, D.C., it was not conventional journalism but Oliver Stone's commercial film JFK that led to the popular agitation that spurred a congressional committee investigating the assassination of Jack Kennedy to ask that the government release all of its documents related to the killing.[30] Across the country, just two weeks after the U.S. Senate's vote on the appointment of Supreme Court Justice Clarence Thomas, viewers of the CBS sitcom *Designing Women* were treated to some of the most stinging criticisms of the Thomas confirmation hearings available on TV, as expressed through the voices of the program's main characters.[31]

In an era when "Bart Simpson's critique of society is more trenchant than that of most newspaper columnists," Katz proclaims, "the culture sparked by rock & roll, then fused with TV and mutated by Hollywood," has fully

obliterated "traditional boundaries between straight journalism and entertainment." [32] While, as I have noted, tabloid journalism is far from new but
rather has an extensive history and indeed a prehistory that can be traced
back hundreds of years,[33] what is distinctive about the current moment is
both the *high* visibility of especially electronic tabloid forms and of popular counterknowledges generally, and the *diminished* visibility of boundaries
between "serious news," "tabloidism," and "entertainment media." People
working in institutions of "serious" journalism report having been "stung
by the mounting evidence that Americans' passions and concerns" stray increasingly far from the most traditional forms of news that journalists associate with "quality." [34] They struggle, in response, to reinscribe fading,
irrelevant, and even counterproductive boundaries by equating their own
practices with "responsibility" and denouncing the growth of popular informational media forms as a "cross between prostitution and Armaged-
don." [35] The irony, however, is that at the same time they increasingly practice various popularizing techniques to regain and retain their audience.

The widely noted circumvention of the "serious press" and its "gatekeep-
ing function" by political candidates during the 1992 presidential election
campaign is a symptom of the blurring of boundaries and the expansion
of alternative popular news and information media that are reshaping the
journalistic culture. During that campaign season, Bill Clinton appeared on
a daytime talk show, played his saxophone on a nighttime one, and spoke
with young people on MTV. Ross Perot declared his presidential candidacy
on a call-in TV chat show. Even George Bush, who had publicly castigated
the popular media for their "weirdness," and who recognized only very late
in the game just how out of touch with "ordinary" Americans he had become, finally agreed, in a desperately futile gesture, to awkwardly entertain
impromptu questions from a White House tour group organized by the producers of a television breakfast program.[36] It is a telling point that during
the 1992 election, voter registration and electoral participation across the
country surged upward for the first time in twenty years.[37] Clinton and Perot
thus helped to end an era of Republicanism by partially bypassing the traditional journalistic gatekeepers of the American political process and ener-
gizing interest among segments of the electorate who had withdrawn from
participation in previous recent elections.

Rather than follow the "high-toned" commentators in their denunciations of the "degeneration" of political campaigning to the level of the
"lowest common denominator," we should therefore be thinking more
carefully about ways in which more progressive polticians might learn to
engage formations of the popular imagination through similar irreverence
toward both the gatekeepers of "serious journalism" and the sacred boundaries they seek to defend. Because so many on the Left have looked for so

long on media culture with little more than disdain and embarrassment and have seen it as "part of the problem," comparatively few have learned to speak to the popular tastes and knowledges that are often catered to by the tabloid and other popular "entertainment" media. This has left that field of potential articulations and rearticulations open to figures like the category-confounding populist Jesse "the Body" Ventura, a former professional wrestler and radio talk show "shock jock" who became "the nation's first governor to have his own action figure doll" when he was elected by Minnesotans in November 1998.[38] Ventura defeated a liberal Democrat and a conservative Republican, both of whom were vastly better funded than he, by appealing to a broad coalition organized around young people, union members, women, gays, and a heavy concentration of people who typically don't vote. Indeed, many of his supporters reported to exit pollsters that they wouldn't have bothered to vote in 1998 if not for Ventura's candidacy.[39]

In mounting his unconventional campaign, Ventura refused all money from PACs and special interest groups and declined to accept any contribution of more than fifty dollars. Consequently, while his opponents spent $4.3 million on their election efforts, Ventura managed just $250,000. (He is, moreover, refunding all unspent campaign contribution money.) The election result thus flies in the face of conventional wisdom, which says that such contests can be won only through the mobilization of immense fortunes. For his campaign's theme music, Ventura chose a song that reflects the power and resource imbalance between himself and his opponents: the title track from the blaxploitation classic *Shaft* (Gordon Parks, 1971), about a suave black detective who goes up against the powerful white Mafia. In addition to tackling the major political parties, Ventura has also, as favorite Minnesota son Garrison Keillor notes, "knocked the struts out from under the religious right."[40] This is not surprising, as Ventura opposes school prayer, school vouchers, and public displays of the Ten Commandments. Ventura has countercultural sympathies as well: "He praises the liberating Sixties, opposes laws against burning the flag, loves rock and roll, and condemns the Vietnam War."[41] (He also opposed Bush's Gulf War.) During campaign appearances Ventura frequently quoted such iconic iconoclasts as Jim Morrison of the Doors and the Grateful Dead's Jerry Garcia, both now dead albeit still resonant in the memories of generations of popular and countercultural mavens. Although in Ventura's incarnation as a popular professional wrestler he wore a gender-bending pink feather boa and sequined tights, his campaign Web site announced that the prototype for the gubernatorial version of his action figure would be a pared-down model with "no strings attached," to match his political philosophy. Among promised additions to the Jesse "the Body" line of accessories were companion dolls of "two-faced career politicians."[42]

Jesse "the Body" Ventura.

Ventura campaigned for abortion rights, gay rights and gun rights, and he "mused publicly about legalizing prostitution and drugs."[43] He supports women in the military and opposes capital punishment. During Minnesota's campaign debates, Ventura was, according to commentator Garry Wills, the only candidate to aggressively denounce a recently passed state law that bans gay marriage. When asked about the law, Ventura replied, "I have two friends that have been together forty-one years. If one of them becomes sick, the other one is not even allowed to be at the bedside. I don't believe government should be so hostile, so mean-spirited. . . . Love is bigger than government."[44] When conservative senator Trent Lott once claimed that sexual preference is determined by individual choice, Ventura responded by asking the senator, "So when did you make yours?"[45] Ventura's iconoclasm extends to the corporate Right as well as the religious one. In one of his most popular campaign commercials, children stage a fight between the Jesse Ventura action figure and a business-suited "Evil Special Interest Man." Once in office, Ventura swiftly alienated Republicans who wanted to turn revenues from a successful Minnesota civil suit against tobacco companies into a tax rebate for the rich; the governor argued that any such refund should be skewed toward the economically dispossessed. Finally, "the Body," who is widely noted for his off-the-cuff wit, his frac-

tured and colorfully blusterous oratorical style, and his penchant for gob-
bling down half-pound cheeseburgers on the campaign trail, sometimes
embraces self-parody as well as iconoclasm, as when he posed as Rodin's
The Thinker in the last commercial for his candidacy.[46] After the election he
also summoned an air of self-parody uncharacteristic of politicians when at
a public appearance he remarked, "I've never held a job for long, so I may
not have a long future in politics."[47]

Significantly, the Minnesota state election that produced "Governor
Body" (the Bakhtinian appellation by which Ventura referred to himself at
a victory rally) boasted the highest voter turnout in the country, despite
widespread media designation of the 1998 California state election as the
"most important" of the year. Indeed, Minnesota's voter turnout during the
Ventura election was almost twice the national average.[48] So many voters
showed up that polling places ran out of ballots, and some people waited
in line for three hours to cast their votes.[49] That more than 60 percent of
the Minnesota electorate participated suggests at once both how successfully the election engaged the interests of that state's voters compared with
those in other parts of the country and how poorly the U.S. political process
manages to do so in general.[50]

Voters for Ventura, whose campaign was laughingly dismissed as a joke
by both serious politicians and the pundits of establishment journalism,
identified with his marginalization as a candidate and thus expressed with
their votes their resentment over their own marginalization by the political
system. One thirty-two-year-old baker from a Minneapolis suburb, for example, told a journalist that he voted for Ventura precisely because of the
other candidates' dismissive attitudes toward the popular former wrestler.[51]
In comments to the media at his victory party, Ventura spoke to the anger
that his supporters feel toward conventional politicians: "They're never
going to take the people lightly again," he opined (no doubt far too opti-
mistically).[52] "They said a vote for me was a wasted vote," he added. "Well
guess what? Those 'wasted' votes wasted *them*."[53] Ventura's campaign had
indeed powerfully mobilized the sentiments of the disaffected. According
to the pastor of a working-class church in suburban Minneapolis, Ventura's
appeal reached deeply into the lowest social strata, beyond the "winners
with good jobs" and the "respectables who may not have good jobs but compensate by seeking respect in their community and church." Ventura found
a way to connect with the "survivors who just get by and the hard-living,
rootless folks who have completely given up on trying to be successful or
live by conventional norms."[54]

Ventura's ability to speak to the disaffected and the nonconforming can
usefully be read against the backdrop of his personal history. Wills observes
that Ventura's "hold on employment" has long been tenuous, and that he

has been unemployed as recently as 1995 and 1996.[55] His campaign's resonance among the ranks of disenfranchised and dispossessed Minnesotans
can also be traced partly to the popular persona Ventura constructed in the
World Wrestling Federation (wwf) and on Minnesota talk radio. As part
of the prehistory of his political activities, it is worth noting that Ventura
grew up listening to his father's seemingly endless criticisms of professional politicians. The elder Ventura, a city street worker who left school
after the eighth grade, reserved his harshest rebukes for Richard M. Nixon,
whom he called a "tail-less rat." [56] In his wwf career, the younger Ventura
constructed a "bad-boy" persona that effectively embodied a hard-bitten,
working-class skepticism that resembled his father's in its iconoclasm. If
as Michael Rogin notes, "Ronald Reagan found out who he was through
the roles he played on film," Jesse "the Body" Ventura began to recognize
his political identity on canvas—that of the wwf.[57] "Win if you can, lose
if you must, but always cheat," he once proclaimed.[58] Ventura thus challenged the sporting ideology that says that success is a product of hard work
and fair play—an ideology that reinforces that of the capitalist economy
by reproducing it in another, relatively autonomous (but ideologically over-
determined) arena. Capitalistic ideologies of economic meritocracy mask
the way in which both power and routine upper-echelon corruption (which
Governor Ventura sometimes calls "high-pocrisy") shape the unequal social distribution of success and failure.[59] What the ideologies of officialdom
hide, however, Ventura's wwf incarnation made explicit, as in the following
exchange between Ventura and wwf commentator Gorilla Monsoon:

> *Ventura:* It ain't cheatin' unless you get caught.
> *Monsoon:* Those are *your* rules, Jess.
> *Ventura:* No, those are *American* rules, the *American way!* [60]

Ventura's "bad-boy" image extended beyond the ring as well, as when
he stirred up trouble with his unsuccessful attempts to form a professional
wrestlers' union. (Incidentally, during his gubernatorial campaign, Ventura often noted that he was the only candidate with a union card.) Later
he successfully sued wwf owners over the issue of wrestlers' rights to
video royalties. Such activities and the "bad-boy" persona that they feed
work to strengthen ideological associations between the media figure that
is Jesse Ventura and various forms of popular counterknowledge. Thus, for
example, while the mainstream press has attributed Ventura's retirement
from professional wrestling to a pulmonary embolism, Web sites report
more populistically that exposure to Agent Orange in Vietnam is responsible, for Agent Orange is a potent symbol of the rank-and-file soldiers'
treacherous betrayal by their own superiors and the U.S. government.[61] I
suspect (though I have no direct evidence to support it) that at the time of his

retirement in 1984, the tabloids also circulated the popular counterexplanation of Ventura's departure from the ring rather than the mainstream medical "truth" of the event as reported by the "respectable" press. For as we have seen, the tabloid media routinely (claim to) make explicit that which is hidden or repressed by officialdom, as does Ventura's version of what constitutes "the American way." Ventura's media persona is also shaped by the fact that his radio talk show was devoted to agendas such as the legalization of marijuana and the identification of the conspirators who assassinated JFK (he cites Oliver Stone's film on the subject as a personal favorite), and that among his acting credits is a guest appearance on *The X-Files*.[62] It is telling that his role in the dissemination of popular counterknowledges would attract the scorn of commentators such as Wills, who derides Ventura for what he, Wills, calls "the demon of paranoid suspicion and conspiratorial distrust that lurks" in the former professional wrestler.[63]

In light of what Wills regards as "conspiratorial distrust" (but which we might see as justified popular skepticism), it is unsurprising that Ventura has long been known as an advocate of open government. Ventura put this advocacy into practice during his one previous stint in public office as mayor of Minneapolis's second-largest suburb, Brooklyn Park, from 1990 to 1994. Perhaps in fear of his open government reformism, Ventura was treated as a threatening outsider by the political establishment during the campaign for that office. He notes indeed that both the Democrats and the Republicans labeled him "the most dangerous man in the city" and banded together to oppose his candidacy. Nevertheless, his former Brooklyn Park colleagues give Ventura credit for "bringing people into the process" of municipal government and for enhancing its accessibility to "the average citizen."[64] He is remembered, for example, for getting Brooklyn Park's city council meetings televised on the local public access cable station. He has also made use of other alternatives to the mainstream political media more recently, for when the establishment politicians and pundits sought to dismiss and marginalize Ventura's gubernatorial campaign, he deployed a cyber-savvy Internet strategy to mobilize popular support. Since his election Ventura has advocated an expanded role for the Internet in Minnesota government to facilitate greater public access to official documents, to cultivate more alternative political candidacies, to enable Minnesotans to more easily hold him and his lieutenant governor "accountable for what they said on the campaign trail," and to "put citizens on an equal footing with lobbyists."[65] He states that one of his aims as governor is to "keep opening the arms of government and make it citizen friendly."[66]

Ventura made overtures in this direction at his inclusive and unconventional inaugural party (which was perhaps the only such event ever to feature a mosh pit). Billed as "the People's Celebration," the event included

The inauguration of Governor Ventura.

musical acts such as folkish alternarockers Soul Asylum, seventies pop icons America, rock legend Warren Zevon, blues prodigy Jonny Lang, and the Sounds of Blackness, a thirty-member ensemble whose work spans the entire gamut of African American music, from R&B to blues, gospel, hip-hop, jazz, reggae, spirituals, and field hollers. Still, entry to the event cost not much more than an urban movie ticket and vastly less than the major political parties' more exclusive soirees (all attendees, including journalists and political contributors, paid a twenty-dollar admission fee). Ventura, wearing earrings, a Jimi Hendrix T-shirt, and a buckskin motorcycle jacket with fringes, joined Zevon onstage and, at a key moment in the performance, tore off his bandanna to reveal the same bare skull that was inscribed with the slogan "Head of State" on T-shirts worn by many of the event's capacity crowd of more than seventeen thousand revelers. In this way, "the Body" upturns the ritualized spectacles of the political process, substituting raucous humor and the signs of countercultural disaffection for the traditional pomp and circumstance of the state. Appropriately enough, a large group of celebrants at the inauguration sported mockingly parodic T-shirts boasting that "our governor can beat up your governor." [67] Like *A Current Affair*'s mode of address, as we saw in chapter 3, the movement for "Governor Body" combines playfully irreverent humor directed against the self-seriousness of the political system (which parallels the tabloid program's lampooning of the serious news) with plainspoken populist indignation. It boisterously expresses resentment over the people's alienation from the power structure and mobilizes political skepticism toward fat cats, bureaucracies, and establishment politicos.

The campaigning styles, strategies, and successes of Jesse "the Body," that epigrammatic figure of popular media culture (professional wrestler, talk radio shock jock, actor in "mass appeal" Hollywood films such as *Running Man*, *Batman and Robin*, and *Predator*, and, incidentally, the only *man* who has ever terminated Arnold Schwarzenegger on-screen—a mark of his status as an iconoclastic giant killer), should be seen not as embarrassments (as they are by, say, the syndicated columnist Bob Greene, who reads them as confirmation of Neil Postman's well-known "amusing ourselves to death" thesis) but as lessons—especially, I hope, to left-leaning political aspirants—about how to converse with subordinated and alienated social formations, how to energize a campaign, and how to make use of the media.[68] Against those who would distinguish neatly between the "puffery" of style and the "meat" of substance, I want to claim that Ventura's political substance lies partly though significantly in his style—a style that is as tabloidized as any: sensationally populist, ironically playful, laughingly skeptical, wildly outrageous, sometimes self-mocking and sometimes self-satisfied, inclusive and participatory, blusterous and averse to euphemism, scandalous, offensive, and often in your face. Ventura is to "respectable" politicians what tabloids are to "respectable" journalism. His success should teach us about some of the failures of the current configuration of U.S. electoral politics, which typically works to exclude the very people with whom Ventura has learned to converse. Increasingly visible popular disruptions of the sacred spheres of "respectable" journalism and elite political discourse, such as the disruption represented by Ventura's election, are signs of a growing crisis: just as the popularity of tabloid media signals a legitimation crisis for the bourgeois "quality press," so does the campaigning success of Jesse "the Body" indicate that a crisis of legitimacy besets the official political system that has worked for so long to secure the interests of the most powerful Americans.

Ventura should also teach us about articulation and rearticulation. These are the cultural processes whereby diverse elements from a variety of discursive, ideological, and representational formations are forged into a new unity that thereby gives rise to the formation of an active social movement that did not previously exist but comes into being around, and is attached to, the newly unified expressive practices.[69] Jesse Ventura succeeded by fusing or *articulating* together certain images and ideological elements that thereby expressed or articulated certain meanings that could be linked or articulated to the newly emergent social movement to which his activities gave rise. The ideological and representational elements that he astutely fused together (gay rights, the 1960s, and pro wrestling, to name a few) were not in themselves novel. It is Ventura's particular arrangement of those diverse elements that was at once unique and powerful in its capacity to both catalyze and forge an expressive connection with an emergent social formation. One Minnesota airport shuttle driver gives apt expression to the sense of frustration that helped to mobilize this formation around Ventura's campaign:

> I don't know what he'll do. But he's going to tell all those Bible-thumpers on the right and the tree-huggers on the left to vote for their own, and he'll unite all the disaffected voters in the middle in a new party. I'm a lifetime DFL-er [Democratic-Farmer-Labor Party of Minnesota], from the "L," but I'm sick of union heads who negotiate contracts that sell out the workers, and I've had it with these professional politicians. We don't have workers running for office anymore, just people who never worked a real 40-hour week in their lives.[70]

Such a perspective helps to explain why Ventura's support was so strong among blue-collar Minnesotans.[71]

Like the tabloid media, Ventura collapses distinctions between politics and entertainment—something I don't believe we should necessarily condemn (as so many have) for reasons that the case of Jesse "the Body" makes clear. Ventura has brought at least some measure of disruption to an all too tight political order that secures the privileges of the few and the exclusion of many. Indeed, the Ventura campaign (and the myriad of dismissive reactions to it) should teach us about the class-cultural basis (and increasing permeability) of the very boundaries between "politics," "news," and "entertainment." Rather than view this permeability as an excuse for further lamentation over the "decline of civilization," we should instead try to identify the opportunities it creates for unsettling and democratizing energies to spill over from the all too often trivialized realms of "entertainment" and popular culture.

Among those who have recently published lamentations over the decline of politics and journalism in the age of television is Pierre Bourdieu. Bourdieu offers a scathing critique of the "structural corruption" of all journalism because of the hegemony of television, which promotes "the fear of being boring and anxiety about being amusing at all costs," so that "real information, analysis, in-depth interviews, expert discussions, and serious documentaries lose out to pure entertainment and, in particular, to mindless talk show chatter."[72] Bourdieu complains further that whereas TV was once used "to raise the taste of the general public," now, "because it must reach the largest audience possible, television is intent on exploiting and pandering to these same tastes."[73] Such an analysis reads ironically alongside Bourdieu's earlier work on popular taste and its various refusals of bourgeois distance, seriousness, and formality in cultural production and consumption (on which I have drawn at a number of points in this book).[74] What seems particularly uncharacteristic is that Bourdieu's analysis of the new news is framed not in terms of the question of its popularity but in terms of the structure of the journalistic field, considered relatively independently of questions about popular taste. The only suggestions Bourdieu's analysis gives regarding popular taste are generally along the lines of such observations as "in the 1990s . . . television is intent on . . . offering viewers what are essentially raw products . . . aimed at satisfying a kind of voyeurism and exhibitionism"; or that, like everyday talk about the weather, TV news is widely accepted because it offends no one and thus "cannot cause trouble."[75] It is doubly ironic that Bourdieu's On Television claims to reveal invisible structures and mechanisms that journalists are unable to see and yet that guide their work, and simultaneously hews very closely at many points to a lament about the decline of journalism that has become conventional among journalists themselves.[76] Accordingly, the medium's culturally uplifting potential is seen to be betrayed by the "populist spontaneism and demagogic capitulation to popular tastes" imposed by the logic of the market and the system of audience ratings.[77] Some U.S. journalists have explained Jesse Ventura's successful campaign in similar terms.

What is at stake for Bourdieu is not just politics and the news, moreover, but the very "conditions necessary for the production and diffusion of the highest human creations," which are jeopardized by television's intrusions into the enclaves of esoteric cultural activity. For example, Bourdieu notes that recent journalism threatens the autonomy of sciences and arts such as physics, jurisprudence, and philosophy by sanctifying some of their most mediocre practitioners, whose relative lack of power within their own fields and want of peer recognition motivates them to seek a kind of compensatory media celebrity that TV journalists are only too happy to promote. Such "heteronomous" dynamics undermine the purity of debate within specialized realms of cultural production and erode "the standards for entry into" the artistic and scientific fields.[78] However, Bourdieu sidesteps the extent to which the autonomy of cultural fields functions as a kind of insulation against the democratizing force of popular counterknowledges like some of those I've analyzed here.[79] A tabloid television program such as Sightings (see chapter 4), for example, is a platform for intervention by heteronomous individuals of a sort: Indian shamans, UFOlogists, alien abductees, and the like. By the same token, Jesse Ventura is a heteronomous figure in the field of politics.

Bourdieu's On Television is not without its merits. Its analysis of the structures and mechanisms whereby mainstream journalism serves as a conduit for the critically unexamined platitudes of official spokespeople is salutary. So too is Bourdieu's indictment of those "sensationalistic" media products that, like some forms of U.S. reality TV (see chapters 1 and 2), play into the hands of right-wing racist populism of the sort associated with Jean-Marie Le Pen's French National Front. Finally, Bourdieu is right to rebuke the triumphal mantras of the marketplace that grow deafening in the age of unrestrained multinational capital: they pose a clear and present danger to democratic practice and to the viability of certain types of oppositional and minority cultural products. Nevertheless, Bourdieu's argument, with its frequent reliance on such inadequately analyzed categories as "human interest news," "tabloid sensationalism," and "pure entertainment," entirely neglects the extent to which commercial pressures have ironically abetted the expansion of certain types of counterhegemonic voices, perspectives, and knowledges, some of which I've discussed in this book. Bourdieu notes that any adequate analysis of the crisis around TV news must steer between two extreme forms of historical interpretation: one that says the current situation is so unique that nothing like it has ever been seen before, and another that claims that things have always been this way. He then goes on to counterpose television against cultural forms that foment "symbolic revolution" and thus challenge our habits of thought and perception (as does the work of an artist such as Manet). By contrast with such forms, Bourdieu insinuates that television works perfectly to uphold the existing "symbolic order." [80] In light of his point about the need to steer between the extremes of historical interpretation, it seems ironic that Bourdieu would situate the social function of television at the very end of a continuum stretching from reproduction of the status quo to symbolic revolution. I would rather navigate an intermediate course: television (and the tabloid media broadly) participates in conflicted and contradictory cultural processes whereby competing discourses and power/knowledges intersect and interact complexly, at once both reproducing and reworking the symbolic order.

Such processes necessarily involve the disturbance of classifying boundaries. In recent times this has entailed the disruption of boundaries between the various modes of news and information discourse available in contemporary U.S. society; indeed, these boundaries appear to be decomposing. Although "serious" journalists have struggled to reinscribe such boundaries, their dissolution nevertheless continues apace. The Ken Starr scandal and the hyper(fune)real media event that erupted around the death of Princess Diana belong to a string of high-visibility happenings whose coverage by "serious" journalism resists easy differentiation from tabloid media, however hard the "respectable" news works to convince itself and its audiences of its definitive difference from lowly tabloidism. For example, seven prime-time network news shows contested a variety of tabloid programs for the first interview with Paula Jones after she accused President Clinton of sexual harassment. Similarly, the *New York Times*, *Washington Post*, and *Los Angeles Times* each averaged almost two stories per day about Olympic figure skater Tonya Harding during the month after Nancy Kerrigan was criminally assaulted by people connected to Harding. In light of such coverage, Thomas B. Rosenstiel of the *Los Angeles Times* writes that "increasingly uncertain of their purpose," journalists "compete with tabloid TV shows for stories and privately wonder whether serious journalism will remain economically viable." According to Rosenstiel, the "dread among many newspeople over whether they can remain relevant" has produced efforts to increase circulation among racial and ethnic minorities and lower-income families and to target audiences that had previously chosen not to read or watch news at all, just as Jesse Ventura and, to a lesser extent, Bill Clinton successfully targeted people who had given up on voting. Thus as more traditionally oriented broadcast and print journalists have watched their audiences shrink while popular definitions of what are considered to be appropriate and important topics for open public discussion and debate have shifted, many have reacted, as noted earlier, by selectively imitating the techniques of their new competitors while simultaneously continuing their efforts to inscribe the kinds of distinctions out of which cultural hierarchies are erected (as when, in 1993, one network executive proclaimed that his goal for a new television magazine program was "*responsible* tabloid" journalism).[81]

Tabloid media are thus positioned on the cutting edge of some significant shifts in the U.S. information culture. Demonized by mainstream journalists and other socially legitimated tastemakers, the tabloids nevertheless engage the popular imagination in ways that serious news organs are likely to continue emulating (while simultaneously continuing to accuse the new forms of popular journalism of "tastelessness" and "trivialization" in their ostensible conversion of the public realm into a "media circus" or an "electronic freakshow"). For us to uncritically accept such demonizing characterizations without interrogating the validation of cultural distinctions they perform would be to aid in the invisibilization of social powers that are exerted through every hierarchical classification of cultural products and consumers. Instead, we must question what it is about tabloid media that provokes widespread popular engagement as well as the disgust and derision of those who loudly proclaim themselves to be endowed with "higher sensibilities."

Appendix: TVQ Scores for Tabloid Programs
by Demographic Audience Category

Empiricist approaches to television audience research, like all forms of empiricism, are highly and notoriously problematic. Television ratings of one form or another, for example, claim merely to measure an empirical entity, "the audience," that purportedly exists in "reality" independently of the ratings discourses that supposedly do nothing but "describe" this reality. As Ien Ang notes, however, it is "in and through the descriptions made by ratings discourse" that "a certain profile of 'television audience' takes shape—a profile that does not exist outside or beyond those descriptions but is produced by them."[1] "Reality" can only ever be accessed through discourse, and all discourses, even statistical ones, are *fictive* in several senses, one of which is that their "descriptions" inevitably and actively select some aspects of the empirical world for inclusion and suppress others. In doing so, they reify allegedly "descriptive" categories that exist in discourse rather than in reality, for categories are techniques of sense making and not empirical objects. Empiricist research fails to grasp, for example, that "people constitute themselves quite differently as audience members at different times." As John Fiske writes, "I am a different television 'audience' when watching my football team from when watching *The A-Team* with my son or *Days of Our Lives* with my wife."[2]

Despite the intractable problems of empiricist audience research, I include here some data that attempt to measure how particular audience groups feel about some of the individual tabloid television programs discussed in this book. Such data can never be conclusive, though if they are approached with caution, I believe they can at least be usefully suggestive. For as Ang again points out, it is not that empiricist data "dream the audience into existence," for they "define a certain field of empirical truth," however fictive.[3] The data presented here are called "Q scores." They are produced by Marketing Evaluations/TvQ, Inc., a New York–based research firm. A Q score doesn't measure the size of a program's audience but rather measures how well the show's audiences like it. Eight times a year, Marketing Evaluations surveys 1,800 to 2,000 people aged six or older from its "cooperating consumer panel," which is made up of more than 55,000 U.S. households. This panel is "structured to be representative of the Continental U.S. population" according to the latest Department of Census estimates.[4] For each TV show, each respondent is asked to rate both his or her familiarity with the program and, if the respondent has seen the show, the degree to which he or she likes it, on a five-point scale that runs from "poor" to "favorite." Each program's Q score is then produced by dividing the percentage of people who identify the show as a favorite by the surveyed population's aggregate level of familiarity with the show. Consequently, if overall audience familiarity with a particular program grows over time but the number of people who select the program as a favorite merely stays the same, that show's Q score will decline. According to Marketing Evaluations spokesman Henry Schafer, "high Q scores signify that viewers are more enthused about a show, more involved with it and pay more attention to it." [5] Schafer reports that a score between twenty-two and twenty-three is, roughly speaking, an average Q score.[6]

Marketing Evaluations provides demographic breakdowns by age and gender for surveys completed by its adult respondents. At the end of the appendix, I have charted select tabloid television program Q scores for a ten-year period stretching from 1988 to 1998 (although not all programs are rated for all years). The programs included are *A Current Affair*, *America's Most Wanted*, *Cops*, *Donahue*, *Final Appeal*, *Jerry Springer*, *Oprah Winfrey*, *Ricki Lake*, *Sightings*, and *Unsolved Mysteries*. The Q scores for these programs are reported for six demographic categories: men age 18–34, men 35–49, men 50+, women 18–34, women 35–49, and women 50+. These data are indicative of the extent to which the programs are liked by the members of different demographic groups. Although the demographic groups are quite broad, I suggest that these Q scores nevertheless provide reference points whereby the social differentiation of tastes over a period of time might at least be roughly and provisionally sketched.

General Trends

Among the most notable general trends in these data are the following: *America's Most Wanted*, *Cops*, and *Unsolved Mysteries* rate consistently among the best-liked tabloid programs for all demographic groups over time, as does *Oprah Winfrey* for women of all ages. (Men consistently like *Oprah* less well, although they tend to like it better the older they are.) *Donahue*, *Jerry Springer*, and *Ricki Lake* are consistently among the least-liked tabloid programs for all years, although some demographic groups buck this trend (for example, in some years, *Donahue* is well liked by women over age fifty). Beyond these basic observations, the data as a whole resist summarization. For example, in some years, within each gender group, viewers like *Jerry Springer* better the younger they are, though this does not hold in other years. The same is true for *A Current Affair*. During several years, within each gender group, viewers like *Unsolved Mysteries* better the older they are, though during other years, for one or both gender groups, the oldest and youngest members like the show better than those in the middle age bracket. Rather than attempting to generalize further from data so resistant to summarization, I simply present graphs that represent each program's average Q score with each demographic group for each television season.

Demographic Breakdown of Q Scores by TV Season

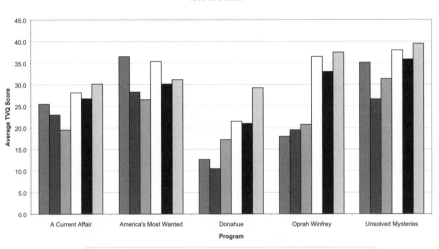

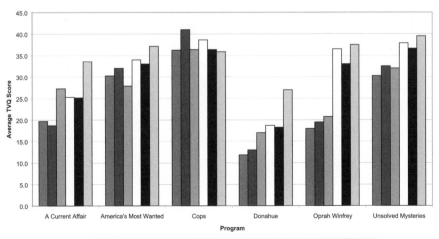

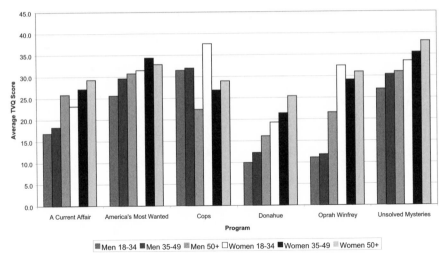

1990-91 Season

Average TVQ Score vs Program

Legend: ■Men 18-34 ■Men 35-49 ■Men 50+ □Women 18-34 ■Women 35-49 Women 50+

Programs: A Current Affair, America's Most Wanted, Cops, Donahue, Oprah Winfrey, Unsolved Mysteries

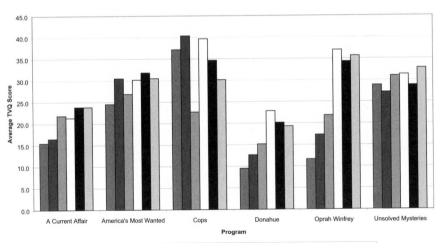

1991-92 Season

Average TVQ Score vs Program

Legend: ■Men 18-34 ■Men 35-49 ■Men 50+ □Women 18-34 ■Women 35-49 Women 50+

Programs: A Current Affair, America's Most Wanted, Cops, Donahue, Oprah Winfrey, Unsolved Mysteries

250   Appendix

1992-93 Season

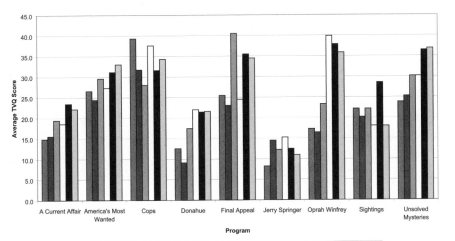

■Men 18-34 ■Men 35-49 ■Men 50+ □Women 18-34 ■Women 35-49 ▓Women 50+

1993-94 Season

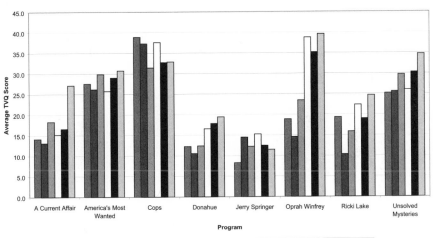

■Men 18-34 ■Men 35-49 ■Men 50+ □Women 18-34 ■Women 35-49 ▓Women 50+

Appendix   251

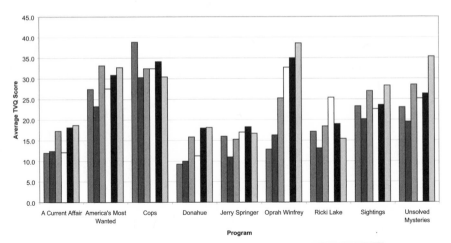

1994-95 Season

Average TVQ Score

Program

A Current Affair | America's Most Wanted | Cops | Donahue | Jerry Springer | Oprah Winfrey | Ricki Lake | Sightings | Unsolved Mysteries

■ Men 18-34 ■ Men 35-49 ■ Men 50+ ☐ Women 18-34 ■ Women 35-49 ▧ Women 50+

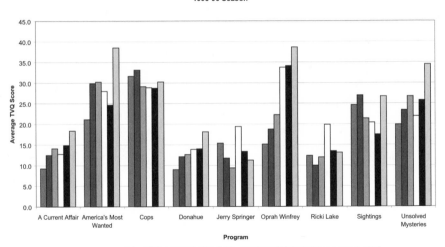

1995-96 Season

Average TVQ Score

Program

A Current Affair | America's Most Wanted | Cops | Donahue | Jerry Springer | Oprah Winfrey | Ricki Lake | Sightings | Unsolved Mysteries

■ Men 18-34 ■ Men 35-49 ■ Men 50+ ☐ Women 18-34 ■ Women 35-49 ▧ Women 50+

1996-97 Season

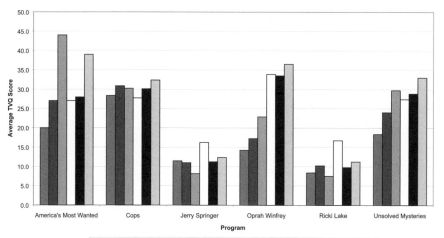

1997-98 Season

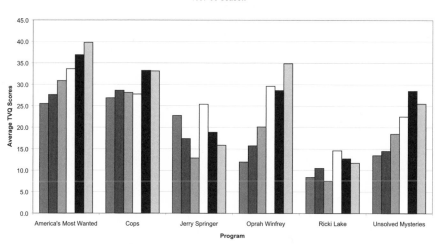

Notes

1 The Genealogy of Tabloid Television

1 Stuart Hall, "What Is This 'Black' in Black Popular Culture?" in *Black Popular Culture*, ed. Gina Dent (Seattle: Bay Press, 1992), 25. Hall adds that "as popular culture has historically become the dominant form of global culture, so it is at the same time the scene, par excellence, of commodification, of the industries where culture enters directly into the circuits of a dominant technology—the circuits of power and capital. It is the space of homogenization where stereotyping and the formulaic mercilessly process the material and experiences it draws into its web, where control over narratives and representations passes into the hands of the established cultural bureaucracies, sometimes without a murmur. It is rooted in popular experience and available for expropriation at one and the same time. I want to argue that this is necessarily and inevitably so" (26).

2 Diane Bartley, "John Walsh: Fighting Back," *Saturday Evening Post*, April 1990, 44.

3 Quoted in Frank J. Prial, "Freeze! You're on TV," *New York Times Magazine*, 25 September 1988, 63.

4 Bartley, "John Walsh," 44–45.

5 Leschorn made this remark during a 1993 episode of *America's Most Wanted*.

6 Quoted in Prial, "Freeze! You're on TV," 58.

7 Bartley, "John Walsh," 44.

8 See the *America's Most Wanted* Web site, http://www.amw.com.

9 See, for example, Graham Knight, "Reality Effects: Tabloid Television News," *Queen's Quarterly* 96, no. 1 (spring 1989): 94–108; John Langer, *Tabloid Television: Popular Journalism and the "Other News"* (London: Routledge, 1998); Monica Collins, "Extra! Extra! Tabloid Clones Invade TV," *TV Guide* (18 November 1989): 14–16; Philip Weiss, "Bad Rap for TV Tabs," *Columbia Journalism Review* 28, no. 1 (May–June 1989): 38–42; Harry F. Waters et al., "Trash TV," *Newsweek*, 14 November 1988, 72–78; J. Max Robins, "Here Come the News Punks," *Channels* (September 1988): 39–43; Roger Simon, "Now It's Tabloid TV: The Shows That Taste Forgot," *TV Guide* (17 September 1988): 51–53; Jay Blumler, "The New Television Marketplace: Imperatives, Implications, Issues," in *Mass Media and Society*, ed. James Curran and Michael Gurevitch (London: Arnold, 1991).

10 Pamela Donovan, "Armed with the Power of Television: Reality Crime Programming and the Reconstruction of Law and Order in the United States," in *Entertaining Crime: Television Reality Programs*, ed. Mark Fishman and Gray Cavender (New York: Aldine de Gruyter, 1998), 117.

11 On the postmodern aspects of television's eclectically hybridized styles, see Jim Collins, "Television and Postmodernism," in *Channels of Discourse, Reassembled: Television and Contemporary Criticism*, ed. Robert C. Allen, 2d ed. (Chapel Hill: University of North Carolina Press, 1992), 327–53, and esp. 336–38.

12 On how this is enhanced by the commercial television production process in the United States, see Todd Gitlin, *Inside Prime Time* (New York: Pantheon Books, 1985), esp. chap. 5.

13 David Morley, *Television, Audiences, and Cultural Studies* (London: Routledge, 1992), 27.

14 Sonia Livingstone and Peter Lunt, *Talk on Television: Audience Participation and Public Debate* (London: Routledge, 1994), 6–7.

15 Tony Bennett, "The Bond Phenomenon: Theorising a Popular Hero," *Southern Review* 16, no. 2 (1983): 209, 219.

16 Ibid., 223.

17 Other scholars have usefully mapped the pretelevision histories and prehistories of tabloid journalism and some of the popular-cultural forms linked historically with it, which can be traced back at least four hundred years. I will not rehearse these prehistories and histories here. Instead, I refer the interested reader to some of the existing work that helpfully maps the historical roots of modern "tabloidism" and some of its historical correlates and contexts in popular culture. Particularly useful are S. Elizabeth Bird, *For Enquiring Minds: A Cultural Study of Supermarket Tabloids* (Knoxville, Tenn.: University of Tennessee Press, 1992); James E. Murphy, "Tabloids as an Urban Response," in *Mass Media between the Wars: Perceptions of Cultural Tension, 1918–1941*, ed. Catherine L. Covert and John D. Stevens (Syracuse, N.Y.: Syracuse University Press, 1984), 55–69; Wayne Munson, *All Talk: The Talkshow in Media Culture* (Philadelphia: Temple University Press, 1993); Jane M. Shattuc, *The Talking Cure: TV Talk Shows and Women* (New York: Routledge, 1997); Joshua Gamson, *Freaks Talk Back: Tabloid Talk Shows and Sexual Nonconformity* (Chicago: University of Chicago Press, 1998); Simon Michael Bessie, *Jazz Journalism: The Story of the Tabloid Newspapers* (New York: E. P. Dutton, 1938); Silas Bent, *Ballyhoo: The Voice of the Press* (New York: Boni and Liveright, 1927).

18 Knight, "Reality Effects," 95. In his *Tabloid Television*, Langer notes similarly that "claims for the specificity" of a journalistic genre that he labels the "'other news' . . . have to be approached cautiously," for "all news on television probably contains elements of the 'other news'" (160). Langer's definition of the "other news" states that the term "is not merely an alternative designation for what sometimes get called 'human interest' stories . . . or for what journalists describe as 'soft news.' . . . Rather, as a descriptive-classificatory formulation, the 'other news' will include human interest or soft news items as well as coverage of fires, accidents, natural, social and personal 'disasters' and the like, all of which are events likely to qualify as 'hard news'" (9). This "other news," the analysis of which is the focus of Langer's book, is derived from a sample of evening news items broadcast mostly in the late 1970s in Melbourne, Australia, and is thus more narrowly constituted than the notion of tabloid television that I'm working with here. For example, Langer excludes daytime talk shows from his study, though they are surely one of the most important—if not the most important—constituents of contemporary U.S. tabloid television (see chapter 5 in this volume). Langer also excludes the more playfully outrageous and, as he terms them, "wild" forms of tabloidism, such as some of those from *A Current Affair* (which I examine in chapter 3), the *Weekly World News*, *Sightings*, and *Unsolved Mysteries* (which I examine in chapter 4).

19 Perhaps the key difference between the tabloid shows (many of which are syndicated) and the prime-time network news divisions' magazine programs, along with those of tone and style, has primarily to do with story selection. The tabloids often cover issues considered marginal, silly, and even "tasteless" by the network news divisions. As prime-time network television is aimed at a more socially central audience, so are its norms, tastes, and values the more socially central ones that tabloid programming frequently offends.

20 Brian Massumi, preface to *The Politics of Everyday Fear*, ed. Brian Massumi (Minneapolis: University of Minnesota Press, 1993), viii. Massumi also notes that "media scare cam-

paigns . . . highlight the materiality of the body as the ultimate object of technologies of fear" (viii), a strategy that is characteristic of tabloid television discourse. Also see Stuart Ewen and Elizabeth Ewen, *Channels of Desire: Mass Images and the Shaping of American Consciousness*, 2d ed. (Minneapolis: University of Minnesota Press, 1992), esp. chap. 1, "Shadows on the Wall."

21 Bahram Haghighi and Jon Sorenson, "America's Fear of Crime," in *Americans View Crime and Justice: A National Public Opinion Survey*, ed. Timothy Flanagan and Dennis Longmire (Thousand Oaks, Calif.: Sage Publications, 1996), 23.

22 Michel Foucault, *Discipline and Punish: The Birth of the Prison*, trans. Alan Sheridan (New York: Vintage Books, 1979).

23 Ibid., 195–228 ("Panopticism"). Foucault writes elsewhere that panopticism entails the imposition of "an inspecting gaze, a gaze which each individual under its weight will end by interiorising to the point that he is his own overseer, each individual thus exercising this surveillance over, and against, himself. A superb formula: power exercised continuously and for what turns out to be a minimal cost." See Michel Foucault, *Power/Knowledge: Selected Interviews and Other Writings, 1972–1977*, ed. Colin Gordon, trans. Colin Gordon et al. (New York: Pantheon Books, 1980), 155.

24 John Fiske, *Power Plays, Power Works* (London: Verso, 1993), 64.

25 Pierre Bourdieu, "The Aristocracy of Culture," *Media, Culture, and Society*, no. 2 (1980): 237. In this book, I draw heavily on Bourdieu's work around the issue of taste, especially his *Distinction: A Social Critique of the Judgement of Taste*, trans. Richard Nice (Cambridge: Harvard University Press, 1984), from which the "Aristocracy of Culture" essay is extracted. More recently, Bourdieu has published a scathingly denunciatory analysis of television journalism and its tabloidization, *On Television*, trans. Priscilla Parkhurst Ferguson (New York: New Press, 1998). I address this book and, briefly, its relationship to Bourdieu's earlier work in chapter 6 of this volume.

26 Mark Pursehouse, "Looking at *The Sun*: Into the Nineties with a Tabloid and Its Readers," *Cultural Studies from Birmingham* 1 (1991): 121. (Thanks to Michael Green for bringing this article to my attention.) Bird finds similar evidence of especially female tabloid readers' enthusiastic participatory engagement with the papers. She notes, for example, that one woman in her study "sends money to unfortunate people featured in the tabloids and feels personally involved in their troubles," and that her research turned up many women who "mentioned the role of the stories and advice columns in helping them sort through their own problems" (Bird, *For Enquiring Minds*, 148–49).

27 Mark Fishman, "Ratings and Reality: The Persistence of the Reality Crime Genre," in Fishman and Cavender, *Entertaining Crime*, 66.

28 See, for example, Anna Williams, "Domestic Violence and the Aetiology of Crime in *America's Most Wanted*," *Camera Obscura* 31 (January 1993): 97–118.

29 Langer cautions against this view, emphasizing instead the influence of long-standing TV news traditions that he groups in a category that he labels "the other news" (see chap. 1, n. 18). Although I agree with Langer's point that the "other news" has been an important source of representational conventions and practices for much of what is currently called "tabloid television," I also think that his particular focus leads him, in his brief concluding remarks on the relationship between the "other news" and the more recent explosion of tabloid television, to understate the important influence of the supermarket tabloid tradition (and the types of popular knowledges it mediates) with regard to the tabloidization of media generally. Thus, for example, as we shall see, UFO and alien encounters, long subjects for consideration by supermarket tabloids, are present

in many forms of tabloid TV, including the issue-oriented daytime talk shows, and such tabloid-style newscasts as *A Current Affair, Hard Copy,* and *Sightings,* and even the more docudramatic *Unsolved Mysteries.*

30 John Fiske, "Popularity and the Politics of Information," in *Journalism and Popular Culture,* ed. Peter Dahlgren and Colin Sparks (London: Sage Publications, 1992), 47–48.

31 Langer notes similarly that the "other news" (see chap. 1, n. 18) has "a more decisive connection with subordinate rather than dominant meaning-systems — instead of endorsing the definitions of reality of the ruling groups, the 'other news' appears to be aligned with the lived experience of the subordinate groups" (Langer, *Tabloid Television,* 154).

32 Fiske, *Power Plays.*

33 Fiske, "Popularity and the Politics of Information," 48.

34 Stuart Hall, "Notes on Deconstructing 'The Popular,'" in *People's History and Socialist Theory,* ed. Raphael Samuel (London: Routledge and Kegan Paul, 1981), 238. For a partially successful account of the history of uses of the term "popular" and a viewpoint that challenges Hall's, see Colin Sparks, "Popular Journalism: Theories and Practice," in Dahlgren and Sparks, *Journalism and Popular Culture,* 24–44. Sparks classifies uses of the term "popular" as either "quantitative," "political," or "aesthetic." Sparks berates theorists for their apparent inability to properly distinguish "which particular sense they are using at a particular moment" and observes that there are general "slippages within the terms themselves" (i.e., between the term's different senses) that problematize the concept of popularity. It seems to me, however, that one of the most valuable developments in cultural studies has been precisely the development of models capable of sliding between Sparks's three senses of popularity.

35 Bourdieu, *Distinction.*

36 Fiske, "Popularity and the Politics of Information," 46. Cf. Fiske, *Power Plays,* esp. ch. 1; Hall, "Notes on Deconstructing 'The Popular.'" Following Fiske, I use the term "social formations" instead of "classes" because it implies a more dynamic model of social processes. "Formations" suggests greater mutability than "classes."

37 See, for instance, Lawrence W. Levine, *Highbrow/Lowbrow: The Emergence of Cultural Hierarchy in America* (Cambridge: Harvard University Press, 1988).

38 Within each of the separate but necessarily interrelated realms of popular and elite culture, there exist, of course, finely grained and complex fields of distinction. Both popular and elite discourses and practices continually produce and reproduce these specialized distinctions, just as they produce and reproduce the basic distinction between elite and popular culture.

39 Hall, "Notes on Deconstructing 'The Popular,'" 238.

40 Fiske, "Popularity and the Politics of Information," 45–46. "The people" are not therefore an empirical entity that can be known objectively, as social science might have it. Bob Connell formulates the problem of masculinity in a way that is helpfully comparable with this culturalist approach to "the power-bloc" and "the people": "I emphasize that terms such as 'hegemonic masculinity' and 'marginalized masculinities' name not fixed character types but configurations of practice generated in particular situations in a changing structure of relationships." See R. W. Connell, *Masculinities* (Berkeley: University of California Press, 1995), 81.

41 Hall, "Notes on Deconstructing 'The Popular,'" 238.

42 For arguments in support of this perspective, see, for example, Michel de Certeau, *The Practice of Everyday Life,* trans. Stephen Rendall (Berkeley: University of California Press, 1984); Rosemary J. Coombe, "Postmodernity and the Rumor: Late Capitalism and the Fetishism of the Commodity/Sign," in *Jean Baudrillard: The Disappearance of Art and Politics,*

ed. William Stearns and William Chaloupkas (London: Macmillan, 1992), 98–108; John Fiske, *Understanding Popular Culture* (Boston: Unwin Hyman, 1989); Hall, "Notes on Deconstructing 'The Popular' "; James C. Scott, *Weapons of the Weak: Everyday Forms of Peasant Resistance* (New Haven, Conn.: Yale University Press, 1986); James C. Scott, *Domination and the Arts of Resistance: Hidden Transcripts* (New Haven, Conn.: Yale University Press, 1990).

43 Coombe, "Postmodernity and the Rumor," 101–2.

44 "P. & G.'s Battles with Rumors," *New York Times*, 22 July 1982, D1, D10, quoted in Coombe, "Postmodernity and the Rumor," 102.

45 "P. & G. Loses Campaign for the Moon and the Stars," *Globe and Mail*, 26 April 1985, B6, quoted in Coombe, "Postmodernity and the Rumor," 102.

46 Coombe, "Postmodernity and the Rumor," 102.

47 Ibid., 105–6.

48 Ibid., 101.

49 Pursehouse, "Looking at *The Sun*," 128.

50 Fiske, "Popularity and the Politics of Information," 46–47.

51 Cf. Stuart Hall's widely influential essay "Encoding, Decoding," in *The Cultural Studies Reader*, ed. Simon During (London: Routledge, 1993), 90–103. Hall writes there that "though the production structures of television originate the television discourse, they do not constitute a closed system. They draw topics, treatments, agendas, events . . . from other sources and other discursive formations within the wider socio-cultural and political structure of which they are a differentiated part," so that "the audience is both the 'source' and the 'receiver' of the television message." Therefore, the audience function is understood to be "reincorporated, via a number of skewed and structured 'feedbacks,' into the production process itself" (92–93).

52 This is a reference to the Birmingham Centre for Contemporary Cultural Studies (CCCS), which was headed by Hall and is usually associated with the emergence of "British cultural studies."

53 Jean Baudrillard, *The Ecstasy of Communication*, ed. Sylvere Lotringer, trans. Bernard Schutze and Caroline Schutze (New York: Semiotext[e], 1988), 27; cf. Fredric Jameson, "Postmodernism and Consumer Society," in *The Anti-aesthetic: Essays on Postmodern Culture*, ed. Hal Foster (Port Townsend, Wash.: Bay Press, 1983), 111–25.

54 John Fiske, *Television Culture* (London: Methuen, 1987), 19; italics mine.

55 Lawrence Grossberg, ed., "On Postmodernism and Articulation: An Interview with Stuart Hall," in *Stuart Hall: Critical Dialogues in Cultural Studies*, ed. David Morley and Kuan-Hsing Chen (London: Routledge, 1996), 138.

56 Jean Baudrillard, *In the Shadow of the Silent Majorities, or The End of the Social, and Other Essays*, trans. Paul Foss, John Johnston, and Paul Patton (New York: Semiotext[e], 1983).

57 In support of this point, I would note that Fiske himself makes use of Baudrillard's postmodern theories in some of his own work. See, for example, Fiske, *Television Culture*, 250–64; "MTV: Post Structural Post Modern," *Journal of Communication Inquiry* 10, no. 1 (1986): 74–79; *Reading the Popular* (Boston: Unwin Hyman, 1989), 87–88; *Media Matters: Everyday Culture and Political Change* (Minneapolis: University of Minnesota Press, 1994), 2. In further support of this point, I would cite a passage from Stuart Hall that begins as a critique of Baudrillard's position but winds up coming rather close indeed to that very position. Hall argues that "in spite of the fact that the popular masses have never been able to become in any complete sense the subject-authors of the cultural practices in the twentieth century, their continuing presence, as a kind of passive historical-cultural force, has constantly interrupted, limited and disrupted everything else. It is as if the masses have kept a secret to themselves while the intellectuals keep running around in circles trying

to make out what it is, what is going on" (Grossberg, "On Postmodernism and Articulation," in Morley and Chen, *Stuart Hall*, 140). Compare this with Baudrillard, who writes
that "it has always been thought—this is the very ideology of the mass media—that it
is the media which envelop the masses. The secret of manipulation has been sought in
a frantic semiology of the mass media. But it has been overlooked, in this naive logic
of communication, that the masses are a stronger medium than all the media, that it is
the former who envelop and absorb the latter. . . . All power silently flounders on this
silent majority. . . . What is to be done with these masses? They are the leitmotiff of every
discourse; they are the obsession of every social project; but all run aground on them"
(*In the Shadow of the Silent Majorities*, 44, 48–49). Now, my point is not to deny the very
real differences between these theorists and their concepts but rather to indicate points
of potential convergence where they might be brought into productive engagement and
interchange with each other.

58   Grossberg, "On Postmodernism and Articulation," in Morley and Chen, *Stuart Hall*, 150.

59   Ibid., 147.

60   Lynn Hunt, "Introduction: History, Culture, and Text," in *The New Cultural History*, ed.
Lynn Hunt (Berkeley: University of California Press, 1989), 8.

61   Stuart Hall identifies a key weakness in Foucault that the addition of a Gramscian dimension might correct. Hall writes that "there are different regimes of truth in the social formation. And these are not simply 'plural'—they define an ideological field of force. There
are subordinated regimes of truth which make sense, which have some plausibility, for
subordinated subjects, while not being part of the dominant episteme. In other words
. . . you have to talk about the relations of power which structure the interdiscursivity,
or the inter-textuality, of the field of knowledge. I don't much care whether you call it
ideology or not. What matters is not the terminology but the conceptualization." By neglecting to "question the relative power and distribution of different regimes of truth in
the social formation at any one time," Hall argues that Foucault "let himself off the hook
of having to re-theorize" the problem of ideology "in a more radical way" (Grossberg,
"On Postmodernism and Articulation," in Morley and Chen, *Stuart Hall*, 136).

62   Jürgen Habermas, *The Structural Transformation of the Public Sphere: An Inquiry into a Category of
Bourgeois Society*, trans. Thomas Burger with Frederick Lawrence (Cambridge: MIT Press,
1989).

63   Anthony Giddens, "Jürgen Habermas," in *The Return of Grand Theory in the Human Sciences*,
ed. Quentin Skinner (Cambridge: Cambridge University Press, 1985), 132.

64   Habermas's divergence from poststructuralism and from the variants of postcolonialism
and multiculturalism that rely on poststructural theory should be immediately apparent
here.

65   Oskar Negt and Alexander Kluge, "Selections from the Proletariat Public Sphere," *Social
Text* 25–26 (1990): 24–32; Nancy Fraser, *Unruly Practices: Power, Discourse, and Gender in Con-
temporary Social Theory* (Minneapolis: University of Minnesota Press, 1989), 113–43; Nancy
Fraser, "Rethinking the Public Sphere: A Contribution to the Critique of Actually Existing
Democracy," *Social Text* 25–26 (1990): 56–80.

66   Jodi Dean, *Aliens in America: Conspiracy Cultures from Outerspace to Cyberspace* (Ithaca, N.Y.:
Cornell University Press, 1998), 11. Quoting Phil Cousineau, *UFOs: A Manual for the Millennium* (New York: Harper-Collins West, 1995), 179, Dean observes that in the United States
there are five times as many UFO believers as there are fundamentalist Christians and
more UFO believers than there were voters for either Reagan, Bush, or Clinton (Dean,
10). She goes on to say that "the idea of the public sphere brings with it presumptions
about truth, discussion, and consensus. Debate in such a sphere, for example, requires

that everyone accept the same conception of reality. Everyone has to agree about what facts look like. . . . Thus, the liberal public is preserved and protected by the bracketing of certain ways of thinking or points of view. This bracketing, in fact, creates the public" (137).

67 Bruce Robbins, "Introduction," *Social Text* 25–26 (1990): 3, quoted in Sonia Livingstone and Peter Lunt, *Talk on Television: Audience Participation and Public Debate* (London: Routledge, 1994), 16.

68 Habermas, *The Structural Transformation of the Public Sphere*, 164, quoted in Shattuc, *The Talking Cure*, 88.

69 Also see, e.g., Paolo Carpignano et al., "Chatter in the Age of Electronic Reproduction: Talk Television and the 'Public Mind,' " *Social Text* 25–26 (1990): 33–55; Shattuc, *The Talking Cure*.

70 Livingstone and Lunt, *Talk on Television*, 32.

71 Jean-François Lyotard, *The Postmodern Condition: A Report on Knowledge*, trans. Geoff Bennington and Brian Massumi (Minneapolis: University of Minnesota Press, 1984).

72 Collins, "Television and Postmodernism," 333.

73 Jameson, "Postmodernism and Consumer Society," 125.

74 Ibid. On the postmodern mode of nostalgia, see Fredric Jameson, "Postmodernism, or The Cultural Logic of Late Capitalism," *New Left Review* 146 (July–August 1984): esp. 64–71.

75 There are interesting similarities here with a phenomenon associated with early campaigning for the year 2000 presidential election. The *New York Times* noted in late July 1999 that recent polls showed Americans feel much more favorably toward President George Bush than they did at the end of his term in office. One month before he was defeated by Clinton, Bush was rated favorably by just 35 percent of the population and unfavorably by 45 percent. So low were these figures that more than 375 of the 400 Republican candidates for public office in 1992 rejected Bush's offers to appear with them in campaign ads. But with his son, George Bush Jr., apparently poised to grab the Republican nomination for the presidency in 2000, the image of the elder Bush has been reactivated by the media and seems to be benefiting from nostalgia-before-its-time; pundits note that President Bush is "basking in the glow of a surprisingly early, and positive, reassessment of his stewardship." What's interesting here is the admixture of historical amnesia and apparent nostalgia-before-its-time that Republican strategists hope to mobilize on behalf of the younger Bush's presidential campaign: amnesia regarding widespread public rancor toward the high unemployment, stagnating wages, and growing social inequalities associated with Bush's continuation of Reaganomic policies, and nostalgia for the warm fuzzies of his "kinder, gentler America," which was in fact widely ridiculed in its day. Richard L. Berke, "As Bush (the Son) Surges, Bush (the Father) Sees a Resurgence," *New York Times*, 25 July 1999, http://www.nytimes.com.

76 This is not to deny that such events are capable of generating great interest and even fascination among many audiences. (Dominick Dunne writes, for example, of "Bel Air dinner parties during the O.J. Simpson trial, when people talked of nothing but that trial for the better part of two years." See "Mr. Dunne Goes to Washington," *Vanity Fair*, May 1999, 91.) Rather, it is to suggest that this interest is met early and head-on by a counterchorus of complaints that ask, in effect, "Haven't we had enough of this story already? Could we please move on?"

77 I'm indebted to Elana Levine for calling these stories to my attention.

78 Fiske, "Popularity and the Politics of Information," 46–62.

79 Lynn Spigel notes that "perhaps not surprisingly, at a time when the ontological status of

the television image was thrown into question by the fraudulent histrionics of the quiz shows, the networks turned to reality-oriented formats with renewed vigor." See "From Domestic Space to Outer Space: The 1960s Fantastic Family Sit-Com," in *Close Encounters: Film, Feminism, and Science Fiction*, ed. Constance Penley, Elisabeth Lyon, Lynn Spigel, and Janet Bergstrom (Minneapolis: University of Minnesota Press, 1991), 212.

80 Edward Bliss Jr., *Now the News: The Story of Broadcast Journalism* (New York: Columbia University Press, 1991), 287.

81 Knight, "Reality Effects"; Sydney W. Head and Christopher H. Sterling, *Broadcasting in America: A Survey of Electronic Media*, brief edition (Boston: Houghton Mifflin Company, 1991); Bliss, *Now the News*; Robert J. Donovan and Ray Scherer, *Unsilent Revolution: Television News and American Public Life* (Cambridge: Cambridge University Press, 1992).

82 Walter Ong, *Orality and Literacy: The Technologizing of the Word* (London: Methuen, 1982), 46.

83 Richard Campbell, "Word vs. Image: Elitism, Popularity, and TV News," *Television Quarterly* 26, no. 1 (1991): 73–81; Karin E. Becker, "Photojournalism and the Tabloid Press," in Dahlgren and Sparks, *Journalism and Popular Culture*, 130–53.

84 David S. Broder, "TV Coverage: Too Close, Too Personal," *San Jose Mercury-News*, 7 July 1985, 7P; italics mine.

85 Mary Ann Doane, *The Desire to Desire: The Woman's Film of the 1940s* (Bloomington: Indiana University Press, 1987), 1.

86 Bliss writes that during the sixties, "the treatment of news changed. Increasingly, news was packaged to attract larger and larger audiences. Consultants advised broadcasters on giving the public what it wanted, rather than what it needed. More emphasis was placed on pictures — the visuals — and on pace. 'Talking heads' were discouraged. And although many broadcasters still acted responsibly, many did not. News had become golden. It was difficult, having a profit center, not to make profit the name of the game" (*Now the News*, 306).

87 Jeff Merron, "Murrow on TV: *See It Now, Person to Person*, and the Making of a 'Masscult Personality,' " *Journalism Monographs* 106 (July 1988).

88 Quoted in Bliss, *Now the News*, 306.

89 Rinker Buck, "What the Cutbacks Really Mean," *Channels* (September 1986): 68.

90 Vernon A. Stone, "Two Decades of Changes in Local News Operations," *Television Quarterly* 25, no. 1 (1990): 41.

91 Knight, "Reality Effects," 95.

92 Bliss, *Now the News*; Head and Sterling, *Broadcasting in America*.

93 Jean Baudrillard, *Revenge of the Crystal: Selected Writings on the Modern Object and Its Destiny, 1968–1983*, ed. and trans. Paul Foss and Julian Pefanis (London: Pluto Press, 1990), 149.

94 Conrad Smith, "News Critics, Newsworkers, and Local Television News," *Journalism Quarterly* 65 (summer 1988): 342.

95 Bourdieu, *Distinction*, 486.

96 Edwin Diamond, *Sign Off: The Last Days of Television* (Cambridge: MIT Press, 1982), 18. Local news is also often cast in terms of its implicit threat to phallic power, as "soft news." See, e.g., Joseph Turow, "Local Television: Producing Soft News," *Journal of Communication* 33, no. 2 (spring 1983): 111–23.

97 Joanmarie Kalter, "Please. Risk It. Bore Me with Reality," *TV Guide* (17 November 1984): 24–25.

98 Michele Hilmes, "Pay Television: Breaking the Broadcast Bottleneck," in *Hollywood in the Age of Television*, ed. Tino Balio (Boston: Unwin Hyman, 1990), 297–318.

99 Head and Sterling, *Broadcasting in America*, 67.

100 Buck, "What the Cutbacks Really Mean."

101 Walter Cronkite, quoted in Fernando Quintero, "Cronkite Tells What Ails Us at First Herb Caen Lecture," *Berkeleyan*, 20 November 1996, 8.

102 James Warren, " 'Tabloid TV's' White Knight," *Chicago Tribune*, 4 August 1989, sec. 5, p. 3.

103 Lane Vernardos, executive producer of the CBS *Evening News*, quoted in Michael Massing, "CBS: Sauterizing the News," *Columbia Journalism Review* 24 (March–April 1986): 31.

104 Massing, "CBS: Sauterizing the News," 30.

105 James S. Ettema, "Journalism in the 'Post-factual' Age," *Critical Studies in Mass Communication* 4, no. 1 (March 1987): 85.

106 Van Gordon Sauter, "In Defense of Tabloid TV," *TV Guide* (5 August 1989): 3.

107 Karl Fleming, quoted in Massing, "Sauterizing the News," 30.

108 Warren, " 'Tabloid TV's' White Knight."

109 Gitlin, *Inside Prime Time*. Herman Gray argues that the previously regnant "principle of least objectionable programming" died during the 1980s. See Gray, *Watching Race: Television and the Struggle for "Blackness"* (Minneapolis: University of Minnesota Press, 1995), 61.

110 Ron Powers, "The Pox of Fox," *Gentlemen's Quarterly*, May 1990, 78.

111 Marc Fisher, "The King of Sleaze," *Gentlemen's Quarterly*, April 1990, 190.

112 John J. Pauly, "Rupert Murdoch and the Demonology of Professional Journalism," in *Media, Myths, and Narratives: Television and the Press*, ed. James W. Carey (Newbury Park, Calif.: Sage Publications, 1988), 246–49.

113 Powers, "The Pox of Fox," 82.

114 Alex Ben Block, "Twenty-First Century Fox," *Channels* (January 1990): 36–40; Peter Ainslie, "Looking for Answers," *Channels* (Field Guide, 1989), 82–83.

115 Buck, "What the Cutbacks Really Mean."

116 Block, "Twenty-First Century Fox," 38.

117 Ron Powers, "Lawyers, Guns, and Money," *Gentlemen's Quarterly*, June 1989, 129–30.

118 Foucault, *Discipline and Punish*, 214.

119 Jane Feuer, *Seeing through the Eighties: Television and Reaganism* (Durham, N.C.: Duke University Press, 1995), 12.

120 Feuer, *Seeing through the Eighties*; Linda Hutcheon, *The Politics of Postmodernism* (London: Routledge, 1989).

121 Diane Rubenstein, "The Anxiety of Affluence: Baudrillard and Sci-Fi Movies of the Reagan Era," in Stearns and Chaloupkas, *Jean Baudrillard*, 65.

122 Diane Rubenstein, "The Mirror of Reproduction: Baudrillard and Reagan's America," *Political Theory* 17, no. 4 (November 1989): 585.

123 Michael Rogin, *Ronald Reagan, the Movie, and Other Episodes in Political Demonology* (Berkeley: University of California Press, 1987), 3.

124 Rubenstein, "The Mirror of Reproduction," 599.

125 Michael Sorkin, "Simulations: Faking It," in *Watching Television: A Pantheon Guide to Popular Culture*, ed. Todd Gitlin (New York: Pantheon Books, 1986), 164.

126 These comments were made on NBC's *Today* show on January 12, 1993.

127 Gray, *Watching Race*, 17.

128 Ibid., 23. Also see Herman Gray, "Television, Black Americans, and the American Dream," *Critical Studies in Mass Communication* 6 (December 1989): 376–87.

129 Jacquelyn Dowd Hall writes that "it may be no accident . . . that the vision of the black man as a threatening beast flourished during the first phase of the southern women's rights movement, a fantasy of aggression against boundary-transgressing women as well as a weapon of terror against blacks. Certainly the rebelliousness of that feminist generation was circumscribed by the feeling that women were hedged about by a 'nameless horror.' " See " 'The Mind That Burns in Each Body': Women, Rape, and Racial Vio-

lence," in *Powers of Desire: The Politics of Sexuality*, ed. Ann Snitow, Christine Stansell, and Sharon Thompson (New York: Monthly Review Press, 1983), 337. It is noteworthy that the 1980s was also a period of increasing backlash against women's movements in the United States. See Susan Faludi, *Backlash: The Undeclared War against American Women* (New York: Crown Publishers, 1991).

130 Richard M. Smith, "The Plague among Us," *Newsweek*, 16 June 1986, 15.

131 See Jimmie L. Reeves and Richard Campbell, *Cracked Coverage: Television News, the Anti-cocaine Crusade, and the Reagan Legacy* (Durham, N.C.: Duke University Press, 1994).

132 Murray Edelman, "The Construction and Uses of Social Problems," in Stearns and Chaloupkas, *Jean Baudrillard: The Disappearance of Art and Politics*, 274.

133 Edelman, "The Construction and Uses of Social Problems," 278–79.

134 Tom Morganthau et al., "Losing the War?" *Newsweek*, 14 March 1988, 18; Smith, "The Plague among Us," 15; Terry E. Johnson, et al., "Urban Murders: On the Rise: Cocaine Is Suspected in a Surge in City Killings," *Newsweek*, 9 February 1987, 30.

135 In *Cracked Coverage*, Reeves and Campbell note that conservatives' need to assert that "the drug economy represents an alien system far removed from the values embraced by the rest of society" clashes with the entrepreneurial motivations of drug traders (36–37).

136 Ted Gest et al., "Victims of Crime," *U.S. News and World Report*, 31 July 1989, 19.

137 John Heinz, "Recognizing the Rights of Crime Victims," *USA Today*, July 1984, 82.

138 Gest et al., "Victims of Crime," 18.

139 Edmund Newton, "Criminals' Rights," *Ladies' Home Journal*, September 1986, 177.

140 Heinz, "Recognizing the Rights of Crime Victims," 80, 83.

141 Quoted in Judith Miller and Mark Miller, "Complaint of Crime Victims: 'Where Are Our Rights?' " *USA Today*, May 1986, 50.

142 Jostein Gripsrud, "The Aesthetics and Politics of Melodrama," in Dahlgren and Sparks, *Journalism and Popular Culture*, 84–95.

143 Quoted in Jane Marion, "Why John Walsh Hunts Killers: 'I Am Still Devastated,' " *TV Guide*, 18 March 1989, 23.

144 Williams, "Domestic Violence and the Aetiology of Crime in *America's Most Wanted*."

145 Fiske, *Media Matters*, 33.

146 Williams, "Domestic Violence and the Aetiology of Crime in *America's Most Wanted*"; Michel Foucault, *Politics, Philosophy, Culture: Interviews and Other Writings, 1977–1984*, ed. Lawrence D. Kritzman, trans. Alan Sheridan et al. (New York: Routledge, 1988), chap. 8.

147 As Thomas L. Dumm puts it, under contemporary regimes of criminological science, "even if the criminal does not speak on his own behalf, even if his motives are not explained by investigation and confession, the body of the criminal itself speaks the 'truth' of the criminal's character." "The New Enclosures: Racism in the Normalized Community," in *Reading Rodney King/Reading Urban Uprising*, ed. Robert Gooding-Williams (New York: Routledge, 1993), 184.

148 By the use of this term "imaginary surveillance," I mean to indicate the development of surveillance and surveillance-like practices that are centered on the generation of images—especially the kinds of images that occupy a central location within the prevailing social imagination of a particular society and, as well, therefore, within the imaginations of many of its inhabitants. I do not mean to suggest, in my use of the concept of the imaginary, something that is false, nonexistent, or "unreal." Imaginary surveillance can be linked with what William Bogard calls "the *imaginary* of surveillant control—a fantastic dream of seeing everything capable of being seen, recording every fact capable of being recorded, and accomplishing these things, whenever and wherever possible, prior to the event itself." See *The Simulation of Surveillance: Hypercontrol in Telematic Societies* (Cam-

bridge: Cambridge University Press, 1996), 4–5. The anticipatory aspect of the surveillant imaginary seeks enhanced control over events (or their deterrence) through advance
preparation.

149 Robert Stam, "Television News and Its Spectator," in *Regarding Television: Critical Approaches
— an Anthology*, ed. E. Ann Kaplan (Frederick, Md.: University Publications of America,
1983), 39.

150 Donovan, "Armed with the Power of Television," 132.

151 On the excision of footage documenting police brutality from broadcasts of the A B C program *American Detective*, see Debra Seagal, "Tales from the Cutting-Room Floor," *Harper's
Magazine*, November 1993, 50–57.

152 *Copswatch: The Media Parasite*, http://www.specmind.com/copswatch.htm.

153 Paul G. Kooistra, John S. Mahoney, and Saundra D. Westervelt, "The World of Crime According to Cops," in Fishman and Cavender, *Entertaining Crime*, 153.

154 John Langer, "Truly Awful News on Television," in Dahlgren and Sparks, *Journalism and
Popular Culture*, 114.

155 Ibid., 123.

156 One statistical content analysis of forty-two *Cops* episodes found that nonwhite offenders were shown to be responsible for thirty-three violent and property crimes, whereas
white offenders were shown to be responsible for only ten such crimes. Furthermore,
all instances of interracial crime in the programs portrayed the violation of *white* victims
by *nonwhite* offenders. See Kooistra, Mahoney, and Westervelt, "The World of Crime According to Cops," 150–53.

157 Mary Beth Oliver and G. Blake Armstrong, "Predictors of Viewing and Enjoyment of
Reality-Based and Fictional Crime Shows," *Journalism and Mass Communication Quarterly* 72,
no. 3 (1995): 559–70; cited in Aaron Doyle, "Cops: Television Policing as Policing Reality,"
in Fishman and Cavender, *Entertaining Crime*, 107.

158 De Certeau notes that handcuffs and billyclubs belong to the stockpile of instruments
used to write the body and so to make of it a socially active bearer of laws and norms (*The
Practice of Everyday Life*, 141).

159 Paolo Carpignano and his colleagues argue that "live" television broadcasts produce a
population of monitors rather than an audience of spectators, and that, moreover, "the
watching of a live space establishes a relationship between an act of monitoring and
a happening" (e.g., the subduction of an unruly "criminal" body). Consequently, "the
more the news is forced to emphasize its live-like quality, the more the act of scanning
of places will be privileged over the reception of reported events." See "Chatter in the
Age of Electronic Reproduction: Talk Television and the 'Public Mind,' " *Social Text* 25–26
(1990): 42.

160 Bogard, *The Simulation of Surveillance*, 9, 19, 30–31.

161 See, for example, Timothy Egan, "Soldiers of the Drug War Remain on Duty," *New
York Times*, 1 March 1999, http://www.nytimes.com. Egan discusses the militarization of
police forces that prevails throughout the United States at the end of the millennium,
thanks to the drug war. He cites the research of professor Peter Kraska, whose national
surveys have found that 90 percent of the police departments in cities with more than
50,000 inhabitants, and 75 percent of those in cities with fewer than 50,000 inhabitants,
now have paramilitary Special Weapons and Tactics (SWAT) units. According to Kraska,
police deployments of paramilitary forces have grown tenfold since the early 1980s. This
is largely attributed to drug war legislation that enables police departments to keep many
of the assets they seize in raids, and to military giveaways of combat artillery to police
departments that want it. For instance, 1.2 million pieces of military hardware such as

grenade launchers and armored personnel carriers were given to police departments by the U.S. Department of Defense between the years of 1995 and 1997 alone.

162 McKenzie Wark, *Virtual Geography: Living with Global Media Events* (Bloomington: Indiana University Press, 1994), 36.

163 Weiss, "Bad Rap for TV Tabs," 42.

2 Cops, Courts, and Criminal Justice: Evidence of Postmodernity in Tabloid Culture

1 Jean Baudrillard, *Baudrillard Live: Selected Interviews*, ed. Mike Gane, trans. George Sale-mohamed et al. (London: Routledge, 1993), 145, 148–49.

2 Jeff Silverman, "Murder, Mayhem Stalk TV: True Tabloid Tales! Television in Frenzy over Sordid Real-Life Sagas," *New York Times*, 22 November 1992, sec. 2, p. 28.

3 Krista Bradford, "The Big Sleaze," *Rolling Stone*, 18 February 1993, 43.

4 In his discussion of Gilles Deleuze and Félix Guattari, Paul Patton makes the point similarly. "The representation of events, in television and print media, has become part of the unfolding of events themselves. . . . While social events have always been constituted in part by the manner in which they were represented or described, the speed of modern telecommunications has undoubtedly accelerated the feedback loop" between events and representations. For Baudrillard, the analytical value of any theoretical distinction between "events" and their "representations" has vanished, so that such distinctions have become more misleading than useful. Paul Patton, "The World Seen from Within: Deleuze and the Philosophy of Events," *Theory and Event* 1, no. 1. *Theory and Event* is an on-line journal available at http://muse.jhu.edu/journals/theory _ & _ event/.

5 John Fiske, *Media Matters: Everyday Culture and Political Change* (Minneapolis: University of Minnesota Press, 1994), 69.

6 Ibid., 62.

7 Zygmunt Bauman, "The Sweet Scent of Decomposition," in *Forget Baudrillard?* ed. Chris Rojek and Bryan S. Turner (London: Routledge, 1993), 24.

8 See, e.g., Briankle G. Chang, "Mass, Media, Mass Media-tion: Jean Baudrillard's Implosive Critique of Modern Mass-Mediated Culture," *Current Perspectives in Social Theory* 7 (1986): 159; Kuan-Hsing Chen, "The Masses and the Media: Baudrillard's Implosive Postmodernism," *Theory, Culture, and Society* 4 (1987): 75; Mark Poster, *The Mode of Information: Poststructuralism and Social Context* (Chicago: University of Chicago Press, 1990), esp. chap. 2; Arthur Kroker, "Television and the Triumph of Culture: Three Theses," *Canadian Journal of Political and Social Theory* 9, no. 3 (fall 1985): 38.

9 Arthur W. Frank, "Twin Nightmares of the Medical Simulacrum," in *Jean Baudrillard: The Disappearance of Art and Politics*, ed. William Stearns and William Chaloupkas (London: Macmillan, 1992), 82–85.

10 William J. Mitchell, *The Reconfigured Eye: Visual Truth in the Post-photographic Era* (Cambridge: MIT Press, 1992), 12–13.

11 Jean Baudrillard, *The Evil Demon of Images*, trans. Paul Patton and Paul Foss (Sydney, Australia: Power Institute Publications, 1987), 27.

12 Jean Baudrillard, *Simulations*, trans. Paul Foss, Paul Patton, and Philip Beitchman (New York: Semiotext[e], 1983), 146.

13 Jean Baudrillard, *Selected Writings*, ed. Mark Poster (Stanford, Calif.: Stanford University Press, 1988), 144.

14 Ibid., 144–45.

15 Ibid., 171.

16 Jean Baudrillard, *Revenge of the Crystal: Selected Writings on the Modern Object and Its Destiny, 1968–1983*, ed. and trans. Paul Foss and Julian Pefanis (London: Pluto Press, 1990), 160.

17 Baudrillard, *Simulations*, 49.

18 Baudrillard, *Revenge of the Crystal*, 149. Baudrillard describes the paradox of hyperreal obscenity through a moribund metaphor: "The real is growing, the real is expanding: one day the whole universe will be real, and when the real becomes universal, it will be death." The death Baudrillard associates with the expansion of hyperreal obscenity is the death of imaginative cultural forms, whose difference from the "real" will have been completely elided.

19 Chang, "Mass, Media, Mass Media-tion," 178.

20 Baudrillard, *Revenge of the Crystal*, 147.

21 Ibid., 27–28.

22 Ibid., 148.

23 Ibid., 146.

24 Baudrillard, *Baudrillard Live*, 84. Also see Judith Williamson, "An Interview with Jean Baudrillard," trans. Brand Thumin, *Block* 15 (1989): 16–19.

25 Baudrillard, *Simulations*, 49–50.

26 *Cops*, 24 October 1992.

27 *American Detective* uses "tiny, wirelike 'lock-down' cameras taped to anything that might provide a view of the scene: car doors, window visors, . . . a gear-shift handle." Debra Seagal, "Tales from the Cutting-Room Floor," *Harper's Magazine*, November 1993, 51.

28 Jon Katz, "Covering the Cops: A TV Show Moves In Where Journalists Fear to Tread," *Columbia Journalism Review* 31, no. 5 (February 1993): 26.

29 Baudrillard, *Revenge of the Crystal*, 175.

30 *Cops*, 7 November 1992.

31 "Mass mediatization . . . is no ensemble of techniques for broadcasting messages; it is the imposition of models. . . . In fact, the essential Medium is the Model. What is mediatized is . . . what is reinterpreted by the sign form, articulated into models, and administered by the code." See Jean Baudrillard, "Requiem for the Media," in *Video Culture: A Critical Investigation*, ed. John G. Hanhardt (Rochester, N.Y.: Visual Studies Workshop Press, 1986), 133. Elsewhere Baudrillard urges that "we must think of media as if they were . . . a sort of genetic code which controls the mutation of the real into the hyperreal. . . . The whole traditional mode of causality is brought into question. . . . We must imagine TV on the DNA model" (*Simulations*, 55–56).

32 Seagal, "Tales from the Cutting-Room Floor," 51.

33 Ibid., 50–52, which I have paraphrased at several points here.

34 Aaron Doyle, "Cops: Television Policing as Policing Reality," in *Entertaining Crime: Television Reality Programs*, ed. Mark Fishman and Gray Cavender (New York: Aldine de Gruyter, 1998), 114.

35 Ibid., 111.

36 *ABC World News Tonight*, 19 November 1993.

37 Doyle, "Cops," 111.

38 Seagal, "Tales from the Cutting-Room Floor," 54.

39 Or, conversely, they are "articulate, meticulously professional, sometimes even laughably solicitous," as when, "on *Cops*, the police thank drunk drivers profusely for cooperating and hand out quarters to teenagers caught driving without licenses so they can call Mom and Dad to come pick them up" (Katz, "Covering the Cops," 26).

40 Seagal, "Tales from the Cutting-Room Floor," 57; italics mine. Seagal asks, "Is it that only by participating in the non-reality of TV can these people feel *more* real?"

41 Susan Faludi, *Backlash: The Undeclared War against American Women* (New York: Crown Publishers, 1991).

42 Along these lines, see Fred Pfeil's compelling analysis of the popular cultural ambivalence around, and struggles over, reconstructions and reassertions of masculinity in postmodern "male rampage films," in his *White Guys: Studies in Postmodern Domination and Difference* (London: Verso, 1995).

43 Dianne Cyr Carmody, "Mixed Messages: Images of Domestic Violence on 'Reality' Television," in Fishman and Cavender, *Entertaining Crime*, 170.

44 Paul G. Kooistra, John S. Mahoney, and Saundra D. Westervelt, "The World of Crime According to *Cops*," in Fishman and Cavender, *Entertaining Crime*, 150. The authors found that 74.8 percent of all crimes depicted on *Cops* culminate in the arrest of a suspect (which is also, of course, depicted on the program). By contrast, according to the *Uniform Crime Reports*, only 21.4 percent of offenses indexed annually lead to an arrest.

45 Jean Baudrillard, *In the Shadow of the Silent Majorities, or The End of the Social, and Other Essays*, trans. Paul Foss, John Johnston, and Paul Patton (New York: Semiotext[e], 1983), 35.

46 Ibid., 43.

47 Kathleen Rowe points out, however, that the grotesquery associated with images of horror, death, and dismemberment—relatively common scenes in *Cops*—work demonically, demotically, and democratically to reveal the leveling materiality of the body. See Kathleen Rowe, *The Unruly Woman: Gender and the Genres of Laughter* (Austin: University of Texas Press, 1995), 33.

48 Lynn Spigel and Henry Jenkins, "Same Bat Channel, Different Bat Times: Mass Culture and Popular Memory," in *The Many Lives of the Batman: Critical Approaches to a Superhero and His Media*, ed. Roberta E. Pearson and William Uricchio (New York: Routledge, 1991), 121.

49 Charlotte Brunsdon's characterization of the dominant view of soap operas, quoted in David Morley, "Changing Paradigms in Audience Studies," in *Remote Control: Television, Audiences, and Cultural Power*, ed. Ellen Seiter et al. (London: Routledge, 1989), 34.

50 Michael Sorkin, "Simulations: Faking It," in *Watching Television: A Pantheon Guide to Popular Culture*, ed. Todd Gitlin (New York: Pantheon Books, 1986), 172.

51 Jean Baudrillard, *Xerox and Infinity*, trans. Agitac (London: Touchepas, 1988). This pamphlet, originally published as *Le Xerox et L'Infini* in Paris in 1987, has no page numbering.

52 "For the law is a second-order simulacrum whereas simulation is third-order, beyond true and false, . . . beyond the rational distinctions upon which function all power and the entire social" (Baudrillard, *Simulations*, 40).

53 Ibid., 25–36.

54 Baudrillard, *Baudrillard Live*, 146.

55 Walter Benjamin, *Illuminations*, ed. Hannah Arendt, trans. Harry Zohn (New York: Schocken, 1968), 217–51.

56 Baudrillard, *Baudrillard Live*, 146.

57 Bradford, "The Big Sleaze," 40.

58 Graham Knight, "Reality Effects: Tabloid Television News," *Queen's Quarterly* 96, no. 1 (spring 1989): 97.

59 Baudrillard, *Baudrillard Live*, 146.

60 According to a brief editor's note appended to Debra Seagal's account of her tenure at *American Detective*, that program was canceled during the summer of 1993 "despite good ratings" (Seagal, "Tales from the Cutting-Room Floor," 57).

61 Fiske, *Media Matters*, 37.

62 E. R. Shipp reports that this view was widespread throughout the black media. See "O.J. and the Black Media," *Columbia Journalism Review* (November–December 1994): 40.

63 See, e.g., Neal Gabler, "O.J.: The News as Miniseries," *TV Guide*, 30 July 1994, 12–17; "Don't Mean Diddly," *New Yorker*, 11 July 1994, 4, 6; Frank Rich, "Another Media Morning After," *New York Times*, 30 June 1994, A23; Frank Rich, "Judge Ito's All-Star Vaudeville," *New York Times*, 2 October 1994, sec. 4, p. 17; Walter Goodman, "The Summer's Top Crime Drama, Continued," *New York Times*, 4 July 1994, sec. 1, p. 40; Jon Katz, "In Praise of O.J. Overkill," *New York*, 25 July 1994, 12–13.

64 Alexander Cockburn, "White Rage: The Press and the Verdict," *Nation*, 30 October 1995, 491.

65 Examples abound. In addition to the ones I discuss in the text, these include "Whodunit?" *Star*, 26 July 1994, 5, 27; "The Picture That Could Free O.J.," *Star*, 18 April 1995, 5; "Drug Gang Killed Nicole," *Globe*, 21 March 1995, 1; Bob Michals, "OJ: Autopsy Shocker: How New Evidence Could Rip Lid off Simpson Case," *Globe*, 14 March 1995, 24–25. Suspicion toward the alternative accounts of events circulating in tabloids was sometimes expressed as bewilderment in the face of a widespread popular, and particularly African American, refusal to accept Simpson's guilt. One commentator writes that "serious people, unwilling to accept what on the face of it seemed to be the facts, offered theories, even to strangers in checkout lines." See John Gregory Dunne, "The Simpsons," *New York Review*, 22 September 1994, 36. Here the invocation of checkout lines (where tabloid newspapers are most commonly found) is tellingly symptomatic of the imaginary proximity of disreputable popular knowledges and the most disreputable branches of the popular press. Another account, this one produced after Simpson's acquittal, tellingly targets "an unreasonable suspicion of law enforcement authorities" harbored by "a paranoid, conspiracy-minded sector of the population that would honestly though irrationally have rejected the state's argument virtually without regard to the evidence." See Randall Kennedy, "After the Cheers," *New Republic*, 23 October 1995, 14.

66 The ensuing discussion of these terms, in this paragraph and the next, is heavily indebted to John Fiske, *Power Plays, Power Works* (London: Verso, 1993), esp. 14–15; and Fiske, *Media Matters*, 3–6, both of which are paraphrased in places here.

67 Fiske, *Power Plays*, 14.

68 Martin Gould, "O.J. Trial Bombshell: I've Found Murder Weapon, Psychic Tells D.A.—and Simpson Didn't Do It," *Star*, 22 November 1994, 6–7.

69 Lawrence Grossberg, ed., "On Postmodernism and Articulation: An Interview with Stuart Hall," in David Morley and Kuan-Hsing Chen, eds., *Stuart Hall: Critical Dialogues in Cultural Studies* (London: Routledge, 1996), 131–50; Gilles Deleuze and Félix Guattari, *A Thousand Plateaus: Capitalism and Schizophrenia*, trans. Brian Massumi (Minneapolis: University of Minnesota Press, 1987).

70 Grossberg, "On Postmodernism and Articulation," 141.

71 Hall gives as an example the Jamaican Rastafarians' disarticulation and rearticulation of elements of Christian religion (generally a reactionary social force) with those of contemporary music culture and social rebellion, and thus the creative production of both a new expressive and ideological formation and a new social movement. As Hall explains, "they did not go back and try to recover some absolutely pure 'folk culture,' untouched by history, as if that would be the only way they could learn to speak. No, they made use of the modern media to broadcast their message. 'Don't tell us about tom-toms in the forest. We want to use the new means of articulation and production to make a new music, with a new message.' This is cultural transformation. It is not something totally new. It is not something which has a straight, unbroken line of continuity from the past. It is

transformation through a reorganization of the elements of a cultural practice, elements which do not in themselves have any necessary political connotations. It is not the individual elements of a discourse that have political or ideological connotations, it is the ways those elements are organized together in a new discursive formation" (Grossberg, "On Postmodernism and Articulation," 143).

72 "The Fuhrman Tapes Uncensored," *Star*, 5 September 1995, 36–37, 39; Ken Harrell, "Fuhrman Race Tapes Shocker," *Globe*, 1 August 1995, 5. Interestingly, in terms of the concerns of this chapter, both the incriminating evidence on Fuhrman and the uncertainty regarding its "reality" or "fictionality" stem from a series of interviews he gave in his capacity as a "consultant on a reality-based movie project about L.A. cops" (Harrell, "Fuhrman Race Tapes Shocker," 5).

73 Ken Harrell and Bob Michals, "O.J. Shocker: Killer Used Two Knives," *Globe*, 21 February 1995, 24–25, 41. Something similar occurs in a story about a 1989 Paramount pictures promotional film starring O.J. Simpson and Leslie Nielsen. In the promo short, Simpson repeatedly tries to stab Nielsen with a large knife. The *Globe* places stills from the film alongside a photo-recreation of the LAPD's scenario of the Simpson and Goldman murders; the placement of the photos creates a seamlessly fluid movement between O.J.'s fictitious character and the tabloid's grisly re-creation. See "The Mad Slasher!" *Globe*, 27 June 1995, 10–11.

74 To those who can only imagine the "postmodern" and its associated concepts in the most grandiose and epochal terms, and who are therefore dismissive of attempts to make use of those concepts, John Fiske offers a helpful formulation: "The postmodern promiscuity of images swamps any attempt to control them; it overwhelms any neat distinction between representation and reality, between fact and fiction. It refuses to allow 'truth' a place in reality alone, for it cannot see that reality still has its own place for truth to make a home in. An image-saturated culture differs from a culture of controlled and organized representations not just in degree, but in kind. And this, postmodernism tells us, is what characterizes its world as generically different from the modern. But we don't live in a completely postmodern world, we live in a world where the modern and the postmodern (and the premodern) coexist uneasily" (Fiske, *Media Matters*, 62). By the same token, we might note the existence of very old cultural forms that prefigure the postmodern.

75 Grossberg, "On Postmodernism and Articulation," 146. Hall makes this criticism of Ernesto Laclau and Chantal Mouffe, *Hegemony and Socialist Strategy: Towards a Radical Democratic Politics*, trans. Winston Moore and Paul Cammack (London: Verso, 1985).

76 S. Elizabeth Bird conducted an ethnographic study of supermarket tabloid readers and concludes that "the tabloids clearly offer millions of Americans something they do not find in other media." In 1992 the *Star* had a circulation of 3,562,367. Because tabloid buyers typically share the papers with family and friends, however, estimates suggest that each issue was read by approximately 11,756,000 people. During that same year, the circulation for the *Globe*, before sharing, was around 1.6 million. Bird notes that the "combined weekly circulation" of the United States' six national supermarket tabloids "hovers around ten million," although their actual readership is "estimated at fifty million." See *For Enquiring Minds: A Cultural Study of Supermarket Tabloids* (Knoxville: University of Tennessee Press, 1992), 7, 35, 37.

77 For a sense of the instability of tabloid perspectives on the Simpson case, consider the difference between the *Globe*'s front covers for July 5, 1994, and October 17, 1995. The former, which appeared not long after Simpson's arrest, features large block letters that read "O.J. Was Framed!" The latter, which appeared not long after Simpson's acquittal, features similar block letters that promise to show "How OJ Got Away with Murder!"

These extreme examples, though published more than a year apart, nevertheless demonstrate a pattern of oscillation that was evident from week to week and even within the same tabloid issue. They also suggest that the tabloids' anti-officialdom is stronger than their belief in either the guilt or innocence of Simpson: here, the *Globe* is on his side when the cops are holding him prisoner, and against him when the courts declare his innocence.

78 "O.J. Couldn't Have Done It," *Star*, 4 April 1995, 5. Similar examples include "Hunt for Nicole's Mystery Lover," *Star*, 14 March 1995, 24–25; "Stunning Evidence That Jury Won't Be Told: What O.J.'s Little Girl Heard on Night of Murders," *Star*, 25 July 1995, 29, 44. The latter reveals "fascinating clues that investigators seemed to ignore in their rush to arrest O.J.—instead of searching for any other suspects" (29). Further examples include Paul Francis, "Two Madmen Killed O.J.'s Wife & Her Pal," *Globe*, 26 July 1994, 36–37, 44; Ken Harrell, "3 Surprise Witnesses Will Set O.J. Free," *Globe*, 11 October 1994, 17; Paul Francis, "Nicole Was the Victim of Deadly Thugs Out to Kill Faye Resnick," *Globe*, 28 March 1995, 24–25, 41.

79 Tony Frost, "O.J.'s Life of Luxury behind Bars," *Star*, 11 July 1995, 6. Similar examples include "Mother's Love," *Star*, 11 October 1994, 2–3; "O.J. Invites Family to Jail for Holiday Get-Together," *Star*, 10 January 1995, 10.

80 "The Juice" is a nickname from O.J.'s days of football stardom and is based on the initials by which he is best known.

81 Tony Frost, "O.J. Gave Sex and Drug Parties for L.A. Cops," *Star*, 6 September 1994, 36–37, 39.

82 This is not to deny that many of the tabloids' stories slotted neatly into those very same racialized narrative grooves but rather to suggest that unlike mainstream media coverage of the case, the tabloids also produced a profusion of stories that went against the racial grain of the serious press and of mainstream white belief in the idea that O.J. committed the murders.

83 My parenthetic mention that the *Globe*'s representation of O.J.'s police mug shot was undarkened is a reference to the infamously darkened image of the mug shot used on the cover of *Time* magazine subsequent to Simpson's arrest. The famous bloody glove was the main piece of evidence linking Simpson with the murders. Prosecutors claimed that it was discovered behind Simpson's house by detective Mark Fuhrman. The defense claimed that Fuhrman planted it there. Its twin was found at the murder scene. The defense's claims were bolstered when in a moment of high courtroom and media drama, Simpson tried to put the glove on his hand but couldn't because it was too small.

84 "Who Really Killed Nicole: Dramatic New Evidence from Globe Readers: $1 Million Reward," *Globe*, 2 August 1994, 44.

85 Ibid., 1.

86 Mike Kerrigan, "Cop Framed O.J.," *Globe*, 2 August 1994, 36–37.

87 LAPD report, quoted in Kerrigan, "Cop Framed O.J.," 37.

88 Kerrigan, "Cop Framed O.J.," 37, 44. The coroner's incompetence is noted often by the tabloids. For example, *Globe* notes that the entire prosecution case may crumble under the weight of fully *sixteen* mistakes made by the coroner's office; see Lo-Mae Lai, "16 Mistakes That Could Set Him Free," *Globe*, 9 August 1994, 36–37. In another issue, the paper reports similarly on ten clues missed by the LAPD; "*Globe* Finds 10 Key Clues Cops Missed," *Globe*, 20 September 1994, 5.

89 Neil Vinetz, quoted in "Who Really Killed Nicole," 44; italics mine.

90 Anonymous informant, quoted in "Who Really Killed Nicole," 44.

91 Reports that Colombians committed the murders also played extensively in the tabloids.

See, for example, Bob Michals, "O.J., Drugs, the Mob—& Murder!" *Globe*, 19 July 1994, 36–37, 40; Tony Frost, "How O.J. Trapped Nicole into Life of Cocaine," *Star*, 30 August 1994, 24–25, 29.

92 S. Elizabeth Bird notes that "even more than [mainstream] newspapers, tabloids place much emphasis on reader response and involvement." See Bird, "The Kennedy Story in Folklore and Tabloids: Intertextuality in Political Communication," in *Politics in Familiar Contexts: Projecting Politics through Popular Media*, ed. Robert L. Savage and Dan Nimmo (Norwood, N.J.: Ablex Publishing, 1990), 259. Although the difference between tabloid and mainstream journalism is best characterized not as a categorical one but as one of degrees, it is nevertheless often helpful to clarify the differences between the points at either end of the continuum, as the instance at hand invites us to do. Still, it should be noted that highly visible "crisis events" such as the Simpson case have a strong tendency to blur distinctions between official or serious and popular or tabloid news forms.

93 Bird, *For Enquiring Minds*; Mark Pursehouse, "Looking at *The Sun*: Into the Nineties with a Tabloid and Its Readers," *Cultural Studies from Birmingham* 1 (1991); Jane M. Shattuc, *The Talking Cure: TV Talk Shows and Women* (New York: Routledge, 1997).

94 If the population of tabloid consumers is relatively high in people who are relatively dispossessed of educational capital, as at least one study has found (see Bird, *For Enquiring Minds*, 108), then the tabloids' acknowledgment of their readers' knowledges and communicative competencies may be an important source of pleasure for some readers; as Pierre Bourdieu suggests, the unequal distribution of educational capital distributes the social validation of competence unequally. See Bordieu, "The Aristocracy of Culture," *Media, Culture, and Society*, no. 2 (1980): 231.

95 Rosemarie Lennon, "Nicole's Amazing Confessions," *Star*, 20 September 1994, 36, 38. The use of the word "confessions" in this title is, to say the least, remarkable. It is not, I should point out, characteristic of the tone of the story itself but does in itself resonate disturbingly with a "blame the victim" ethos, about which I shall have more to say hereafter.

96 To cite another example along similar lines, *Globe* reports on its discovery of a secret eighty-five-page "bombshell" dossier that reveals more than twenty repressed incidents of violence perpetrated against Nicole by O.J., which describes O.J. as "an obsessed stalker who bragged about spying on Nicole and knowing her day-to-day movements." See Paul Francis, "Nicole: Top-Secret File Lists 20 Cases of Abuse by Juice!" *Globe*, 24 January 1995, 36.

97 Tony Frost, "Nicole's Final Hours on Earth," *Star*, 24 January 1995, 22, 24–25, 29; Tony Frost, "Nicole Put on a Sexy Sun Dress and a Sweet Smile, Then Begged O.J. 'Take Me Back'; at That Moment She Signed Her Death Warrant," *Star*, 20 June 1995, 26–28.

98 Frost, "Nicole's Final Hours on Earth," 24.

99 Tony Frost, "It Was Just One Year Ago: O.J. & Nicole's Easter Break," *Star*, 4 April 1995, 24.

100 Ibid., 27.

101 "O.J. Takes America by Storm," *Star*, 26 July 1994, 43.

102 Quoted in Frost, "Nicole Put on a Sexy Sun Dress and a Sweet Smile," 28.

103 Tony Frost, "Nicole Uncensored," *Star*, 25 October 1994, 25–27.

104 Hillary Sweeney, "How This Dog May Hold Key to O.J. Case," *Star*, 6 December 1994, 37.

105 On January 1, 1989, Nicole made a desperate call to "911" emergency services while she was being viciously beaten by O.J. Los Angeles prosecutors leaked a recording of the chilling phone call to the news media, who broadcast the tape repeatedly for days. The *Star* used the word "savage" both on its November 8, 1994, cover and in the subtitle of that issue's feature story on the beating and "911" call. The tabloid further primitivizes

O.J. in its description of how "the onetime football superstar . . . broke down a door" and "dragged Nicole around the estate by her long blonde hair" before "pummeling her with his fists so badly she had to go to the hospital." See Tony Frost, "I Watched in Terror as O.J. Beat Nicole," *Star*, 8 November 1994, 24. What I want to point out here is the characterization of O.J. in Neanderthalean terms (he dragged Nicole by her hair), and the careful inclusion of Nicole's hair color (blonde as a powerful signifier of whiteness), which work together in what should be obvious racially significant ways.

106 Frost, "I Watched in Terror as O.J. Beat Nicole," 27.

107 Tony Frost, "Nicole's Dance with Death," *Star*, 31 January 1995, 39.

108 Frost, "Nicole's Dance with Death," 36–37.

109 Quoted in Michael Rogin, *Ronald Reagan, the Movie, and Other Episodes in Political Demonology* (Berkeley: University of California Press, 1987), 207.

110 "O.J.'s Defense," *Globe*, 27 September 1994, 2–5.

111 Ken Harrell, "O.J. Will Take the Stand," *Globe*, 4 April 1995, 36–37.

112 Ken Harrell, "Chilling New Murder Puts O.J. in the Clear: Brentwood Ripper Killed Nicole & Ron," *Globe*, 23 May 1995, 5.

113 Ibid. Other examples along these lines include Dave LaFontaine, Yasmin Brennan, and Tony Frost, "Nicole's Mystery Link to Nightclub Murder," *Star*, 11 October 1994, 5, 8; Tony Frost, "Nicole & Goldman: The Secret Love Affair," *Star*, 23 May 1995, 36–37.

114 "O.J.'s Defense," 2–3.

115 Another such example is Marie Terry, "I Saw Nicole's Killers," *Globe*, 23 August 1994, 36–37.

116 Caroline Glines, "Is This the Face of the Real O.J. Killer?" *Globe*, 9 August 1994, 36.

117 Bob Temmey, "O.J.'s Roots: Startling Struggle from Slavery to Superstardom," *Globe*, 25 October 1994, 24–25, 32.

118 "Exposed! Sickening Racist Rampages of Simpson Trial's Notorious Rogue Cop: Raging Bully!" *Globe*, 3 October 1995, 24–25.

119 Ken Harrell, "Avenging Angel Denise Is Plotting to Kidnap OJ's Kids," *Globe*, 24 October 1995, 6–7.

120 Ken Harrell, "Neighbors Shun 'Butcher of Brentwood,'" *Globe*, 24 October 1995, 24–25.

121 Tabloid homophobia around the Simpson affair was implicit rather than explicit. For example, in some stories, reports that O.J.'s father was gay or that Nicole Brown Simpson and Faye Resnick had a sexual relationship were treated as "shocking" revelations. On the other hand, some stories about Nicole and Resnick treated their sexual relationship as loving and healthy, especially by contrast with the Simpsons' abusive marriage. See, for example, Paul Francis, "O.J.'s Dad Was Gay—and Died of AIDS," *Globe*, 12 July 1994, 4–5; "New Nicole Scandal Sends O.J. into Jailhouse Rage," *Globe*, 4 October 1994, 36–37, 44; Tony Frost, "Nicole Fell in Love with Best Girlfriend," *Star*, 27 September 1994, 39, 41; Tony Frost, "Nicole's Gay Affair Drove O.J. to Tears," *Star*, 18 July 1995, 20.

122 "O.J. Didn't Do It!" *Star*, 27 June 1995, 36; "How Nicole Seduced O.J.'s Best Pal—under His Nose," *Star*, 27 June 1995, 36–37.

123 "What You Didn't Hear on TV: Shocking Story behind 911 Tapes: Why O.J. Was in Rage," *Star*, 12 July 1994, 29; Jennifer Bialow, "Nicole's Sexy Spend, Spend Life of Fast Cars, Drugs & Young Men," *Star*, 12 July 1994, 36–37. Cf. "Money-Loving Nicole Kept O.J. on a String," *Globe*, 5 July 1994, 36.

124 Tony Frost, "Revealed! Truth about Nicole & O.J.'s Best Pal," *Star*, 20 June 1995, 5, 29; "Revealed! Cops' Secret File on Marcus Allen," *Star*, 8 August 1995, 5, 36–37. Also see, along similar lines, "The Day O.J. Caught Gal Pal Tawny in Bed with Another Guy," *Star*, 12 September 1995, 5. There, a former girlfriend of O.J.'s, Tawny Kitaen, says, among

other things, "I never saw anything that would stand out and make me say, 'Yes, it's possible, he [committed the murders].' " She adds that "his girlfriend Paula and his ex-wife Marguerite all say the same thing."

125 "O.J. Sobs in Jail As He Tapes Secret Message to the World," *Globe*, 24 January 1995, 36–37.

126 The tabloids are full of accounts of her sex life with O.J., as well as with Marcus Allen, who is also African American. This suggests a mapping of the age-old "virgin-whore" dualism onto a *racial* binary. On the "blackening" of Nicole through the strategy of appealing both to her boundary-violating sexual associations with black men and to the discourses of addiction, consider the following tabloid passage: " 'Nicole was addicted to sex,' confides a pal. 'She met O.J. when she was just 17 and he molded her sexually. Nic told me she and O.J. had sex five times a day. They both had huge sexual appetites.' " See "Nicole's Tragic Search for Love," *Globe*, 1 August 1995, 45. Another story about Nicole's "tragic life of addiction to sex and drugs" says that she "made no attempt to hide her addiction to sex." After her divorce from O.J., the story reports, a "distraught" Nicole penned the following lines in her diary: "It was hard for me to adjust to the fact that I wasn't having constant sex. But I never found another man who could turn me on the way that O.J. did—except for one." The story reveals that "that one" was Marcus Allen. See "Sex & Drugs Secrets of Nicole Simpson's Private Diary," *Globe*, 6 December 1994, 17.

127 Ken Harrell, "Nicole Stalked O.J.!" *Globe*, 30 August 1994, 7. This story quotes a friend who says that Nicole "was a coke freak with an attitude—and she used that attitude to torment a man who loved her very much."

128 "Nicole's Tragic Search for Love," 45; "Sex & Drugs Secrets of Nicole Simpson's Private Diary," 17.

129 While this tendency could be located in many of the tabloid stories, reports where it is particularly pronounced include Bob Michals, "O.J. Horror over New Autopsy Pics," *Globe*, 11 April 1995, 41; Bob Burns, "Silence of the Lambs," *Globe*, 20 June 1995, 36–37.

130 "The Last Run," *Star*, 5 July 1994, 26.

131 See, e.g., Frank Rich, "Addicted to O.J.," *New York Times*, 23 June 1994, A23.

132 Andy Patrizio, "Paging Service Beeps Users for Car Chases," *TechWeb: The Technology News Site*, 29 January 1999, http://www.techweb.com.

133 Valerie Cannon, quoted in Ken Harrell, "Dear O.J.," *Globe*, 13 September 1994, 3.

134 Jeffrey Toobin, "A Horrible Human Event," *New Yorker*, 23 October 1995, 46; italics mine.

135 John Fiske, *Media Matters*, rev. ed. (Minneapolis: University of Minnesota Press, 1996), 264. My point here is *in no way* meant to suggest that African Americans are incapable of understanding DNA science (an inference drawn by one critic of my argument when it was presented in another form). Rather, my point is that the very idea that science in general, including DNA science, produces "objective," "politically neutral," "value-free" knowledge is a product of the Eurocentric discourses that underlie the particular scientific formation that is currently the hegemonic one. This does not, of course, mean that all blacks reject all scientific ways of knowing, nor that no blacks have contributed to the development of the modern Western sciences. Conversely, I call a particular formation of skepticism toward scientism's naive and power-bearing objectivism "a black knowledge" not because I believe that it is the *only* black knowledge, or that it exhaustively describes *all* the black knowledges there are. Rather, there is a historically specific skepticism toward Eurocentric scientism's naive objectivism that is part of a distinctively black knowledge (among other black knowledges) *because it is a product of the material, cultural, social African American experience*, whose history has been shaped in part by the many nefarious uses of Eurocentric science against people of color. Hence there is *a* black knowledge (though it is not the only black knowledge) that deeply and with histori-

cal justification distrusts the sciences' claims to "objectivity," and this particular black knowledge has been made an object of disdain and ridicule within many quadrants of the white-dominated society that is the contemporary United States. On the continued persistence of scientific racism in mainstream criminology, see Thomas L. Dumm, "The New Enclosures: Racism in the Normalized Community," in *Reading Rodney King/Reading Urban Uprising*, ed. Robert Gooding-Williams (New York: Routledge, 1993), 178–95.

136   "So Who Did Kill Nicole?" *Star*, 17 October 1995, 5, 29.

137   Fiske, *Media Matters*, rev. ed., 271–72.

138   David Margolick, "Simpson Judge Sets Hearing on TV and Radio Coverage," *New York Times*, 4 October 1994, A19.

139   Sophfronia Scott Gregory, "Oprah! Oprah in the Court!" *Time*, 6 June 1994, 30–31.

140   Gil Garcetti, quoted in Gregory, "Oprah! Oprah in the Court!" 31.

141   Gregory, "Oprah! Oprah in the Court!" 31.

142   Ibid., 30.

143   Jeffrey Toobin, "The Marcia Clark Verdict," *New Yorker*, 9 September 1996, 66.

144   Ibid., 66–67.

145   Fiske, *Power Plays*.

146   Louise Mengelkoch, "When Checkbook Journalism Does God's Work," *Columbia Journalism Review* (November–December 1994): 35–38.

147   Stuart Hall, "Encoding, Decoding," in *The Cultural Studies Reader*, ed. Simon During (London: Routledge, 1993), 101.

148   Mengelkoch, "When Checkbook Journalism Does God's Work," 38.

149   Michael Eric Dyson, *Reflecting Black: African-American Cultural Criticism* (Minneapolis: University of Minnesota Press, 1993); Fiske, *Power Plays*, chap. 11; Fiske, *Media Matters*, rev. ed., 264–75. Dyson writes that "ghetto residents must often flip a coin to distinguish Los Angeles' police from its criminals" (218).

150   Rich, "Judge Ito's All-Star Vaudeville," 17; Jerry Spence, quoted in "Simpson Case Backlash Keeps Cameras Out of Other Courtrooms," *New York Times*, 17 September 1995, sec. 1, p. 35.

151   George Curry, quoted in Shipp, "O.J. and the Black Media," 41.

152   In terms of the hypervisibilization of black men as "poster children" for psychosexual pathologies, consider the following lines from a tabloid story about Simpson's request to the court for permission to have conjugal jailhouse visits during his trial: "Frustrated O.J. Simpson is going 'stir crazy' after a year in jail and has told his team of lawyers: 'I need sex!' . . . He told [defense attorney Robert] Shapiro 'If I don't have a woman soon, I'll go outta my mind.' [According to] a source close to the disgraced gridiron great, . . . 'he's crawling up the walls of his cell, he won't take "no" for an answer.' . . . At one stage, sex-starved Simpson told his attorney: 'Imagine how I feel in that courtroom every day. There are women parading in front of me . . .' Simpson was one of Hollywood's most voracious studs before his imprisonment last year." See "O.J. Begs Court: Give Me a Love Break," *Star*, 13 June 1995, 36–37, 39.

153   Mark Riley, quoted in Shipp, "O.J. and the Black Media," 41.

154   Harry Edwards, quoted in Shipp, "O.J. and the Black Media," 40.

155   Mary Ann Norbom, "OJ Killed 'Em!" *Globe*, 17 October 1995, 4–5, 8. Mike Davis gives an example of Gates's racism in the form of a statement made by the chief after fifteen African Americans were killed by a choke hold that the department taught its officers to use against suspects. As Davis notes, Gates here advances "the extraordinary theory that the deaths were the fault of the victims' racial anatomy, not excessive police force." Said Gates, "we may be finding that in some Blacks when [the carotid choke hold] is applied,

the veins or arteries do not open up as fast as they do on normal people." Quoted in Mike Davis, *City of Quartz: Excavating the Future in Los Angeles* (London: Verso, 1990), 272.

156 Pierre Bourdieu, *Distinction: A Social Critique of the Judgement of Taste*, trans. Richard Nice (Cambridge: Harvard University Press, 1984).

157 Baudrillard, *In the Shadow of the Silent Majorities*, 9–10, 35. I quote Baudrillard's use of the term "the masses" here not because I concur with the view that popular social formations can be properly understood in such homogenizing terms but rather because I think this term captures the notion of the people that is inscribed within the discourses of backlash and moral panic.

158 See, e.g., Rosemary J. Coombe, "Postmodernity and the Rumor: Late Capitalism and the Fetishism of the Commodity/Sign," in *Jean Baudrillard: The Disappearance of Art and Politics*, ed. William Stearns and William Chaloupkas (London: Macmillan, 1992), 98–108; Liz Ferrier, "Postmodern Tactics: The Uses of Space in Shoppingtowns," manuscript on file with the author.

159 Baudrillard, *In the Shadow of the Silent Majorities*, 48–58.

3   Bodies of Popular Knowledge: The High, the Low, and A Current Affair

1 Terry Ann Knopf, "Sleazy Does It," *Boston Magazine*, September 1990, 70–71.

2 Maury Povich with Ken Gross, *Current Affairs: A Life on the Edge* (New York: Berkeley Books, 1991), 109.

3 Monica Collins has dubbed *A Current Affair* "the elder/punk statesman of the [tabloid] genre." See Monica Collins, "Extra! Extra! Tabloid Clones Invade TV," *TV Guide*, 18 November 1989, 14. During 1989 it was estimated that each weeknight, the program reached 7.2 million people in 146 U.S. television markets. See Kristin McMurran, "Two Hearts Beating in Prime Time," *People Weekly*, 10 April 1989, 119.

4 Povich with Gross, *Current Affairs*, 190.

5 David Kamp, "The Tabloid Decade," *Vanity Fair*, February 1999, 75.

6 Ron Powers, *The Beast, the Eunuch, and the Glass-Eyed Child: Television in the '80s* (San Diego: Harcourt Brace Jovanovich, 1990), 185.

7 Mikhail Bakhtin, *Rabelais and His World*, trans. Hélène Iswolsky (Bloomington: Indiana University Press, 1984).

8 Povich with Gross, *Current Affairs*, 124. Bakhtin writes that "not only parody in its narrow sense but all the other forms of grotesque realism degrade, bring down to earth, turn their subject into flesh. . . . Degradation here means coming down to earth, the contact with earth as an element that swallows up and gives birth at the same time." Bakhtin, *Rabelais and His World*, 20–21. Povich's equation of tabloid journalism with the juxtaposition of "blood and gore," "happy mischief," and "life" suggests an earthy principle that is closely related to the attitude embodied in Bakhtinian grotesque realism. As Kathleen Rowe observes, "dismemberment, horror, death, and taboo are essential elements of the grotesque. They are reminders of the totality of life, possessing a demonic power to unsettle all that would conceal the democratic materiality of the body." See *The Unruly Woman: Gender and the Genres of Laughter* (Austin: University of Texas Press, 1995), 33.

9 On the culturally low status of tabloid journalism, see, e.g., S. Elizabeth Bird, *For Enquiring Minds: A Cultural Study of Supermarket Tabloids* (Knoxville: University of Tennessee Press, 1992).

10 Dick Hebdige, *Hiding in the Light: On Images and Things* (London: Routledge, 1988), 243.

11 Aben Kandel, "A Tabloid a Day," *Forum* 77, no. 3 (March 1927): 379–80. The discursive figure of the audience that is more vulnerable than the critic who invokes it is an impor-

tant agent in the production of cultural distinction and therefore in the exertion of social control.

12 Howard Rosenberg, "New Channel 2 News Director Sets Off a Storm," *Los Angeles Times*, 4 March 1992, F1.

13 Harry F. Waters et al., "Trash TV," *Newsweek*, 14 November 1988, 73–74.

14 Jane M. Shattuc, *The Talking Cure: TV Talk Shows and Women* (New York: Routledge, 1997), 182.

15 Carl Bernstein, "The Idiot Culture," *New Republic*, 8 June 1992, 24.

16 Ibid., 24–25.

17 It is worth noting that anxieties around viral phenomena and therefore contagion became particularly acute during the 1980s, in the wake of the HIV epidemic and the recognition of our growing dependence on virally vulnerable computer networks in an increasingly cybernetic society.

18 "This Is What You Thought: 80% Think TV Has Become Too Trashy," *Glamour*, May 1989, 179.

19 Pierre Bourdieu, *Distinction: A Social Critique of the Judgement of Taste*, trans. Richard Nice (Cambridge: Harvard University Press, 1984), 99.

20 Ian Mitroff and Warren Bennis, *The Unreality Industry: The Deliberate Manufacturing of Falsehood and What It Is Doing to Our Lives* (Secaucus, N.J.: Birch Lane Press, 1989).

21 Mitroff and Bennis, *The Unreality Industry*, quoted in Bill Thomas, "Finding Truth in the Age of 'Infotainment,'" *Editorial Research Reports* 1, no. 3 (19 January 1990): 45.

22 Mike Drew, "Sleaze! Spats! Payoffs!" *Milwaukee Journal*, 23 May 1993, T3.

23 Alvin Boskoff, quoted in Charles Walston, "Tabloid TV Has Changed the Rules," *Atlanta Constitution*, 17 November 1991, G1, G5.

24 Daniel Schorr, "The Show Business of TV News," *San Francisco Chronicle*, 10 June 1990, This World section, 20.

25 Norman J. Ornstein and Michael J. Robinson, "Do You Give Viewers Good Journalism or the Sensationalism They Prefer?" *TV Guide*, 17 December 1988, 4–5. Ornstein and Robinson are scholars discussing their research in the popular press.

26 Peter M. Herford, "In News, Public Choice Is a Disaster," *New York Times*, 4 August 1990, 15.

27 John Hartley, "Invisible Fictions: Television Audiences, Paedocracy, Pleasure," in *Television Studies: Textual Analysis*, ed. Gary Burns and Robert J. Thompson (New York: Praeger, 1989).

28 Richard Campbell, "Word vs. Image: Elitism, Popularity, and TV News," *Television Quarterly* 26, no. 1 (1991): 79, 81.

29 John Fiske, *Understanding Popular Culture* (Boston: Unwin Hyman, 1989), 114.

30 Peter Stallybrass and Allon White, *The Politics and Poetics of Transgression* (Ithaca, N.Y.: Cornell University Press, 1986).

31 Quoted without attribution in Marc Fisher, "The King of Sleaze," *Gentlemen's Quarterly*, April 1990, 196.

32 Richard Wolkomir, "With Tabloids, 'Zip! You're in Another World!'" *Smithsonian*, October 1987, 240.

33 Stallybrass and White, *The Politics and Poetics of Transgression*, 5.

34 Howard Kurtz, "Though Public Says It's Fed Up, It Maintains an Appetite for the Story," *Washington Post*, 12 February 1998, A1.

35 Waters et al., "Trash TV," 74.

36 Bourdieu, *Distinction*, 6–7.

37 John Waters, "Why I Love the *National Enquirer*," *Rolling Stone*, 10 October 1985, 44.

38 Overholser made these comments in 1989 during a televised round table discussion sponsored by the American Society of Newspaper Editors and entitled "Who's a Journalist? Talk Show Sensationalism."

39 See, e.g., Natalie Zemon Davis, *Society and Culture in Early Modern France* (Stanford, Calif.: Stanford University Press, 1965); Mary Russo, "Female Grotesques: Carnival and Theory," in *Feminist Studies, Critical Studies*, ed. Teresa de Lauretis (Bloomington: Indiana University Press, 1986), 213–29.

40 Stallybrass and White, *The Politics and Poetics of Transgression*, 23.

41 Michel de Certeau, *The Practice of Everyday Life*, trans. Stephen Rendall (Berkeley: University of California Press), 141, 147–48.

42 Margaret Morse, "The Television News Personality and Credibility: Reflections on the News in Transition," in *Studies in Entertainment: Critical Approaches to Mass Culture*, ed. Tania Modleski (Bloomington: Indiana University Press, 1986), 55–79.

43 Morse notes elsewhere, moreover, that the discursive structure of television news—its ongoing and fragmented flow of images—requires "the constant discursivity of a story-teller" to hold it together. See Morse, "Talk, Talk, Talk," *Screen* 26, no. 2 (March–April 1985): 5.

44 Robert Stam, "Television News and Its Spectator," in *Regarding Television: Critical Approaches—an Anthology*, ed. E. Ann Kaplan (Frederick, Md.: University Publications of America, 1983), 28–29.

45 Morse, "The Television News Personality and Credibility," 57.

46 Quoted in Maura Sheehy, "Crocodile Povich and the Aussie-fication of American Television," *Manhattan, Inc.*, April 1989, 78.

47 Pierre Bourdieu, "The Aristocracy of Culture," *Media, Culture, and Society*, no. 2 (1980): esp. 239–44.

48 Bernstein, "The Idiot Culture," 22.

49 Victor Hugo, *Les Miserables*, trans. N. Denny, vol. 2 (Harmondsworth: Penguin, 1980), 369, quoted in Stallybrass and White, *The Politics and Poetics of Transgression*, 141.

50 Stallybrass and White, *The Politics and Poetics of Transgression*, 141. Hugo vividly describes the sewer's elision of the difference between high and low: "A livid foetus is wrapped in the spangles, which last Shrove Tuesday danced at the Opera, a wig which passed judgement on men wallows near the decay which was the skirt of Margoton" (Hugo, *Les Miserables*, vol. 2, 369, quoted in Stallybrass and White, *The Politics and Poetics of Transgression*, 141).

51 Bernstein, "The Idiot Culture," 22.

52 Ibid.

53 Bird, *For Enquiring Minds*, esp. chap. 5; Sue Brower, "Inside Stories: Gossip and Television Audiences," in *Communication and Culture: Language, Performance, Technology, and Media*, ed. Sari Thomas and William A. Evans (Norwood, N.J.: Ablex Publishing, 1990), 225–35.

54 Patricia Mellencamp, *High Anxiety: Catastrophe, Scandal, Age, and Comedy* (Bloomington: Indiana University Press, 1992), 177, 179.

55 For a feminist analysis of the subversive potential of gossip, see Patricia Meyer Spacks, *Gossip* (New York: Alfred A. Knopf, 1985). Note, however, that despite her positive re-valuation of gossip, Spacks is no fan of the tabloid media.

56 See Rosemary J. Coombe, "Postmodernity and the Rumor: Late Capitalism and the Fetishism of the Commodity/Sign," in *Jean Baudrillard: The Disappearance of Art and Politics*, ed. William Stearns and William Chaloupkas (London: Macmillan, 1992), 98–108, for a fascinating argument along these lines.

57 Sheehy, "Crocodile Povich and the Aussie-fication of American Television," 75.

58 Philip Weiss, "Bad Rap for TV Tabs," *Columbia Journalism Review* 28, no. 1 (May–June 1989): 39.

59 Povich with Gross, *Current Affairs*, 49.

60 Bakhtin, *Rabelais and His World*.

61 John Fiske, *Television Culture* (London: Methuen, 1987), 241.

62 Bakhtin, *Rabelais and His World*, 11.

63 Ibid., 33–34.

64 Hugo, *Les Miserables*, vol. 2, 369, quoted in Stallybrass and White, *The Politics and Poetics of Transgression*, 140–41.

65 Povich with Gross, *Current Affairs*, 61–62.

66 Weiss, "Bad Rap for TV Tabs," 42. Weiss's description of Povich recalls the signficance of sexuality as a primary site for normalization.

67 Bakhtin, *Rabelais and His World*, 11–12.

68 Powers, *The Beast, the Eunuch, and the Glass-Eyed Child*, 187.

69 The feminization of mass culture is, as Andreas Huyssen has shown, one of the primary strategies for its delegitimation in patriarchal society. See Andreas Huyssen, "Mass Culture as Woman: Modernism's Other," in Modleski, *Studies in Entertainment*, 188–207.

70 Powers, *The Beast, the Eunuch, and the Glass-Eyed Child*, 189–90.

71 Sheehy, "Crocodile Povich and the Aussie-fication of American Television," 76.

72 Cf. Morse, "The Television News Personality and Credibility," 58–60, 78. There Morse describes the network news anchor as an "overarching presence" and a "supersubject" who, like a "paraclete," speaks as a messenger of God. The figure of the network anchor bears no slight resemblance to Bakhtin's classical body: positioned somewhere beyond the world while watching over it, the anchor's body represents the convergence of authority and judgment. The anchor is charged with a solemn social obligation: the dispensation, from a god's-eye view, of the truths needed for the proper functioning of a democracy. The attitude of the anchor's body projects a proper distance from the world whose truths he (or she) narrates. Direct contact with the "real world" and its people is mediated by field reporters. The body of the anchor marks a disembodied nexus of taste, seriousness, and normality.

73 Povich with Gross, *Current Affairs*, 100–101.

74 The popular British tabloid the *Sun* compares interestingly with *A Current Affair* along these lines. Mark Pursehouse notes that "in its mocking headline puns," the *Sun* "seems keen to laugh at its own sense of humour," and that "the paper takes an ironic stance in relation to traditional expectations of the serious nature of headlines." See Mark Pursehouse, "Looking at *The Sun*: Into the Nineties with a Tabloid and Its Readers," *Cultural Studies from Birmingham* 1 (1991): 96.

75 Povich with Gross, *Current Affairs*, 172–73.

76 My description of the prank played by Elliott on Trump, in this and the previous paragraph, is based on Povich with Gross, *Current Affairs*, 175–76, from which the quotes here are drawn and which I have paraphrased in places.

77 Povich with Gross, *Current Affairs*, 177.

78 Compare James Curran and Colin Sparks on British tabloids' coverage of the royal family: "Tabloid speculation about whether the Prince of Wales has one screw loose and gets on badly with his father; whether his wife is anorexic, neglects her children and is bored by her husband; whether Prince Edward is a 'wimp'; and whether Princess Anne is on speaking terms with the country's future queen strips away the traditional mystique of the monarchy and undermines the status of royal family as revered figures of authority." See

James Curran and Colin Sparks, "Press and Popular Culture," *Media, Culture, and Society* 13 (1991): 233.

79 Mikhail Bakhtin, *Problems of Dostoevsky's Poetics*, ed. and trans. Caryl Emerson (Minneapolis: University of Minnesota Press, 1984), 123–24. Bakhtin describes the "mock crowning and subsequent decrowning of the carnival king" as "the primary carnivalistic act."

80 Along with Kandel, "A Tabloid a Day," see Oswald Garrison Villard, "Tabloid Offenses," *Forum* 77, no. 4 (April 1927): 485–91.

81 For recent examples of this tendency in the criticism of journalism, see Serge Halimi, "Myopic and Cheapskate Journalism," trans. Ed Emery, *Le Monde Diplomatique*, November 1998, 14–15; William Pfaff, "Entertainment Coup, or America's Politics of Illusion," *International Herald Tribune*, 18 December 1997.

82 In his *Tabloid Television: Popular Journalism and the "Other News"* (London: Routledge, 1998), John Langer characterizes the journalistic traditionalists' reaction against the "other news" as "the lament." Langer's "other news" includes "items about fires, floods, accidents, civic rituals, twists of fate, heroic acts of humble people, victims . . . beauty contests, celebrities, peculiar occupations and hobbies," in short, all "those 'trivialities' which take audiences away from 'intellectual activation' " (29–30, 32).

83 Cf. Curran and Sparks, "Press and Popular Culture." Curran and Sparks note that the development of British "entertainment"-oriented tabloids, within a highly competitive commercial context, has generated a set of interesting ideological contradictions because it has led to the production of stories about the royal family that subvert the tabloids' official pro-royalist stance and is thus "beginning to weaken a central institution of authority in Britain," the monarchy (233). It would seem that the shrill outcry about the role of the paparazzi in the accident that caused the death of Princess Diana six years after the appearance of Curran and Sparks's article is symptomatic of a partially displaced and latent recognition of the tabloids' contradictory subversion of the monarchy. That is, although Diana was of course no longer a member of the royal family, and indeed contributed to the subversion of their image through her savvy use of the very tabloid media said to have "exploited" her, nevertheless the public reaction against the paparazzi was motivated by an awareness of the tabloids' cheeky and dogged fascination with the lives and relationships of the royals.

84 As Fiske notes, the people's current reorientation of their informational tastes away from "serious" treatments of the official political system and "towards those domains where popular interests may be best promoted . . . may be a worrying shift, but at least it is a shift of politics, not its extinction." See Fiske, "Popularity and the Politics of Information," in *Journalism and Popular Culture*, ed. Peter Dahlgren and Colin Sparks (London: Sage Publications, 1992), 47.

85 Hebdige, *Hiding in the Light*, 194.

86 Frank P. Tomasulo, " 'I'll See It When I Believe It': Rodney King and the Prison-House of Video," in *The Persistence of History: Cinema, Television, and the Modern Event*, ed. Vivian Sobchack (New York: Routledge, 1996), 70. This follows Fredric Jameson's argument that postmodern cultural production "can no longer gaze directly on some putative real world, at some reconstruction of a past history which was once itself a present; rather, as in Plato's cave, it must trace our mental images of that past upon its confining walls. If there is any realism left here, therefore, it is a 'realism' which is meant to derive from the shock of grasping that confinement, and of slowly becoming aware of a new and original historical situation in which we are condemned to seek History by way of our own pop images and simulacra of that history, which itself remains forever out of reach." See

"Postmodernism, or The Cultural Logic of Late Capitalism," *New Left Review* 146 (July–August 1984): 71.

87   Geraldo Rivera with Daniel Paisner, *Exposing Myself* (New York: Bantam, 1991), 216. Aware of his own status as a living emblem of media tabloidization, Rivera notes that he has "passed into the lexicon, a caricature for columnists, cartoonists, and commentators seeking a shorthand way of describing all that ails the popular culture. Want to get an easy laugh or start a cocktail party argument? Just mention *Geraldo*" (463).

88   See Theodore L. Glasser and James S. Ettema, "Investigative Journalism and the Moral Order," *Critical Studies in Mass Communication* 6, no. 1 (March 1989): 1–20; James S. Ettema and Theodore L. Glasser, "Narrative Form and Moral Force: The Realization of Innocence and Guilt through Investigative Journalism," *Journal of Communication* 38, no. 3 (summer 1988): 8–26.

89   Glasser and Ettema, "Investigative Journalism and the Moral Order." The phrase "culture of objectivity" appears on p. 14.

90   Ibid., 3.

91   Jack Katz, "What Makes Crime 'News'?" *Media, Culture, and Society* 9 (1987): 66.

92   Peter Brooks, *The Melodramatic Imagination: Balzac, Henry James, Melodrama, and the Mode of Excess* (New Haven: Yale University Press, 1976). It should be noted, however, that despite its pervasiveness in twentieth-century popular culture, and its commonplace, pejorative associations with "schlock," melodrama also has important historical links with the bourgeoisie and takes bourgeois cultural forms at particular historical moments; see Geoffrey Nowell-Smith, "Minnelli and Melodrama," in *Home Is Where the Heart Is: Studies in Melodrama and the Woman's Film*, ed. Christine Gledhill (London: BFI Publishing, 1987), 70–74; Gledhill, "The Melodramatic Field: An Investigation," in *Home Is Where the Heart Is*, 5–39.

93   Bourdieu notes that "conspicuous formality, both in art and in life," implies "a sort of censorship of the expressive content which explodes in the expressiveness of popular language" and enacts "a distancing" that amounts to a kind of "refusal to communicate concealed at the heart of the communication itself" (*Distinction*, 34).

94   Ibid.

95   Such criticisms are reminiscent of Bourdieu's discussion of "pure" aesthetic judgment in the Kantian tradition. The pure aesthete obstinately refuses cultural forms that give him or her "the sense of being treated like any Tom, Dick or Harry who can be seduced by tawdry charms" (*Distinction*, 486).

96   Brooks, *The Melodramatic Imagination*, 12.

97   Christine Gledhill notes that "the typical role of the melodrama heroine/victim" is to function as the "symbol of moral value"; her "perseverance to the end, against danger and public opinion, leads to public recognition of the truth." See "Pleasurable Negotiations," in *Female Spectators: Looking at Film and Television*, ed. E. Deidre Pribram (London: Verso, 1988), 77.

98   Rita Kempley, "Sex, Lies, and Videotape," *Washingtonpost.com*, 11 August 1989. Washingtonpost.com is the on-line version of the *Washington Post* and is available at http://www.washingtonpost.com.

99   Weiss, "Bad Rap for TV Tabs," 40. Mellencamp also notes that the tabloids have undertaken "a revision of domesticity (and romance). Rather than being a soothing, calm respite from the turmoil and travail of the public sphere, the domestic, or the private, has become a fount of trouble, conflict, anguish, and crime" (*High Anxiety: Catastrophe, Scandal, Age, and Comedy*, 196).

100 Robin Wood, "Return of the Repressed," *Film Comment* 14, no. 4 (July–August 1978): 25–32. Also see Tania Modleski, "The Terror of Pleasure: The Contemporary Horror Film and Postmodern Theory," in Modleski, *Studies in Entertainment*, 155–66.

101 Lynne Spigel uses this phrase on p. 219 of her discussion of how sixties sitcoms like *I Dream of Jeanie* and *Bewitched* "provided a cultural space in which anxieties about everyday life could be addressed, albeit through a series of displacements and distortions" (214). See Lynn Spigel, "From Domestic Space to Outer Space: The 1960s Fantastic Family Sit-Com," in *Close Encounters: Film, Feminism, and Science Fiction*, ed. Constance Penley, Elisabeth Lyon, Lynn Spigel, and Janet Bergstrom (Minneapolis: University of Minnesota Press, 1991), 205–33.

102 Stallybrass and White, *The Politics and Poetics of Transgression*, 19.

103 Brooks, *The Melodramatic Imagination*.

104 Lynne Joyrich, "All That Television Allows: TV Melodrama, Postmodernism, and Consumer Culture," *Camera Obscura* 16 (January 1988): 138.

105 Quoted in Mike Drew, "TV Tabloids are Confusing Audiences: Some Viewers Can't Tell the Difference between Them and Real News Shows," *Dallas Morning News*, 29 May 1993, 1W. O'Boyle worked as a substitute for Povich before his departure from *A Current Affair*, after which she became the program's primary anchor.

106 This phrase is enclosed in quotation marks to question the idea of a "natural" (anatomical) "sex" that putatively precedes the cultural assignment of gender identity. See Judith Butler, *Gender Trouble: Feminism and the Subversion of Identity* (New York: Routledge, 1990).

107 Graham Knight, "Reality Effects: Tabloid Television News," *Queen's Quarterly* 96, no. 1 (spring 1988): 98. Also see Richard V. Ericson et al., *Visualizing Deviance: A Study of News Organization* (Toronto: University of Toronto Press, 1987).

108 "Acts, gestures, and desire produce the effect of an internal core or substance, but produce this *on the surface* of the body. . . . Such acts, gestures, enactments, generally construed, are *performative* in the sense that the essence or identity that they otherwise purport to express are *fabrications* manufactured and sustained through corporeal signs and other discursive means. That the gendered body is performative suggests that it has no ontological status apart from the various acts which constitute its reality. This also suggests that if that reality is fabricated as an interior essence, that very interiority is an effect and function of a decidedly public and social discourse" (Butler, *Gender Trouble*, 136).

109 This point parallels Jacques Derrida's deconstruction of what he calls Western philosophy's "metaphysics of presence." The metaphysics of presence is based on the idea that "presence" and "absence" exist in a mutually exclusive relation to each other ("something cannot be simultaneously present and absent," says the Western metaphysician), and that something that is present can be known *in itself*. Derrida questions these assumptions. He argues that because the meaning of something construed as "present" is necessarily grounded in meanings assigned to the absent "thing," against which the identity of the present "thing" is defined, therefore the trace of that which is absent is always already *a constitutive part* of that which is thought simply present "in itself." Thus although that which is present is thought to be self-substantiating (e.g., the phallus), it is in fact dependent on that absent other, by whose exclusion it constitutes its own identity as a present "thing." For Derrida, the metaphysics of presence constitutes the master binary that subsumes all the other binaries with which Western thought is replete: male/female, reason/madness, truth/falsity, inside/outside, speech/writing, identity/difference, and so on, ad infinitum. While Western thought claims that these binaries are merely neutral and descriptive, Derrida argues persuasively that one of each binary's terms is invariably, in thought and practice, privileged over the other (usually it is

the term associated with *presence; e.g.*, masculinity is both *privileged* and based on the idea of the *presence* of the phallus). See Derrida, *Of Grammatology*, trans. Gayatri Chakravorty Spivak (Baltimore, Md.: Johns Hopkins University Press, 1976).

110 Butler, *Gender Trouble*, 136–37; Butler's italics.

111 The slash is intended to equate "gender" with "performance," or to at least suggest that the two things are so closely related as to be inseparable.

112 Drag is a "double inversion that says, 'appearance is an illusion.' Drag says 'my "outside" appearance [my clothing, etc.] is feminine, but my essence "inside" is masculine.' At the same time it symbolizes the opposite inversion; 'my appearance "outside" [my physique] is masculine but my essence "inside" is feminine.' " See Esther Newton, *Mother Camp: Female Impersonators in America* (Chicago: University of Chicago Press, 1972), 103, quoted in Butler, *Gender Trouble*, 137. Butler adds that these "claims to truth" made implicitly by the drag performer "contradict one another and so displace the entire enactment of gender significations from the discourse of truth and falsity." One might object that a typical response to the story of Billy Tipton would agree that Tipton's gender was purely performative but maintain that this is aberrant, that "normal" subjects *do* possess a stable, coherent, and interior gender identity. Nevertheless, by emphasizing the credibility of Tipton's performance, the story implicitly asserts the *possibility* that *all* enactments of gender are similarly performative.

113 Michel Foucault, *The Foucault Reader*, ed. Paul Rabinow, trans. Josué V. Harari et al. (New York: Pantheon Books, 1984), 76–100.

114 Ibid., 88. On Foucault's use of the term "disparity," see p. 98 n. 14.

115 Ibid., 79, 88, 94.

116 That U.S. voters have continually forgiven Bill Clinton his apparent extramarital activities may indicate a partial and ongoing realignment of normality around nonmonogamous marriage. It suggests, at least, a widespread acceptance of the inevitability of marital infidelity that combines interestingly with popular skepticism toward the power-bloc. As a thirty-two-year-old "homemaker" observed at the height of the Ken Starr scandal, "If a pure moral character and lack of extramarital affairs were the criteria for holding office, there wouldn't be anyone in Washington" (Debbie Schapiro, quoted in Paula Span and Libby Ingrid Copeland, "Women Voice Sympathy, and Disgust," *Washington Post*, 14 September 1998, A1).

117 Allon White, "The Dismal Sacred Word: Academic Language and the Social Reproduction of Seriousness," *Journal of Literature Teaching Politics* 2 (1983): 9.

4 Fantastic Populism: A Walk on the Wild Side of Tabloid Culture

1 Alan Sheridan, *Michel Foucault: The Will to Truth* (London: Tavistock Publications, 1980), 222.

2 Wayne A. Saroyan, "Keeping Tabs: Aliens with Bad Ties and Bad Attitudes, and Other Bits of Supermarket Lore," *Chicago Tribune*, 7 July 1991, 3.

3 Ibid.

4 See S. Elizabeth Bird, *For Enquiring Minds: A Cultural Study of Supermarket Tabloids* (Knoxville: University of Tennessee Press, 1992).

5 See also S. Elizabeth Bird, "Storytelling on the Far Side: Journalism and the Weekly Tabloid," *Critical Studies in Mass Communication* 7, no. 4 (December 1990): 377–89.

6 There are six major U.S. supermarket tabloids: the *National Enquirer*, the *Star*, the *Weekly World News*, the *Globe*, the *National Examiner*, and the *Sun*. The first three are published by

MacFadden Holdings Inc., the last three by Globe Communications. Of these six, the *Weekly World News* and the *Sun* are clearly the most fantastic. The weekly circulation of the *News* has been estimated at 1,021,708 (*The Standard Periodical Directory*, 15th ed. [New York: Oxbridge Communications, 1992], 1058). Estimates place the *Sun*'s weekly circulation at 500,000 (Bird, *For Enquiring Minds*, 37). These figures represent direct sales only, however. They do not reflect the total weekly readership for the *News* and the *Sun*, which, according to Bird, increases considerably after individual issues have been traded or shared among several family members and friends, as typically they are.

7   Pierre Bourdieu, *Distinction: A Social Critique of the Judgement of Taste*, trans. Richard Nice (Cambridge: Harvard University Press, 1984).

8   In a commentary on Bourdieu, Fiske concisely explicates the metaphor of cultural capital. For those who have it, cultural capital produces a "social 'return' in terms of better job prospects, of enhanced social prestige and thus of a higher socio-economic position. Cultural capital thus works hand in hand with economic capital to produce social privilege and distinction." See John Fiske, "The Cultural Economy of Fandom," in *The Adoring Audience: Fan Culture and Popular Media*, ed. Lisa A. Lewis (London: Routledge, 1992), 31.

9   Fiske, "The Cultural Economy of Fandom."

10 In his fascinating analysis of the complicated relationship between the economic interests of the cultural industries and the cultural interests of fans, Fiske notes that popular tastes and competencies, unlike official ones, receive little if any social legitimation or institutional support ("The Cultural Economy of Fandom," 31). No journalism college teaches fantastic tabloid newswriting. Public schools exclude tabloid stories, whether fantastic or not, from the category of current events. In general, popular tastes and competencies are supported only by fans themselves, and by the commercial industries that profit from them. Of course, the institutions of official culture thoroughly demonize the "crass commercialism" of these industries. The inferiority of crass commercial culture leads to the derogation of its inferior consumers (to whom the cultural industries "pander").

11 Fiske, "The Cultural Economy of Fandom," 33.

12 Mikhail Bakhtin, *Rabelais and His World*, trans. Hélène Iswolsky (Bloomington: Indiana University Press, 1984), 39.

13 Mikhail Bakhtin, *Problems of Dostoevsky's Poetics*, ed. and trans. Caryl Emerson (Minneapolis: University of Minnesota Press, 1984), 113.

14 See especially Michel Foucault, *The History of Sexuality, Volume 1: An Introduction*, trans. Robert Hurley (New York: Pantheon Books, 1978); *Discipline and Punish: The Birth of the Prison*, trans. Alan Sheridan (New York: Vintage Books, 1979); *Power/Knowledge: Selected Interviews and Other Writings, 1972–1977*, ed. Colin Gordon, trans. Colin Gordon, Leo Marshall, John Mepham, and Kate Soper (New York: Pantheon Books, 1980); *The Foucault Reader*, ed. Paul Rabinow, trans. Josué V. Harari et al. (New York: Pantheon Books, 1984).

15 Bakhtin, *Problems of Dostoevsky's Poetics*, 114.

16 Philip Holland, "Robert Burton's *Anatomy of Melancholy* and Menippean Satire, Humanist and English" (Ph.D. diss., University of London, 1979), 36–37, quoted in editor's footnote, Bakhtin, *Problems of Dostoevsky's Poetics*, 107.

17 Bakhtin, *Problems of Dostoevsky's Poetics*, 107.

18 Ibid., 115–16.

19 "Guardian Angel Michael Landon Appears to 8 People!" *Weekly World News*, 20 August 1991, 2–4. In recent years, U.S. media have devoted increasing coverage to their "discovery" of widespread popular belief in angels.

20 Bakhtin, *Problems of Dostoevsky's Poetics*, 116–17.

21 In the latter category, see, for instance, T. Carlton, "Battered and Bruised Gardener Claims, 'A Space Alien Attacked Me—& Tried to Mate with My Weed Eater!' " *Weekly World News*, 24 July 1990, 1.

22 David Burton, "Top Psychic Splits Herself into 2 People . . . & Says You Can Do It Too!" *Weekly World News*, 9 July 1991, 46–47.

23 L. Tarragon, "Sweet Old Lady, 74, Shows Boxers How to Fight," *Sun*, 15 May 1990, 4; Dr. Bruno Grosse, "Blind Old Man Has X-Ray Vision," *Sun*, 17 April 1990, 5.

24 John Fiske, *Understanding Popular Culture* (Boston: Unwin Hyman, 1989), 114.

25 "Sex-Change Dad Is Now Son's 2nd Mom," *Sun*, 1 May 1990, 11.

26 Bakhtin, *Problems of Dostoevsky's Poetics*, 117.

27 See, for example, "Woman Gives Birth at Bingo Game—and Keeps On Playing," *Sun*, 1 May 1990, 1; T. Keene, "Woman Wills $500g . . . to a Houseplant," *Weekly World News*, 4 September 1990, 3; "Wife Drives Dead Hubby All over the Country . . . Looking for a Graveyard to Bury Him In!" *Weekly World News*, 22 January 1991, 27.

28 "George Washington Grew Pot," *Weekly World News*, 9 July 1991, 35; K. O'Hara, "3 U.S. Presidents Were Gay!" *Sun*, 1 May 1990, 35.

29 Cf. John Fiske, *Reading the Popular* (Boston: Unwin Hyman, 1989), chap. 7.

30 S. Miller, "Scientists Dig 9-Mile-Deep Hole and Claim, 'We Drilled through the Gates of Hell,' " *Weekly World News*, 24 April 1990, 45.

31 As Andrew Ross notes, "in the popular mind, the allegiances of many of the sciences to elite interests—military, corporate, and state—and to the cause of superindustrialism have underscored the perception that they are far from democratic in practice." See introduction to *Science Wars*, ed. Andrew Ross (Durham, N.C.: Duke University Press, 1996), 2.

32 M. Kramer, "Is Ric Flair Running the White House? Pro Wrestler Talked Bush into Sending Troops to Saudi Arabia!" *Weekly World News*, 5 February 1991, 3; "73-Year-Old JFK Photographed in White House Window!" *Weekly World News*, 29 January 1991, 4–5; N. Mann, "Space Alien Meets with President Bush!" *Weekly World News*, 14 May 1991, 4–5.
     The saga of the space alien mentioned in the last reference dates back at least as far as October 30, 1990. The headline of the *Weekly World News* for that date reads, "Alien Captured by U.S. Agents." The accompanying story reports on the secret detention of the creature by the CIA ("Alien Captured by U.S. Agents!" *Weekly World News*, 30 October 1990, 1). In its November 20, 1990, edition, the *Weekly World News* reports that the alien had escaped from a "CIA safe house in Washington" after incapacitating "11 guards and agents" ("Captured Alien Escapes!" *Weekly World News*, 20 November 1990, 24). In May 1991, the *News* reported that the alien had participated in an important Camp David meeting with George Bush. The alien promised to "provide the education, technology and strategic know-how to achieve lasting peace on Earth by 1997." The story also notes that the alien planned to meet with Mikhail Gorbachev in the Kremlin during June 1991 (Mann, "Space Alien Meets with President Bush!" 4). In July 1992 the *News* wrote that the alien had met with Ross Perot, probably to discuss "trade and cooperation initiatives between the alien's home planet and the United States." According to *News* source Nathaniel Dean, a UFO researcher, the meeting between the alien and Perot indicates that "Perot's candidacy is much more serious and viable than many would like to think" (quoted in N. Mann, "Space Alien Meets with Ross Perot!" *Weekly World News*, 14 July 1992, 4). Finally, in August 1992 the *News* wrote that the alien was endorsing Bill Clinton and that according to "sources close to Perot," the alien's endorsement of Clinton had "figured prominently in the billionaire's decision to drop out of the [presidential] race." The story also disclosed that Clinton and the alien had met and discussed "the environment,

health care, world peace and social issues, but the emphasis was on the economic situa-tion." According to Nathaniel Dean (who is quoted in the story), "the alien is from a planet that has grown from tough economic beginnings to become the most successful planet in the universe." Dean said the alien gave Clinton information on how his planet "turned the economy around and created more jobs in a relatively short period of time" (J. Alexander, "Space Alien Endorses Bill Clinton," *Weekly World News*, 11 August 1992, 24–25). In each *News* story, the alien's various meetings with Bush, Perot, and Clinton are photographically documented.

33 Dialogue from the first episode of the Fox Network's *The X-Files*, quoted in Robert Wester-felhaus and Teresa A. Combs, "Criminal Investigations and Spiritual Quests: *The X-Files* as an Example of Hegemonic Concordance in a Mass-Mediated Society," *Journal of Com-munication Inquiry* 22, no. 2 (April 1998): 208.

34 Robert Stam, *Subversive Pleasures: Bakhtin, Cultural Criticism, and Film* (Baltimore, Md.: Johns Hopkins University Press, 1989), 221, 227.

35 Dr. Bruno Grosse, "Lightning Turns Man into Woman: Electric Shock Destroyed Her Genes," *Sun*, 12 September 1989, 29.

36 Stam, *Subversive Pleasures*, 234.

37 Ibid., 95.

38 Cf. Michel de Certeau, *The Practice of Everyday Life*, trans. Stephen Rendall (Berkeley: Uni-versity of California Press), 15–28. De Certeau writes, for example, about Brazilian peas-ants' utopian tales of Frei Damiao, a legendary, charismatic popular religious hero who visited "celestial punishments" upon his enemies. The miraculous stories of Frei Damiao expressed social protest and loudly proclaimed "the unacceptability of an order which is nevertheless established" (15). Because the oppressive social order worked so hard to naturalize itself, the people required a supernatural hero to tell each other insistently and continuously, through the constant repetition of his stories, just how profoundly unjust were their current conditions. The Frei Damiao legend therefore fulfilled the cru-cial political function of maintaining a *will to resistance* in the face of massive technologies of domination, relentlessly long odds, and oppressors who strove endlessly to convince the people of the naturalness, acceptability, and inevitability of their current lot. The uto-pian Frei Damiao stories were both a symptom and an agent of popular disbelief in the ideologies whose acceptance would enslave them.

39 Henry Jenkins III, "*Star Trek* Rerun, Reread, Rewritten: Fan Writing as Textual Poaching," *Critical Studies in Mass Communication* 5, no. 2 (June 1988): 88–89. Also see Henry Jenkins, *Textual Poachers: Television Fans and Participatory Culture* (New York: Routledge, 1992).

40 Jenkins, "*Star Trek* Rerun, Reread, Rewritten," 96.

41 B. Ray, "Washer Turns into a Time Machine: Woman Puts in Sheets—and Pulls Out a 200-Year-Old Coat!" *Weekly World News*, 17 April 1990, 15.

42 Bakhtin, *Problems of Dostoevsky's Poetics*, 147.

43 John Fiske, *Television Culture* (London: Methuen, 1987), 94–99.

44 Tabloids have a complex and contradictory relationship to mainstream science. They are happy to invoke its authority opportunistically, but even happier to problematize such invocations with fantastic examples for which "the experts" can provide what is at best an only partially satisfactory explanation, if any at all.

45 Bird, whose research involved a small group of regular tabloid readers, writes that their comments contradict the stereotype of "tabloid reading as a solitary, guilty pleasure" (*For Enquiring Minds*, 142). Bird's readers use the papers as an important cultural resource in their everyday social relations. She finds that men tend to evaluate and circulate tab-loid stories on the basis of their informational content, whereas women typically "use

the stories as springboards for sharing opinions about their own lives — 'what would you do, how would you feel' " (150).

46 Ted Corners, "Brain Surgeon Turns Patients into Helpless Robots," *National Examiner*, 6 June 1989, 15.

47 Corners, "Brain Surgeon Turns Patients into Helpless Robots," 15.

48 Bird, *For Enquiring Minds*, 107–9.

49 For example, Eileen Lehnert and Mary J. Perpich, "An Attitude Segmentation Study of Supermarket Tabloid Readers," *Journalism Quarterly* 59 (1982): 104–11.

50 Bird, *For Enquiring Minds*, 112.

51 Bird writes that tabloid readers are "quite selective about the particular phenomena they choose to believe in," and that "the relationship between 'belief' and tabloid reading is more subtle and complex than the image of totally gullible readers would allow" (*For Enquiring Minds*, 120, 122).

52 This is not to conflate racism with class dynamics, as some analyses do, but rather to recognize that the absence of adequate political structures for the organization and expression of opposition to social domination can lead to the unnecessary articulation of various popular resentments to racist discourses and therefore to the intensification of racisms.

53 Fiske, "The Cultural Economy of Fandom," 33.

54 Quoted in Chuck Ross, "Another Contender in Tabloid TV Pack," *San Francisco Chronicle*, 12 August 1989, C8.

55 Alan Shapiro, "The Star Trekking of Physics," *Ctheory: Theory, Technology, and Culture* 20, no. 3 (October 1997). *Ctheory* is an on-line journal available at http://www.ctheory.com/.

56 Bird, *For Enquiring Minds*, 202.

57 Ibid., 64–67.

58 On the idea that it is really only the ruling classes and their children who subscribe to dominant capitalist ideologies, see Nicholas Abercrombie et al., *The Dominant Ideology Thesis* (London: G. Allen and Unwin, 1980).

59 Jay Blumler, "The New Television Marketplace: Imperatives, Implications, Issues," in *Mass Media and Society*, ed. James Curran and Michael Gurevitch (London: Arnold, 1991), 192–215.

60 Steve Behrens, "A Finer Grind from the Ratings Mill," *Channels* (Field Guide, December 1987): 16.

61 Ibid.

62 John Langer, *Tabloid Television: Popular Journalism and the "Other News"* (London: Routledge, 1998), 164. As I've suggested in a previous footnote, however (see chap. 1, n. 18), I think that Langer's conception of the tabloid perspective that has been cut loose from its previous moorings is too narrowly circumscribed, focused as it is on the influences associated with Langer's "other news," and excluding as it does the "wilder" forms of tabloidism as well as the daytime talk shows, whose place in the discursive universe of tabloid television is extremely significant.

63 *A Current Affair*, for example, has lost much of its ironically playful and skeptical irreverence and adopted a more conventional approach to less unconventional and fantastic stories since anchor Maury Povich (see chapter 3) left to host his own tabloid talk show.

64 Mark Allen Peterson, "Aliens, Ape Men, and Whacky Savages: The Anthropologist in the Tabloids," *Anthropology Today* 7, no. 5 (October 1991): 4.

65 Jane Feuer, "The Concept of Live Television: Ontology as Ideology," in *Regarding Television: Critical Approaches — an Anthology*, ed. E. Ann Kaplan (Frederick, Md.: University Publications of America, 1983), 14.

66   As Paolo Carpignano and his colleagues point out, "there is no distinction in terms of truth between live pictures and framed events, not because the equation between live and real is ideological but because reality as such is socially constructed." See "Chatter in the Age of Electronic Reproduction: Talk Television and the 'Public Mind,' " *Social Text* 25–26 (1990): 42.

67   Work that comments on the participatory inclusiveness of print tabloids includes S. Elizabeth Bird, "The Kennedy Story in Folklore and Tabloids: Intertextuality in Political Communication," in *Politics in Familiar Contexts: Projecting Politics through Popular Media*, ed. Robert L. Savage and Dan Nimmo (Norwood, N.J.: Ablex Publishing, 1990), 247–68; Mark Pursehouse, "Looking at *The Sun*: Into the Nineties with a Tabloid and Its Readers," *Cultural Studies from Birmingham* 1 (1991): 88–133.

68   Jimmie L. Reeves, Mark C. Rodgers, and Michael Epstein, "Rewriting Popularity: The Cult Files," in *Deny All Knowledge: Reading "The X-Files*," ed. David Lavery, Angela Hague, and Marla Cartwright (Syracuse, N.Y.: Syracuse University Press, 1996), 35. Also see Westerfelhaus and Combs, "Criminal Investigations and Spiritual Quests," 208; Jodi Dean, *Aliens in America: Conspiracy Cultures from Outerspace to Cyberspace* (Ithaca, N.Y.: Cornell University Press, 1998), 17–18.

69   Defenders of scientific rationalism typically argue, for example, that the hallmark of its epistemology lies in the flexible recognition that the "truth" is always open to challenge and reformulation. *In social practice*, however, the invocation of science and scientific authority serves almost perfectly inverted ends: to foreclose debate, to silence alternative voices, to deflect challenge, to depoliticize and to authorize and serve powerful military, industrial, and governmental interests. See Ross, *Science Wars*; Jennifer Daryl Slack and M. Mehdi Semati, "Intellectual and Political Hygiene: The 'Sokal Affair,' " *Critical Studies in Mass Communication* 14, no. 3 (September 1997): 201–7; John Michael, "Science Friction and Cultural Studies: Intellectuals, Interdisciplinarity, and the Profession of Truth," *Camera Obscura* 37 (January 1996): 125–55.

70   Leon Jaroff, "Weird Science," *Time*, 15 May 1995, 75.

71   See John Fiske, *Power Plays, Power Works* (London: Verso, 1993), esp. 147.

72   Gordon has also determined, based on eyewitness accounts, that the 662d Air Force Radar Squadron was involved in the Kecksburg recovery operations. Gordon believes that this squadron was part of a larger unit conducting top-secret UFO investigations. The log book of the 662d Squadron contains no entry for December 9, 1965, the night of the Kecksburg incident. Says Gordon, "that tells us that somebody apparently wanted to keep all information associated with the unit's involvement in that site away from public information. I think that we can very plainly see the fact that the government has not told us everything they know about the Kecksburg case."

73   One way it does this is by eschewing the discursive authoritarianism of the serious news, whereby the truth is dispensed authoritatively by journalistic paracletes (see chapter 3). "The following program deals with controversial subjects. The theories expressed are not the only possible interpretation. The viewer is invited to make a judgment based on all available information," states a title that opens each episode of *Sightings*. Such a disclaimer would seem jarringly out of place before mainstream newscasts, which rarely encourage viewers to question the programs' contents.

74   Charlotte Brunsdon and David Morley, *Everyday Television: "Nationwide"* (London: British Film Institute, 1978), 87.

75   Bird, *For Enquiring Minds*, 122–23.

76   This follows the Foucauldian view that a statement can be "true" or "false" only within the terms of a particular discourse that establishes conditions for the determination of

truth and falsity, but which is not itself "true" or "false." In other words, truth is determined not by "reality" but rather by "discourse," which is conceived of as a system of rules for producing statements that are either true or false. There is, of course, a different level of "truth" that pertains precisely to whether the abduction of humans by aliens has "actually happened." I do not mean to suggest that the answer to this is a trivial matter. Indeed, far from trivializing this issue, I wish to understand the complex sociocultural forces that make it so hard for so many to even listen seriously to, much less believe in the "truth" of, statements made by thousands of people who insist they have been abducted by aliens.

77 John Fiske, "Cultural Studies and the Culture of Everyday Life," in *Cultural Studies*, ed. Lawrence Grossberg, Cary Nelson, and Paula Treichler (New York: Routledge, 1992), 162.

78 The discourses of "post-abortion syndrome" have become important knowledge weapons in anti-choice efforts to regulate women's access to medical treatment. See, e.g., "Recognizing Post Abortion Syndrome," 12 March 1996, at http://www.infinet.com/~life/aborted/seepas.htm, part of the Ohio Right to Life Web site.

79 Alan Nadel, *Containment Culture: American Narratives, Postmodernism, and the Atomic Age* (Durham, N.C.: Duke University Press, 1995).

80 Dean, *Aliens in America*, 180.

81 Michael Rogin, *Ronald Reagan, the Movie, and Other Episodes in Political Demonology* (Berkeley: University of California Press, 1987), 265.

82 Ibid., 266.

5 Normalization and Its Discontents: The Conflictual Space of Daytime Talk Shows

1 Joy Overbeck, "I Can't Believe What My Kid Sees on TV," *TV Guide*, 14 August 1993, 13.

2 Elayne Rapping, "Daytime Inquiries," *Progressive* 55, no. 10 (October 1991): 37.

3 Joshua Gamson, *Freaks Talk Back: Tabloid Talk Shows and Sexual Nonconformity* (Chicago: University of Chicago Press, 1998), 25–26.

4 William Bennett, quoted in Jonathan Alter, "Culture Wars: Next: 'The Revolt of the Revolted,' " *Newsweek*, 6 November 1995, 46.

5 Mark Schone, "Talked Out," *Spin*, May 1996; "Conservatives Take on Daytime 'Trash TV,' " *Dallas–Fort Worth Heritage*, March 1996, an on-line monthly Christian newspaper available at http://www.fni.com/heritage/. The *Dallas–Fort Worth Heritage* article quotes Lieberman as follows: "These shows increasingly make the abnormal normal and set up the most perverse role models for our children and adults. The result is an increasingly debased culture that rejects rather than reflects the basic values that most Americans share."

6 Rapping, "Daytime Inquiries," 37. With regard particularly to "sex and gender nonconformists," Joshua Gamson adds that "for people whose life experience is so heavily tilted toward invisibility, whose nonconformity, even when it looks very much like conformity, discredits them and disenfranchises them, daytime TV talk shows are a big shot of visibility and media accreditation" (*Freaks Talk Back*, 5).

7 John Fiske, *Media Matters: Everyday Culture and Political Change* (Minneapolis: University of Minnesota Press, 1994), 116.

8 Michel Foucault, *Discipline and Punish: The Birth of the Prison*, trans. Alan Sheridan (New York: Vintage Books, 1979); *The History of Sexuality, Volume 1: An Introduction*, trans. Robert Hurley (New York: Pantheon Books, 1978).

9 Foucault, *Discipline and Punish*, 199–200.

10 A condition can only be pronounced "normal" within the parameters of a preexisting

field of knowledge that makes such a pronouncement possible. Scientific rationalism has produced rigorous rules for the determination of the normal, which in social practice has both quantitative and normative dimensions. Other discourses, such as religion, have no concept of "normality," except insofar as they borrow one from scientific rationalism.

11   Mark Philp, "Michel Foucault," in *The Return of Grand Theory in the Human Sciences*, ed. Quentin Skinner (Cambridge: Cambridge University Press, 1985), 73.

12   Foucault, *Discipline and Punish*, 184.

13   Michel Foucault, *Power/Knowledge: Selected Interviews and Other Writings, 1972–1977*, ed. Colin Gordon, trans. Colin Gordon et al. (New York: Pantheon Books, 1980), 151–52.

14   Foucault, *Discipline and Punish*, 184.

15   William Connolly, "Taylor, Foucault, and Otherness," *Political Theory* 13, no. 3 (August 1985); Stephen K. White, "Poststructuralism and Political Reflection," *Political Theory* 16, no. 2 (May 1988).

16   Philp, "Michel Foucault," 67–68.

17   Michel Foucault, *Politics, Philosophy, Culture: Interviews and Other Writings, 1977–1984*, ed. Lawrence D. Kritzman, trans. Alan Sheridan et al. (New York: Routledge, 1988), 178–210.

18   Philp, "Michel Foucault," 75.

19   Christopher Lasch, "The Moynihan Report: Rethinking Family," in *Social Theory: The Multicultural and Classic Readings*, ed. Charles Lemert (Boulder, Colo.: Westview Press, 1993), 437.

20   Moynihan made these comments on the NBC news program *Meet the Press*, June 19, 1994. Compare some of the mainstream journalistic criticisms of tabloid television discussed in chapter 3 (for example, that of Carl Bernstein).

21   Foucault, *Discipline and Punish*, 304. Foucault describes the norm as "a new form of 'law' " that combines "legality and nature, prescription and constitution." Thus "the activity of judging has increased precisely to the extent that the normalizing power has spread."

22   Fiske, *Media Matters*, 4.

23   Neil Postman and Steve Powers, *How to Watch TV News* (New York: Penguin Books, 1992), 94.

24   Laura Grindstaff, "Producing Trash, Class, and the Money Shot: A Behind-the-Scenes Account of Daytime TV Talk Shows," in *Media Scandals: Morality and Desire in the Popular Culture Marketplace*, ed. James Lull and Stephen Hinerman (New York: Columbia University Press, 1997), 196.

25   Fiske, *Media Matters*, 236. In *Freaks Talk Back*, Gamson details many of the strategies of manipulation and control pressed into service by producers and hosts because of the high pressures exerted by demanding production schedules and unforgiving profit motives. In a study of *Sally Jesse Raphael* and *Oprah*, Janice Peck analyzes both the ideological mechanisms that work hard to contain talk show discourse within dominant ideological frames and the ruptures that inevitably occur because of the way in which the programs must necessarily grant some control over the production of speech to those who are socially disempowered. As Peck puts it, "this is the irreconcilable contradiction of TV talk shows: in order to carry out the ideological work of mediating and managing the meaning of social conflicts, they must give voice to those who live them." See "TV Talk Shows as Therapeutic Discourse: The Ideological Labor of the Televised Talking Cure," *Communication Theory* 5, no. 1 (February 1995): 75.

26   Judith Butler, *Bodies That Matter: On the Discursive Limits of "Sex"* (New York: Routledge, 1993), 237; Butler's italics removed.

27   Foucault, *Discipline and Punish*.

28 Patricia Mellencamp, *High Anxiety: Catastrophe, Scandal, Age, and Comedy* (Bloomington: Indiana University Press, 1992), 214. Numerous commentators have made essentially the same point about the talk shows' prioritization of the experiential knowledges of ordinary people and their typical creation of spaces for the expression of skepticism toward, or refusal of, ostensibly objective expert knowledges. See, for example, Paolo Carpignano et al., "Chatter in the Age of Electronic Reproduction: Talk Television and the 'Public Mind,'" *Social Text* 25–26 (1990): 33–55; Rapping, "Daytime Inquiries"; Wayne Munson, *All Talk: The Talkshow in Media Culture* (Philadelphia: Temple University Press, 1993); Jane M. Shattuc, *The Talking Cure: TV Talk Shows and Women* (New York: Routledge, 1997); Gamson, *Freaks Talk Back*. For an alternative perspective, see Lisa McLaughlin, "Chastity Criminals in the Age of Electronic Reproduction: Re-viewing Talk Television and the Public Sphere," *Journal of Communication Inquiry* 17, no. 1 (winter 1993): 41–55. McLaughlin invokes Gramsci to argue against the idea that talk shows generally express ordinary knowledges that challenge expert ones, since "the social formation of common sense . . . can be seen as rising out of 'official'—scientific, medical, legal, political—discourses" (47). Ordinary common sense, for McLaughlin, is thus produced through "intervention" and "colonization" by dominant ideologies (48). Although I think McLaughlin is right to suggest that "official" scientific and ordinary "commonsense" discourses are not simply and binarily opposed to each other in any neat and mutually exclusive way, I also think that she comes too close to the obliteration of any sense of difference between these knowledge formations, ultimately suggesting that opposition toward dominant ideologies can come only from discourses that exist somehow in a relation of complete externality to dominant ones. Indeed, her theoretical framework strikes me as one that comes closer to Althusserian structural Marxism than to Gramscianism, which has greater room to accommodate ongoing contestation over meanings. Along these lines, it is telling that McLaughlin criticizes cultural studies reception and audience approaches for ignoring "the location of the subject by the text" (53).

29 One might read patriarchy's "normal" positioning of women in submissive roles as the "dysfunctional cause" of these guests' desires to dominate men, though this was clearly not implied by the questioner's general tone and demeanor.

30 Anne McClintock, "Screwing the System: Sexwork, Race, and the Law," *boundary 2* 19, no. 2 (1992): 76.

31 McClintock, "Screwing the System," 76.

32 George Bataille writes that "the low prostitute, because she has become a stranger to the taboo without which we should not be human beings, falls to the level of the beasts; she generally excites a disgust like the one most civilizations claim to feel for sows." See *Death and Sensuality: A Study in Eroticism and Taboo*, trans. Mary Dalwood (New York: Walker Press, 1962), 134, quoted in Kathleen Rowe, *The Unruly Woman: Gender and the Genres of Laughter* (Austin: University of Texas Press, 1995), 43.

33 McClintock, "Screwing the System," 76.

34 McClintock is writing in support of the efforts of sex workers to achieve more control over their work and its legal regulation, and against the version of feminism that condemns prostitutes "for becoming complicit in commodity fetishism." She asks, therefore, "Doesn't the argument that prostitutes sell *themselves* [italics mine] bear an uncanny and perilous resemblance to the sanctioned male view that a woman's identity is *equivalent* to her sexuality? Prostitutes do not sell themselves; rather, like all workers (including feminists), they exchange specific services for cash and carefully negotiate with their clients what services they provide, at what rate, and for how long." She adds that "as a result, working-class women and women of color are able to educate themselves, find

social mobility, and raise their children in the comfort and security usually given to only good white girls" (McClintock, "Screwing the System," 94–95). When Donahue asked of the phone caller who described herself as a prostitute, "How's business?" she replied, with a chuckle, "The recession hasn't hit us!"

35 Christine Gledhill, "Pleasurable Negotiations," in *Female Spectators: Looking at Film and Television*, ed. E. Deidre Pribram (London: Verso, 1988), 67–68. Gledhill explains the Gramscian derivation of this notion of negotiation. "According to Gramsci, since ideological power in bourgeois society is as much a matter of persuasion as of force, it is never secured once and for all, but has continually to be re-established in a constant to and fro between contesting groups. 'Hegemony' describes the ever shifting, ever negotiating play of ideological, social and political forces through which power is maintained and contested" (68).

36 Foucault, *The History of Sexuality*, 101. Foucault offers a similar example from the history of European psychiatry: "There is no question that the appearance in nineteenth-century psychiatry, jurisprudence, and literature of a whole series of discourses on the species and subspecies of homosexuality . . . made possible a strong advance of social controls into this area of 'perversity'; but it also made possible the formation of a 'reverse' discourse: homosexuality began to speak in its own behalf, to demand that its legitimacy or 'naturality' be acknowledged, often in the same vocabulary, using the same categories by which it was medically disqualified."

37 Cindy Patton, *Inventing AIDS* (New York: Routledge, 1990).

38 Jodi Dean, *Aliens in America: Conspiracy Cultures from Outerspace to Cyberspace* (Ithaca, N.Y.: Cornell University Press, 1998), 104.

39 Ibid., 106–7. Pulitzer Prize–winning Harvard psychiatrist John E. Mack was made painfully aware of the costs of defying official orthodoxies regarding the alien abduction phenomenon when the university tried to revoke his tenure because of the 1994 book in which he published the results of his close work with thirteen abductees and supported their claims.

40 Patton, *Inventing AIDS*, 129.

41 Foucault, *The History of Sexuality*, 157.

42 Judith Butler, *Gender Trouble: Feminism and the Subversion of Identity* (New York: Routledge, 1990), 97. Against both essentialism and sexual liberationism, Foucault argues that "by saying yes to sex," one merely "tracks along the course" laid out by dominating power in its "general deployment of sexuality" (since "sex" is not "on the side of reality" but is instead the product of sexuality) (Foucault, *The History of Sexuality*, 157).

43 Butler, *Gender Trouble*, 149.

44 Gamson, *Freaks Talk Back*.

45 David Plotz, "Assessment," *Slate*, 21 March 1998. *Slate* is an on-line magazine available at http://www.slate.com/toc/FrontPorch.asp.

46 Gloria-Jean Masciarotte, "C'mon, Girl: Oprah Winfrey and the Discourse of Feminine Talk," *Genders*, no. 11 (fall 1991): 84–85.

47 Rapping, "Daytime Inquiries," 37.

48 Alison Bass, "Talk Shows Faulted as Trivial, Exploitive," *Wisconsin State Journal*, 17 October 1993, 1F–2F. It should be noted that this sort of simplistic cause/effect perspective isolates television, rather than social differences and inequalities, as the "cause" of whatever modalities social conflict assumes. By extension, television audiences are construed as the recipients of television's "effects" and are thus seen as (more or less) passive victims of the cathode-ray tube.

49 Quoted in Maria Glod, "Springer Mania: Too Hot for Parents and Teachers!" *Washington Post*, 27 April 1998, A1.

50 Rapping, "Daytime Inquiries," 38.

51 Ibid.

52 Mikhail Bakhtin, *Rabelais and His World*, trans. Hélène Iswolsky (Bloomington: Indiana University Press, 1984), 10.

53 Emily Prager, "Oprah's Opera," *Village Voice*, 10 March 1987, 45.

54 Carpignano et al., "Chatter in the Age of Electronic Reproduction," 47.

55 Jaffe Cohen, "Land o' Lake," *Harvard Gay and Lesbian Review* 2, no. 4 (fall 1995): 36.

56 Cohen, "Land o' Lake," 37.

57 It is a telling point that in their search for good guests, the talk shows provide airtime for people such as transsexual activist Susan Stryker, who has developed strategies for the presentation of theoretical ideas on the tabloid programs. Says Stryker, "It's code switching. If I wanted to get on the talk show and do my, you know, transgender theory, poststructuralist, queer-inflected thing, it would not fly. So I found that what worked was telling stories about yourself that have some kind of hook with someone else's experience, like talking with nontranssexual women who are going through menopause or who have fibroid tumors or have their ovaries out for whatever reason, and they're doing these things that alter their body in a way that calls into question their gender identity for themselves" (quoted in Gamson, *Freaks Talk Back*, 182).

58 Gamson, *Freaks Talk Back*, 109–25.

59 Cohen, "Land o' Lake," 37.

60 See, for example, John Fiske, *Television Culture* (London: Methuen, 1987); Henry Jenkins, *Textual Poachers: Television Fans and Participatory Culture* (New York: Routledge, 1992); Mary Ellen Brown, *Soap Opera and Women's Talk: The Pleasure of Resistance* (Thousand Oaks, Calif.: Sage Publications, 1994).

61 Jane Shattuc notes, for example, that "slowly, across twenty-five years, talk shows have created a community of women who believe in their right to speak about their experiences as part of the body politic" (*The Talking Cure*, 197).

62 Shattuc, *The Talking Cure*, p. 195.

63 S. Elizabeth Bird, *For Enquiring Minds: A Cultural Study of Supermarket Tabloids* (Knoxville: University of Tennessee Press, 1992), 150.

64 Shattuc, *The Talking Cure*, 172.

65 Gamson, *Freaks Talk Back*, 113.

66 During "I'm Gay, You're Gay," Timmie complicates the idea of "casual sex" and confounds neat distinctions between "promiscuity" and monogamy with an anecdote about how he initiated what would become a three-year-long relationship when, at an airport, he fondled the genitals of an absolute stranger.

67 On "scientific racism" as a form of normalizing power that abnormalizes people of color, see Thomas L. Dumm, "The New Enclosures: Racism in the Normalized Community," in *Reading Rodney King/Reading Urban Uprising*, ed. Robert Gooding-Williams (New York: Routledge, 1993), 178–95. For a more recent overview of work on the normalization of whiteness in the United States and related issues, also see Janice Radway, "What's in a Name? Presidential Address to the American Studies Association, 20 November 1998," *American Quarterly* 51, no. 1 (March 1999): 1–32.

68 This white notion of "underdeveloped" black initiative coincides powerfully with white First World attitudes about the putative immaturity or "underdevelopment" of the industries and economies of the nonwhite "Third World." Along these lines, Kobena Mercer

notes that "the term/ethnic minorities/ . . . connotes the black subject as a minor, an abject childlike figure necessary for the legitimation of paternalistic ideologies of assimilation and integration." See Mercer, " '1968': Periodizing Politics and Identity," in *Cultural Studies*, ed. Lawrence Grossberg, Cary Nelson, and Paula Treichler (New York: Routledge, 1992), 429.

69 I am not at this point asking readers to "take it on faith" that this woman's claims about the institutional racism of the D.C. police department are "true" (as one critic suggested when I presented this argument in another form). Rather, I am demonstrating for readers that the often trivialized tabloid talk shows are significant in part for their openness to perspectives that challenge dominant ideological ones. Such challenges are always and inevitably politically significant, regardless of the issue of their "truth" (which is also, of course, a very important issue). For further clarification of my position on this issue, see my discussion of the terms "knowledge," "truth," and "discourse" in chapter 2.

70 See, e.g., Gamson, *Freaks Talk Back*, 57–65.

71 Shattuc, *The Talking Cure*, 101–2.

72 Schone, "Talked Out," 69.

73 Ibid., 71.

74 Quoted in Schone, "Talked Out," 74.

75 Barbara Ehrenreich, "In Defense of Talkshows," *Time*, 4 December 1995, 92; Shattuc, *The Talking Cure*; Gamson, *Freaks Talk Back*.

76 Schone, "Talked Out," 75.

77 Janice Peck, "Talk about Racism: Framing a Popular Discourse of Race on *Oprah Winfrey*," *Cultural Critique* (spring 1994): 89–126.

78 Peck uses Stuart Hall's concept of "inferential racism," which entails those "apparently naturalized representations of events and situations relating to race" that, despite the (often explicitly antiracist) intentions of the social agents who invoke them, nevertheless "have racist premises and propositions inscribed into them as a set of unquestioned assumptions." See Stuart Hall, "The Whites of Their Eyes: Racist Ideologies and the Media," in *Silver Linings*, ed. George Bridges and Rosalind Brunt (London: Lawrence and Wishart, 1981), 36, quoted in Peck, "Talk about Racism," 93.

79 Peck, "TV Talk Shows as Therapeutic Discourse," 63.

80 Foucault, *The History of Sexuality*, 96.

81 Ibid., 95–96. Elsewhere Foucault writes similarly that "power *is* 'always already there,' . . . one is never 'outside' it, . . . there are no 'margins' for those who break with the system to gambol in. But this does not entail the necessity of accepting an inescapable form of domination or an absolute privilege on the side of the law. To say that one can never be 'outside' power does not mean that one is trapped and condemned to defeat no matter what. . . . Resistance to power does not have to come from elsewhere to be real, nor is it inexorably frustrated through being the compatriot of power. It exists all the more by being in the same place as power; hence, like power, resistance is multiple and can be integrated in global strategies" (Foucault, *Power/Knowledge*, 141–42).

82 Gamson, *Freaks Talk Back*, 147.

83 Stephen Schiff, "Geek Shows," *New Yorker*, 6 November 1995, 9–10.

84 Foucault, *The History of Sexuality*, 59.

85 Ibid., 61.

86 See, e.g., Gamson, *Freaks Talk Back*.

87 Patricia Joyner Priest, *Public Intimacies: Talk Show Participants and Tell-All TV* (Cresskill, N.J.: Hampton Press, 1995), 177.

88 *TV Nation*, summer 1994.

89 Comments made by Jerry Springer on *The Jerry Springer Show*, 16 November 1994.

90 Lisa Millman, Heather's friend, quoted in Ben Relles, "UW Pranksters to Appear on National TV: Students Masquerade as Sexual Deviants on Tonight's *The Jerry Springer Show*," *Badger Herald*, 16 November 1994, 1.

91 Relles, "UW Pranksters to Appear on National TV," 1.

92 Heather Stoneman, quoted in Relles, "UW Pranksters to Appear on National TV," 1.

93 Relles, "UW Pranksters to Appear on National TV," 2.

94 Gamson, *Freaks Talk Back*, chap. 3.

95 See, e.g., Shattuc, *The Talking Cure*, 154–69.

96 Plotz, "Assessment."

97 "Sally Blames Jerry Springer for Fake Fights," Associated Press, 22 September 1998, http://tvtalkshows.com/sallyjessyraphael/news/1998/fake; Michael Starr, "Sally Does a 'Springer,' Films Back Stage Fights," *New York Post*, 18 September 1998, http://www.nypostonline.com.

98 Quoted in Starr, "Sally Does a 'Springer.'"

99 This point does not presume that Raphael's maneuver is motivated by a sincere desire to demonstrate the "authenticity" of her program. Even if we wish to view her strategy as a cynical attempt at product differentiation to increase her program's market share, her public explanation of this strategy is in itself symptomatic of the hyperreal cultural conditions within which such an explanation can make sense to others, and within which there is a demand for "reality TV" that Raphael can capitalize on in this way.

6 Conclusion: Cultural Struggle, the New News, and the Politics of Popularity in the Age of Jesse "the Body" Ventura

1 Jon Katz, "Rock, Rap, and Movies Bring You the News," *Rolling Stone*, 5 March 1992, 33.

2 Historian Stanley Kutler, on how future historians will likely view the end of the twentieth century. Quoted in Scott Milfred, "Tabloid Culture: Is That How History Will See Us?" *Wisconsin State Journal Online*, 12 October 1998, http://www.madison.com:80/wsj/.

3 Dialogue from a fourth-season episode entitled "Postmodern Prometheus." This episode was unusually but postmodernistically self-reflective about the close connection between *The X-Files* and the tabloid media—so much so that it included a brief segment from *The Jerry Springer Show*.

4 Anne Swarsdon, "Driver of Diana's Car Said to Be Drunk," *Washington Post*, 2 September 1997, A1.

5 Roxanne Roberts, "The Princess and the Press: A Dance Ending in Death," *Washington Post*, 4 September 1997, D1.

6 Christine Spolar, "At the Palace Gates, Flowers and Tears—and Anger at the Press," *Washington Post*, 1 September 1997, A27.

7 "Princess Diana's Death," *Washington Post*, 1 September 1997, A20.

8 Roberts, "The Princess and the Press," D1.

9 Richard Cohen, "Serving Up a Story Line," *Washington Post*, 4 September 1997, A19.

10 Howard Kurtz, "Extra! Read All About It! Overcoverage Shocks Press!" *Washington Post*, 5 September 1997, D1.

11 Quoted in Kurtz, "Extra! Read All About It!" D1.

12 Jonathan Yardley, "Media Culpa," *Washington Post*, 15 September 1997, B2.

13 Quoted in Sophfronia Scott Gregory, "Oprah! Oprah in the Court!" *Time*, 6 June 1994, 31. This obviously does not "prove" the "effects" of "Oprahization" on real juries. Rather, it demonstrates that nervous officials are aware of the fluidity of popular skepticism, and

that there is a high level of official anxiety over the existence of alternative ways of sense making, as I have argued.

14 Gregory, "Oprah! Oprah in the Court!" 30–31.

15 Ibid. The result in this case was the declaration of a mistrial. The consequence of this defense in terms of its racial meanings is quite contradictory. On the one hand, it signifies a recognition that all behavior occurs within determinative social contexts, which creates pressure to displace conservative notions of "individual responsibility" that contribute to the increasing incarceration of young African American men. On the other, it coincides too neatly with white racist unconcern for black-on-black violence in urban centers. As the Reverend Ralph Waldo Emerson of Fort Worth put it, the Osby mistrial says that " 'these folks' can't help shooting each other. . . . And it says to already nervous law-enforcement officials that they'd better be ready to draw when they stop someone in our community" (quoted in Gregory, "Oprah! Oprah in the Court!" 31).

16 The Gramscian theory of historical conjuncture is an alternative to the logic of "cause" and "effect" as a way of explaining the relationships that link events to other events. When two events are conjuncturally related, it is not that one is the "cause" of the other but rather that they are mutually determinative by virtue of their common situatedness within a particular historically conjunctural moment. See, e.g., Stuart Hall, "Gramsci's Relevance for the Study of Race and Ethnicity," in *Stuart Hall: Critical Dialogues in Cultural Studies*, ed. David Morley and Kuan-Hsing Chen (London: Routledge, 1996), 411–40.

17 Sophfronia Scott Gregory, "Black Rage: In Defense of a Mass Murder," *Time*, 6 June 1994, 31.

18 Carlo Ginzburg, *The Cheese and the Worms: The Cosmos of a Sixteenth-Century Miller*, trans. John Tedeschi and Anne Tedeschi (New York: Dorset Press, 1989).

19 Jodi Dean, *Aliens in America: Conspiracy Cultures from Outerspace to Cyberspace* (Ithaca, N.Y.: Cornell University Press, 1998), 8.

20 According to this poll, 46 percent of people between the ages of eighteen and thirty-four believe in UFOs, but only 25 percent believe in the continued viability of social security. See "Youths Give UFOs Edge over Security," *Wisconsin State Journal*, 27 September 1994, 6B.

21 Howard Kurtz, "Clintons Long under Siege by Conservative Detractors," *Washington Post*, 28 January 1998, A1; Richard Morin and Claudia Deane, "President's Popularity Hits a High: Majority in Poll Say Political Enemies Are Out to Get Him," *Washington Post*, 1 February 1998, A1.

22 George Johnson, "Pierre, Is That a Masonic Flag on the Moon?" *New York Times*, 24 November 1996, http://www.nytimes.com.

23 Mark Poster, "Cyberdemocracy: Internet and the Public Sphere," in *Internet Culture*, ed. David Porter (New York: Routledge, 1997), 211.

24 Dean notes that "what happens in cyberia is an unending disruption of settled beliefs and ideas . . . produced by the possibility of available alternatives" (*Aliens in America*, 138). Jon Stratton observes further that when "silenced groups, such as the Chiapas Amerindians in Mexico can speak out on the Internet . . . not only the organization of the media and the construct of the audience, but also the formation of a unified and distinct imagined community—a disciplined and disciplinary public sphere—and the very understanding of the nation-state itself are transformed. The Internet is one more vector in the global flows that have shifted nation-state rhetoric from homogeneity to multiculturalism." This, he suggests, helps explain, beyond mere economic rationales, the urgency of both government and business leaders to reconstruct the Internet in a way that much more

closely approximates the structures of other modern mass media ("Cyberspace and the Globalization of Culture," in Porter, *Internet Culture*, 265).

25 By characterizing poststructuralism in this way, I am choosing to give that term a Foucauldian "spin" while equally inflecting it with a sense of Vološinov's critique of structural linguistics. See V. N. Vološinov, *Marxism and the Philosophy of Language*, trans. Ladislav Matejka and I. R. Titunik (Cambridge: Harvard University Press, 1973). There are, of course, other varieties of poststructuralist theory, most notably, perhaps, the Derridean one. Unlike Foucault's and Vološinov's criticisms of structuralism, Derrida's tend to center around a theory of the nature of language itself, rather than ideas about the social mobilization of meanings. Nevertheless there are significant social implications that arise from the Derridean version of poststructuralism that some commentators seem to overlook. See Jacques Derrida, *Of Grammatology*, trans. Gayatri Chakravorty Spivak (Baltimore: Johns Hopkins University Press, 1974).

26 Graham Knight, "Reality Effects: Tabloid Television News," *Queen's Quarterly* 96, no. 1 (spring 1989): 99.

27 Michel Foucault, *Power/Knowledge: Selected Interviews and Other Writings, 1972–1977*, ed. Colin Gordon, trans. Colin Gordon et al. (New York: Pantheon Books, 1980), 138.

28 Elayne Rapping, "Daytime Inquiries," *Progressive* 55, no. 10 (October 1991): 36.

29 Katz, "Rock, Rap, and Movies Bring You the News," 33.

30 Ibid.

31 Andrew Ross, "The Private Parts of Justice," in *Race-ing Justice, En-gendering Power*, ed. Toni Morrison (New York: Pantheon Books, 1992), 59. Katz notes that "for millions of Americans," *Designing Women*'s treatment of the Thomas/Hill hearings was "a more relevant hashing of the matter than they would get on any Sunday-morning" news discussion program (Katz, "Rock, Rap, and Movies Bring You the News," 36).

32 Katz, "Rock, Rap, and Movies Bring You the News," 33.

33 This all depends on how loosely and elastically one wishes to draw the boundaries around various tabloid forms and how wide a net one chooses to cast in the search for historical cultural practices that prefigure contemporary tabloidism. Wayne Munson, for example, traces the talk show's roots in seventeenth-century European salon and coffeehouse culture. See Munson, *All Talk: The Talkshow in Media Culture* (Philadelphia: Temple University Press, 1993), 20. Similarly, S. Elizabeth Bird links supermarket tabloids to seventeenth-century "broadside ballads and newsbooks . . . packed with tales of strange and wondeful happenings — murders, natural disasters, unusual births, and omens." See *For Enquiring Minds: A Cultural Study of Supermarket Tabloids* (Knoxville: University of Tennessee Press, 1992), 9.

34 Katz, "Rock, Rap, and Movies Bring You the News," 36.

35 Jon Katz, "Beyond Broadcast Journalism," *Columbia Journalism Review* 30, no. 6 (March–April 1992): 23.

36 Jon Katz, "The Plugged-In Voter," *Rolling Stone*, 10 December 1992, 116.

37 Ibid., 117.

38 Marc Fisher, "Minnesota's Surprise: 'Governor Body': Populist Ex-Wrestler Ventura Appears to Have Pinned 2 Rivals," *Washington Post*, 4 November 1998, A1.

39 Andrew Stern, "Minnesota's Governor-Elect Says He's No Rebel," *Excite News*, 4 November 1998, http://nt.excite.com; Garry Wills, "The People's Choice," *New York Review of Books* 46, no. 13 (12 August 1999), http://www.nybooks.com.

40 Quoted in Wills, "The People's Choice."

41 Wills, "The People's Choice."

42 Fisher, "Minnesota's Surprise," A1.

43 Pam Belluck, "A 'Bad Boy' Wrestler Ignores the Script," *New York Times*, 5 November 1998, http://www.nytimes.com.

44 Quoted in Wills, "The People's Choice."

45 This is a paraphrase of the line ascribed to Ventura in stories reported by Wills in "The People's Choice."

46 Fisher, "Minnesota's Surprise"; Benno Groeneveld, "Ex-Wrestler Ventura Sworn In as Minnesota Governor," *Excite News*, 4 January 1999, http://nt.excite.com.

47 Jesse Ventura, quoted in Wills, "The People's Choice."

48 Micah L. Sifry, "Working Class Hero?" *Salon*, 11 January 1999, http://www.salonmagazine.com.

49 Katherine Lanpher, "The Mind," 27 November 1998, http://news.mpr.org. This commentary was originally broadcast on Minnesota Public Radio.

50 This statistic comes from Groeneveld, "Ex-Wrestler Ventura Sworn In as Minnesota Governor."

51 Belluck, "A 'Bad Boy' Wrestler Ignores the Script."

52 Jesse Ventura, quoted in Fisher, "Minnesota's Surprise," A1.

53 Jesse Ventura, quoted in Belluck, "A 'Bad Boy' Wrestler Ignores the Script."

54 Rev. Jerry O'Neill, quoted in Sifry, "Working Class Hero?"

55 Wills, "The People's Choice."

56 David Hanners, "Governor Is Yet Another Venture in Jesse's Unusually Varied Career," *Pioneer Planet*, 9 December 1998, http://www.pioneerplanet.com.

57 Michael Rogin, *Ronald Reagan, the Movie, and Other Episodes in Political Demonology* (Berkeley: University of California Press, 1987), 3.

58 Quoted in Hanners, "Governor Is Yet Another Venture in Jesse's Unusually Varied Career."

59 "High-pocrisy" is quoted in Wills, "The People's Choice."

60 Quoted in Hanners, "Governor Is Yet Another Venture in Jesse's Unusually Varied Career."

61 Matt Bai and David Brauer, "Jesse Ventura's 'Body' Politics," *Newsweek*, 16 November 1998, http://www.newsweek.com; Hanners, "Governor Is Yet Another Venture in Jesse's Unusually Varied Career."

62 Bai and Brauer, "Jesse Ventura's 'Body' Politics."

63 Wills, "The People's Choice."

64 Hanners, "Governor Is Yet Another Venture in Jesse's Unusually Varied Career."

65 "Interim Page," *Official Site of the Jesse Ventura Volunteer Committee*, http://www.jesseventura.org/interim.htm; Jesse Ventura, "How I Will Use the Internet," 28 December 1998, http://www.jesseventura.org/internet/howuse.htm; Dane Smith, "Ventura Creates Web Site to Influence 2000 Presidential Race," *Minneapolis Star-Tribune*, 9 February 1999, http://www.startribune.com.

66 Jesse Ventura, quoted in Groeneveld, "Ex-Wrestler Ventura Sworn In as Minnesota Governor."

67 This account of Ventura's inauguration is drawn from Jim Derogatis, "Politics as Usual in Minnesota," *Chicago Sun-Times*, 18 January 1999, http://www.suntimes.com.

68 Bob Greene, "The Voice of America Has Spoken: 'Amuse Me,' " *Chicago Tribune*, 11 November 1998, http://chicagotribune.com; Neil Postman, *Amusing Ourselves to Death: Public Discourse in the Age of Show Business* (New York: Viking Press, 1986).

69 Lawrence Grossberg, ed., "On Postmodernism and Articulation: An Interview with Stuart Hall," in Morley and Chen, *Stuart Hall*, 141–45.

70 Quoted in Sifry, "Working Class Hero?"
71 Cf., e.g., Sifry, "Working Class Hero?"
72 Pierre Bourdieu, *On Television*, trans. Priscilla Parkhurst Ferguson (New York: New Press, 1998), 2–3, 17.
73 Ibid., 48.
74 Cf. Pierre Bourdieu, *Distinction: A Social Critique of the Judgement of Taste*, trans. Richard Nice (Cambridge: Harvard University Press, 1984).
75 Bourdieu, *On Television*, 44, 48.
76 On the conventionality of this lament (of which Bourdieu's is a left-wing version), see John Langer, *Tabloid Television: Popular Journalism and the "Other News"* (London: Routledge, 1998). It should be noted that Bourdieu does observe that "these days, print journalists, in particular those who occupy a dominated position within" the journalistic field, "are elaborating a discourse that is highly critical of television" (*On Television*, 49).
77 Bourdieu, *On Television*, 48.
78 Ibid., 65.
79 This is not to say that Bourdieu is entirely oblivious to this issue. He notes, for example, that along with the fortification and elevation of the "fees" for entry into esoteric fields of cultural production, specialists must also "reinforce the duty to get out, to share what we have found, while at the same time improving the conditions and the means for doing so" (*On Television*, 65). Still, Bourdieu does not, to my mind, speak adequately to this problem.
80 Bourdieu, *On Television*, 16, 43–46. Bourdieu asserts that "if a vehicle as powerful as television were oriented even slightly toward . . . symbolic revolution, I can assure you that everyone would be rushing to put a stop to it" (45). Events like William Bennett's conservative assault on daytime talk shows (see chapter 5) suggest that television does sometimes provoke forms of backlash that are not entirely dissimilar to those that Bourdieu is imagining here.
81 Thomas B. Rosenstiel, "To Journalists, Technology Is a Blessing—and a Curse," *Los Angeles Times*, 24 September 1994, A1; italics mine.

Appendix   TVQ Scores for Tabloid Programs by Demographic Audience Category

1 Ien Ang, *Desperately Seeking the Audience* (London: Routledge, 1991), 60.
2 John Fiske, "Moments of Television: Neither the Text nor the Audience," in *Remote Control: Television, Audiences, and Cultural Power*, ed. Ellen Seiter et al. (London: Routledge, 1989), 56.
3 Ang, *Desperately Seeking the Audience*, 60.
4 http://www.qscores.com/about.html.
5 Richard Katz, "Cable Gets Its First Q Ratings," *Variety.com*, 5 August 1999, http://www.variety.com.
6 Henry Schafer, telephone interview by author, 24 August 1999.

Works Cited

Abercrombie, Nicholas, Stephen Hill, and Bryan S. Turner. *The Dominant Ideology Thesis*. London: G. Allen and Unwin, 1980.

Ainslie, Peter. "Looking for Answers." *Channels Field Guide* (1989): 82–83.

Alexander, J. "Space Alien Endorses Bill Clinton." *Weekly World News*, 11 August 1992, 24–25.

"Alien Captured by U.S. Agents!" *Weekly World News*, 30 October 1990, 1.

Allen, Robert C., ed. *Channels of Discourse, Reassembled: Television and Contemporary Criticism*. 2d ed. Chapel Hill: University of North Carolina Press, 1992.

Alter, Jonathan. "Culture Wars: Next: 'The Revolt of the Revolted.'" *Newsweek*, November 1995, 46.

Bai, Matt, and David Brauer. "Jesse Ventura's 'Body' Politics." *Newsweek*, November 1998. http://www.newsweek.com.

Bakhtin, Mikhail. *Problems of Dostoevsky's Poetics*. Ed. and trans. Caryl Emerson. Minneapolis: University of Minnesota Press, 1984.

———. *Rabelais and His World*. Trans. Hélène Iswolsky. Bloomington: Indiana University Press, 1984.

Balio, Tino, ed. *Hollywood in the Age of Television*. Boston: Unwin Hyman, 1990.

Bartley, Diane. "John Walsh: Fighting Back." *Saturday Evening Post*, April 1990, 44–47.

Bass, Alison. "Talk Shows Faulted as Trivial, Exploitive." *Wisconsin State Journal*, 17 October 1993, sec. F, pp. 1–2.

Bataille, George. *Death and Sensuality: A Study in Eroticism and Taboo*. Trans. Mary Dalwood. New York: Walker Press, 1962.

Baudrillard, Jean. *Baudrillard Live: Selected Interviews*. Ed. Mike Gane. Trans. George Salemohamed et al. London: Routledge, 1993.

———. *The Ecstasy of Communication*. Ed. Sylvere Lotringer. Trans. Bernard Schutze and Caroline Schutze. New York: Semiotext(e), 1988.

———. *The Evil Demon of Images*. Trans. Paul Patton and Paul Foss. Sydney, Australia: Power Institute Publications, 1987.

———. *In the Shadow of the Silent Majorities, or The End of the Social, and Other Essays*. Trans. Paul Foss, John Johnston, and Paul Patton. New York: Semiotext(e), 1983.

———. "Requiem for the Media." In *Video Culture: A Critical Investigation*, ed. John G. Hanhardt, trans. Charles Levin, 124–43. Rochester, N.Y.: Visual Studies Workshop Press, 1986.

———. *Revenge of the Crystal: Selected Writings on the Modern Object and Its Destiny, 1968–1983*. Ed. and trans. Paul Foss and Julian Pefanis. London: Pluto Press, 1990.

———. *Selected Writings*. Ed. Mark Poster. Trans. Charles Levin et al. Stanford, Calif.: Stanford University Press, 1988.

———. *Simulations*. Trans. Paul Foss, Paul Patton, and Philip Beitchman. New York: Semiotext(e), 1983.

———. *Xerox and Infinity*. Trans. Agitac. London: Touchepas, 1988.

Bauman, Zygmunt. "The Sweet Scent of Decomposition." In *Forget Baudrillard?* ed. Chris Rojek and Bryan S. Turner, 22–46. London: Routledge, 1993.

Becker, Karin E. "Photojournalism and the Tabloid Press." In *Journalism and Popular Culture*, ed. Peter Dahlgren and Colin Sparks, 130–53. London: Sage Publications, 1992.

Behrens, Steve. "A Finer Grind from the Ratings Mill." *Channels* Field Guide (December 1987): 10, 12, 16.

Belluck, Pam. "A 'Bad Boy' Wrestler Ignores the Script." *New York Times*, 5 November 1998. http://www.nytimes.com.

Benjamin, Walter. *Illuminations*. Ed. Hannah Arendt. Trans. Harry Zohn. New York: Schocken, 1968.

Bennett, Tony. "The Bond Phenomenon: Theorising a Popular Hero." *Southern Review* 16, no. 2 (1983): 195–225.

Bent, Silas. *Ballyhoo: The Voice of the Press*. New York: Boni and Liveright, 1927.

Berke, Richard L. "As Bush (the Son) Surges, Bush (the Father) Sees a Resurgence." *New York Times*, 25 July 1999. http://www.nytimes.com.

Bernstein, Carl. "The Idiot Culture." *New Republic*, June 1992, 22–25, 28.

Bessie, Simon Michael. *Jazz Journalism: The Story of the Tabloid Newspapers*. New York: E. P. Dutton, 1938.

Bialow, Jennifer. "Nicole's Sexy Spend, Spend Life of Fast Cars, Drugs & Young Men." *Star*, 12 July 1994, 36–37.

Bird, S. Elizabeth. *For Enquiring Minds: A Cultural Study of Supermarket Tabloids*. Knoxville: University of Tennessee Press, 1992.

———. "The Kennedy Story in Folklore and Tabloids: Intertextuality in Political Communication." In *Politics in Familiar Contexts: Projecting Politics through Popular Media*, ed. Robert L. Savage and Dan Nimmo, 247–68. Norwood, N.J.: Ablex Publishing, 1990.

———. "Storytelling on the Far Side: Journalism and the Weekly Tabloid." *Critical Studies in Mass Communication* 7, no. 4 (December 1990): 377–89.

Bliss, Edward, Jr. *Now the News: The Story of Broadcast Journalism*. New York: Columbia University Press, 1991.

Block, Alex Ben. "Twenty-First Century Fox." *Channels* (January 1990): 36–40.

Blumler, Jay. "The New Television Marketplace: Imperatives, Implications, Issues." In *Mass Media and Society*, ed. James Curran and Michael Gurevitch, 192–215. London: Arnold, 1991.

Bogard, William. *The Simulation of Surveillance: Hypercontrol in Telematic Societies*. Cambridge: Cambridge University Press, 1996.

Bourdieu, Pierre. "The Aristocracy of Culture." *Media, Culture, and Society*, no. 2 (1980): 225–54.

———. *Distinction: A Social Critique of the Judgement of Taste*. Trans. Richard Nice. Cambridge: Harvard University Press, 1984.

———. *On Television*. Trans. Priscilla Parkhurst Ferguson. New York: New Press, 1998.

Bradford, Krista. "The Big Sleaze." *Rolling Stone*, February 1993, 39–43, 69.

Bridges, George, and Rosalind Brunt, eds. *Silver Linings*. London: Lawrence and Wishart, 1981.

Broder, David S. "TV Coverage: Too Close, Too Personal." *San Jose Mercury-News*, 7 July 1985, sec. P, p. 7.

Brooks, Peter. *The Melodramatic Imagination: Balzac, Henry James, Melodrama, and the Mode of Excess*. New Haven: Yale University Press, 1976.

Brower, Sue. "Inside Stories: Gossip and Television Audiences." In *Communication and Culture: Language, Performance, Technology, and Media*, ed. Sari Thomas and William A. Evans, 225–35. Norwood, N.J.: Ablex Publishing, 1990.

Brown, Mary Ellen. *Soap Opera and Women's Talk: The Pleasure of Resistance*. Thousand Oaks, Calif.: Sage Publications, 1994.

Brunsdon, Charlotte, and David Morley. *Everyday Television: "Nationwide."* London: British Film Institute, 1978.

Buck, Rinker. "What the Cutbacks Really Mean." *Channels* (September 1986): 67–69.

Burns, Bob. "Silence of the Lambs." *Globe*, 20 June 1995, 36–37.

Burns, Gary, and Robert J. Thompson, eds. *Television Studies: Textual Analysis.* New York: Praeger, 1989.

Burton, David. "Top Psychic Splits Herself into 2 People . . . & Says You Can Do It Too!" *Weekly World News*, 9 July 1991, 46–47.

Butler, Judith. *Bodies That Matter: On the Discursive Limits of "Sex."* New York: Routledge, 1993.

———. *Gender Trouble: Feminism and the Subversion of Identity.* New York: Routledge, 1990.

Campbell, Richard. "Words vs. Image: Elitism, Popularity, and TV News." *Television Quarterly* 26, no. 1 (1991): 73–81.

"Captured Alien Escapes!" *Weekly World News*, 20 November 1990, 24–25.

Carey, James W., ed. *Media, Myths, and Narratives: Television and the Press.* Newbury Park, Calif.: Sage Publications, 1988.

Carlton, T. "Battered and Bruised Gardener Claims, 'A Space Alien Attacked Me—& Tried to Mate with My Weed Eater!' " *Weekly World News*, 24 July 1990, 1.

Carmody, Dianne Cyr. "Mixed Messages: Images of Domestic Violence on 'Reality' Television." In *Entertaining Crime: Television Reality Programs*, ed. Mark Fishman and Gray Cavender, 159–74. New York: Aldine de Gruyter, 1998.

Carpignano, Paolo, Robin Anderson, Stanley Aronowitz, and William DiFazio. "Chatter in the Age of Electronic Reproduction: Talk Television and the 'Public Mind.' " *Social Text*, nos. 25–26 (1990): 33–55.

Chang, Briankle G. "Mass, Media, Mass Media-Tion: Jean Baudrillard's Implosive Critique of Modern Mass-Mediated Culture." *Current Perspectives in Social Theory* 7 (1986): 157–81.

Chen, Kuan-Hsing. "The Masses and the Media: Baudrillard's Implosive Postmodernism." *Theory, Culture, and Society* 4 (1987): 71–88.

Cockburn, Alexander. "White Rage: The Press and the Verdict." *Nation*, October 1995, 491.

Cohen, Jaffe. "Land o' Lake." *Harvard Gay and Lesbian Review* 2, no. 4 (fall 1995): 36–37.

Cohen, Richard. "Serving Up a Story Line." *Washington Post*, 4 September 1997, A19.

Collins, Jim. "Television and Postmodernism." In *Channels of Discourse, Reassembled: Television and Contemporary Criticism*, ed. Robert C. Allen, 327–53. 2d ed. Chapel Hill: University of North Carolina Press, 1992.

Collins, Monica. "Extra! Extra! Tabloid Clones Invade TV." *TV Guide*, November 1989, 14–16.

Connell, R. W. *Masculinities.* Berkeley: University of California Press, 1995.

Connolly, William. "Taylor, Foucault, and Otherness." *Political Theory* 13, no. 3 (August 1985).

"Conservatives Take On Daytime 'Trash TV.' " *Dallas–Fort Worth Heritage* 4, no. 9 (March 1996). http://www.fni.com/heritage.

Coombe, Rosemary J. "Postmodernity and the Rumor: Late Capitalism and the Fetishism of the Commodity/Sign." In *Jean Baudrillard: The Disappearance of Art and Politics*, ed. William Stearns and William Chaloupkas, 98–108. London: Macmillan, 1992.

Copswatch: The Media Parasite. http://www.specmind.com/copswatch.htm.

Corners, Ted. "Brain Surgeon Turns Patients into Helpless Robots." *National Examiner*, 6 June 1989, 15.

Cousineau, Phil. *UFOs: A Manual for the Millennium.* New York: Harper-Collins West, 1995.

Covert, Catherine L., and John D. Stevens, eds. *Mass Media between the Wars: Perceptions of Cultural Tension, 1918–1941.* Syracuse, N.Y.: Syracuse University Press, 1984.

Curran, James, and Michael Gurevitch, eds. *Mass Media and Society.* London: Arnold, 1991.

Curran, James, and Colin Sparks. "Press and Popular Culture." *Media, Culture, and Society* 13 (1991): 215–37.

Dahlgren, Peter, and Colin Sparks, eds. *Journalism and Popular Culture*. London: Sage Publications, 1992.

Davis, Mike. *City of Quartz: Excavating the Future in Los Angeles*. London: Verso, 1990.

Davis, Natalie Zemon. *Society and Culture in Early Modern France*. Stanford, Calif.: Stanford University Press, 1965.

"The Day O.J. Caught Gal Pal Tawny in Bed with Another Guy." *Star*, 12 September 1995, 12.

de Certeau, Michel. *The Practice of Everyday Life*. Trans. Stephen Rendall. Berkeley: University of California Press, 1984.

de Lauretis, Teresa, ed. *Feminist Studies, Critical Studies*. Bloomington: Indiana University Press, 1986.

Dean, Jodi. *Aliens in America: Conspiracy Cultures from Outerspace to Cyberspace*. Ithaca, N.Y.: Cornell University Press, 1998.

Deleuze, Gilles, and Félix Guattari. *A Thousand Plateaus: Capitalism and Schizophrenia*. Trans. Brian Massumi. Minneapolis: University of Minnesota Press, 1987.

Dent, Gina, ed. *Black Popular Culture*. Seattle: Bay Press, 1992.

Derogatis, Jim. "Politics As Usual in Minnesota." *Chicago Sun-Times*, 18 January 1999. http://www.suntimes.com.

Derrida, Jacques. *Of Grammatology*. Trans. Gayatri Chakravorty Spivak. Baltimore, Md.: Johns Hopkins University Press, 1976.

Diamond, Edwin. *Sign Off: The Last Days of Television*. Cambridge: MIT Press, 1982.

Doane, Mary Ann. *The Desire to Desire: The Woman's Film of the 1940s*. Bloomington: Indiana University Press, 1987.

Donovan, Pamela. "Armed with the Power of Television: Reality Crime Programming and the Reconstruction of Law and Order in the United States." In *Entertaining Crime: Television Reality Programs*, ed. Mark Fishman and Gray Cavender, 117–37. New York: Aldine de Gruyter, 1998.

Donovan, Robert J., and Ray Scherer. *Unsilent Revolution: Television News and American Public Life*. Cambridge: Cambridge University Press, 1992.

"Don't Mean Diddly." *New Yorker* 70, no. 20 (July 1994): 4, 6.

Doyle, Aaron. " 'Cops': Television Policing as Policing Reality." In *Entertaining Crime: Television Reality Programs*, ed. Mark Fishman and Gray Cavender, 95–116. New York: Aldine de Gruyter, 1998.

Drew, Mike. "Sleaze! Spats! Payoffs!" *Milwaukee Journal*, 23 May 1993, sec. T, p. 3.

———. "TV Tabloids Are Confusing Audiences: Some Viewers Can't Tell the Difference between Them and Real News Shows." *Dallas Morning News*, 29 May 1993, sec. W, p. 1.

"Drug Gang Killed Nicole." *Globe*, 21 March 1995, 1.

Dumm, Thomas L. "The New Enclosures: Racism in the Normalized Community." In *Reading Rodney King/Reading Urban Uprising*, ed. Robert Gooding-Williams, 178–95. New York: Routledge, 1993.

Dunne, Dominick. "Mr. Dunne Goes to Washington." *Vanity Fair*, May 1999, 88–93, 146–49.

Dunne, John Gregory. "The Simpsons." *New York Review*, September 1994, 34–39.

During, Simon, ed. *The Cultural Studies Reader*. London: Routledge, 1993.

Dyson, Michael Eric. *Reflecting Black: African-American Cultural Criticism*. Minneapolis: University of Minnesota Press, 1993.

Edelman, Murray. "The Construction and Uses of Social Problems." In *Jean Baudrillard: The Disappearance of Art and Politics*, ed. William Stearns and William Chaloupkas, 263–80. London: Macmillan, 1992.

Egan, Timothy. "Soldiers of the Drug War Remain on Duty." *New York Times*, 1 March 1999. http://www.nytimes.com.

Ehrenreich, Barbara. "In Defense of Talkshows." *Time*, December 1995, 92.

Ericson, Richard V., Patricia M. Baranek, and Janet B. L. Chan. *Visualizing Deviance: A Study of News Organization*. Toronto: University of Toronto Press, 1987.

Ettema, James S. "Journalism in the 'Post-factual' Age." *Critical Studies in Mass Communication* 4, no. 1 (March 1987): 82–86.

Ettema, James S., and Theodore L. Glasser. "Narrative Form and Moral Force: The Realization of Innocence and Guilt through Investigative Journalism." *Journal of Communication* 38, no. 3 (summer 1988): 8–26.

Ewen, Stuart, and Elizabeth Ewen. *Channels of Desire: Mass Images and the Shaping of American Consciousness*. 2d ed. Minneapolis: University of Minnesota Press, 1992.

"Exposed! Sickening Racist Rampages of Simpson Trial's Notorious Rogue Cop: Raging Bully!" *Globe*, 3 October 1995, 24–25.

Faludi, Susan. *Backlash: The Undeclared War against American Women*. New York: Crown Publishers, 1991.

Ferrier, Liz. "Postmodern Tactics: The Uses of Space in Shoppingtowns." 1987. Manuscript on file with the author.

Feuer, Jane. "The Concept of Live Television: Ontology as Ideology." In *Regarding Television: Critical Approaches—an Anthology*, ed. E. Ann Kaplan, 12–22. Frederick, Md.: University Publications of America, 1983.

———. *Seeing through the Eighties: Television and Reaganism*. Durham, N.C.: Duke University Press, 1995.

Fisher, Marc. "The King of Sleaze." *Gentlemen's Quarterly*, April 1990, 185–98.

———. "Minnesota's Surprise: 'Governor Body': Populist Ex-Wrestler Ventura Appears to Have Pinned 2 Rivals." *Washington Post*, 4 November 1998, sec. A, p. 1.

Fishman, Mark. "Ratings and Reality: The Persistence of the Reality Crime Genre." In *Entertaining Crime: Television Reality Programs*, ed. Mark Fishman and Gray Cavender, 59–75. New York: Aldine de Gruyter, 1998.

Fishman, Mark, and Gray Cavender, eds. *Entertaining Crime: Television Reality Programs*. New York: Aldine de Gruyter, 1998.

Fiske, John. "The Cultural Economy of Fandom." In *The Adoring Audience: Fan Culture and Popular Media*, ed. Lisa A. Lewis, 30–49. London: Routledge, 1992.

———. "Cultural Studies and the Culture of Everyday Life." In *Cultural Studies*, ed. Lawrence Grossberg, Cary Nelson, and Paula Treichler, 154–73. New York: Routledge, 1992.

———. *Media Matters*. Rev. ed. Minneapolis: University of Minnesota Press, 1996.

———. *Media Matters: Everyday Culture and Political Change*. Minneapolis: University of Minnesota Press, 1994.

———. "Moments of Television: Neither the Text nor the Audience." In *Remote Control: Television, Audiences, and Cultural Power*, ed. Ellen Seiter, Hans Borchers, Gabriele Kreutzner, and Eva-Maria Warth, 56–78. London: Routledge, 1989.

———. "MTV: Post Structural Post Modern." *Journal of Communication Inquiry* 10, no. 1 (1986): 74–79.

———. "Popularity and the Politics of Information." In *Journalism and Popular Culture*, ed. Peter Dahlgren and Colin Sparks, 45–63. London: Sage Publications, 1992.

———. *Power Plays, Power Works*. London: Verso, 1993.

———. *Reading the Popular*. Boston: Unwin Hyman, 1989.

———. *Television Culture*. London: Methuen, 1987.

———. *Understanding Popular Culture*. Boston: Unwin Hyman, 1989.

Flanagan, Timothy, and Dennis Longmire, eds. *Americans View Crime and Justice: A National Public Opinion Survey.* Thousand Oaks, Calif.: Sage Publications, 1996.

Foster, Hal, ed. *The Anti-aesthetic: Essays on Postmodern Culture.* Port Townsend, Wash.: Bay Press, 1983.

Foucault, Michel. *Discipline and Punish: The Birth of the Prison.* Trans. Alan Sheridan. New York: Vintage Books, 1979.

———. *The Foucault Reader.* Ed. Paul Rabinow. Trans. J. Harari et al. New York: Pantheon Books, 1984.

———. *The History of Sexuality, Volume 1: An Introduction.* Trans. Robert Hurley. New York: Pantheon Books, 1978.

———. *Politics, Philosophy, Culture: Interviews and Other Writings, 1977–1984.* Ed. Lawrence D. Kritzman. Trans. Alan Sheridan et al. New York: Routledge, 1988.

———. *Power/Knowledge: Selected Interviews and Other Writings, 1972–1977.* Ed. Colin Gordon. Trans. Colin Gordon, Leo Marshall, John Mepham, and Kate Soper. New York: Pantheon Books, 1980.

Francis, Paul. "Nicole: Top-Secret File Lists 20 Cases of Abuse by Juice!" *Globe,* 24 January 1995, 36.

———. "Nicole Was the Victim of Deadly Thugs Out to Kill Faye Resnick." *Globe,* 28 March 1995, 24–25, 41.

———. "O.J.'s Dad Was Gay—and Died of AIDS." *Globe,* 12 July 1994, 4–5.

———. "Two Madmen Killed O.J.'s Wife & Her Pal." *Globe,* 26 July 1994, 36–37, 44.

Frank, Arthur W. "Twin Nightmares of the Medical Simulacrum: Jean Baudrillard and David Cronenberg." In *Jean Baudrillard: The Disappearance of Art and Politics,* ed. William Stearns and William Chaloupkas, 82–97. London: Macmillan, 1992.

Fraser, Nancy. "Rethinking the Public Sphere: A Contribution to the Critique of Actually Existing Democracy." *Social Text,* nos. 25–26 (1990): 56–80.

———. *Unruly Practices: Power, Discourse, and Gender in Contemporary Social Theory.* Minneapolis: University of Minnesota Press, 1989.

Frost, Tony. "How O.J. Trapped Nicole into Life of Cocaine." *Star,* 30 August 1994, 24–25, 29.

———. "I Watched in Terror As O.J. Beat Nicole." *Star,* 8 November 1994, 24–27.

———. "It Was Just One Year Ago: O.J. & Nicole's Easter Break." *Star,* 4 April 1995, 24–25, 27.

———. "Nicole & Goldman: The Secret Love Affair." *Star,* 23 May 1995, 36–37.

———. "Nicole Fell in Love with Best Girlfriend." *Star,* 27 September 1994, 39, 41.

———. "Nicole Put On a Sexy Sun Dress and a Sweet Smile, then Begged O.J. 'Take Me Back'; at That Moment She Signed Her Death Warrant." *Star,* 20 June 1995, 26–28.

———. "Nicole Uncensored." *Star,* 25 October 1994, 24–27.

———. "Nicole's Dance with Death." *Star,* 31 January 1995, 36–37, 39.

———. "Nicole's Final Hours on Earth." *Star,* 24 January 1995, 22, 24–25, 29.

———. "Nicole's Gay Affair Drove O.J. to Tears." *Star,* 18 July 1995, 20.

———. "O.J. Gave Sex and Drug Parties for L.A. Cops." *Star,* 6 September 1994, 36–37, 39.

———. "O.J.'s Life of Luxury behind Bars." *Star,* 11 July 1995, 6–7.

———. "Revealed! Truth about Nicole & O.J.'s Best Pal." *Star,* 20 June 1995, 5, 29.

"The Fuhrman Tapes Uncensored." *Star,* 5 September 1995, 36–37, 39.

Gabler, Neal. "O.J.: The News as Miniseries." *TV Guide* 42 (July 1994): 12–17.

Gamson, Joshua. *Freaks Talk Back: Tabloid Talk Shows and Sexual Nonconformity.* Chicago: University of Chicago Press, 1998.

"George Washington Grew Pot." *Weekly World News,* 9 July 1991, 35.

Gest, Ted, et al. "Victims of Crime." *U.S. News and World Report,* July 1989, 16–19.

Giddens, Anthony. "Jürgen Habermas." In *The Return of Grand Theory in the Human Sciences*, ed. Quentin Skinner, 121–39. Cambridge: Cambridge University Press, 1985.

Ginzburg, Carlo. *The Cheese and the Worms: The Cosmos of a Sixteenth-Century Miller*. Trans. John Tedeschi and Anne Tedeschi. New York: Dorset Press, 1989.

Gitlin, Todd. *Inside Prime Time*. New York: Pantheon Books, 1985.

——, ed. *Watching Television: A Pantheon Guide to Popular Culture*. New York: Pantheon Books, 1986.

Glasser, Theodore L., and James S. Ettema. "Investigative Journalism and the Moral Order." *Critical Studies in Mass Communication* 6, no. 1 (March 1989): 1–20.

Gledhill, Christine. "The Melodramatic Field: An Investigation." In *Home Is Where the Heart Is: Studies in Melodrama and the Woman's Film*, ed. Christine Gledhill, 5–39. London: BFI Publishing, 1987.

——. "Pleasurable Negotiations." In *Female Spectators: Looking at Film and Television*, ed. E. Deidre Pribram, 64–89. London: Verso, 1988.

——, ed. *Home Is Where the Heart Is: Studies in Melodrama and the Woman's Film*. London: BFI Publishing, 1987.

Glines, Caroline. "Is This the Face of the Real O.J. Killer?" *Globe*, 9 August 1994, 36.

"Globe Finds 10 Key Clues Cops Missed." *Globe*, 20 September 1994, 5.

Glod, Maria. "Springer Mania: Too Hot for Parents and Teachers!" *Washington Post*, 27 April 1998, A1.

Gooding-Williams, Robert, ed. *Reading Rodney King/Reading Urban Uprising*. New York: Routledge, 1993.

Goodman, Walter. "The Summer's Top Crime Drama, Continued." *New York Times*, 4 July 1994, sec. 1, p. 40.

Gould, Martin. "O.J. Trial Bombshell: I've Found Murder Weapon, Psychic Tells D.A. — and Simpson Didn't Do It." *Star*, 22 November 1994, 6–7.

Gray, Herman. "Television, Black Americans, and the American Dream." *Critical Studies in Mass Communication* 6 (December 1989): 376–87.

——. *Watching Race: Television and the Struggle for "Blackness."* Minneapolis: University of Minnesota Press, 1995.

Greene, Bob. "The Voice of America Has Spoken: 'Amuse Me.'" *Chicago Tribune*, 11 November 1998. http://chicagotribune.com.

Gregory, Sophfronia Scott. "Black Rage: In Defense of a Mass Murder." *Time*, June 1994, 31.

——. "Oprah! Oprah in the Court!" *Time*, June 1994, 30–31.

Grindstaff, Laura. "Producing Trash, Class, and the Money Shot: A Behind-the-Scenes Account of Daytime TV Talk Shows." In *Media Scandals: Morality and Desire in the Popular Culture Marketplace*, ed. James Lull and Stephen Hinerman, 164–202. New York: Columbia University Press, 1997.

Gripsrud, Jostein. "The Aesthetics and Politics of Melodrama." In *Journalism and Popular Culture*, ed. Peter Dahlgren and Colin Sparks, 84–95. London: Sage Publications, 1992.

Groeneveld, Benno. "Ex-Wrestler Ventura Sworn In as Minnesota Governor." *Excite News*, 4 January 1999. http://nt.excite.com.

Grossberg, Lawrence. "On Postmodernism and Articulation: An Interview with Stuart Hall." In *Stuart Hall: Critical Dialogues in Cultural Studies*, ed. David Morley and Kuan-Hsing Chen, 131–50. London: Routledge, 1996.

Grossberg, Lawrence, Cary Nelson, and Paula Treichler, eds. *Cultural Studies*. New York: Routledge, 1992.

Grosse, Bruno, Dr. "Blind Old Man Has X-Ray Vision." *Sun* 8 (April 1990): 5.

———. "Lightning Turns Man into Woman: Electric Shock Destroyed Her Genes." *Sun* (September 1989): 29.

"Guardian Angel Michael Landon Appears to 8 People!" *Weekly World News*, 20 August 1991, 2–4.

Habermas, Jürgen. *The Structural Transformation of the Public Sphere: An Inquiry into a Category of Bourgeois Society*. Trans. Thomas Burger with Frederick Lawrence. Cambridge: MIT Press, 1989.

Haghighi, Bahram, and Jon Sorenson. "America's Fear of Crime." In *Americans View Crime and Justice: A National Public Opinion Survey*, ed. Timothy Flanagan and Dennis Longmire, 16–30. Thousand Oaks, Calif.: Sage Publications, 1996.

Halimi, Serge. "Myopic and Cheapskate Journalism." Trans. Ed Emery. *Le Monde Diplomatique* (November 1988): 14–15.

Hall, Jacquelyn Dowd. " 'The Mind That Burns in Each Body': Women, Rape, and Racial Violence." In *Powers of Desire: The Politics of Sexuality*, ed. Ann Snitow, Christine Stansell, and Sharon Thompson, 328–49. New York: Monthly Review Press, 1983.

Hall, Stuart. "Encoding, Decoding." In *The Cultural Studies Reader*, ed. Simon During, 90–103. London: Routledge, 1993.

———. "Gramsci's Relevance for the Study of Race and Ethnicity." In *Stuart Hall: Critical Dialogues in Cultural Studies*, ed. David Morley and Kuan-Hsing Chen, 411–40. London: Routledge, 1996.

———. "Notes on Deconstructing 'The Popular.' " In *People's History and Socialist Theory*, ed. Raphael Samuel, 227–40. London: Routledge and Kegan Paul, 1981.

———. "What Is This 'Black' in Black Popular Culture?" In *Black Popular Culture*, ed. Gina Dent, 21–33. Seattle: Bay Press, 1992.

———. "The Whites of Their Eyes: Racist Ideologies and the Media." In *Silver Linings*, ed. George Bridges and Rosalind Brunt, 28–52. London: Lawrence and Wishart, 1981.

Hanhardt, John G., ed. *Video Culture: A Critical Investigation*. Rochester, N.Y.: Visual Studies Workshop Press, 1986.

Hanners, David. "Governor Is Yet Another Venture in Jesse's Unusually Varied Career." *Pioneer-Planet*, 9 December 1998. http://www.pioneerplanet.com.

Harrell, Ken. "Avenging Angel Denise Is Plotting to Kidnap OJ's Kids." *Globe*, 24 October 1995, 6–7.

———. "Chilling New Murder Puts O.J. in the Clear: Brentwood Ripper Killed Nicole & Ron." *Globe*, 23 May 1995, 5.

———. "Dear O.J." *Globe*, 13 September 1994, 2–5.

———. "Fuhrman Race Tapes Shocker." *Globe*, 1 August 1995, 5.

———. "Neighbors Shun 'Butcher of Brentwood.' " *Globe*, 24 October 1995, 24–25.

———. "Nicole Stalked O.J.!" *Globe*, 30 August 1994, 6–7.

———. "O.J. Will Take the Stand." *Globe*, 4 April 1995, 36–37.

———. "3 Surprise Witnesses Will Set O.J. Free." *Globe*, 11 October 1994, 17.

Harrell, Ken, and Bob Michals. "O.J. Shocker: Killer Used Two Knives." *Globe*, 21 February 1995, 24–25, 41.

Hartley, John. "Invisible Fictions: Television Audiences, Paedocracy, Pleasure." In *Television Studies: Textual Analysis*, ed. Gary Burns and Robert J. Thompson, 223–43. New York: Praeger, 1989.

Head, Sydney W., and Christopher H. Sterling. *Broadcasting in America: A Survey of Electronic Media*. Brief ed. Boston: Houghton Mifflin, 1991.

Hebdige, Dick. *Hiding in the Light: On Images and Things*. London: Routledge, 1988.

Heinz, John. "Recognizing the Rights of Crime Victims." *USA Today* 113, no. 2470 (July 1984): 80–83.

Herford, Peter M. "In News, Public Choice Is a Disaster." *New York Times*, 4 August 1990, 15.

Hilmes, Michele. "Pay Television: Breaking the Broadcast Bottleneck." In *Hollywood in the Age of Television*, ed. Tino Balio, 297–318. Boston: Unwin Hyman, 1990.

Holland, Philip. "Robert Burton's *Anatomy of Melancholy* and Menippean Satire, Humanist and English." Ph.D. diss., University of London, 1979.

"How Nicole Seduced O.J.'s Best Pal—under His Nose." *Star*, 27 June 1995, 36–37.

Hugo, Victor. *Les Miserables*. Trans. N. Denny. Harmondsworth: Penguin, 1980.

"Hunt for Nicole's Mystery Lover." *Star*, 14 March 1995, 24–25.

Hunt, Lynn. "Introduction: History, Culture, and Text." In *The New Cultural History*, ed. Lynn Hunt, 1–22. Berkeley: University of California Press, 1989.

———, ed. *The New Cultural History*. Berkeley: University of California Press, 1989.

Hutcheon, Linda. *The Politics of Postmodernism*. London: Routledge, 1989.

Huyssen, Andreas. "Mass Culture as Woman: Modernism's Other." In *Studies in Entertainment: Critical Approaches to Mass Culture*, ed. Tania Modleski, 188–207. Bloomington: Indiana University Press, 1986.

"Interim Page." *Official Site of the Jesse Ventura Volunteer Committee*. http://www.jesseventura.org/interim.htm.

Jameson, Fredric. "Postmodernism and Consumer Society." In *The Anti-aesthetic: Essays on Postmodern Culture*, ed. Hal Foster, 111–25. Port Townsend, Wash.: Bay Press, 1983.

———. "Postmodernism, or The Cultural Logic of Late Capitalism." *New Left Review*, no. 146 (July 1984–August 1984): 53–92.

Jaroff, Leon. "Weird Science." *Time*, May 1995, 75.

Jenkins, Henry. "*Star Trek* Rerun, Reread, Rewritten: Fan Writing as Textual Poaching." *Critical Studies in Mass Communication* 5, no. 2 (June 1988): 85–107.

———. *Textual Poachers: Television Fans and Participatory Culture*. New York: Routledge, 1992.

Johnson, George. "Pierre, Is That a Masonic Flag on the Moon?" *New York Times*, 24 November 1996. http://www.nytimes.com.

Johnson, Terry E., et al. "Urban Murders: On the Rise: Cocaine Is Suspected in a Surge in City Killings." *Newsweek*, February 1987, 30.

Joyrich, Lynne. "All That Television Allows: TV Melodrama, Postmodernism, and Consumer Culture." *Camera Obscura*, no. 16 (January 1988): 129–53.

Kalter, Joanmarie. "Please. Risk It. Bore Me with Reality." *TV Guide*, November 1984, 24–25.

Kamp, David. "The Tabloid Decade." *Vanity Fair*, February 1999, 64–66, 68, 70, 75–76, 78, 80, 82.

Kandel, Aben. "A Tabloid a Day." *Forum* 77, no. 3 (March 1927): 378–84.

Kaplan, E. Ann, ed. *Regarding Television: Critical Approaches—An Anthology*. Frederick, Md.: University Publications of America, 1983.

Katz, Jack. "What Makes Crime 'News'?" *Media, Culture, and Society* 9 (1987): 47–75.

Katz, Jon. "Beyond Broadcast Journalism." *Columbia Journalism Review* 30, no. 6 (March–April 1992): 19–23.

———. "Covering the Cops: A TV Show Moves In Where Journalists Fear to Tread." *Columbia Journalism Review* 31, no. 5 (February 1993): 25–30.

———. "In Praise of O.J. Overkill." *New York*, July 1994, 12–13.

———. "The Plugged-In Voter." *Rolling Stone*, December 1992, 115–17, 201.

———. "Rock, Rap, and Movies Bring You the News." *Rolling Stone*, March 1992, 33, 36–37, 40, 78.

Katz, Richard. "Cable Gets Its First Q Ratings." *Variety.Com*, August 1999. http://www.variety.com.

Keene, T. "Woman Wills $500g . . . to a Houseplant." *Weekly World News*, 4 September 1990, 3.

Kempley, Rita. "Sex, Lies, and Videotape." *Washingtonpost.Com*, 11 August 1989. http://www. washingtonpost.com.

Kennedy, Randall. "After the Cheers." *New Republic*, October 1995, 14, 16–18.

Kerrigan, Mike. "Cop Framed O.J." *Globe*, August 1994, 36–37, 44.

Knight, Graham. "Reality Effects: Tabloid Television News." *Queen's Quarterly* 96, no. 1 (spring 1989): 94–108.

Knopf, Terry Ann. "Sleazy Does It." *Boston Magazine*, September 1990, 70–73.

Kooistra, Paul G., John S. Mahoney, and Saundra D. Westervelt. "The World of Crime According to 'Cops.' " In *Entertaining Crime: Television Reality Programs*, ed. Mark Fishman and Gray Cavender, 141–58. New York: Aldine de Gruyter, 1998.

Kramer, M. "Is Ric Flair Running the White House? Pro Wrestler Talked Bush into Sending Troops to Saudi Arabia!" *Weekly World News*, 5 February 1991, 3.

Kroker, Arthur. "Television and the Triumph of Culture: Three Theses." *Canadian Journal of Political and Social Theory* 9, no. 3 (fall 1985): 37–47.

Kurtz, Howard. "Clintons Long under Siege by Conservative Detractors." *Washington Post*, 28 January 1998, A1.

———. "Extra! Read All about It! Overcoverage Shocks Press!" *Washington Post*, 5 September 1997, D1.

———. "Though Public Says It's Fed Up, It Maintains an Appetite for the Story." *Washington Post*, 12 February 1998, A1.

Laclau, Ernesto, and Chantal Mouffe. *Hegemony and Socialist Strategy: Towards a Radical Democratic Politics*. Trans. Winston Moore and Paul Cammack. London: Verso, 1985.

LaFontaine, Dave, Yasmin Brennan, and Tony Frost. "Nicole's Mystery Link to Nightclub Murder." *Star*, 11 October 1994, 5, 8.

Lai, Lo-Mae. "16 Mistakes That Could Set Him Free." *Globe*, 9 August 1994, 36–37.

Langer, John. *Tabloid Television: Popular Journalism and the "Other News."* London: Routledge, 1998.

———. "Truly Awful News on Television." In *Journalism and Popular Culture*, ed. Peter Dahlgren and Colin Sparks, 113–29. London: Sage Publications, 1992.

Lanpher, Katherine. "The Mind." November 1998. http://news.mpr.org.

Lasch, Christopher. "The Moynihan Report: Rethinking Family." In *Social Theory: The Multicultural and Classic Readings*, ed. Charles Lemert, 436–42. Boulder, Colo.: Westview Press, 1993.

"The Last Run." *Star*, 5 July 1994, 26–27.

Lavery, David, Angela Hague, and Marla Cartwright, eds. *Deny All Knowledge: Reading "The X-Files."* Syracuse, N.Y.: Syracuse University Press, 1996.

Lehnert, Eileen, and Mary J. Perpich. "An Attitude Segmentation Study of Supermarket Tabloid Readers." *Journalism Quarterly* 59 (1982): 104–11.

Lemert, Charles, ed. *Social Theory: The Multicultural and Classic Readings*. Boulder, Colo.: Westview Press, 1993.

Lennon, Rosemarie. "Nicole's Amazing Confessions." *Star*, 20 September 1994, 36–38.

Levine, Lawrence W. *Highbrow/Lowbrow: The Emergence of Cultural Hierarchy in America*. Cambridge: Harvard University Press, 1988.

Lewis, Lisa A., ed. *The Adoring Audience: Fan Culture and Popular Media*. London: Routledge, 1992.

Livingstone, Sonia, and Peter Lunt. *Talk on Television: Audience Participation and Public Debate*. London: Routledge, 1994.

Lull, James, and Stephen Hinerman, eds. *Media Scandals: Morality and Desire in the Popular Culture Marketplace*. New York: Columbia University Press, 1997.

Lyotard, Jean-François. *The Postmodern Condition: A Report on Knowledge*. Trans. Geoff Bennington and Brian Massumi. Minneapolis: University of Minnesota Press, 1984.

"The Mad Slasher!" *Globe*, 27 June 1995, 10–11.

Mann, N. "Space Alien Meets with President Bush!" *Weekly World News*, 14 May 1991, 4–5.

———. "Space Alien Meets with Ross Perot!" *Weekly World News*, 14 July 1992, 4–5.

Margolick, David. "Simpson Judge Sets Hearing on TV and Radio Coverage." *New York Times*, 4 October 1994, sec. A, p. 19.

Marion, Jane. "Why John Walsh Hunts Killers: 'I Am Still Devastated.' " *TV Guide* 37, no. 11 (March 1989): 22–24.

Masciarotte, Gloria-Jean. "C'mon, Girl: Oprah Winfrey and the Discourse of Feminine Talk." *Genders*, no. 11 (fall 1991): 81–110.

Massing, Michael. "CBS: Sauterizing the News." *Columbia Journalism Review* 24 (March–April 1986): 27–37.

Massumi, Brian, ed. *The Politics of Everyday Fear*. Minneapolis: University of Minnesota Press, 1993.

———. Preface to *The Politics of Everyday Fear*, ed. Brian Massumi, vii–x. Minneapolis: University of Minnesota Press, 1993.

McClintock, Anne. "Screwing the System: Sexwork, Race, and the Law." *boundary 2* 19, no. 2 (1992): 70–95.

McLaughlin, Lisa. "Chastity Criminals in the Age of Electronic Reproduction: Re-viewing Talk Television and the Public Sphere." *Journal of Communication Inquiry* 17, no. 1 (winter 1993): 41–55.

McMurran, Kristin. "Two Hearts Beating in Prime Time." *People Weekly* 31, no. 14 (April 1989): 119.

Mellencamp, Patricia. *High Anxiety: Catastrophe, Scandal, Age, and Comedy*. Bloomington: Indiana University Press, 1992.

Mengelkoch, Louise. "When Checkbook Journalism Does God's Work." *Columbia Journalism Review* (November–December 1994): 35–38.

Mercer, Kobena. " '1968': Periodizing Politics and Identity." In *Cultural Studies*, ed. Lawrence Grossberg, Cary Nelson, and Paula Treichler, 424–49. New York: Routledge, 1992.

Merron, Jeff. "Murrow on TV: *See It Now, Person to Person*, and the Making of a 'Masscult Personality.' " *Journalism Monographs* 106 (July 1988).

Michael, John. "Science Friction and Cultural Studies: Intellectuals, Interdisciplinarity, and the Profession of Truth." *Camera Obscura*, no. 37 (January 1996): 125–55.

Michals, Bob. "O.J., Drugs, the Mob—& Murder!" *Globe*, 19 July 1994, 36–37, 40.

———. "O.J. Horror over New Autopsy Pics." *Globe*, 11 April 1995, 41.

———. "OJ: Autopsy Shocker: How New Evidence Could Rip Lid off Simpson Case." *Globe*, 14 March 1995, 24–25.

Milfred, Scott. "Tabloid Culture: Is That How History Will See Us?" *Wisconsin State Journal Online*, 12 October 1998. http://www.madison.com:8o/wsj/.

Miller, Judith, and Mark Miller. "Complaint of Crime Victims: 'Where Are Our Rights?' " *USA Today*, May 1986, 50–52.

Miller, S. "Scientists Dig 9-Mile-Deep Hole and Claim, 'We Drilled through the Gates of Hell.' " *Weekly World News*, 24 April 1990, 45.

Mitchell, William J. *The Reconfigured Eye: Visual Truth in the Post-photographic Era*. Cambridge: MIT Press, 1992.

Mitroff, Ian, and Warren Bennis. *The Unreality Industry: The Deliberate Manufacturing of Falsehood and What It Is Doing to Our Lives*. Secaucus, N.J.: Birch Lane Press, 1989.

Modleski, Tania, ed. *Studies in Entertainment: Critical Approaches to Mass Culture*. Bloomington: Indiana University Press, 1986.

———. "The Terror of Pleasure: The Contemporary Horror Film and Postmodern Theory." In

Studies in Entertainment: Critical Approaches to Mass Culture, ed. Tania Modleski, 155–66. Bloomington: Indiana University Press, 1986.

"Money-Loving Nicole Kept O.J. on a String." *Globe*, 5 July 1994, 36.

Morganthau, Tom, et al. "Losing the War?" *Newsweek*, March 1988, 16–18.

Morin, Richard, and Claudia Deane. "President's Popularity Hits a High: Majority in Poll Say Political Enemies Are Out to Get Him." *Washington Post*, 1 February 1998, A1.

Morley, David. "Changing Paradigms in Audience Studies." In *Remote Control: Television, Audiences, and Cultural Power*, ed. Ellen Seiter, Hans Borchers, Gabriele Kreutzner, and Eva-Maria Warth, 16–43. London: Routledge, 1989.

———. *Television, Audiences, and Cultural Studies*. London: Routledge, 1992.

Morley, David, and Kuan-Hsing Chen, eds. *Stuart Hall: Critical Dialogues in Cultural Studies*. London: Routledge, 1996.

Morrison, Toni, ed. *Race-ing Justice, En-gendering Power*. New York: Pantheon Books, 1992.

Morse, Margaret. "Talk, Talk, Talk." *Screen* 26, no. 2 (March–April 1985): 2–15.

———. "The Television News Personality and Credibility: Reflections on the News in Transition." In *Studies in Entertainment: Critical Approaches to Mass Culture*, ed. Tania Modleski, 55–79. Bloomington: Indiana University Press, 1986.

"Mother's Love." *Star*, 11 October 1994, 2–3.

Munson, Wayne. *All Talk: The Talkshow in Media Culture*. Philadelphia: Temple University Press, 1993.

Murphy, James E. "Tabloids as an Urban Response." In *Mass Media between the Wars: Perceptions of Cultural Tension, 1918–1941*, ed. Catherine L. Covert and John D. Stevens, 55–69. Syracuse, N.Y.: Syracuse University Press, 1984.

Nadel, Alan. *Containment Culture: American Narratives, Postmodernism, and the Atomic Age*. Durham, N.C.: Duke University Press, 1995.

Negt, Oskar, and Alexander Kluge. "Selections from the Proletariat Public Sphere." *Social Text*, nos. 25–26 (1990): 24–32.

"New Nicole Scandal Sends O.J. into Jailhouse Rage." *Globe*, 4 October 1994, 36–37, 44.

Newton, Edmund. "Criminals' Rights." *Ladies' Home Journal*, September 1986, 106–7, 170, 174, 177.

Newton, Esther. *Mother Camp: Female Impersonators in America*. Chicago: University of Chicago Press, 1972.

"Nicole's Tragic Search for Love." *Globe*, 1 August 1995, 45.

Norbom, Mary Ann. "OJ Killed 'Em!" *Globe*, 17 October 1995, 4–5, 8.

Nowell-Smith, Geoffrey. "Minnelli and Melodrama." In *Home Is Where the Heart Is: Studies in Melodrama and the Woman's Film*, ed. Christine Gledhill, 70–74. London: BFI Publishing, 1987.

O'Hara, K. "3 U.S. Presidents Were Gay!" *Sun* 8 (May 1990): 35.

"O.J. Begs Court: Give Me a Love Break." *Star*, 13 June 1995, 36–37, 39.

"O.J. Couldn't Have Done It." *Star*, 4 April 1995, 5, 27.

"O.J. Didn't Do It!" *Star*, June 1995, 5, 36.

"O.J. Invites Family to Jail for Holiday Get-Together." *Star*, 10 January 1995, 10.

"O.J.'s Defense." *Globe*, 27 September 1994, 2–5.

"O.J. Sobs in Jail As He Tapes Secret Message to the World." *Globe*, 24 January 1995, 36–37.

"O.J. Takes America by Storm." *Star*, 26 July 1994, 43.

Ohio Right to Life. "Recognizing Post Abortion Syndrome." March 1996. http://www.infinet.com/~life/aborted/seepas.htm.

Oliver, Mary Beth, and G. Blake Armstrong. "Predictors of Viewing and Enjoyment of Reality-Based and Fictional Crime Shows." *Journalism and Mass Communication Quarterly* 72, no. 3 (1995): 559–70.

Ong, Walter. *Orality and Literacy: The Technologizing of the Word*. London: Methuen, 1982.

Ornstein, Norman J., and Michael J. Robinson. "Do You Give Viewers Good Journalism or the Sensationalism They Prefer?" *TV Guide* 36, no. 51 (December 1988): 4–7.

Overbeck, Joy. "I Can't Believe What My Kid Sees on TV." *TV Guide* 41, no. 33 (August 1993): 12–13.

"P. & G. Loses Campaign for the Moon and the Stars." *Globe and Mail*, 26 April 1985, sec. B, p. 6.

"P. & G.'s Battles with Rumors." *New York Times*, 22 July 1982, sec. D, pp. 1, 10.

Patrizio, Andy. "Paging Service Beeps Users for Car Chases." *TechWeb: The Technology News Site*, 29 January 1999. http://www.techweb.com.

Patton, Cindy. *Inventing AIDS*. New York: Routledge, 1990.

Patton, Paul. "The World Seen from Within: Deleuze and the Philosophy of Events." *Theory and Event* 1, no. 1. http://muse.jhu.edu/journals/theory_&_event/.

Pauly, John J. "Rupert Murdoch and the Demonology of Professional Journalism." In *Media, Myths, and Narratives: Television and the Press*, ed. James W. Carey, 246–61. Newbury Park, Calif.: Sage Publications, 1988.

Pearson, Roberta E., and William Uricchio, eds. *The Many Lives of the Batman: Critical Approaches to a Superhero and His Media*. New York: Routledge, 1991.

Peck, Janice. "Talk about Racism: Framing a Popular Discourse of Race on Oprah Winfrey." *Cultural Critique* (spring 1994): 89–126.

———. "TV Talk Shows as Therapeutic Discourse: The Ideological Labor of the Televised Talking Cure." *Communication Theory* 5, no. 1 (February 1995): 58–81.

Penley, Constance, Elisabeth Lyon, Lynn Spigel, and Janet Bergstrom, eds. *Close Encounters: Film, Feminism, and Science Fiction*. Minneapolis: University of Minnesota Press, 1991.

Peterson, Mark Allen. "Aliens, Ape Men, and Whacky Savages: The Anthropologist in the Tabloids." *Anthropology Today* 7, no. 5 (October 1991): 4–7.

Pfaff, William. "Entertainment Coup, or America's Politics of Illusion." *International Herald Tribune*, December 1997.

Pfeil, Fred. *White Guys: Studies in Postmodern Domination and Difference*. London: Verso, 1995.

Philp, Mark. "Michel Foucault." In *The Return of Grand Theory in the Human Sciences*, ed. Quentin Skinner, 65–81. Cambridge: Cambridge University Press, 1985.

"The Picture That Could Free O.J." *Star*, 18 April 1995, 5.

Plotz, David. "Assessment." *Slate*, March 1998. http://www.slate.com/toc/FrontPorch.asp.

Porter, David, ed. *Internet Culture*. New York: Routledge, 1997.

Poster, Mark. "Cyberdemocracy: Internet and the Public Sphere." In *Internet Culture*, ed. David Porter, 201–17. New York: Routledge, 1997.

———. *The Mode of Information: Poststructuralism and Social Context*. Chicago: University of Chicago Press, 1990.

Postman, Neil. *Amusing Ourselves to Death: Public Discourse in the Age of Show Business*. New York: Viking Press, 1986.

Postman, Neil, and Steve Powers. *How to Watch TV News*. New York: Penguin Books, 1992.

Povich, Maury, with Ken Gross. *Current Affairs: A Life on the Edge*. New York: Berkeley Books, 1991.

Powers, Ron. *The Beast, the Eunuch, and the Glass-Eyed Child: Television in the '80s*. San Diego: Harcourt Brace Jovanovich, 1990.

———. "Lawyers, Guns, and Money." *Gentlemen's Quarterly*, June 1989, 129–32.

———. "The Pox of Fox." *Gentlemen's Quarterly*, May 1990, 78–82.

Prager, Emily. "Oprah's Opera." *Village Voice*, March 1987, 45, 48.

Prial, Frank J. "Freeze! You're on TV." *New York Times Magazine*, September 1988, 56–68.

Pribram, E. Deidre, ed. *Female Spectators: Looking at Film and Television*. London: Verso, 1988.

Priest, Patricia Joyner. *Public Intimacies: Talk Show Participants and Tell-All TV.* Cresskill, N.J.: Hampton Press, 1995.

"Princess Diana's Death." *Washington Post,* 1 September 1997, A20.

Pursehouse, Mark. "Looking at *The Sun:* Into the Nineties with a Tabloid and Its Readers." *Cultural Studies from Birmingham,* no. 1 (1991): 88–133.

Quintero, Fernando. "Cronkite Tells What Ails Us at First Herb Caen Lecture." *Berkeleyan,* 20 November 1996, 1, 8.

Radway, Janice. "What's in a Name? Presidential Address to the American Studies Association, 20 November 1998." *American Quarterly* 51, no. 1 (March 1999): 1–32.

Rapping, Elayne. "Daytime Inquiries." *Progressive* 55, no. 10 (October 1991): 36–38.

Ray, B. "Washer Turns into a Time Machine: Woman Puts in Sheets—and Pulls Out a 200-Year-Old Coat!" *Weekly World News,* 17 April 1990, 15.

Reeves, Jimmie L., and Richard Campbell. *Cracked Coverage: Television News, the Anti-cocaine Crusade, and the Reagan Legacy.* Durham, N.C.: Duke University Press, 1994.

Reeves, Jimmie L., Mark C. Rodgers, and Michael Epstein. "Rewriting Popularity: The Cult Files." In *Deny All Knowledge: Reading "The X-Files,"* ed. David Lavery, Angela Hague, and Marla Cartwright, 22–35. Syracuse, N.Y.: Syracuse University Press, 1996.

Relles, Ben. "UW Pranksters to Appear on National TV: Students Masquerade as Sexual Deviants on Tonight's 'The Jerry Springer Show.'" *Badger Herald* 26, no. 53 (November 1994): 1–2.

"Revealed! Cops' Secret File on Marcus Allen." *Star,* 8 August 1995, 5, 36–37.

Rich, Frank. "Addicted to O.J." *New York Times,* 23 June 1994, sec. A, p. 23.

———. "Another Media Morning After." *New York Times,* 30 June 1994, sec. A, p. 23.

———. "Judge Ito's All-Star Vaudeville." *New York Times,* 2 October 1994, sec. 4, p. 17.

Rivera, Geraldo, with Daniel Paisner. *Exposing Myself.* New York: Bantam, 1991.

Robbins, Bruce. "Introduction." *Social Text,* nos. 25–26 (1990): 3–7.

Roberts, Roxanne. "The Princess and the Press: A Dance Ending in Death." *Washington Post,* 4 September 1997, D1.

Robins, J. Max. "Here Come the News Punks." *Channels* (September 1988): 39–43.

Rogin, Michael. *Ronald Reagan, the Movie, and Other Episodes in Political Demonology.* Berkeley: University of California Press, 1987.

Rojek, Chris, and Bryan S. Turner, eds. *Forget Baudrillard?* London: Routledge, 1993.

Rosenberg, Howard. "New Channel 2 News Director Sets Off a Storm." *Los Angeles Times,* 4 March 1992, sec. F, pp. 1, 5–7.

Rosensteil, Thomas B. "To Journalists, Technology Is a Blessing—and a Curse." *Los Angeles Times,* 25 September 1994, sec. A, p. 1.

Ross, Andrew. Introduction to *Science Wars,* ed. Andrew Ross, 1–15. Durham, N.C.: Duke University Press, 1996.

———. "The Private Parts of Justice." In *Race-ing Justice, En-gendering Power,* ed. Toni Morrison, 40–60. New York: Pantheon Books, 1992.

———, ed. *Science Wars.* Durham, N.C.: Duke University Press, 1996.

Ross, Chuck. "Another Contender in Tabloid TV Pack." *San Francisco Chronicle,* 12 August 1989, sec. C, p. 8.

Rowe, Kathleen. *The Unruly Woman: Gender and the Genres of Laughter.* Austin: University of Texas Press, 1995.

Rubenstein, Diane. "The Anxiety of Affluence: Baudrillard and Sci-Fi Movies of the Reagan Era." In *Jean Baudrillard: The Disappearance of Art and Politics,* ed. William Stearns and William Chaloupkas, 65–81. London: Macmillan, 1992.

———. "The Mirror of Reproduction: Baudrillard and Reagan's America." *Political Theory* 17, no. 4 (November 1989): 582–606.

Russo, Mary. "Female Grotesques: Carnival and Theory." In *Feminist Studies, Critical Studies*, ed. Teresa de Lauretis, 213–29. Bloomington: Indiana University Press, 1986.

"Sally Blames Jerry Springer for Fake Fights." *Associated Press*, 22 September 1998. http://tvtalk-shows.com/sallyjessyraphael/news/1998/fake.

Samuel, Raphael, ed. *People's History and Socialist Theory*. London: Routledge and Kegan Paul, 1981.

Saroyan, Wayne A. "Keeping Tabs: Aliens with Bad Ties and Bad Attitudes, and Other Bits of Supermarket Lore." *Chicago Tribune*, 7 July 1991, 1, 3.

Sauter, Van Gordon. "In Defense of Tabloid TV." *TV Guide* 37, no. 31 (August 1989): 3–5.

Savage, Robert L., and Dan Nimmo, eds. *Politics in Familiar Contexts: Projecting Politics through Popular Media*. Norwood, N.J.: Ablex Publishing, 1990.

Schiff, Stephen. "Geek Shows." *New Yorker* 71, no. 35 (November 1995): 9–10.

Schone, Mark. "Talked Out." *Spin* 12, no. 2 (May 1996): 66–72, 74–75, 118.

Schorr, Daniel. "The Show Business of TV News." *San Francisco Chronicle*, 10 June 1990, This World, p. 20.

Scott, James C. *Domination and the Arts of Resistance: Hidden Transcripts*. New Haven: Yale University Press, 1990.

———. *Weapons of the Weak: Everyday Forms of Peasant Resistance*. New Haven: Yale University Press, 1986.

Seagal, Debra. "Tales from the Cutting-Room Floor." *Harper's Magazine*, November 1993, 50–57.

Seiter, Ellen, Hans Borchers, Gabriele Kreutzner, and Eva-Maria Warth, eds. *Remote Control: Television, Audiences, and Cultural Power*. London: Routledge, 1989.

"73-Year-Old JFK Photographed in White House Window!" *Weekly World News*, 29 January, 1991, 4–5.

"Sex & Drugs Secrets of Nicole Simpson's Private Diary." *Globe*, 6 December 1994, 17.

"Sex-Change Dad Is Now Son's 2nd Mom." *Sun* 8 (May 1990): 11.

Shapiro, Alan. "The Star Trekking of Physics." *Ctheory: Theory, Technology, and Culture* 20, no. 3 (October 1997). http://www.ctheory.com/.

Shattuc, Jane M. *The Talking Cure: TV Talk Shows and Women*. New York: Routledge, 1997.

Sheehy, Maura. "Crocodile Povich and the Aussie-fication of American Television." *Manhattan, Inc.* (April 1989): 75–81.

Sheridan, Alan. *Michel Foucault: The Will to Truth*. London: Tavistock Publications, 1980.

Shipp, E. R. "O.J. and the Black Media." *Columbia Journalism Review* (November–December 1994): 39–41.

Sifry, Micah L. "Working Class Hero?" *Salon*, January 1999. http://www.salonmagazine.com.

Silverman, Jeff. "Murder, Mayhem Stalk TV: True Tabloid Tales! Television in Frenzy over Sordid Real-Life Sagas." *New York Times*, 22 November 1992, sec. 2, pp. 1, 28–29.

Simon, Roger. "Now It's Tabloid TV: The Shows That Taste Forgot." *TV Guide* 36, no. 38 (September 1988): 51–53.

"Simpson Case Backlash Keeps Cameras out of Other Courtrooms." *New York Times*, 17 September 1995, sec. 1, p. 35.

Skinner, Quentin, ed. *The Return of Grand Theory in the Human Sciences*. Cambridge: Cambridge University Press, 1985.

Slack, Jennifer Daryl, and M. Mehdi Semati. "Intellectual and Political Hygiene: The 'Sokal Affair.'" *Critical Studies in Mass Communication* 14, no. 3 (September 1997): 201–27.

Smith, Conrad. "News Critics, Newsworkers, and Local Television News." *Journalism Quarterly* 65, no. 2 (summer 1988): 341–46.

Smith, Dane. "Ventura Creates Web Site to Influence 2000 Presidential Race." *Minneapolis Star-Tribune*, 9 February 1999. http://www.startribune.com.

Smith, Richard M. "The Plague among Us." *Newsweek*, June 1986, 15.

Snitow, Ann, Christine Stansell, and Sharon Thompson, eds. *Powers of Desire: The Politics of Sexuality*. New York: Monthly Review Press, 1983.

"So Who Did Kill Nicole?" *Star*, 17 October 1995, 5, 29.

Sobchack, Vivian, ed. *The Persistence of History: Cinema, Television, and the Modern Event*. New York: Routledge, 1996.

Sorkin, Michael. "Simulations: Faking It." In *Watching Television: A Pantheon Guide to Popular Culture*, ed. Todd Gitlin, 162–82. New York: Pantheon Books, 1986.

Spacks, Patricia Meyer. *Gossip*. New York: Alfred A. Knopf, 1985.

Span, Paula, and Libby Ingrid Copeland. "Women Voice Sympathy, and Disgust." *Washington Post*, 14 September 1998, A1.

Sparks, Colin. "Popular Journalism: Theories and Practice." In *Journalism and Popular Culture*, ed. Peter Dahlgren and Colin Spark, 24–44. London: Sage Publications, 1992.

Spigel, Lynn. "From Domestic Space to Outer Space: The 1960s Fantastic Family Sit-Com." In *Close Encounters: Film, Feminism, and Science Fiction*, ed. Constance Penley, Elisabeth Lyon, Lynn Spigel, and Janet Bergstrom, 205–33. Minneapolis: University of Minnesota Press, 1991.

Spigel, Lynn, and Henry Jenkins. "Same Bat Channel, Different Bat Times: Mass Culture and Popular Memory." In *The Many Lives of the Batman: Critical Approaches to a Superhero and His Media*, ed. Roberta E. Pearson and William Uricchio, 117–48. New York: Routledge, 1991.

Spolar, Christine. "At the Palace Gates, Flowers and Tears—and Anger at the Press." *Washington Post*, 1 September 1997, A27.

Stallybrass, Peter, and Allon White. *The Politics and Poetics of Transgression*. Ithaca, N.Y.: Cornell University Press, 1986.

Stam, Robert. *Subversive Pleasures: Bakhtin, Cultural Criticism, and Film*. Baltimore, Md.: Johns Hopkins University Press, 1989.

———. "Television News and Its Spectator." In *Regarding Television: Critical Approaches—an Anthology*, ed. E. Ann Kaplan, 23–43. Frederick, Md.: University Publications of America, 1983.

The Standard Periodical Directory. 15th ed. New York: Oxbridge Communications, 1992.

Starr, Michael. "Sally Does a 'Springer,' Films Back Stage Fights." *New York Post*, 18 September 1998. http://www.nypostonline.com.

Stearns, William, and William Chaloupkas, eds. *Jean Baudrillard: The Disappearance of Art and Politics*. London: Macmillan, 1992.

Stern, Andrew. "Minnesota's Governor-Elect Says He's No Rebel." *Excite News*, 4 November 1998. http://nt.excite.com.

Stone, Vernon A. "Two Decades of Changes in Local News Operations." *Television Quarterly* 25, no. 1 (1990): 41–48.

Stratton, Jon. "Cyberspace and the Globalization of Culture." In *Internet Culture*, ed. David Porter, 253–75. New York: Routledge, 1997.

"Stunning Evidence That Jury Won't Be Told: What O.J.'s Little Girl Heard on Night of Murders." *Star*, 25 July 1995, 29, 44.

Swarsdon, Anne. "Driver of Diana's Car Said to Be Drunk." *Washington Post*, 2 September 1997, A1.

Sweeney, Hillary. "How This Dog May Hold Key to O.J. Case." *Star*, 6 December 1994, 37.

Tarragon, L. "Sweet Old Lady, 74, Shows Boxers How to Fight." *Sun* 8 (May 1990): 4.

Temmey, Bob. "O.J.'s Roots: Startling Struggle from Slavery to Superstardom." *Globe*, 25 October 1994, 24–25, 32.

Terry, Marie. "I Saw Nicole's Killers." *Globe*, 23 August 1994, 36–37.

"This Is What You Thought: 80% Think TV Has Become Too Trashy." *Glamour*, May 1989, 179.

Thomas, Bill. "Finding Truth in the Age of 'Infotainment.'" *Editorial Research Reports* 1, no. 3 (January 1990).

Thomas, Sari, and William A. Evans, eds. *Communication and Culture: Language, Performance, Technology, and Media*. Norwood, N.J.: Ablex Publishing, 1990.

Tomasulo, Frank P. "'I'll See It When I Believe It': Rodney King and the Prison-House of Video." In *The Persistence of History: Cinema, Television, and the Modern Event*, ed. Vivian Sobchack, 69–88. New York: Routledge, 1996.

Toobin, Jeffrey. "A Horrible Human Event." *New Yorker* (October 1995): 40–46, 48–49.

———. "The Marcia Clark Verdict." *New Yorker* 72, no. 26 (September 1996): 58–62, 64–67, 69–71.

Turow, Joseph. "Local Television: Producing Soft News." *Journal of Communication* 33, no. 2 (spring 1983): 111–23.

Ventura, Jesse. "How I Will Use the Internet." December 1998. http://www.jesseventura.org/internet/howuse.htm.

Villard, Oswald Garrison. "Tabloid Offenses." *Forum* 77, no. 4 (April 1927): 485–91.

Vološinov, V. N. *Marxism and the Philosophy of Language*. Trans. Ladislav Matejka and I. R. Titunik. Cambridge: Harvard University Press, 1973.

Walston, Charles. "Tabloid TV Has Changed the Rules." *Atlanta Constitution*, 17 November 1991, sec. G, pp. 1, 5.

Wark, McKenzie. *Virtual Geography: Living with Global Media Events*. Bloomington: Indiana University Press, 1994.

Warren, James. "'Tabloid TV's' White Knight." *Chicago Tribune*, 4 August 1989, sec. 5, pp. 1, 3.

Waters, Harry F., Peter McKillop, Bill Powell, and Janet Huck. "Trash TV." *Newsweek*, November 1988, 72–76, 78.

Waters, John. "Why I Love the National Enquirer." *Rolling Stone*, October 1985, 43–44, 71–72.

Weiss, Philip. "Bad Rap for TV Tabs." *Columbia Journalism Review* 28, no. 1 (May–June 1989): 38–42.

Westerfelhaus, Robert, and Teresa A. Combs. "Criminal Investigations and Spiritual Quests: The X-Files as an Example of Hegemonic Concordance in a Mass-Mediated Society." *Journal of Communication Inquiry* 22, no. 2 (April 1998): 205–20.

"What You Didn't Hear on TV: Shocking Story behind 911 Tapes: Why O.J. Was in Rage." *Star*, 12 July 1994, 29.

White, Allon. "The Dismal Sacred Word: Academic Language and the Social Reproduction of Seriousness." *Journal of Literature Teaching Politics* 2 (1983): 4–15.

White, Stephen K. "Poststructuralism and Political Reflection." *Political Theory* 16, no. 2 (May 1988).

"Who Really Killed Nicole: Dramatic New Evidence from Globe Readers: $1 Million Reward." *Globe*, August 1994, 44.

"Whodunit?" *Star*, 26 July 1994, 5, 27.

"Wife Drives Dead Hubby All over the Country . . . Looking for a Graveyard to Bury Him In!" *Weekly World News*, 22 January 1991, 27.

Williams, Anna. "Domestic Violence and the Aetiology of Crime in *America's Most Wanted*." *Camera Obscura* 31 (January 1993): 97–118.

Williamson, Judith. "An Interview with Jean Baudrillard." Trans. Brand Thumin. *Block* 15 (1989): 16–19.

Wills, Garry. "The People's Choice." *New York Review of Books* 46, no. 13 (August 1999). http://www.nybooks.com.

Wolkomir, Richard. "With Tabloids, 'Zip! You're in Another World!' " *Smithsonian*, October 1987, 240.

"Woman Gives Birth at Bingo Game—and Keeps On Playing." *Sun* 8 (May 1990): 1.

Wood, Robin. "Return of the Repressed." *Film Comment* 14, no. 4 (July–August 1978): 25–32.

Yardley, Jonathan. "Media Culpa." *Washington Post*, 15 September 1997, B2.

"Youths Give UFOs Edge over Security." *Wisconsin State Journal*, 27 September 1994, sec. B, p. 6.

Index

MacDonald, Jeffrey, 61–62
Marketing Evaluations/TvQ, Inc., 247–248
Masciarotte, Gloria-Jean, 198
Masculinity: in *Cops*, 55–56
McClintock, Anne, 191, 193
McGuire, Charles/Catherine, 138–141
Mellencamp, Patricia, 113
Melodrama, 126; and domesticity, 128–130; and investigative tabloidism, 124–125; and transgenderism, 141–142. *See also* Postmodernity: and melodrama
Mengelkoch, Louise, 96
Menippean satire. *See* Bakhtin, Mikhail: on menippean satire
"Metaphysics of presence." *See* Derrida, Jacques: on the "metaphysics of presence"
Miller, David Lee, 129
Minow, Newton, 20
Mitroff, Ian, 104–105
Modernist epistemologies, 47–48, 58–59, 93; contemporary struggles over, 229; and normalization, 185–187, 189. *See also* Scientific rationalism
Monti, John, 69–70
Morley, David, 3, 171
Morse, Margaret, 111
Moynihan, Daniel Patrick, 187
Multiculturalism, 232; and cultural boundaries, 103; talk shows as popular media form of, 211–212
Multidiscursivity, 187–188, 190
Murdoch, Rupert, 27–28
Murrow, Edward R., 22

National Examiner, 154, 156
Niche broadcasting. *See* Post-Fordism: and TV programming
Noriega, Manuel, 125
"Normal"/"abnormal," 104, 133; in postmodernity, 187–188
Normalization, 185–189, 217–218
Nostalgia-before-its-time, 19, 261 n.75

Oakes, Kitty, 132–135, 137
Obscenity, postmodernist definition of. *See* Baudrillard, Jean: on "obscenity"
Official journalism, 6–7, 10, 148; the body in, 111–112; communicative authoritarianism of, 79; "newsworthiness" in, 24; and the power-bloc, 20, 95
Ong, Walter, 21
Oprah, 212–213
"Oprahization," 94–95, 228
Overholser, Geneva, 109–110

Paparazzi, 225–226, 280 n.83
Patton, Cindy, 196
Pauly, John J., 28
Peck, Janice, 212, 216
Performativity, gender as, 134–136, 282 n.108
Philp, Mark, 186
Popular culture, 8–9, 115, 159
Popular knowledges, 7, 69; and cultural insurgency, 12; gossip, rumor, and, 113–114, 171; and the "public sphere," 16. *See also* Counterknowledges, popular
Popular memory: *A Current Affair* and, 123
Popular skepticism, 66, 74, 78, 90, 178, 183; and institutional politics, 148–150, 157–159, 228–229; toward scientific rationalism, 69, 148, 165, 171–172. *See also* Ventura, Jesse
Popular tastes: for participatory culture, 5. *See also* Bourdieu, Pierre: on bourgeois vs. popular tastes
Pornography: discussion of, on *The Jerry Springer Show*, 219–221
Poster, Mark, 230
Post-Fordism, and TV programming, 161–162
Postman, Neil, 188
Postmodernism, 58–59, 61, 63; and cultural boundaries, 103; and cultural studies, 13–14; and tabloidism, 47–48, 70
Postmodernity, 17–19, 58, 64–65, 224; articulation, rearticulation, and, 71–72, 75–76; and extradiscursive "reality," 227, 231–232; gossip, rumor, and, 114; and image recycling, 122–123; and melodrama, 131–132. *See also* Fiske, John: on postmodernity; Reaganism: postmodern characteristics of
Poststructuralism: and cultural studies, 14; Derridean, 297 n.25; Foucauldian, 231. *See also* Discourse: knowledge, power, and
Poussaint, Alvin, 90–92

Kevin Glynn is Lecturer in American Studies at the University of Canterbury in New Zealand.

Library of Congress Cataloging-in-Publication Data
Glynn, Kevin, 1963–
Tabloid culture : trash taste, popular power, and the transformation of American television / Kevin Glynn.
p. cm. — (Console-ing passions)
Includes bibliographical references and index.
ISBN 0-8223-2550-0 (cloth : alk. paper)
ISBN 0-8223-2569-1 (pbk. : alk. paper)
1. Reality television programs—United States.
2. Talk shows—United States. I. Title. II. Series.
PN1992.8.R43 G59 2000 791.45′6—dc21 00-030865